# ACCIDENTAL GODS

# ACCIDENTAL
# GODS

—

*On Men Unwittingly*
*Turned Divine*

## ANNA DELLA SUBIN

METROPOLITAN BOOKS

Henry Holt and Company

New York

Metropolitan Books
Henry Holt and Company
*Publishers since 1866*
120 Broadway
New York, New York 10271
www.henryholt.com

Metropolitan Books® and ▥® are registered trademarks of
Macmillan Publishing Group, LLC.

Library of Congress Cataloging-in-Publication Data

Names: Subin, Anna Della, author.
Title: Accidental gods : on men unwittingly turned divine / Anna Della Subin.
Description: First edition. | New York : Metropolitan Books ; Henry Holt & Company, 2021. |
    Includes index.
Identifiers: LCCN 2021002258 (print) | LCCN 2021002259 (ebook) | ISBN 9781250296870
    (hardcover) | ISBN 9781250296887 (ebook)
Subjects: LCSH: Apotheosis. | Religious leaders—Biography. | Kings and rulers—Biography. |
    Heroes—Biography. | Religion and politics. | Religion and sociology.
Classification: LCC BL465 .S83 2021 (print) | LCC BL465 (ebook) | DDC 202/.130922—dc23
LC record available at https://lccn.loc.gov/2021002258
LC ebook record available at https://lccn.loc.gov/2021002259

Our books may be purchased in bulk for promotional, educational, or business use. Please
contact your local bookseller or the Macmillan Corporate and Premium Sales Department at
(800) 221-7945, extension 5442, or by e-mail at MacmillanSpecialMarkets@macmillan.com.

First Edition 2021

Printed in the United States of America

1  3  5  7  9  10  8  6  4  2

for Ismael & Hussein

*I am not God.*
    —Haile Selassie I

*I am not God.*
    —Mohandas Karamchand Gandhi

*But what is my God?*

*I put my question to the earth. It answered, "I am not God," and all things on earth declared the same.*
    —Saint Augustine, *Confessions*

# CONTENTS

## III: WHITE GODS

*How whiteness was deified in the New World*

# ACCIDENTAL GODS

# First Rites

In the beginning, it was the serpent who first proposed that mankind might become divine. *Ye shall be as gods*, he advised, as the fruit waited. Sorrow and shame and wisdom came into the world, but whether man was any nearer to godliness, who could say? The creature, cursed to slither, appeared again when Saint Paul was shipwrecked on an island. The apostle had gathered a pile of wood for a fire when the snake crawled out and bit his hand. The islanders, looking on, waited for the stranger to drop dead, and supposed that he must have been a murderer to have met such a fate. But after seeing that no harm had befallen him, they changed their minds and declared that Paul was a god. It wasn't his first time: earlier on the saint's travels, while Paul was preaching the word, a man, unable to walk, had leapt to his feet. When the people saw what had happened, they determined that Paul was Mercury and his companion Barnabas was Jupiter, and began to shout, *The gods are come down to us in the likeness of men.* A priest prepared to sacrifice an ox. But the two apostles tore at their clothes and ran among the people, crying out, *Sirs, why do ye these things? We are men of like passions with you.* A new trap had been set, rewiring the serpent's words. One might be shaped like a god, colored like a god, imperious, impervious, or violent like a god. One might just be in the right place at the right time. Mistakes happen.

✦  ✦  ✦

A fleet of ships appeared on the horizon, swarming the boundary between heaven and earth. Confusing them for the vessels of their own king, in 307 BCE the people of Athens allowed a foreign conqueror to enter the harbor of Piraeus, and dropped their shields. The commander, Demetrius Poliorcetes, didn't land, but issued a proclamation that he would return to liberate the city and restore it to democracy, and sailed off again. When he reappeared several months later and captured Athens, Demetrius was surprised to find himself hailed as a divinity. The people lined the streets of the city, bearing garlands, dancing, and shouting as the new god passed by. They sang a hymn, which the historian Douris of Samos recorded:

> *The other gods dwell far away,*
> *Or have no ears, or pay us no mind.*
> *But you are here, and you we see,*
> *Not carved in wood or stone but real—*
> *So to you we pray.*

The other gods were sleeping, but Demetrius was there, present before them. He was handsome and laughed like a god. He was luminous like the sun and his entourage was like the stars. Unlike the inert idols of wood and stone, Demetrius was energetic and able to initiate change. At the place where his foot touched down from a chariot, an altar sprang up. Inside newly built temples to Demetrius, priests robed in clouds of incense poured out libations to the Descender. The conqueror found himself besieged with prayers and requests, above all to bring peace. "Even Demetrius himself was filled with wonder at the things that took place," the statesman Demochares recounted. He noted that, while Demetrius found some aspects of his worship enjoyable, others were distressing and embarrassing to the new god, especially an intrusive temple, erected for his legendarily beautiful mistress, Lamia.

The idea that a man might turn divine, even without intending or willing it, was to ancient Greece a natural and perfectly rational occurrence. Traffic flowed between earth and the dwelling place of the gods in the sky. In his *Theogony*, the poet Hesiod sang of the births of gods in a genealogy often crossed with that of humans. He told of mortals who became daemons, or deific spirits; of the half-gods, born of mixed parentage; of the man-gods, or heroes, venerated for their deeds. The theorist Euhemerus claimed he found, on a desert island, a golden pillar inscribed with the birth and death dates of the immortal Olympians. According to his hypothesis, all gods were originally men who had once lived on earth, yet their roots did not impinge upon their cosmic authority, nor make them any less divine. The ranks of the gods swelled with warriors and thinkers, from the Spartan general Lysander to the materialist philosopher Epicurus, deified after his death. In his *Parallel Lives*, the biographer Plutarch recorded that someone among the older, established gods was evidently displeased by the newcomer, Demetrius. A whirlwind tore apart Demetrius's robe, severe frost disrupted his procession, and tendrils of hemlock, unusual in the region, sprouted up around the man's altars, menacingly encircling them.

In ancient Rome, the borders between heaven and earth fell under Senate control, as deification by official decree became a way to legitimize political power. Building upon Greek traditions of apotheosis, the Romans added a new preoccupation with protocol, the rites and rituals that could effect a divine status change. For his conquests, Julius Caesar was divinized, while still alive, by a series of Senate measures that bestowed upon him rights as a living god, including a state temple and license to wear Jupiter's purple cloak. Yet if it seemed like a gift of absolute power, it was also a way of checking it, as Caesar knew. One could constrain a powerful man by turning him into a god: in divinizing Julius, the Senate also laid down what the virtues and characteristics of a god *should be*. In their speeches, senators downplayed domination and

exalted magnanimity and mercy as the divine qualities that defined Caesar's godhood. As a new deity, Julius would have to live up to his god self,
to pardon his political enemies and respect the republican institutions
of Rome. On the Capitoline Hill, the Senate installed an idol of Julius
with the globe at his feet, but "he erased from the inscription the term
'demigod,'" the statesman Cassius Dio related. Caesar sensed that state-
sanctioned godhood could be at once a blessing and a curse.

When, not long after his deification, Julius was stabbed to death
twenty-three times, Octavian rose to power as Augustus, the first Emperor
of Rome, yet he and subsequent emperors would demur from being
turned into living gods. Divinity had become ominously tinged with
death, whether through the threat of provoking human jealousy, or
a connection more existential. Augustus blocked the construction of
a sacred "Augusteum," Claudius forbade sacrificial rituals to himself,
and Tiberius eschewed any portraits, unless they were placed far away
from those of the gods. Vespasian resisted claims of his divinity, though
even the animal kingdom seemed to acknowledge it—it was said that
an ox once broke free from its yoke, charged into the emperor's dining
room, and prostrated itself at his feet. After an emperor's demise, his
successor would lead the state ritual to turn the deceased into a deity. As
his wax effigy burned on a funeral pyre, an eagle was released from the
flames, a winged transport to the heavens. The fact of death in no way
compromised the politician's claim to immortality. Death was simply a
shedding of the body, like a snake sheds its skin.

As a tool of statecraft, apotheosis consolidated political dynasties, and
it was also an expression of love and devastation, often for those who
perished in unexpected, tragic ways. The emperor Hadrian deified both
his wife and mother-in-law, but the highest heavens were reserved for
Antinous, his young lover who drowned in the Nile under clouded circumstances. When Julia Drusilla was stricken by a virus at twenty-two,
she was divinized by her maximalist brother Caligula as Panthea, or "all
the gods." In February of 45 BCE, when Cicero's daughter Tullia died a
month after giving birth, the bereaved statesman became determined to
turn her into a god, and set his keen intellect to the task of how best
to achieve apotheosis. To raise public awareness of the new deity, Cicero

decided to build her a shrine, and had an architect draw up plans. Yet the senator became fixated on the question of what location would be optimal, indoors or outside, and worried about how the land in the future could change ownership. He fretted over how best to introduce Tullia to Rome, to win the approval of both the immortal gods and mortal public opinion. "Please forgive me, whatever you think of my project . . ." Cicero wrote in a letter to a friend, and wondered aloud if his strange endeavor would make him feel even worse. But to the statesman, supernatural in his grief, the urge was irrepressible. Deification was a kind of consolation.

The century that reset time began with a man perhaps inadvertently turned divine. It is hard to see him, for the earliest gospels were composed decades after his death at Golgotha, and the light only reaches so far into the dark tombs of the past. The scholars who search for the man-in-history find him embedded in the politics of his day: a Jewish dissident preacher who posed a radical challenge to the gods and governors of Rome. They find him by the banks of the Jordan with John the Baptist. He practices the rite of baptism as liberation, from sin and from the bondage of the empire that occupied Jerusalem. Jesus, like many in his age, warns that the apocalypse is near: the current world order, in its oppressions and injustices, will soon come to an end and the kingdom of the Israelites will be restored, the message for which he will be arrested for high treason. In what scholars generally agree was the first written testimony, that of Mark, Jesus never claims to be divine, nor speaks of himself as God or God's Son. In the early scriptures, when asked if he is the messiah, "the anointed one," at every turn he appears to eschew, deflect, or distance himself from the title, or refers to the messiah as someone else, yet to come. He performs miracles under a halo of reluctance, the narrative ever threatening to slip from his grasp. When he cures a deaf man, he instructs bystanders not to tell anyone, *but the more He ordered them, the more widely they proclaimed it*, Mark relates.

In the decades after the crucifixion, just as the gospels were being composed and circulated, the apotheosis of Roman emperors had become so routine that Vespasian, as he lay on his deathbed in 79 CE, could quip,

"Oh dear, I think I'm becoming a god." Refusing homage to the deified
dictators of Rome, early Christians wrested the titles bestowed upon
them—"God," "Son of God," "the Lord," "Divine Savior," "Redeemer,"
"Liberator"—and gave them to the man Rome had executed as a criminal. In the writings of the apostle Paul, aglow with a vision of the resurrected Christ, Jesus appears as a new species of cosmic being, God's
eternal Son. While pagan politicians ascended to heaven, transported
on the steep journey by eagle, Jesus simply lowered himself; he emptied
himself, in Paul's words, into the form of a peasant. Although Paul was
horrified when he found himself mistaken for a pagan god, the apostle preached the mystical possibility that all humankind might join in
Christ's divinity. Transcending earthly politics, the dissident turned into
a deity to surpass the godlings of Rome. As the Almighty made flesh, Jesus
became a power that could conquer the empire—and eventually, He did.

According to the Gospel of John, among the last to be written, on
the eve of his crucifixion, Jesus compared himself to a serpent, the one
Moses had set upon a pole at God's command to save his people from
the plague. Like the reptile, Christ would point the way toward the divinity ever coiled within each man. In the second century, the sect of the
Ophites worshipped Jesus in his form as serpent, invoking the fact that
human entrails resemble a snake. It was recorded they celebrated the
Eucharist by inviting a snake onto the table to wind itself around the loaf
of bread. By the third century, the Greek convert Clement of Alexandria could declare that divinity now "pervades all humankind equally."
All who followed the teachings of Christ "will be formed perfectly in
the likeness of the teacher—made a god going about in flesh." Theologians avidly debated the possibility of *theosis*—"becoming god"—a word
coined to distinguish Christian doctrine from the pagan *apotheosis*.
Among Christians in the second and third centuries, the notion was
commonplace that each person had a deified counterpart or divine
twin, whom they might one day encounter.

In 325 CE, the emperor Constantine gathered together two thousand
bishops at the Council of Nicaea to officially define the nature of Jesus's
divinity for the first time. Against those who maintained he had been created by God as a son, perfect but still to some extent human, the bishops

pronounced Jesus as Word Incarnate on earth, equal to and made of the same substance as God the Father, whatever it may be. Other notions of Jesus's essence were branded as heresies and suppressed, and gospels deemed unorthodox were destroyed. Through the mandates of the Nicene Creed, the idea of divinity itself became severed from its old proximities to ordinary mortal life. In the work of theologians such as Augustine, who shaped Christian orthodoxy for centuries to come, the chasm between humankind and divinity grew ever more impassable.

Though mystics might strive for union with the godhead, veiled in metaphors, the idea that a man could transform into an actual deity became absurd. God is absolutely different from us, the theologians maintained; the line between Creator and His creation clearly drawn. Away from its pagan closeness, away from the dust and turmoil of terrestrial life, Christian doctrine pushed the heavens from the earth. "I asked the sea and the chasms of the deep and the living things that creep in them," Augustine writes in the *Confessions*. "I spoke to all the things that are about me, all that can be admitted by the door of the senses," but they said in their myriad voices, *I am not God*. "And I said, 'Since you are not my God, tell me about him.'"

✦ ✦ ✦

My story begins with a light, appearing in the darkness of an unknown shore.

It was "like a small wax candle that rose and lifted up," recorded the mariner, sighting a campfire on land after five weeks on the open sea. In the daylight, as he anchored his ship off the coast, crowds of curious islanders gathered on the beach. "They threw themselves into the sea swimming and came to us," Christopher Columbus wrote in his diary on October 14, 1492. "We understood that they asked us if we had come from heaven," he reported, although he could not understand a word of their language. "One old man came into the boat, and others cried out, in loud voices . . . to come and see the men who had come from heaven." Hundreds surrounded the admiral, and begged him to take them aboard his craft, thinking the divinities would soon return to the sky. A week later, Columbus related he was again hailed as a celestial deity, now on an island so densely flocked by parrots they concealed the sun. The natives "held our arrival to be a great marvel, believing that we came from heaven," he wrote of people wearing gold nose rings that he found disappointingly small.

Having sailed in the wrong direction to China, the admiral never knew where he had landed, and underestimated the size of the sea. His error was an origin point, such that a historian could claim in 1982, "We are all direct descendants of Columbus, it is with him that our genealogy begins, insofar as the word *beginning* has a meaning." In a green lagoon at this beginning, Columbus reported that he killed a serpent. "I am bringing its skin to Your Highnesses," he promised Ferdinand and Isabella, offering a sacrifice of scales. Conquest followed apotheosis: of every island he found, again and again filled with people reportedly mistaking him for divine, the mariner took possession for Spain. He would read an indecipherable declaration and pause for the refusal that could not occur. "No opposition was offered to me," Columbus wrote.

I will tell you not of one god but of many.

I will speak of the lost explorers, the captains and militants, the officer who died on a hill far from home. I will tell of the presidents and prime ministers, the anthropologists, the optometrist, the teenager who bathed on the beach. I will sing of the marginal avatars, the abortive sects and misfired devotions, of the gods only briefly, unstably divine. Though the idea that a man could become deified may appear an archaic and arcane theological puzzle, a dream jettisoned from an enchanted past, with the accident that was the alleged dawn of the modern age, the flood of sanctifications begins to rise.

In the earliest stream, from the fifteenth century on, the sailors, missionaries, and settlers who came in the footsteps of Columbus collected myriad accounts of Europeans mistaken for gods, the unexpected side effect of their civilizing mission. In the high age of empire, as Europe spanned the earth in quest of wealth, the stories poured forth of colonial officers, soldiers, and bureaucrats who in going about their administrative duties were irritated to find themselves worshipped as living deities. They were surprised to observe their dead colleagues appeased at tomb shrines with offerings of biscuits and gin. With the rise of nationalism and liberation movements in the twentieth century come the politicians and activists, secularists and modernists, who were dismayed to learn of their own apotheoses, as tales of their miracles contradicted their political agendas. The accidental god haunts modernity. He, always he, walks bewildered into the twenty-first century, striving for a secular authority yet finding himself sacred instead. He appears on every continent on the map, at times of colonial invasion, nationalist struggle, and political unrest.

To speak of men unwittingly turned divine is to sing a history of how the modern world came to be. With the incursion of Europe and Christendom onto a new shore, the idea of the West was born with the deaths, over the coming century, of an estimated sixty million of its inhabitants. According to modernity's own creation myth, Columbus's revelation ushered in the high age of exploration and conquest, the crashing waves of the Enlightenment, and the onward cruise of industrialization and progress. Philosophers chased superstitions and spirits out of the shadows and exposed them in the clear light of reason, and even God Himself was pronounced dead on the scene. ("Who will wipe this blood from us?" the messenger Nietzsche asked.) Freed from the irrational reverences that defined the past, the modern age grew disenchanted, it was said. Condemned first as heretical, and then as nonsensical, ideas of deification had no place in the canon of the West's modernity, a tradition predicated on the exclusion of other ways of thinking about transcendence and how, on earth, we should live. But all the while, what became seen as "Western thought" was built upon two altars, of Greco-Roman classicism and Christian creed, both of which had men-becoming-gods at their centers.

Europe's imperialists interpreted exotic accounts of celestial ascent as the delusions of primitive societies, isolated atolls, and fetishistic minds. These stories, however, were coauthored creations, as much the product of Europe's sailors, soldiers, and scholars as the islanders, chieftains, and shamans they described in their encounters. The narratives often hinged upon problems of meaning: What word do you translate as "god"—and what do you intend by it? The colonizers kept telling them, for they were useful, as a means to legitimize conquest and hold

on to territories ever on the verge of slipping away. Though these incidents may seem no more than a fleeting curiosity in the annals of the
sacred, I will relate how ideas of accidental divinity persist in a hidden
way, entrenched in something else we mistake as eternal: the modern
concept of race.

But I will sing, too, of a mystical mutiny, of how to fight old myths with
the new. If deified men have propped up empires, they have also brought
them down, heralding new visions of government. Into the twenty-first
century, apotheosis has been a form of resistance against imperialism and
injustice, and a response to modernity's spectacular displays of state violence. It has been a powerful political tool of blessed rage, posing new
answers to the contentious question of what a god looks like. Deification
has been defiance: from the depths of abjection, creating gods has been a
way to imagine alternative political futures, wrest back sovereignty, and
catch power. Accidental deities have also cured illnesses, bestowed children, and controlled the weather.

This book does not seek to determine whether people believed in the
unwitting gods. For the very idea of "belief" has a history of its own, as
a specific rather than universal concept, for which many languages did
not, and still do not, have a corresponding word. Rather than making
claims as to what people really believed—for one can never truly know—
let us ask why these stories exist, why they have been constructed and
retold, and how they have shaped our world. Let us unravel the ways stories are woven together and reproduced, treasured and manipulated, used
to exalt and to degrade—to create what successive generations will hold
as true. Our scriptures are found in diaries and interviews, in scholarly
accounts, newspaper clippings, telegrams, films, in handwritten gospels,
police archives, court records, even a conversation with a deity who is a
friend. Some gods are living and some are dead. There is no single definition of what it means to be a god, or divine. Divinity emerges not as
an absolute state, but a spectrum, able to encompass an entire range of
meta-persons: living gods, demigods, avatars, ancestor deities, divine
spirits who possess human bodies in a trance. We call a female deity a
"goddess," as if something less than a god, and there are few of them

here, an absence taken on at the heart of this book, which examines how a military general worshipped as a god became an icon of modern masculinity and a role model for how a man should be.

There is no single method or set of criteria to determine when someone is deified, or to distinguish between religious worship and a more colloquial adoration. Let us search for the presence, or allegations, of what we have come to understand as the defining features of a religion: sacred texts, shrines or houses of worship, ritual practices, icons, a set of shared convictions and tenets. But let us do so while asking how these ingredients of a "religion" came to be—for it will turn out that involuntary gods were present at its birth. The deities who appear here are profoundly modern in character: their divinity rests on concepts that are not timeless but modern in origin—religion, gender, and race—and draws upon new technologies of transport, communication, and warfare. Their godhood confounds the artificial distinctions between conceptual worlds, such as sacred versus secular, that make enchanted things seem misplaced in a disenchanted world, or the appearance of divinity in politics seem like a strange intrusion. The accidental god has a history, extending from a beach in 1492 to the dark holes of the internet, and his story has not yet been told.

✦   ✦   ✦

Gods are born ex nihilo and out of lotuses, from the white blood of the sea-foam, or the earwax of a bigger god. They are also birthed on dining room tables and when spectacles of power are taken too far. They are born when men find themselves at the wrong place at the wrong time. Gods are made in sudden deaths, violent accidents; they ascend in the smoke of a pyre, or wait, in their tombs, for offerings of cigars. But gods are also created through storytelling, through history-writing, cross-referencing, footnoting, repeating. They ascend in acts of translation and misunderstanding. If to translate is to carry words from one language into another, it is also "to carry or convey to heaven without death." Gods are made when language goes beyond its intentions. Occasionally, a god is born out of an excess of love. As the third-century theologian Origen wrote, in his commentary on the Song of Songs, "It should be known that it is impossible for human nature not always to love something." It is also impossible for human nature not to love too much.

It may be that the surest way to find out what it means to be human is to ask what it means to be inadvertently, unwittingly, ingloriously divine.

I follow the serpent.

I

# LATE THEOGONY

As for this generation of the 20th Century, you have no knowledge how worlds are built.
  And upon what trigger Kingdoms are set.

—Fitz Balintine Pettersburg, *The Royal Parchment Scroll of Black Supremacy*

Paradise is a person. Come into this world.

—Charles Olson, "Maximus, at the Harbor"

# 1

---

# In the Light of Ras Tafari

"A strange new fish emits a blinding green light," the article in *National Geographic* announced. Off the coast of Bermuda, an intrepid correspondent curled up inside a Bathysphere, a round steel chamber with a porthole, had been lowered by rope into depths where no man had gone before. His deep-sea observations, appearing in the June 1931 issue, were followed by the account of an even greater curiosity: the coronation of an African king. On November 2, 1930, Ras Tafari Makonnen had been crowned His Imperial Majesty Haile Selassie I, Emperor of Ethiopia, King of Kings, Elect of God, and Conquering Lion of the Tribe of Judah, in a spectacular weeklong celebration in Addis Ababa. In sixty-eight pages of text and color photography, the magazine described how world leaders and monarchs, film crews, and chieftains in prickly lion-mane headdresses had converged from all directions on the landlocked Christian kingdom, the last uncolonized territory in Africa. From Great Britain came the Duke of Gloucester, King George V's son, bearing a crown and scepter once stolen from the country as well as a traditional English coronation cake. From Italy came the Prince of Udine with the gift of an airplane; from America, President Herbert Hoover's emissary came laden with an electric refrigerator, five hundred rosebushes, and a complete bound set of *National Geographic*.

"The studded doors of the Holy of Holies open ponderously," recounted the diplomat Addison E. Southard, who served as United States consul general in Ethiopia and was reporting on the ceremony for the magazine. At dawn, the Conquering Lion and His Empress, Menen Asfaw, entered the throne room, aglow with a red-gold light. Forty-nine bishops in groups of seven had been reciting the Psalms for seven days and seven nights, stationed in the seven corners of the cathedral. The Ethiopian royal dynasty had remained unbroken, Southard noted, from the mistiest dawn of the past, "with time out, naturally," for the Flood. Ras Tafari, who could trace his lineage back to the union of King Solomon and the Queen of Sheba—in the Ethiopian version of the story, they sired a child—was anointed with seven oils that dripped down his face and hair. As the chanting grew from the sea "of priestly throats," Tafari Makonnen rose above his title of *Ras*, meaning "head" or duke, and took on his sanctified baptismal name, Haile Selassie, "Power of the Trinity." He was duly vested with the symbols of power: the imperial scepter and the orb, a jeweled sword, a ring inlaid with diamonds, two gold filigree lances, unfathomably long scarlet robes, and the crown, glistening with emeralds. "Nothing disturbed the impressive solemnity save the staccato exhaust of low-flying airplanes which circled above," observed the *National Geographic* staff photographer W. Robert Moore. "Otherwise the centuries seemed to have slipped suddenly backward into Biblical ritual."

Outside in the daylight, lining streets recently paved and shaded with eucalyptus, perched upon the distant hilltops as far as the eye could see, were the multitude of Ethiopian citizens, wrapped in white robes and carrying white parasols, awaiting word of the sovereign. There were thousands of Ethiopian soldiers in starched uniforms, guarding newly erected monuments to the King of Kings, alongside the leagues of warriors from the interior in full tribal dress. The sunlight danced off the surfaces of their gilded rhinoceros shields. "The country is surrounded, or embraced, we might say, by African colonial possessions of Great Britain, France, and Italy," Southard noted.

They had now gathered inside the throne room: the representatives of a world that had tried to colonize Ethiopia and failed, delegates of a global system that self-destructed in the stock market crash only a year before. Haile Selassie sat upon his scarlet throne and serenely watched, in Southard's words, as "the princes then made obeisance on bended knee." The cannons fired a 101-gun salute. "There is the fanfare of a thousand trumpets," the US consul proclaimed. "The triumphant ululation of tens of thousands of waiting women is released in waves over the city of the 'New Flower.'" The Lion and his empress drove off to their luncheon in a horse-drawn carriage, last seen at the court of Kaiser Wilhelm II.

◆  ◆  ◆

On the other side of the earth, on the island of Jamaica, several people had the same idea almost simultaneously. At first it was just an inkling, a rising suspicion, the glimmer of a thought, but of a kind that could tear apart the universe and build it anew. It began to circulate without anyone thinking to consult the Ethiopian monarch, to ask for his opinion or consent, or even notify him with a telegram. A thirty-five-year-old theorist, Leonard Percival Howell, convened a meeting to announce the idea in public, in a marketplace known as Redemption Ground in downtown Kingston. The crowds that gathered around him were small at first, but as Howell took his message from one street corner to the next, and to the neighboring parishes, moving east along the coast, his listeners grew. He handed out flyers; discarded on the street, they skittered along the pavement and floated when they caught the breeze.

> *King of Kings and Lord of Lords of Ethiopia*
> *BLACK PEOPLE! BLACK PEOPLE!*
> *Arise and shine for the Light is come*

God was a living man, alive on earth right now. He had high cheekbones, all-seeing eyes, a dark beard and black skin, and wore velvet robes of scarlet and gold. By April 18, 1933, when police officers first began to take note, two hundred people had gathered around the apostle, poised atop a wooden barrel. "I heard Leonard Howell, the speaker, said to the hearers: 'The Lion of Judah has broken the chain, and we of the black race are now free. George the Fifth is no more our King,'" an officer reported. On an island still under British colonial rule, Howell spoke of how the British king's own son had made obeisance on bended knee to a new messiah. He passed around a photograph of the Duke of Gloucester, looking dazed in Addis Ababa beneath his furry busby hat. One must not pay taxes nor rent to the British government, Howell instructed, for Jamaica now belonged to the children of the new god. "'The white people will have to bow to the Negro Race,'" the police transcribed, and dispatched the report to Jamaica's crown solicitor. "The man is a stupid ranter who puts forward an imaginary being or person who he calls 'Ras Tafari' and whom he describes as Christ as well as King of Ethiopians," the solicitor wrote in a letter of advice to the attorney general. Fearing that pressing charges of sedition against Howell would only serve to advertise his message, he suggested "the Lunatic Asylum" instead.

Preaching was in Leonard Howell's blood; his father, Charles, when he wasn't tending the family fields in Clarendon parish, had worked as a lay minister in the Anglican church, the conduit to the Almighty authorized by Jamaica's overlords. As a teenager, Leonard was shipped off to Panama for work, then became a cook on US marine ships during the First World War before settling in New York in the 1920s. He worked construction jobs on Long Island and opened a tearoom on 136th Street in Harlem, where it was said he also provided certain mystical services. In 1931, Howell was imprisoned at Sing Sing for eighteen months for selling medicines without a pharmacist license and serving ganja in his "tea pad." The following year, he was deported.

Back in Jamaica, he took up the mantle of his father, but he preached a different deity. To a people vilified and dehumanized for the shade of their skin, Howell told that God was a black man. And He resembled the faces in the crowd, such as those who gathered in late May 1933. "You are God and every one of you is God," Howell said, according to the notes of one British corporal. When it became clear the police would not let Howell out of their sights, the charismatic apostle had strolled into the station and invited the officers to attend his sermons.

The corporal, flanked by two armed reinforcements, had taken up the offer and recorded Howell's words:

> I am here to inform You my dear Ethiopians that I can bring the Governor of Jamaica, but he cannot understand me as it is too deep for him.

✦ ✦ ✦

Haile Selassie appears as the first of my testaments, for of all men god-swept into divinity in the modern age, he would obtain the greatest number of worshippers; he alone found nearly a million devotees. It had long been foretold that Ethiopia would be the site of a new theogony, among those in the New World living in the obscenity of injustice. From the forced labor camps of scenic plantations to the destitute city slums of the American north, currents of Ethiopianism, a black emancipatory movement, had begun to emerge in the late eighteenth century. *Ethiopia*, "the land of burnt faces," the Greek word used for the continent in the Bible, stood as the driving image of liberation, for all Africa and its diaspora. It was the password to access hope. "God decrees to thy slave his rights as a man," the New York City preacher Robert Alexander Young declared to the white slave owner in his 1829 *Ethiopian Manifesto*. "This we issue forth as the spirit of the black man or Ethiopian's right, established from the Ethiopian's Rock, the foundation of his civil and religious rights." The distant, mysterious kingdom would be the stone slab upon which a new power would rise.

In 1896, Ethiopia became the only territory to survive Europe's rapacious "scramble for Africa," stunning the globe when it defeated an attempted Italian invasion in the Battle of Adwa. This confirmed, for many, its status as the spiritual home of the black diaspora, even if very few families in the New World had ancestral roots in its mountainous terrain. If the white imperialist world, constructed upon the back of black enslavement, was Babylon, city of captivity, Ethiopia was Zion, site of exile and future return. Young had ended his *Manifesto* with the news that God was preparing the next John the Baptist, to spread word of a coming messiah. "How shall you know this man?" he asked.

A new Zion would require a new scripture, and in 1924, a text was published in Newark, New Jersey, that aimed to supplant the King James Bible. The earlier teachings had become corrupt, for passages such as the vague "curse of Ham" in Genesis 9 were notoriously used to justify slavery. When a drunken Noah was found naked in his tent, his sons Shem and Japheth covered him but Ham in some way humiliated him, and Noah condemned his descendants, supposedly the black race, to servitude. If the Bible upheld centuries of oppression upon the figment of a petty, obscure crime, the true route to salvation would require not only other interpretations, but a different book.

"Now in the year of 1917 A.D., Shepherd Athlyi first went about the City of Newark, New Jersey, U.S.A., telling of the Law . . ." So told the revelation of *The Holy Piby*, which appeared, in a large print run, the same year the US government passed a racist law halting Afro-Caribbean immigration to the United States. Its author was Robert Athlyi Rogers, a black pastor hailing from Anguilla. In the *Piby*, a word whose origin is unknown, Athlyi told of a new creation myth, of an Adam and Eve who were "of a mixed complexion." He described his own divine annunciation as messenger, the flashing light that had appeared, splitting the heavens open, and the angels who called out: "*Athlyi. . . . Athlyi . . .*" In a climax of holiness, Athlyi wrote, in the third person, of how he came face-to-face with God Himself—an Abyssinian Almighty. "Athlyi advanced towards the Lord with open arms and cried out, 'O God of Ethiopia, I pray, redeem me, wash me clean and separate me from all gospels that pollute the righteousness of thy name . . .'" And the God of Ethiopia spoke to him, saying, "Reach out and touch me." When the shepherd stretched out his right hand, "the eyes of Athlyi lit up like a torch."

The Ethiopianists saw clearly the paradox: for centuries, white rulers had claimed moral rectitude, to have superior knowledge of God and His ethics, and yet dispossessed, enslaved, and dehumanized fellow men in a way that could only be described as evil—or, to turn their clinical language against them, insane. Why did the God that men like Athlyi or Howell were raised to worship permit the inordinate suffering of the black race? When they prayed, were their words directed to the wrong god? The Ethiopianists knew that sometimes, one paradox could only be surmounted by another.

In *The Holy Piby*, Newark's shepherd prophesied a coronation scene. He told of how Elijah placed a crown, inlaid with a star of infinite light, upon the head of a "natural man," and the heavens rejoiced. "And it came to pass," Athlyi wrote, "that I saw a great host of Negroes marching upon the earth. . . . I looked towards the heaven and behold I saw the natural man standing in the east and the star of his crown gave light to the pathway of the children of Ethiopia." Six years later, the verses in the *Piby* would prove oracular, beyond even what Athlyi himself had imagined. When news of Haile Selassie's ascension flooded the airwaves, Athlyi had left New Jersey and was residing in Jamaica. Leonard Howell and his disciples took up his *Piby* as prophecy and sang its verses as hymns. On August 24, 1931, the same summer the *National Geographic* issue appeared, Robert Athlyi Rogers decided to take his own life. He was only forty, but his followers would say that, having heard the news of Haile Selassie's coronation, having seen the photographs, his mission on earth was complete. The shepherd walked across the beach, into the waves, and kept walking until he drowned in the deep.

✦   ✦   ✦

It was not only Howell or Athlyi who had the idea. There was Joseph Nathaniel Hibbert, a Jamaican who moved to Costa Rica as a teenager to toil on a plantation. Esoteric by nature, Hibbert devoured occultist tomes, cabbalistic mysteries, and searched for clues in a translation of the fourteenth-century Ge'ez epic *Kebra Nagast*, which sang of the Solomonic kings. He joined a society of black Freemasons, the Ancient Mystic Order of Ethiopia, and scaled its ranks. In 1931, not long after Haile Selassie's coronation, the thirty-seven-year-old Hibbert returned to Jamaica, where he began to preach on street corners that the Ethiopian king was divine. Hibbert had come to this realization without any contact with Howell, whom he only met after he moved to Kingston and found someone already spreading his word. Yet Howell would gain a much larger following, for Hibbert, sometimes glimpsed in full masonic regalia—green satin robes, yellow turban, saber, heavy Star of David, and adornments of red, green, and gold—was so occult that he declined to share the innermost secrets with others.

There was also the Jamaican sailor Henry Archibald Dunkley, who worked for the United Fruit Company. He was standing on a dock in Hoboken, New Jersey, when he heard news over the radio, "that they crown a strange king in Africa." "Immediately after the announcement came," Dunkley remembered, "snow fell same time, it fell fast, and I said to myself same time: from 1909 I have been looking for this individual, this King of Kings." Guided by the light of his blizzard epiphany, Dunkley quit his job and returned to Jamaica in early December. Before long, the sailor found himself robbed of all his earthly belongings. "After that," he said, "I went on a very high place . . ." Renouncing all materialistic pursuits, Dunkley decided to read through the King James Bible page by page, to find evidence for his conviction that Haile Selassie was the messiah returned. Two years of close reading, and verses in Ezekiel, Isaiah, Timothy, and especially Revelation 19 assured him:

*His eyes were as a flame of fire, and on his head were many crowns . . .*
*And he hath on his vesture and on his thigh a name written,* KING OF
KINGS, AND LORD OF LORDS.

By mid-1933, independently of Howell or Hibbert, Dunkley had
opened his own mission in Kingston. His sermons drew a burgeoning
crowd of curious listeners and armed police. When he refused to stop
preaching, Dunkley was dragged down from his platform and thrown in
jail. A medical examiner was called in to evaluate him. "Lock him up, he
is mad," the doctor said.

But the idea could not be contained. Among the earliest converts
were the Bedwardites, who added their numbers to the swelling ranks
of Leonard Howell's flock. To a people who had endured centuries in
chains, only to find in Jamaica's 1834 emancipation continuing enslavement under another name, the revivalist teacher Alexander Bedward
spoke of liberation. He rejected the versions of Christianity that upheld
white imperialist rule, preaching instead in the tradition of Jamaica's
Native Baptist churches, which drew upon African healing traditions.
With a keen sense of injustice, Bedward had fought for years against
the deep structural inequalities of Jamaica, an island where the majority lacked the right to vote and poverty was eternal. On an infamous
New Year's Eve in 1920, Bedward and his chief disciple, Robert Hinds,
had assembled their followers by the banks of the Hope River. They
announced the hour had come for them to escape the confines of their
tropical prison and fly up to heaven in a rapturous ascent.

Some say Bedward waited, at midnight, aboard his chariot, a chair
perched in a tree, but nothing happened. Others say that at the appointed
time, everyone jumped from the treetops, breaking numerous arms and
legs. In the wake of their attempted flight, ridiculed in the Jamaican
press, Bedward and Hinds were tried at the Half Way Tree Courthouse
and sentenced to imprisonment in Bellevue, Jamaica's grim psychiatric
asylum. While Hinds was released, Bedward would languish there for
nine years. Six days after Haile Selassie's coronation, Bedward divested
his body in his prison cell. Having heard the good news, the Jamaican

preacher determined his terrestrial work was done. *His father called him home*, his tombstone read.

There were others, who identified the divinity of Haile Selassie in an entirely different way. The ancestors from the Kongo region, kidnapped and sold into the Atlantic slave trade, had brought with them Kumina, rites of drumming, dancing, and trances in worship of an Old World pantheon of deities and spirits. They knew that whatever befell them, Kumina was a space of inviolability deep within, out of the slave owner's reach. They knew it would sustain them, as did a later wave of Kongo-lese immigrants who arrived in Jamaica after abolition as indentured laborers and kept Kumina aflame. In 1930, the island was plagued by a drought, yet just as reports of the coronation came over the radio, the rain came down. Kumina adepts declared that Haile Selassie was *Nzambi a Mpungu*, the supreme Creator in Kongo cosmology, who also went by the name Mbùmba. He was a deity often depicted as a gigantic serpent, resting by the edge of the sea.

In Kumina, it was not considered strange for a god to incarnate as a man; its philosophy was unburdened by any vast theological chasm between heaven and earth. It was thought that adepts themselves could become divine momentarily in spirit possession rituals, when gods and ancestral spirits entered them and acted through them. *Nzambi* was also the power of the soul, a creative life force that stands at the beginning of all things, a concept that would lend its misunderstood syllables to the word *zombie*. In Haiti, when a group of enslaved freedom fighters met in secret in a sheltering forest on an August night in 1791, the invoca-tions that sparked the Haitian Revolution were chanted in the name of this same deity. This was the first modern anti-colonial uprising, which led the French colony to independence and broke the shackles of white rule. As *Nzambi a Mpungu*, Haile Selassie was recognized, alive a cen-tury later, as the revolution's patron god.

Leonard Howell could often be spotted in Kingston, standing on the steps of a Methodist church, preaching that heaven was a white man's trick. Black people were taught to reject wealth in this life and remain quiescent as they awaited the silver and gold of the next—while the whites grew rich off their myth. Heaven was not in the clouds, like Christian priests taught, or even as Bedward had imagined: it was a real place on earth, Howell maintained, and Haile Selassie was organizing a plan to repatriate Africans there. The steamships that would carry home the black diaspora would arrive on August 1, 1934, the centenary of Jamaica's abolition of slavery.

Howell sold five thousand portraits of Haile Selassie in his kingly robes for a shilling, copied from a photograph in the *Illustrated London News*. If one wrote one's troubles on the back and mailed the portrait to the palace in Addis Ababa, Ras Tafari would resolve any grievances and answer all prayers. Better still, the cards would serve as passports when the ships to Ethiopia drew near. It was, in its way, an idea that *National Geographic* had cultivated, that a photograph could be a passport to another place. There was debate, among the growing hundreds of Howell's followers, as to whether they would need steamships at all. Some said the people would enter the sea, and the waters would part for them, as if in restitution for the voyage in the other direction. They would take a straight path across the Atlantic sea floor, passing the bones of ancestors, in a procession of redemption and deliverance, with the distant light of Ethiopia showing the way.

✦ ✦ ✦

Atop the soil where Tafari Makonnen's umbilical cord was buried, a church was raised. In the remote province of Harar, a month's journey to the east on horseback from Addis Ababa, a princess gave birth nine times. Each child born to Yeshimebet, the beautiful wife of the governor Ras Makonnen, was stillborn or died in infancy, but the tenth child, born in 1892, lived. When his mother died, in labor once more, the young Tafari was placed under the care of his uncle and aunt. He saw little of his illustrious father, who was preoccupied with his work managing and modernizing Harar. Ras Makonnen led Ethiopian forces to victory against the Italians at Adwa, and served on diplomatic missions for his cousin, the Emperor Menelik II, who named him as successor to the throne. Despite his absence, the young Tafari would grow to resemble

his father in his slight frame and delicate features, eyes that saw everything, and the understated way he exuded power. When Makonnen lay
dying of typhoid, he sent the emperor a letter charging him with guard-
ianship of his son. "Protect him well, and be assured that I will hold you
to account for this in the Afterlife before a Higher Judge," he wrote. The
orphaned Tafari was brought to the palace in Addis Ababa, where he
began to discreetly observe the mechanics of power.

After the Emperor Menelik suffered a series of strokes, he announced
that his grandson, Lij Iyasu, would be his successor. The conservative
elite was dismayed, for many viewed the handsome, hotheaded Iyasu as
radical and disrespectful of tradition. The son of a Muslim father forced
to convert to Christianity, Iyasu vowed to grant equality to Ethiopia's suppressed Muslim and Oromo populations and seemed poised to threaten
the old feudal hierarchies. Vilified as a secret Muslim and a conspicuous
womanizer, Lij Iyasu was excommunicated from the Orthodox Church,
never crowned, and deposed in a coup led by Menelik's widow, the formidable Empress Taitu. Her stepdaughter, Princess Zauditu, became the
first woman to reign over Ethiopia since the mythical Sheba, with Ras
Tafari appointed as prince regent and heir. It was said the petite Tafari
was chosen because he was so obsequious and well behaved, ingratiating
himself to everyone at court. The princes of the Ethiopian empire, who
possessed private armies and enjoyed autonomy in fiefdoms far from the
capital, thought Tafari unlikely to encroach upon their rule.

It may also be that he was so wily no one noticed his maneuverings as
he spun a web of strategic alliances. He swiftly began to strengthen the
central government in Addis, building institutions, imposing reforms,
and circulating his own newspaper, the *Light's Revealer*. He saw his work
as a tireless attempt to awaken Ethiopia into modernity after a long sleep.
"My country, you see, is like Sleeping Beauty in her castle in the forest,
where nothing has changed for two thousand years," he told an interviewer. "I have to struggle . . . against the inertia of my people, who prefer
to close their eyes against that dazzling light."

Imperialist Europe was wide-awake, and eyed Ethiopia with a preda-
tor's gaze. Under the wartime Treaty of London, secretly signed in 1915,
Britain and France promised Italy more territory in East Africa in the

event of victory if it joined the Allied side. When Italy sought to claim
its Abyssinian prize, the European powers enforced a weapons embargo
that left Ethiopia without the means to defend itself. Attempting to preserve its sovereignty, Ras Tafari successfully negotiated its acceptance
into the League of Nations, as the first independent African member, in
a further triumph for Ethiopianism. He embarked on an international
state tour, accompanied by the noblemen he didn't trust enough to leave
at home. Whether glimpsed in a Parisian motorcade or conferring with
Pope Pius XI in Rome, the travels of the exotic prince regent were avidly
followed by the press. Just as the Shepherd Athlyi was prophesying hosts
of cherubs in *The Holy Piby*, Ras Tafari was in Jerusalem, where, as he
strolled through the white stone alleyways of the city, he heard a heavenly music. It was the sound of a marching band of forty Armenian
orphans, survivors of the genocide. The future god was so moved that
he decided to adopt them and bring them to Addis Ababa to serve as his
imperial brass band. He would call them his angels.

"There is nothing that is human which can avoid returning to dust,"
he wrote, proclaiming the news in April 1930 that the Empress Zauditu
had met her demise. In preparation for his coronation, Ras Tafari began
to transform the city, building electrical poles and plywood triumphal
arches, telegraph lines to carry the word, and accommodations for the
delegates from all corners of the earth. To bring them to Addis Ababa
would be a powerful display for his enemies among Ethiopia's provincial
rulers, known to plot coups. He commissioned kingly accoutrements for
himself and his wife, the statuesque Princess Menen, and sent a friend
back to Jerusalem to acquire a slab of rock hewn from Solomon's temple,
upon which to position their thrones. He ordered thirteen lion-mane
headdresses from London's Savile Row, using the same milliner who
fashioned bearskins for the king's guards. He worked in haste to dispel the cloud of illegitimacy that hung over his ascent, for Iyasu, Menelik's rightful heir, was still alive and kept imprisoned. He instructed the
Armenian angels to debut an Ethiopian national anthem. On the eve of
the ceremony, at an ungodly hour of the night, the British consul was
surprised to catch sight of Tafari himself, attending to a last-minute task.

"I saw a little group of men in the twilight in the middle of the road,"

Major R. E. Cheesman recalled. "I got out of the car and walked towards them and someone said in a subdued tone: *'Janhoy!'* [Majesty!] There he was with a handful of men, within a few hours of his Coronation, inspecting a patch in the road which was being mended with a steamroller."

✦  ✦  ✦

While *National Geographic* raved about the magnificence of the coronation, accounts in other publications had painted a vastly different scene. The journalist Ellen La Motte, writing for *Harper's*, was in a bad mood after a night spent in a renovated cowshed, besieged by ants. Addis Ababa was filthy and lacked culture, La Motte complained; there weren't even any handicrafts for sale, let alone any seraphic splendor. "A primitive people like the Abyssinians, without genius, has created nothing," she declared. "Once in a while a hut is capped with an empty Perrier bottle." Reporting for the *Times*, Evelyn Waugh described the preparations in a state of unfinished disarray, "a complex of hysteria and apathy, majesty and farce," with the crown unceremoniously stashed in a cardboard box. When no one was paid to train the new imperial stallions, the restive horses toppled Wilhelm's carriage, killing a footman.

Many newspapers related that the emperor had bankrupted his country to pay for the celebrations, levying tax after tax while crooked officials skimmed off the top. At the ceremony, there were a hundred chairs reserved for foreigners that went empty—the Ethiopians, journalists reported, who walked barefoot for weeks across the country to reach the capital were not permitted to sit in them. In one of the more florid sections of the *National Geographic* coverage, Southard recounted the majestic "review of the troops" ritual, in which Ethiopia's tribal chieftains and their warriors were given the chance to show off their military prowess in traditional costume. *Harper's* reported that during the mock battle there appeared to be a mutiny: suddenly, combatants began to charge the stage, threatening Haile Selassie with sharpened spears, as the foreign guests overturned their chairs in fear and confusion. While the press had little idea what was going on, *National Geographic* focused on the wild beauty of the event, glossing over the rest: "How many elephants, how many lions, how many men . . . !"

For *National Geographic* the diversity of the planet was glorious—so long as it remained at a distance, like a picture in a book. Through the 1940s, the National Geographic Society excluded black people from membership, forbade them from using the library at its headquarters in Washington, DC, and enforced a whites-only policy at lectures. For the most part, the magazine avoided writing about America's own black population. Although it embraced the exotic for the thrill of discovery, it published pieces in favor of colonialist conquest, against immigration, and in support of eugenics. While it would never dare to print pictures of white women topless, its photographs of African women—in the name of science—provided the first glimpse of a breast for generations of enthralled American schoolboys. Haile Selassie was himself an avid collector of the magazine, and an enthusiastic member of the society, in what might seem a rare exception to its rules. Yet Haile Selassie did not consider himself "black"—he was a descendant, not of Noah's cursed son Ham, but of Shem, and *National Geographic* concurred that he was "decidedly Semitic."

Perhaps there is paradox attendant at the birth of every deity, but, searching in the deep waters of the distant past, we rarely have enough light to see it. A magazine that pursued racist policies and championed imperialism would inadvertently serve as scripture in the theogony of a black divine. "God is the grief of irony," the philosopher Emil Cioran once wrote, for He rises above any contradictions or sarcasms surrounding His birth. That the celestial throne of black power should welcome a man who did not think of himself as black might seem a greater paradox still. The new religion that formed around Him would be called "Rasta-fari," yet Waugh had noted that, ever since the emperor had taken on his imperial name of Haile Selassie, "a heavy fine is threatened to anyone overheard referring to him as Tafari."

At odds with his mortal self, the emperor's godhead transcended any single identity, or name, or pigment of skin. It encompassed all that stood opposite to the white hegemonic order, to the injustices the white world had wrought, ever since Columbus, on May 5, 1494, spied a new land. "There, silhouetted against the evening sky, arose sheer and darkly green Xamayca," the admiral reported, as the Taíno people assembled their defenses on shore. The admiral's style of discovery writing would be preserved in the explorer narratives of *National Geographic*. It was on this second voyage, when he found Jamaica, that Columbus sailed back to Europe with thousands bound in captivity for a human auction, in what marked the first passage of the transatlantic slave trade.

Addison Southard himself would seem an unlikely scribe of a revelation of black power. The white, Kentucky-born bureaucrat's appointment as ambassador to Ethiopia was controversial, given America's many well-qualified black politicians who might have been chosen instead. At his embassy desk, Southard was visited by a theopoetic muse. He closed his exhilarated account of the coronation with details from his own travels, across Ethiopia's steep canyons and pastoral valleys, its thriving marketplaces where traders dealt in leopard skins and honey, to paint a vision of a promised land, beautiful beyond compare. Proud camels carried corrugated iron for modern roofing on their humps, tied up with a bow. While *Harper's* spoke of cesspools and parasites, in *National Geographic* a cherubic Abyssinian played a harp. It was as if to lend proof to the psalmist King David's line that Ethiopia is the place "where God loves to dwell." To a readership deep in the Great Depression, the magazine presented the miraculous image of an elegant Ethiopian cook holding a platter upon which rested a single white ostrich egg, able to feed twenty-four.

By the 1950s, an anthropologist in Kingston would observe that men on the street corners were preaching with the Bible in one hand and a weathered copy of *National Geographic* in the other. They would read at length from Southard's descriptions, pausing at certain sentences to interpret and debate the meaning with their listeners. They dwelled on the diplomat's line about how the princes of the earth "made obeisance on bended knee before the Emperor." Brother Yendis, a teenager at the time, remembered the moment when he became convinced that Ras Tafari is God. "A man come from Cuba and give me a book. And the book is a underwater book, Geographic book . . . Well, in the middle of the Geographic book, it have the entire crowning of His Majesty. And when me read all them things, me get powerful, you know . . ." Copies of the scripture were precious, and hard to find.

✦ ✦ ✦

The coronation was not the only prophecy that Athlyi Rogers had divined. The Ethiopian God, Athlyi wrote, had also sent an apostle to earth, to lead the way. He was a barrel-chested trade unionist by the name of Marcus Mosiah Garvey, and at first, Athlyi felt ambivalent about him.

> In the year of 1921 Garvey spake saying: "*I have no time to teach religion.*" Because of this saying Athlyi took up his pen and was about to declare him not an apostle of the twentieth century. And it came to pass that the word of the Lord came to Athlyi saying, "*Blame not this man for I the Lord God hath sent him to prepare the minds of Ethiopia's generations, verily he shall straighten up upon the map.*"

Living in Harlem, the Jamaican-born black activist dreamed of a future "United States of Africa" to rival American power. In 1914, Garvey founded the Universal Negro Improvement Association, dedicated to promoting black unity, liberation, and progress. Observing the world around him, Garvey asked: Where were the black kings and black prime ministers, the black scientists, engineers, entrepreneurs? To promote black independence from the structural racism endemic to the white economy, Garvey founded the Black Star Line, a shipping company that would raise revenue through cargo transport and provide passage for anyone in the diaspora who desired to return to Africa. In the wake of World War I, membership in Garvey's UNIA soared, drawing activists such as Leonard Howell. "There will be no democracy in the world until the Negro rules," Garvey announced in 1919.

For Garvey, the barbarism of World War I had clearly demonstrated that white men were unfit to rule the earth. The "white man's war," in which black soldiers sacrificed their lives, had shattered any last illusion that there was anything innately superior about European civilization. Everything about how the world was constructed, ordered, and valued would radically need to change, including notions of God upon which the edifice of white Christian hegemony was built. If the Bible provided the images and myths that powered the imperialists, the only way forward would be to wrest them back, by sacralizing black politics. "Since the white people have seen their God through white spectacles, we have only now started out, late though it be, to see our God through our spectacles," Garvey wrote. "We shall worship Him through the spectacles of Ethiopia."

In 1927, after two years spent wrongfully imprisoned on false charges of mail fraud, Marcus Garvey was deported from the US to Jamaica. His Black Star Line had not proved seaworthy; several vessels sank, and the entire venture was abandoned. But still he returned to a hero's welcome among many Jamaicans; attempting to avoid further prison time, he found the adulation uncomfortable, particularly the prophecies of the *Piby* and a hymn that told of Garvey hoisting a serpent on top of a pole. An official from Kingston's UNIA headquarters sent a letter to the Jamaican daily, the *Gleaner*, distancing itself from Athlyi's inflammatory ideas, denouncing "as swindlers the gentlemen who have elevated Marcus Garvey to the rank of prophet and have painted the Almighty in sable hue." Garvey didn't want to be associated with any new Ethiopianist "cult." For his own part, he took Haile Selassie's claim to the lineage of the Israelite king Solomon seriously; he considered the emperor to be Jewish and wrote him off as a black ally.

Yet in the origin myth of a new religion, Garvey became inextricably linked with an oracle attributed to him: *Look to Africa, when a black king shall be crowned, for the day of deliverance is at hand*, words there is no evidence that he actually said. On the occasion of Haile Selassie's coronation, he did, however, write in an editorial in his newspaper the *Blackman*, "The Psalmist prophesied that Princes would come out of Egypt and Ethiopia would stretch forth her hands unto God. We have no doubt that the time is now come." If he meant only to mark the geopolitical occasion, Garvey's words took on a meaning far beyond their intentions. Adding to his predicament, he had staged a prescient play in Kingston only a few months earlier, called *The Coronation of the King and Queen of Africa*. In the religion of Rastafari, Marcus Garvey was inescapably John the Baptist, whether he liked it or not. He was the herald whom Young had foreseen in his *Ethiopian Manifesto*, the one whose ideas paved the way; the next head to be served on a plate. Like divine speech, it was as if every time Garvey pronounced something, it was so. *"Marcus Garvey is but a John the Baptist in the wilderness,"* Garvey had said in a rhetorical flourish in 1923, warning that a more powerful version of himself, a more formidable enemy to injustice, would soon appear.

In 1926, Marcus Garvey had made an enigmatic appearance as "the Pilot" in a searing and sacred text dreamed by a Jamaican reverend, Fitz Balintine Pettersburg. It was titled *The Royal Parchment Scroll of Black Supremacy*, and it took on a phantasm that had haunted print for at least a century. According to the *Oxford English Dictionary*, the phrase "white supremacy" had first appeared in a tract apprehensively titled *Emancipation: Or Practical Advice to British Slave-holders*. Its author, T. S. Winn, looked to the revolution in Haiti to advise slave owners that liberation was in their own best economic interest, for the entire system was on the verge of collapse. They must not wait until their slaves inevitably rose up and rebelled, Winn wrote, "or it may be too late by any means, however wisely and honestly attempted, to reduce them to

order and obedience under White supremacy." From its first passage
into print, white supremacy embodied its own fear of slipping away. It is
a concept with a blood-drained pallor, as if it had just glimpsed a vision
of its future death.

By 1920, when the Harvard scholar Lothrop Stoddard published his
best-selling *The Rising Tide of Color Against White World-Supremacy*,
the phrase had become ever more entrenched. "The white man could
think, could create, could fight superlatively well," Stoddard theorized,
for this archetypal man had been steeled in the furnace of Europe's harsh
medieval ages. "No wonder that redskins and negroes feared and adored
him as a god, while the somnolent races of the Farther East, stunned
by this strange apparition rising from the pathless ocean, offered no
effective opposition." But in the wake of the pale world's first "interne-
cine" war, with declining white birth rates and the influx of immigrants
branded "the colored peril," white power began to ebb. Facing his own
extinction, the white supremacist reaches for the ultimate claim: that
others are less than human. "The black people have no historic pasts,"
Stoddard declared, in a text so iconic of its time it was cited in *The Great
Gatsby*. "Never having evolved civilizations of their own, they are practi-
cally devoid of that accumulated mass of beliefs, thoughts, experiences,"
he wrote, listing the things that constitute a collective humanity.

How to even begin to fight such a claim? Reverend Balintine took it
back to the Garden, wielding the sword of a new scripture. Whiteness
was a curse dating back to Eve, and to an apple that beckoned from a
tree, he countered in *The Royal Parchment Scroll of Black Supremacy*.
"That looks pretty and respectable to your eyes. Don't it?" he joked. "We
have given Our Blood, Souls, Bodies, and Spirits to REDEEM Adam-
Abraham-Anglo-Saxon the white man from his DREADFUL downfall
and Leprosy," Balintine narrated. He wrote of how Africans had not only
sacrificed their lands, bodies, and labor before the altar of the white
man, but even the sites and characters of the Bible itself. "We have given
him access to the Tree of Life, we gave him the Garden of Eden, we gave
him Egypt, Palestine. . . . We gave him The Life, Soul, and Body of Jesus
Christ . . . The Body of the Black Virgin . . . and they took Joseph also.
We gave Ourselves to be Slaves for Hundreds of Years . . . Now we are

Perfectly DISGUSTED OF THEM," Balintine declared. "We wash our hands of THEM, for life." The new world system would be called "black supremacy," a phrase that has still never been recognized by the *OED*.

Observing Jamaican society, and recalling his years spent living in New York, Balintine knew that the trappings of bureaucratic authority were invaluable tools to conceal and deploy white power. This included the endless need for identification, registration, paperwork, and data in communities in which many were never given the chance to learn how to read. As officiousness constructs white supremacy, so Balintine, in his new sacred text, would take the form of the census, the affidavit, the marriage certificate, the diploma, the patent, the pay slip—and subvert them into documents authorizing a new regime. "All Governments and 'PROFESSIONS' must be REGISTERED in The Royal OFFICE of Black Supremacy," the *Scroll* declared. Scraps of boilerplate became scripture; bits of legalese became liturgy that sanctified blackness. "We are Creators of Creation, Dynasties and Kingdoms, Holy Genealogy and Holy Theocracy, and Celestial and Terrestrial Mediator if you wish to know Our Professions," the *Scroll* relayed. "Black Supremacy has taken Charge of White Supremacy, K.A.Q.O.," Balintine announced, using an enigmatic, official-seeming acronym.

Deep within the *Scroll* was a prophecy: of a royal couple who, on the morning of their coming coronation, were "very busy" with preparations. They were King Alpha and Queen Omega—the mysterious K.A.Q.O.— "The Lion and His Lioness," the "Head and Pillow-Monarchs" of a divine nuptial bed. Balintine even reproduced their "Marriage Diploma." The "Copyright of Holy Time" was Theirs. While Balintine had previously thought of himself and his wife Lula May as Alpha and Omega, with the passing of the year 1930, a more compelling identification, for readers of the *Scroll*, was Haile Selassie and Empress Menen.

By October 1933, according to complaints filed with the police, Leonard Howell was preaching alongside Balintine on street corners, using what the *Gleaner* would call a "weird doctrine": excerpts from the *Piby* and the *Scroll*. The idea, the notion that flickered, and rose, and glowed, could not be extinguished. To declare that Haile Selassie was God was to insist, against the white supremacist, that black people were human—and made of the same material as the divine. "He told us that

Christ was back on the earth. I couldn't understand it," one of Howell's original followers, Jephet Wilson, would recall. "But after him put it to me several times and I read the Scriptures, I saw that he was coming off the Bible . . . When he started to teach with the Bible and this same Black Supremacy book, I take it home. I had visions in my sleep at night."

*Alpha & Omega, The Black man & his wife was, here on Earth before*
*Adam and Eve & ABRAHAM & Anglo-Saxon if you please.*
*We, are the Type-Setters for Time and Eternity, if you please.*
*Our appointment is an Eternal Appointment if you please.*
*We are His & Her Register General of Black Supremacy if you please.*

✦ ✦ ✦

In 1934, nearly all the early Rastafari preachers were arrested by the colonial authorities, among them Howell, Hibbert, and Hinds. In mid-March, standing trial on charges of sedition, Leonard Howell became the first to defend the divinity of Haile Selassie in a British court of law. Howell was accused of inciting hatred and contempt for the British government, of calling the late Queen Victoria a "harlot," and convincing British colonial subjects that they were Ethiopians. "He took with him into the dock sheaths of documents and a few books of unusual proportions," the *Gleaner* reported. Before a courtroom packed with supporters, outraged hecklers, and amused voyeurs, Howell stood his ground.

CROSS-EXAMINATION:
*You rather preached that Ras Tafari is the Messiah come back to earth?*
Yes, Your Worship.
*Have you had any communication with Ras Tafari?*
No.
*Never?*
—No.

The apostle invoked the spectacle of the coronation in his defense. Hadn't the powers of the earth sent diplomats bearing gold, frankincense, and myrrh? Hadn't George V sent his own son? "All kings of the earth had to bow down," Howell avowed. Robert Hinds testified that he first learned of Haile Selassie's ascension in the pages of a magazine. Hinds couldn't read, but he saw the photographs and counted how Ras Tafari's crown had twelve stars, just as in Revelation 12:1. Hinds warned of the fall of empires: the Persian, Greek, Roman, and the British to come— before a judge with a notorious past. In Nyasaland in 1915, Judge Robert William Lyall-Grant had presided over the sentencing of the followers of John Chilembwe, who led a messianic rebellion against British rule. Lyall-Grant was knighted for his unsparing "justice"; the revolutionaries were executed en masse.

Outside the courthouse a crowd gathered, and watched as a rooster ascended the steps and crowed after each time Howell spoke. It was the duppy, or daemonic spirit, of a Baptist minister, Paul Bogle, people said, who had come to provide punctuation. In 1865, led by Bogle, hundreds of destitute Jamaicans rose up against injustice and set the courthouse on fire. When the governor declared martial law, over four hundred Jamaicans were killed by British troops and Bogle was hanged from the smoldering archway. "I said, 'People, you are poor but you are rich, because God planted mines of diamond and gold for you in Africa your home,'" Howell recalled, when asked to recount the contents of his sermons. As he spoke of the billions of pounds stolen from Africa by the British, the rooster crowed. Howell went on, repeating that "Christianity was only idolatry." If God is alive on earth right now, any religion that banishes Him to a distant sky, exiling Him from human affairs, must be worshipping the wrong deity. The British may have spread their faith far and wide, yet everywhere Christian churches were closing, he testified, becoming only "empty shells." The true god, Ras Tafari, lived elsewhere—and a gigantic meteor, Howell added, was headed toward Britain. "I told them: 'As it was in the beginning, so shall it be in the end.'"

After only fifteen minutes of deliberation, the jury found Howell guilty, and the judge announced a sentence of two years. "Asked if he had anything to say, Howell said he would appeal the conviction. The Chief Justice said there was no appeal," the *Gleaner* reported. "Howell paused for a little while." Then he said that "Ras Tafari would deliver him, very very soon."

✦ ✦ ✦

*I wish to state to you my dear Readers, that Ethiopia is a Country of great contrasts largely unexplored and is populated by Black People whose attitude towards this so called Western civilization has not changed within the last six thousand years. . . .*

Leonard Howell was confined by barbed wire and iron bars, but the landscape inside his cell was Addis Ababa as he wrote the foundational text of Rastafari, *The Promised Key*. The scripture began as if with the bourgeois tone of a travel magazine, but subverted, shredded, repurposed. "The Emperor attended to most of his preparations for the reception of his thousands of guests himself," Howell wrote, "and day after day could be seen rushing about in his scarlet car seeing how the white laborers were getting on with the new road he had ordered." All the powers of the earth were about to arrive. Alongside details from *National Geographic* and the British daily papers, Howell wove together and rewrote lines from *The Holy Piby* and the *Scroll*.

He would captivate his fellow inmates by recounting for them how King George's son made obeisance to Ras Tafari on bended knee. "'Master, Master my father has sent me to represent him sir,'" Howell narrated. "'He is unable to come and he said that he will serve you to the end.'" It may have appeared, to an outside eye, that Howell was locked in his bleak cage at Saint Catherine's in Spanish Town, first built as a slave trading market, and which had seamlessly evolved into the colonial prison. But the theorist was inside the throne room, aglow with a red-gold light. A scepter was being passed from one king to the next. "Upon His Majesty Ras Tafari's head are many diadems and on His garment a name written King of Kings and Lord of Lords oh come let us adore him," Howell prayed.

*The air you are breathing this minute is for King Ras Tafari.*
*The barbed wire eternity is his;*
    *the brimstone is his.*
*I want you to know that the firmament is his,*

he wrote.

    *Instead of saying Civilization hereafter we all shall say Black Supremacy*
    *Black People Black People arise and shine for the light has come.*

To deify a man is to look for him everywhere. It is to search every source and sign, to wade into the flows of information and events with the solemnity of a baptizee, headed underwater. At his King of Kings Mission, Robert Hinds ordered subscriptions for all his disciples to the *Pittsburgh Courier*, a popular black middle-class weekly, for he needed to interpret its pages as prophecy for an unfolding war. In April 1936, as hundreds of thousands of Italian troops and mercenary soldiers cut a gruesome path toward Addis Ababa, the deity was forced from his kingdom in fear of his life. "He did not seem to know where he was putting his feet," a *Times* correspondent reported. The haunted emperor and his family, along with an alleged thirty thousand pounds of luggage, boarded a train to French Somaliland, then on to Djibouti, where they escaped onto a British navy ship, eventually landing in the quiet city of Bath.

While Ethiopia's fighters had formidably stood against an invading force twice their size, the Italians resorted to chemical warfare. From circling fighter jets, Italian commanders launched poison gas, choking soldiers and civilians with an agonizing death that rained down from above. Over the next five years, nearly half a million Ethiopians were killed during the country's occupation by Italy. Carabinieri prowled the streets, enforcing a system of apartheid between Ethiopians and white settlers. Thousands of priests were slaughtered as they sheltered inside monasteries and churches, and villages were burned down on a whim. *National Geographic*, meanwhile, published a glowing panegyric to Mussolini, proclaiming the rebirth of the Roman Empire: "As we lunched informally with Il Duce in a little Littoria restaurant, I learned upon what meat this modern Caesar feeds."

To Marcus Garvey, Haile Selassie had been fatally unprepared to defend Ethiopia; he failed to mobilize resources and was, in Garvey's scathing phrase, "a cowardly lion," who "allowed himself to be conquered, by playing white." Yet for the growing legions of Jamaican Rastafarians, the war, despite going badly, only served to strengthen and define their faith. "What you have taught us about Jesus, is fulfilling in the land of Ethiopia right now: with the said same Romans," wrote a new convert, L. F. C. Mantle, in the Jamaican journal *Plain Talk*. "These are the said people who crucified Jesus 2,000 years ago." The new religion swiftly identified its Satan, in the cassocked shape of Pope Pius XI.

Across the island, Rastafarians fasted, protested, prayed, raised funds, organized battalions, and attempted, without success, to repeal a British law that barred Jamaicans from joining a foreign military. If they could not enlist in Haile Selassie's troops themselves, they would send an army of duppies to fight alongside the living. Because these ancestral warriors were already dead, they would be even more powerful against the forces of imperialism. To those who countered that the war was decisively lost, Rastafarians spoke of Haile Selassie's vast navy, hidden in a lake deep in the Ethiopian highlands, of the factories in mountain caves that churned out ammunition, and of His conscripts: lions and leopards who waited in the dead of night to feed on Italian invaders. "Snakes, caterpillars, scorpions and all sorts of poisonous reptiles and insects are said to have been conscripted and regimented for war service," a report detailed.

As he parsed the *Pittsburgh Courier*, Robert Hinds would dwell in particular on a pulp fiction serial starring a brainiac superhero, Dr. Belsidus. A black autocrat to rival Mussolini, the genius Belsidus played out a fantasy of revenge against white Europe, wielding gadgets and laser death rays. "White world supremacy must be destroyed, my lad, and it will be destroyed," Belsidus tells his secretary in the sci-fi series, penned by the journalist George Schuyler under a pseudonym. "It sounds mad, doesn't it?" As he leads the liberation movement of the Black Internationale, Belsidus establishes a state cult of religion, centered around a fifty-foot-tall, chiseled nude of a black god—an idol who is, ultimately, Belsidus himself. Identifying the pulp deity as code for Haile Selassie, Hinds had his disciple transcribe every episode of the serial into a logbook. It was read aloud during liturgies for the latest news from the war, as police informants in the shadows jotted down notes. If British officials were dismayed by these subversive rites of interpretation, they couldn't ban such prosaic papers as the *Pittsburgh Courier*, or for that matter, *National Geographic*.

Nor could they ban the *Jamaica Times*, which reprinted a piece of Italian propaganda that had been circulating in European newspapers. The author, masked by the pseudonym Frederico Philos, claimed that Haile Selassie had gathered a secret confederation of twenty million black people, with the goal of igniting a race war. This "black peril," which had limitless resources of gold and counted all the black soldiers serving in Europe's armies as members, called itself *Nyabinghi*, or "Death to Whites." "Haile Selassie is regarded as a veritable messiah, a savior to colored people everywhere," Philos wrote. "Whenever one mentions the word 'Negus,' the eyes of the blacks gleam with mad fanaticism. They worship him as an idol. He is their God. To die for the Negus is to ensure admission to paradise." The text then called upon Italian fascists to depose the dangerous demiurge. For many Rastafarian readers of the *Times*, the article was an uncanny, astoundingly public confirmation of their own beliefs. Soon, many islanders wanted to join the mysterious league. It was unclear where the Italian propagandist had found the word *Nyabinghi*: some say she was a nineteenth-century Ugandan queen, or a group of female warriors who led an uprising against the British, or even a lioness, avatar of the Egyptian goddess Sekhmet. Seizing and subverting the absurd, fearmongering screed, Jamaican brethren founded the first mansion, or denomination, within the Rastafari religion. They called it the House of Nyabinghi.

It is not known at precisely what point Haile Selassie became aware that, as he lost his empire on one side of the earth, he was growing a divine kingdom on the other. There are no direct comments or statements preserved from this time, although with the outpouring of Rastafari support for the war effort and the widespread coverage of Howell's trial in British papers, news must have reached him. From the depths of his dispossession, the exiled deity began to speak like his devotees. "In a word, it is international morality that is at stake," Haile Selassie announced as he took the stage in Geneva before the League of Nations, to deliver an impassioned appeal begging the world's powers to intervene in the Ethiopian genocide. Defending himself in the courthouse, Leonard Howell had similarly declared that "what is needed to-day is international salvation, not individual salvation." Sin was not personal or private but structural, the Rastafarians maintained, residing not in the failings of a heart but in the corporations, nations, and empires that made up the modern Babylon. Much like Howell, Haile Selassie was heckled and shouted at as he took the stand; though his oratory was by many accounts moving, it had no effect. The large majority of League members voted to lift sanctions on Italy, which argued in its defense that civilizing Ethiopia was "her sacred duty." Disillusioned, Haile Selassie returned to a frigid England, where the royal family sold its monogrammed lion silver to raise money for coal.

On an evening in 1937, the police stormed a public gathering in Kingston's Coronation Market, where Robert Hinds was using Revelation 17—in particular the woman astride a scarlet, seven-headed beast with MYSTERY written on her forehead—to interpret another unlikely text. Hinds had a copy of *Coronation Commentary* by Geoffrey Dennis, an awkwardly timed book on the British monarchy that appeared just after Edward VIII abdicated the throne to marry the American divorcée Wallis Simpson. While the Duke of Windsor threatened to sue Dennis for defamation for his final chapter, which described his "dereliction from duty" ("he had to have more freedom from godhead (the bores, the bowing) . . .") and insulted Simpson as "shop-soiled," Hinds saw Dennis's gospel as proof of the imminent downfall of the British Empire. Interrupting his sermon, the police attacked him with metal-tipped batons. "When you look 'pon Hinds, him was washed in bare blood," a follower remembered of that night.

But Hinds, weaving in and out of prison, did not give up his theological search to learn more about the nature and workings of the divine. He sought understanding in the sublimest testaments and in the lowest detritus of news; he combed through libel and vitriol and pulp. He spoke to all things that were around him, to every book at hand, all the news fit to print, and he asked for word of his god. In a house on Kelston Road, Haile Selassie huddled by a warm stove and gave no reply.

While both the emperor and his John the Baptist, Marcus Garvey, were living in grim circumstances in England, Haile Selassie declined an invitation to meet. In 1940, residing in London, Garvey was paralyzed following a stroke. A few months later, news mistakenly broke of his death and was picked up by the international press. As Garvey sat reading a stack of his own obituaries, some of them unflattering evaluations of his life, he suffered another stroke and died two weeks later. Yet for the Rastafarians, the prophet Garvey could not possibly be dead. If God was alive and breathing, what was the nature of death? What alchemy did the flesh and spirit undergo, and to what end? For the Rastafari death remained untheorized, unritualized, unspeakable. One might say a person "transitioned," or that their passing was proof they had fallen away from the living god, for the Rasta faithful would never experience death. In 1950, when Robert Hinds died of illness in a Kingston hospital, his followers refused to attend his funeral and only his sister was present.

Marcus Garvey was kept alive: stories circulated that he was living in the Congo, that he had avatared in the form of President William Tubman of Liberia, that he cursed a follower who betrayed him to wander dressed in a burlap sack. In life, Garvey had refused to associate with the Rastafari movement and forbade Howell from selling portraits of the emperor outside the UNIA headquarters in Kingston. In death he remained as living prophet, even if he had criticized and scolded God. "If death has power, then count on me in death to be the real Marcus Garvey I would like to be," Garvey said in a 1924 address smuggled out of an Atlanta prison, in which he swore to keep up the fight for black liberation, no matter what befell him. He said it not knowing that in death one can become other than oneself, too.

> *Would I not go to hell a million times for you?*
> *Would I not like Macbeth's ghost, walk the earth forever for you?*
> *Would I not lose the whole world and eternity for you?*
> *Would I not cry forever before the footstool of the Lord Omnipotent for you?*
>     *. . . Look for me in the whirlwind*, Garvey had said.

◆   ◆   ◆

Freed from prison, in 1939 Leonard Howell secured funding to purchase hundreds of acres atop one of Jamaica's highest peaks. In a way that moved beyond theory, beyond theology, Pinnacle became the site of a Rastafari exercise in building the New World anew. To the mountainous commune with a dizzying view, seven hundred of Howell's acolytes relocated, establishing a counter-society free from any dependency on Babylon. Anticipating that all their earthly needs would be provided for, some destroyed their possessions before they began the trek across rolling hills, moving closer to the sky.

Upon the rock of the Ethiopian divine, the inhabitants of Pinnacle strove to live, in Howell's words, "a socialistic life," led by the charismatic apostle, who some said was an incarnation of Haile Selassie Himself. The people planted cassava, plantains, yams, red peas, gungo peas, and the sacred herb with which Rastafarians would become permanently associated. On the anniversary of the coronation each year, they fasted. They raised chickens, herded goats, and developed complex methods of creating things from nothing. People fashioned violins from oak branches and vines. "It was paradise," recalled Howell's son Bill, who grew up at Pinnacle as a child.

But utopias are threatening to the authorities, even though the drive to colonize the ends of the earth could not have been other than utopian. The cultivation of ganja gave the colonial police a convenient excuse for frequent, destructive raids and mass arrests. In the predawn hours before an invasion in July 1941, Leonard Howell was warned by a dream. By the time the cops arrived, the apostle had disguised himself as an elderly woman, and participated in the manhunt for himself. It was said that the seventy-two men thrown into prison in Spanish Town that day were the seventy-two nations present at the coronation. All the powers of the earth had arrived.

By the late 1950s, Jamaica's colonial government determined it had "a problem." The idea could not be contained: engulfing the island like wildfire, the Rastafari religion had divided in myriad factions, mansions, and sects, from the Howellites to the Nyabinghis to the Bobo Shanti, a priestly order led by the turbaned prophet Prince Emmanuel. A younger generation, the Youth Black Faith, growing up in the slums of Trench Town, wore manes of matted locks, in defiance of the colonial mores of "civility." No word became more charged than *dread*: it meant a mass of tangled hair or a sense of apprehension and fear, but it was also fearlessness in the fight for freedom, and a sense of duty and obligation to the faith. "They used to say I was very 'dreadful,'" one of the Faith's leaders, Brother Wato, recalled. To be dread was to reclaim, through the majesty of Haile Selassie, a black selfhood denied for centuries, and to let the imperialists tremble.

Beyond their persecution by the police, the dreads were despised as dangerous criminals by the Jamaican middle class, many of whom were pious churchgoers and were content with the stability of British rule. "Rasta a foolishness!" people would shout, deeming them backward, blasphemous, and sinful. In 1944, Jamaica had won universal adult suffrage, and there was a growing sense that the island was moving in the direction of progress, with a new elite of faintly mixed-race politicians, such as Alexander Bustamante, taking the helm. Yet for the Rastafari this was only an illusion, a fantasy of a creole multiracialism that masked the perpetuation of white power over a black majority, who lived, in the Jamaican philosopher Sylvia Wynter's phrase, in a "miasma of borrowed beliefs."

If language creates and maintains meaning and order, then the words themselves would have to change. With a new language could come a new history. At a court appearance, Leonard Howell had spoken in tongues, addressing cryptic syllables to Haile Selassie. It was not an ecstatic glossolalia but a rejection of the imperial order that was so profound even the Queen's English, language of the colonizers, had to be overthrown. ("Anglo Militant fallen Angels tongues," Howell would say.) Over the years, the Rastafari, and particularly the Youth Black Faith, began to develop the language known as Iyaric, after the Ethiopian Amharic. While the emperor himself used the royal *we*, albeit inconsistently, Rastafarians took on a doubled form of I, the "I-and-I," a pronoun that encompassed both one's inner and outer selves, and the relation of those selves to God. The one who spoke as "I-and-I"—long dismissed by Babylon as invisible, as no one at all—insisted that they possessed a personhood that was multilayered and sanctified, a part of the godhead itself. The pronoun reminded the listener that it is, after all, the letter *I* that ends the word *Rastafari*, embedding the prophecy: *So the last shall be first, and the first last.*

Moving from the end to the beginning, the letter *I* would start new words in Iyaric. To reappropriate English but purify it of hatred, the Rasta philologists sought out all negativities imbedded in words with positive meanings. *Sincerely*—containing *sin*—became *incerely*. The word *divinity* embodied division, and so one would speak of *ivinity* instead. Words with the sound of *death* were avoided: *dedicate* became *livicate*. "To understand" became "to overstand": if you have mastered an idea, you must stand over it and not beneath it. The word *oppressor* sounded too uplifting: for Rastafari the *downpressors* were the colonialists and capitalists, the police, politicians, and priests who built Babylon, beginning with the appearance of Columbus in Xamayca, hunting for gold. Scouring away centuries of exploitation masked as civilization, the dread linguists insisted that words must sound like what they mean.

A core tenet of the doctrine was still the imminent return to Africa, which, as the Rastafarians suffered raids, mass arrests, and the forced shaving of dreads, became ever more urgent. On March 20, 1958, the prophet of the priestly Bobo Shanti order, Prince Emmanuel, sent a telegram:

```
To Her Majesty Queen Elizabeth the Second Buckingham
Palace London: WE THE DESCENDANTS OF ANCIENT
ETHIOPIA CALL UPON YOU FOR OUR REPATRIATION FOR THIS
IS THE 58TH YEAR EMERGENCY ANSWER.
```

"Who are these?!" the palace secretary commented, forwarding a copy to the Colonial Office. The Rastafari reverend Claudius Henry, founder of the African Reform Church, made multiple, fruitless attempts to reach the queen. "We . . . have tried hard to get in touch with representatives of Her Majesty's Government, but we have been always treated with utter dis-regard," he wrote. Nonetheless, declaring himself leader of a new "Lepers' Government," Henry predicted October 5, 1959, as the date when British ships would arrive to transport Jamaicans, and, like Howell before him, distributed thousands of blue cards as passports. Leading up to the decisive day, many passport holders sold their belongings to buy provisions for the trip. When the Royal Navy failed to appear off the Kingston coast, the reverend's followers were left despondent, some without money to get home, and Henry decided to adopt a more militant approach. The reverend began to plot the actual overthrow of Jamaica's colonial government, in league with his son Ronald. In the Bronx, Ronald was training a band of guerrilla fighters, the First Africa Corps, and raising funds through heists.

"The plan is this," he wrote to his father. "To gather a force of about 600 and leave secretly and land on the shore of certain Colony, take the capital and proceed to occupy the place and round up all the Europeans and either kill or ship the hell to their ice box Europe." In an April 1960 raid on Claudius Henry's headquarters, the police found conch shells, seventy machetes, two guns, "several sticks" of dynamite, and over four thousand detonators for homemade bombs. They also discovered letters addressed to Fidel Castro, informing him that, as the Rastafarians were about to depart for Ethiopia, they would be ceding control of the island to him. Henry had interpreted Castro's recent revolution to mean that the native peoples of the Americas had risen up and taken back the territories that were rightfully theirs—land that must also include Jamaica. Repatriation would not only return the descendants of Africa to their homeland but would restore America to the Americans, righting the injustice that had been done in the conquest of the New World. The reverend was charged with treason and Ronald, now in Jamaica, was captured and hanged.

In the aftermath of the Henrys' coup, Jamaican authorities violently persecuted anyone displaying Rastafari sympathies, yet they also began, for the first time, to take seriously their ideas about repatriation. "If the 20,000 hard core were loaded on ships and set down on an African shore, Jamaica would be free of this cancer," the American consul general wrote in a memo to the US State Department. Claudius Henry had previously been informed by the British Colonial Office that there was zero chance any African country would accept the Rastafarians. But as if by a miracle, it turned out that acres of land in Zion had been allocated for them, years earlier. In gratitude for the support of the African diaspora during the Italian invasion, after being restored to the throne in 1941, Haile Selassie had set aside five hundred acres to be used as land grants for anyone who wished to repatriate to Ethiopia. The territory, located at Shashamane in the fertile Rift Valley, initially received only a small number of settlers, and it remained waiting, a promised land. As the brutality wielded against Rastafarians by the Jamaican police continued to worsen, the editor in chief of the *Gleaner* wrote to the Ethiopian Ministry of Foreign Affairs, which confirmed that the gift, made long ago, was real.

In 1961, a state-sponsored "Back to Africa" mission set out from Kingston to explore possibilities for resettlement, a delegation of nine men that included three Rastafari leaders. They christened themselves the "Apostles of the Negus": Mortimo Planno, a weaver and prominent teacher; Philmore Alvaranga, a shoemaker and renowned drummer; and Douglas Mack, a mechanic and visionary. To the three dreads, their pilgrimage to H.I.M. was "likened spiritually to the visit of the three wise men who journeyed from the West to the East to visit the Baby Jesus, bringing with them gold, frankincense and myrrh," they wrote in the "Minority Report" they appended to the delegation's official report, since they felt the original did not convey events from their point of view. Their flight path took them from Kingston to New York, to London, Rome, and Khartoum, where they embarked on the final stretch aboard an Ethiopian Airlines jet. In his memoir, *The Earth Most Strangest Man: The Rastafarian*, Mortimo Planno wrote the verse,

> Leave our home and family
> to travel with the Lord of Love
> Travel, travel travel travel
> Travel with the Lord of Love.

❖ ❖ ❖

They found an Almighty suspended, in space and time, between His own tragedies. Only a few months before his apostles arrived, while Haile Selassie was on a state visit to Brasília, high-ranking palace officials staged a coup. Outraged by government inaction as millions across the Ethiopian provinces dwelled in abject poverty and died of hunger, the conspirators seized control of the capital, held loyalists hostage, and enlisted the support of the emperor's eldest son, Crown Prince Asfa-Wossen. On Radio Addis Ababa, he proclaimed himself Ethiopia's sovereign and announced a new age of reform. Yet the rebels failed to win over the army or the powerful clergy, and by the time Haile Selassie returned on his plane, the revolt had been suppressed, with hundreds dead. "We would have been very proud of you if We were coming to attend your funeral . . ." the emperor remarked to the son who betrayed him, now prostrate on the tarmac at his feet. The chiefs of his own Imperial Body-guard, palace security, and police had been among the plotters, leaving the emperor steeped in paranoia and unease. He decided to sleep in a new residence, for at his palace Guenete Leul, "Paradise of Princes," Haile Selassie found a bullet hole in his bedroom mirror, positioned just off to the side of his lion-crested canopy bed. When I visited in 2011, another year of failed revolutions, I thought it seemed far too narrow for a god.

He was nearly seventy; dwelling on the edge of loss, he buried himself between his bedsheets for naps. He hadn't been able to stop the death of his favorite son, Prince Makonnen, Duke of Harar, when he crashed on the road to the Ethiopian town of Nazareth in May 1957. The emperor wept at his grave but couldn't resurrect him, and so he spoke, at his son's funeral, of how he wished he had died before him. He had already lost three daughters: his eldest, Romanework, was imprisoned by the Italians and died in captivity; Tsehai died in childbirth; and fifteen-year-old Zenebework died suddenly amid allegations of mistreatment by her husband. More tragedy was to come: the demise of his wife, Empress Menen, and only a few weeks later, of his youngest son, Prince Sahle Selassie, who died of illness at age thirty-one. His grandson Lij Samson followed, killed driving drunk after an evening in an Addis nightclub, in a spate of months that also witnessed the deaths of three of the emperor's closest friends. That he could not bring people back to life, nor for that matter prevent the Italian invasion, nor centuries of slavery, would need to be worked out in Rastafari theory. Was it anger or vengeance, part of a larger divine plan? It was observed in the Jubilee Palace that H.I.M. pre-ferred the company of small children and smaller dogs. He loved apple strudel, according to his Viennese chef. He fed the lions their breakfast each morning by hand. Planno would sing:

> Run away Run away Run away Haile Salassie I call you
> Bright angels are waiting Bright angels are waiting

*To carry the tiding Home*
*Blackman.*

✦   ✦   ✦

Only a few hours after the mission landed in Addis Ababa, the Arch-bishop of the Ethiopian Orthodox Church invited the Rastafari travelers to his residence, to discuss a pressing matter. The austere, conservative Abuna Basilios warned the brethren not to mention Haile Selassie's god-hood in his presence, as His Majesty was unaware and would be dis-pleased by such blasphemy. "If He does not believe He is god, we know that He is god," the apostles countered, for "*he that humbleth himself shall be exalted, and he that exalteth himself shall be abased.*" According to the Minority Report, the Rastafarians reasoned with the Abuna, assiduously reciting one scriptural passage after the next as proof that Haile Selassie was at least the Christ returned, until eventually the elderly patriarch became exhausted and conceded "that the Bible can be interpreted that way." "We had tea and honey wine with him," Brother Philmore wrote of an afternoon considered victorious. Over the following days, as they awaited their summons to the palace, the apostles toured coffee and sugar plantations, craft workshops, community centers, and the fertile land of Shashamane. On Friday, April 21, 1961, at ten a.m., the matted Magi finally stood in the presence of God.

In the gilded drawing room of the Imperial Palace, all was solemn and still, but the walls were spinning with the earth's rotation as God spoke in Amharic and was translated by his minister. His Majesty wel-comed the men of the mission as "brothers, of one blood and race," presented each with a gold medal, and said that Ethiopia would always be open to those in the African diaspora who wished to return. The emperor added that he hoped Jamaica would "send the right people." While the rest of the delegation set out on a palace tour, the three dreads remained in the halo of His proximity, as they came bearing gifts. When Alvaranga offered a carved wooden box with a map of Africa and a portrait of H.I.M. on the lid, the deity spoke in English for the first time.

*That's Africa. Is it from the Rastafarian Brethren?*

"(That showed that he knew us before)," Brother Phil recounted. "We said 'Yes.'"

From Brother Mack, photographs of the Rastafari community in Jamaica.

*Photographs; Thank you.*

From Brother Planno, a scarf in red, gold, and green.

*Is it you that wove it?* "Yes." *Thank you again.*

Their final offering to H.I.M. was a photograph of a Jamaican widow and her six children; her Rastafari husband had been shot and killed by the police.

*Who is taking care of them now?* the god asked.

Upon their return to Kingston, the apostles were confronted by a doubting Thomas, in the form of a certain Clyde Hoyte. The editor of the weekly paper *Public Opinion*, Hoyte interrogated Planno as to whether they had asked Haile Selassie forthrightly about his divine nature. When Planno said they hadn't broached the subject, Hoyte challenged him as to what he would have said if His Imperial Majesty had demurred. "I would have faced him and said: 'You, Haile Selassie I, are God,'" Planno replied. Remaining antagonistic, Hoyte wrote to the emperor's personal secretary over the issue, requesting that His Imperial Majesty respond to survey questions about whether he considered himself a deity. Soon after, Hoyte received a letter from the emperor's Press Office:

*It is the fervent desire of his Imperial Majesty that the Ras Tafarians should discard this belief.*

Hoyte rushed to Planno's house to gloat, but found the apostle away in New York. He published the letter, along with photographs of it and the envelope as proof, on his front page. But it had no effect on Haile Selassie's worshippers, for compliance was the least important of His attributes.

Facing the ineluctable fact of his apotheosis, the pious emperor, a friend to the Pope and evangelicals such as Billy Graham, later announced he would dispatch missionaries from the Ethiopian Orthodox Church to the Caribbean. He appointed the Ethiopian bishop Abba Laike Mandefro to preach to a wayward West. "I didn't want to go," Abba Mandefro recalled, "but the Emperor said: 'I want to help these people. My heart is broken because of the situation of these people. Help them to find the True God. Teach them.'" The bishop started packing his liturgical tools: "It was the Emperor's order, and I could not refuse." When he arrived in Jamaica, he was welcomed by the occult elder Joseph Hibbert, and much to the chagrin of Jamaican officials, Mandefro appeared to become swayed by the beauty of Rasta belief.

The priest knew that many of the thousands of Rastas who underwent his ritual of baptism did so only because he was an emissary of the Living God, and Haile Selassie and Christ were the same. But Abba Mandefro would not denounce them, and found it a challenge to refute their argument that Christianity had been used to legitimize their ancestors' enslavement. The priest gently reminded them of the commandment: *Thou shall have no other gods before me—for I am a jealous God.* He spoke of how Haile Selassie himself fervently prayed for an hour every morning to that same God. But it was also rumored that in private, the emperor would ask the palace secretary to read aloud the letters mailed to him from the Rastafarians, and he would listen, profoundly moved.

From 1964, a stream of Rastafarians began to flow in the direction of God to Shashamane. The population grew to two thousand brethren, with each pioneer allotted land to cultivate, and Haile Selassie himself visited several times. But there were no legal structures in place for repatriated Rastas to receive Ethiopian citizenship, and Shashamane was, in its own way, stolen land. It had not been empty, awaiting Rasta settlers, but belonged to Oromo people, who had long suffered oppression and enslavement under the ruling Amhara elite, alleging them nomadic tres-passers on Amhara land. Although Haile Selassie himself had Oromo ancestry on his father's side, the emperor sought to colonize and unite Ethiopia's provinces under a myth of Amhara identity, and did not tol-erate any displays of Oromo nationalism, viewing Ethiopia's Oromo majority as "a people without history."

Though he was an anti-colonialist, Pan-Africanist icon, toward his own people the emperor behaved like the imperialists he stood against. During the Italian war, certain Oromo leaders saw an opportunity for self-determination and collaborated with the enemy; Oromo farmers in Shashamane later interpreted the emperor's callous grants of their land as retribution. While Rastafarians considered themselves as Ethiopians returning home, the native inhabitants of Zion could not but see them as immigrants, and their worship of Haile Selassie as liberator utterly non-sensical. The Rasta brethren might have been destitute in Jamaica, yet they were still generally wealthier than the Ethiopians they displaced, breeding resentment. But for the pilgrims, there was only space for one struggle, only one map of redemption for their own centuries of loss. There was no place for the Oromo in the biblical prophecy playing out.

Planno: *for I an I sing—*

> *Ethiopia is a better land Ethiopia is a better land Ethiopia is a better land Oh yes Rastafari oh Yes.*

◆  ◆  ◆

The people had begun to arrive the night before, from all corners of the island, by foot, on buses and trucks, by whatever means they could. Rain poured from the sky as thousands gathered in waiting at Kingston's Palisa-does Airport on the morning of April 21, 1966. They sang hymns, waved flags of red, green, and gold, and kept time with the beat of the drum. They stared up at the heavens as the rain came down. Although some brethren had made the crossing to Shashamane, the Jamaican govern-ment had found that large-scale repatriation was a costly and logistically

difficult solution to the "Rasta problem." Led by the conservative Jamaica Labour Party, it decided to pursue a new tactic: Haile Selassie was invited on his first official state visit to the newly independent nation, with the hope that he might publicly deny his divinity in front of the islanders. The aim was that they would see him in his conspicuously human form.

When the Ethiopian Airlines plane broke through the clouds and touched down on earth, the sun followed, beaming onto the crowd. The diminutive monarch, wearing his beige military uniform and a plumed cap, appeared in the cabin doorway and surveyed the surging multitudes on the tarmac. The crowd rushed forward, stampeding over barriers and trapping H.I.M. inside the airplane for nearly an hour. "*WILD WELCOME FOR NEGUS: And the Emperor Wept*," ran the front page of the *Gleaner*. "*SAVAGE JOY SWAMPS.*" Beneath the belly of the jet, the people lit chalices of weed while leftover gasoline trickled out, tempting fate. "Tears came to his eyes as he held up his hands in what could have been half a royal gesture and half a call for calm," the *Gleaner* reported, and wondered whether these were tears of sorrow at Jamaican misguidedness, or delight.

The emperor recognized Mortimo Planno in the sea of faces and called for his help. Planno ascended the stairs to the cabin door, dressed all in white. It was said that the Rastafari teacher had recently undergone throat surgery and had lost his voice. But when the emperor reached out for his hand, his voice came back, and Planno shouted loudly to the crowd to give way. As the King of Kings descended the plane and was hurried into a car, people cried, "God is with us!" "Let me touch the hem of His garment!" They called out, "Prepare a place for me in Thy kingdom!" The emperor waved from his motorcade, slowly weaving through the masses along the airport road. Rita Marley saw the black stigmata in Haile Selassie's palm, and would convert her husband Bob to the new religion.

At an intimate reception with the emperor the next day, he presented Rastafari leaders with gifts of gold medallions, along with gentle admonitions. "Do not worship me: I am not God," he urged, ever so politely, in the account of the Rasta activist Barbara Makeda Blake Hannah. Haile Selassie's great-nephew, Asfa-Wossen Asserate, records that the emperor spoke in his royal plural. "We are not God. We are not a prophet," His Majesty advised; "We are a slave of God." Certain Rastas remembered the reception differently. "*I am who you think I am*," He said. Any humble denials only served as further theological evidence, and the sight of dreadlocks in the hallowed governor's hall was a powerful, legitimizing force. "He lifted us from the dust of the earth and let us sit between princes and kings," reported the Rastafari brethren who had been privileged to attend the junket of cocktail parties and speeches. Middle-class Jamaicans, the very same who ordinarily refused to employ them or accept them as tenants, eagerly conversed with the Rastafarians, and the police paused their arrests. With God right there, they were protected.

For the dread theologians, the 1966 visit was Haile Selassie's *parousia*, from the Greek New Testament word for the presence or arrival of Christ. The aging Leonard Howell had refused to witness it, however, for its logistics were irreparably tainted by "politricks." Howell had made the difficult decision to boycott the state visit, for he felt the right-wing JLP party was exploiting the power of Rastafari for its own gain without seriously accommodating its principles. Yet for a younger generation of Rastafari leaders, Haile Selassie's parousia was clear proof that a new kind

of engagement with Babylon was possible. The idea that began as a glimmer in the Kingston rain became able to shift the tides of party politics.

The dread orator Samuel Elisha Brown had formed the Suffering
People's Party in 1961 and became the first Jamaican Rasta to stand in an
election. He had been scorned at the time, garnering less than a hundred
votes. But now, more Rastafarians began to participate in party politics
and run for office, not only in Jamaica but across the Caribbean, from
the Virgin Islands to Trinidad to the coast of Guyana, on platforms of
democratic socialism. "We are those who shall right all wrongs and bring
ease to the suffering bodies, and peace to all people," Brown declared
in a treatise, published the same month that Haile Selassie appeared in
Jamaica in the flesh. "We are the vanguard of 144,000 celestial selectees,"
Brown wrote, invoking the number in Revelation of those marked on
their foreheads for salvation.

In a speech, Haile Selassie had proclaimed that "Jamaica is a part of
Africa," words that Rasta activists interpreted to mean they must strive
for the betterment of their immediate isle first, before looking east. "Liberation before repatriation" became the rallying cry among those who
sought to fight injustice and poverty at home. There was so much work
to be done: Jamaica might have won independence in 1962, but too
many remnants of the colonizer remained, from economic ties to the old
Westminster system of rule to the hollow value the state placed on black
lives. The JLP had treated the dreads like dignitaries for a day, but soon
after they authorized the destruction of hundreds of Rasta homes in the
slums of Back-O-Wall, in the name of a government "clean-up" campaign. How could the Rasta leaders take flight to Zion when hundreds
of destitute families were left to sleep in a cemetery?

Leading up to the 1972 election, Jamaica's leftist opposition, the People's National Party, recognized that to change the nation's direction,
they would need to draw upon Rasta idioms of sanctity. For his campaign, the PNP's candidate Michael Manley, of largely white ancestry,
incorporated the ideas of dread philosophers, appeared alongside Rastafari musicians, and solicited the support of an unlikely ally—the radical
reverend Claudius Henry, freed from prison. When Henry circulated a
pamphlet depicting "the Trinity of the God-Head"—with Haile Selassie

at the top, flanked by Manley and himself—JLP rivals lambasted Manley as having "joined forces with some strange elements." Manley had even paid a visit to Addis Ababa, where the emperor presented him with a carved ivory-tipped staff. In his campaign speeches, Manley would slice the sky with the scepter, underlining his sentences. It became known as his "Rod of Correction," able to repair injustice and imbued with a supernatural charge. "Everywhere he appeared people wanted to touch this potent source of power, a few ascribing to it healing properties," one observer noted.

Jamaicans who had once shunned voting flocked to the polls, and Manley won the election by a large majority, going on to serve three terms as prime minister. Over his years in power, the democratic socialist established a minimum wage and equal pay for women, introduced free education, universal healthcare, and maternity leave, and redistributed idle land to farmers, among many other reforms. The adoration of a distant Ethiopian autocrat had served, in a concrete and effectual way, as a democratizing force. Manley started to investigate how to liberate the island entirely from the British monarchy, to create a Jamaican republic unburdened by any crown. But he held on to the ivory staff, as if to remind his flock that politics is ever a continuation of the sacred, under a new name.

✦　✦　✦

In November 1974, the world appeared to receive confirmation that Ethiopia was Eden, the cradle of man. In the Awash valley, paleontologists exhumed bones belonging to the most ancient skeleton as of then unearthed, the 3.2-million-year-old female they called Lucy. Yet her paradise was in the grip of famine; in the surrounding provinces of Wollo and Tigray, an estimated eighty thousand people died of starvation after a year without rain. Ethiopia might be where God loved to dwell, but life expectancy was at thirty years of age. No miracles of loaves or fishes were forthcoming; Haile Selassie's government refused to acknowledge the famine and exported a heaping surplus of grain. The emperor invited all the powers of the earth to return to Addis Ababa for his eightieth birthday party, recalling in twilight the splendor of the coronation. The

Swiss delegate arrived with the offering of a watch, the Germans brought wine, while the Ethiopians closest to H.I.M. hoped he would take the opportunity to gracefully retire from the throne.

The journalist Oriana Fallaci traveled to Addis Ababa to interview the emperor and found his eyes "swollen with forgetfulness." She fixated on his not quite human appearance. "Eyebrows, whiskers, beard, and hair all over him like feathers," she wrote. "Beneath that bird's head with the pharaoh's face, the body twisted and turned, as fragile as a child's body made up to look like an old man." The journalist asked him a series of questions. Later, Rastafarians would say it was the devil himself who had come to tempt the emperor in the form of the strikingly beautiful Italian inquisitor. ("Her name Fallaci like fallacy . . . Full-a-cheese.")

Q: Your Majesty, of all the monarchs still occupying their thrones you are the one that has ruled the longest. Moreover, in an age that has seen the ruinous downfall of so many kings, you are the only absolute monarch. Do you ever feel lonely in a world so different from the one you grew up in?

H.I.M.: It is our opinion that the world hasn't changed at all. . . .

Q: Your Majesty, what is your opinion of democracy?

H.I.M.: Democracy, republic, what do these words signify? What have they changed in the world? Have men become better, more loyal, kinder? Are the people happier? All goes on as before, as always. Illusions, illusions . . .

Beneath the veil of high bureaucracy, a group of military officers covertly began to organize, calling themselves the Derg, or "council." One by one, they dismantled Haile Selassie's institutions, from his Ministry of the Pen to the Crown Council, arrested his advisors, governors, and noblemen, and convinced his Imperial Bodyguards to abandon him. The emperor closed his eyes to the slow coup unfolding all around him, preserving instead his daily routines, the apple strudel and the naps. His great-nephew Asfa-Wossen recalled watching his own father, Ras Asserate, still prostrate himself to the telephone while on a call with His

Majesty, as he beseeched H.I.M. to seek asylum. When Ras Asserate was arrested, another son, Mulugeta, desperately sought the emperor's help, and was admitted into His Majesty's bedchamber, where he found the Lord of Lords forlorn but composed. The emperor said to him, "What can a mother cat do when her kittens have been taken away from her? Scratch, that's all, and that's exactly what we're going to do."

On the Ethiopian eve of the New Year, Derg officials forced the emperor to watch a broadcast, on state TV, of a British documentary on the famine that had scandalized the rest of the globe, and which his imperial regime had banned. Amid scenes of emaciated children, the Derg had spliced footage from Haile Selassie's birthday party and other royal fêtes, images of cake and champagne and the marble tombstone of his departed dog Lulu. The next morning, with the airport shut down and phone lines cut, the Derg, led by Colonel Mengistu Haile Mariam, bundled the indignant monarch into the back of a sky-blue Beetle and drove him to army head-quarters. For weeks, the Derg interrogated him as to the location of thirty million dollars in famine aid allegedly stashed in Swiss banks. When no fortune was to be found, he was moved to the Imperial Palace compound and imprisoned in an octagonal tower. Inside a dark, moldering wine cellar nearby, forty-seven of his ministers, generals, and princes were incarcerated for weeks and then massacred without trial. "One emperor was replaced by 108 emperors," a Derg officer later recalled, as the committee terrorized a country in chaos, torturing dissenters and forcing families to repay the cost of the bullet to retrieve their dead.

The man who was worshipped as god was so slight he would sometimes disappear behind the drapes as he gazed out the window, to the alarm of his prison guards. Stories circulated that he could transform into a bird and fly from his cage, but then he was always back again, in his detention, watching TV and reading Psalms. His butler, Eshetu Tekle-Mariam, remained with him, serving meals prepared by his usual cook and sleeping on a camp bed outside his chamber. On an August night in 1975, Eshetu was taken away by the Derg and locked in a different wing. "In the morning, I was let out to attend to the emperor's breakfast," Eshetu later testified. "I thoroughly washed my hands as usual, arranged the breakfast on a tray and carried it into the emperor's bedroom." He found the old man's pillow not beneath his head, but next to it, and laced with an overpowering smell of ether. His face had turned the shade of the god Vishnu, the deep blue of the next world.

✦ ✦ ✦

"Check me now," said Bob Marley to an interviewer. "Many people, dey scoffers, many people say to me, 'Backside, your God he dead.' How can he be dead? How can God die?" Despite the flood of press coverage, no one could say where Haile Selassie was buried, or even the cause of his demise, for it would be twenty years before the testimonies of Eshetu and others came to light. Though reporters relished confronting the Rastafarians, just to see what they would make of the news, for them it was evident that the living God was not, could not, be dead. "If him eighty-three today, tomorrow you see him and he twenty-eight. And next mornin' him a baby, and today him a bird," Marley said. "Yeah man, Jah Live! Ya cyaan kill God." The Lion had gone into occultation, vanishing in a burst of flames. His ear still listened to grievances and justice still flowed from his hand.

In 1992, remains were unearthed in a cement casket, buried vertically at a depth of thirteen feet, beneath a latrine across from Mengistu's office, just to be certain, as a Derg officer admitted, "that the dead man would not be resurrected." Rastafarians were unconvinced the skeleton had anything to do with the god. "I was at the river and he just came down in his white colored cape," the Nyabinghi drummer Ras Michael recalled. "Him said to me, say, 'They say I'm dead. But, I'm not dead. I'm just floating through the passage of time.'" There was no cause for any crisis of faith. The divinity of Haile Selassie had always been beyond Himself, existing in each person, in the infinity of the I-and-I. *Thou settest a crown of pure gold on his head*, reads Psalm 21. *He asked life of thee, and thou gavest it him, even length of days for ever and ever.*

Leonard Howell was living in a small house at the foothills of his former Pinnacle, when, in 1980, a gang of twelve men attacked the eighty-one-year-old and tried to cut out his tongue. Badly wounded, the prophet decided to move into the Kingston Sheraton, where Haile Selassie had attended a cocktail party on his state visit. Howell stayed there for two months, paying for his hotel room each day in cash, until one morning he drank a glass of fresh-squeezed orange juice and left the earth. With the deaths of the first fathers, new leaders bring the doctrine of Rastafari into the twenty-first century, ever constructing the human and the divine anew. In the Blue Mountains above Kingston, the priest Dermot Fagan and his School of Vision await the return of Haile Selassie in "a galactical advent," aboard a fleet of spacecraft to be used for repatriation to the hereafter. This is the Third Coming, as the messiah already came for a second time, in the form of the midcentury monarch. "I'll show you mystery," Ras Dermot says.

The new generations draw upon an instantaneous network of connection: a realm of power and venom, pulp and poetry set above terrestrial life. "I would be much quicker to question His Divinity if he stated 'Yes, I am God,'" writes sisMenenI on the Rastafari forum Africa Speaks, interpreting quotations from the state visit. "Nah, God wouldn't say that." They analyze a viral photograph, purportedly capturing Queen Elizabeth II and Prince Philip, with their backs turned, making obeisance on bended knee before the black messiah at his Silver Jubilee. The chandelier above the supposed Philip's head casts a halo. "Let's define, what is divinity?" asks the bespectacled theologian Ras Iadonis Tafari in one of his many video posts, as he pulls out his *Webster's New World College Dictionary*, bound in a red canvas cloth. Haile Selassie's divine nature is so obvious he closes the book. "It's like debating whether the earth is round."

The San Francisco theologian Abba Yahudah Berhan Sellassie recently undertook a scriptural exegesis of the June 1931 issue of *National Geographic*, page by page. No text contains within it deeper mystery. He drew upon the tools of numerology, paying close attention to the numbers embedded in paragraphs to derive meaning from things that might seem purely coincidental. Inside the throne room, suffused with a red-gold light, the numbers add up to 360, signifying "infinity, completeness, and perfection," Abba Yahudah wrote, "encompassing the whole cycle of life." In footage shot in Shashamane in 2013 by the Italian art collec-

tive Invernomuto, a man holds a magazine with a familiar, faded-yellow cover. He flips to a page with a photograph showing thousands of Ethiopians in white robes, waiting in the streets of the city as far as the eye can see. Under the Derg, the Rastafarians of Shashamane suffered persecution, as leftover worshippers of the deposed regime, but the community survived on the land. The man reads aloud, "Well they say, 'Blessed be the King of Israel.' Bless, *barakat*, you understand?"

In a radio interview, Haile Selassie was once asked what he thought of the fact that hundreds of thousands of people were convinced he is God. "I have heard of that idea," the emperor replied. "I also met certain Rastafarians. I told them clearly that I am a man, that I am mortal, and that I would be replaced by the oncoming generation; and that they should never make a mistake in assuming or pretending that a human being is emanated from a deity." The dread scholar Ras Iadonis took on the thorny recording in a video exegesis. "Now I know some of y'all will say, 'He's just saying he's a man, he's a mortal . . . What is this a fairytale or something like that?'" he reasons. "But nowhere in there does he ever say, 'I deny my divinity.'" For Iadonis, Haile Selassie was clearly offering a theological warning to the brethren against the ancient philosophy of Neoplatonism. "What is 'emanated'?? . . . Where in the Bible is 'emanate' or 'emanation' mentioned?" Haile Selassie heaped scorn upon this third-century metaphysics, Iadonis argued, which considered all reality to emanate from a vague "the One," to which the human mind or *nous* sought to return. "He wasn't emanated like a spirit or a spook," Ras Iadonis reasoned. "He said, 'It is I, real flesh and blood, walking on this water here, you understand?' He said, 'Hey Thomas, come here and touch this, put your finger in my side, go ahead . . . I'm real.'"

✦  ✦  ✦

When he returns to earth, the light of Ras Tafari will reach the shores of New Zealand first. A circle of Māori Rastas has existed since the late 1970s in the town of Ruatoria on the North Island, a land said to have been a strange, gigantic fish pulled from the ocean and left to dry. They live in the shadow of Mount Hikurangi, "the tail of heaven." Lying just west of the International Date Line, the mountain is thought to be the first place in the world to see the light of each new day. It was here, standing on Hikurangi, that Jah said, *Let there be light.* Some say Rastafari had always been there, that Haile Selassie had come and revealed Himself to the Māori ancestors of the Ngāti Porou community at the dawn of time. The Māori brother Ras Gideon just woke up as a Rastafarian one morning, and covered the walls of his home, a converted sheep-shearing shed, with scripture, written with a felt pen. *Blessed be thou Ethiopia forever and forever; the people at the end of the known world, and world unknown, shall look for the coming of thy children*, the Shepherd Athlyi had prayed. The Māori were there at the ends of the earth, or the beginning.

With little direct contact with Jamaica, Rastafari took root in the antipodes as a doctrine of resistance against the white colonial appropriation of Māori land. Ever since James Cook sighted Aotearoa in 1769, the gate was forced open: to the gold prospectors and traders, the settlers who razed forests to build Britain in the South Seas, and the missionaries, tasked with making the Māori adore the trespassers' god. Contending with the immensity of dispossession and loss, Māori liberationists in the 1970s found in Rastafari a new sanctity. For the dreads of the Ngāti Porou, blackness stood against everything the white settler world represented. The Māori had never left paradise: they are the cherubs, the Rasta elder Hone Heeney relates, who guard Eden with swords aflame, protecting its people from invaders.

Vilified by outsiders as criminals, the dreads took on the pronoun *tatou tatou*, as equivalent to the Jamaican "I-and-I." They inked intricate face tattoos, or *moko*, in ancestral patterns but with new letters, spelling out His name. The activist Ras Arama had been languishing in prison when his girlfriend gave him a book about Haile Selassie and his rise to the throne. When he was freed, Ras Arama had the name of *Jah* tattooed on his forehead, alongside *Io*, the Māori term for the hidden origin of things, translated as *God* by the Christian evangelists who claimed superior knowledge of Him. *And they shall see his face; and his name shall be on their foreheads*, spoke the prophecies of Revelation. It is how Haile Selassie will know them when he descends for the third time.

When he returns, he will come from the east, with all his angels behind him, to restore the land once taken from the Māoris. All the powers of the earth will convene in this remote place for the second coronation. "All nations will be gathering on the mountain to see his light, eh, just like that, one day," Ras Arama prophesies. "They want to see his light hit here first; but that light might be too bright for them, eh? They'll be looking to see the light, and next minute that light was Jah. The brightest light in there, that's Him, that's Him there, the brightest light. In one second, man, the world done, their wickedness gone. . . . We'll be all clean."

2

---

# The Gospel of Philip

Coiled inside a red earthenware jar, not far from the skeleton of a monk, was a parchment scripture from the late second century that didn't seem authorized by Yahweh or any other god at all. Its title was *Peuaggelion pkata Philippos*, or the "Gospel of Philip." *In the beginning, God created humankind*, the scroll, written in Coptic, narrated. *But now humankind creates God. This is the way it is in the world—human beings invent gods and worship their creation. It would be more fitting for the gods to worship men!* The gospel sang of error, of divine fallibility, of a universe in which intention and outcome, cause and effect, were like so many strands of seaweed brushing up against one another in the sea. Condemned as heretical by the Council of Nicaea, the codex, along with others, had been buried in the desert cliffs of Nag Hammadi, in Upper Egypt. It remained undiscovered until 1945, when a man digging for soil to use as fertilizer stumbled across the vessel, full of different ways of constructing religious truth. *The world came into being through a mistake*, the Gospel of Philip revealed. *The creator wanted to make it incorruptible and immortal, but he failed and did not get what he hoped for.*

The text, itself disintegrating, sang of Adam and Eve and their transgression, of the floodwaters and the ark of salvation that glided above. It told that there is no ultimate good nor absolute evil in this world: all things are mixed. The scripture sang of wine and oil, of marriage and hell, of nakedness and virgins in the bridal chamber, and baptism using both water and light. The scroll radiated mystery and irreverence, its corners torn off or decomposed in the vicissitudes of time. *Some have gone into heaven's kingdom laughing, and they have come out laughing*, spoke the good news according to Philip.

◆ ◆ ◆

In early August 1774, a distant fire in the darkness steered Captain James Cook, commanding the *Resolution*, to a South Pacific island as yet uncharted by Europe. As the ship drew closer, the crew realized the light was a glowing volcano, emitting sparks and sulphuric smoke into the troposphere. When the *Resolution* anchored in a bay, islanders gathered on the shore, armed with bows and spears. The sailors fired muskets above their heads to scare them, but the natives were not overawed. "One fellow shewed us his backside, in a manner which plainly conveyed his meaning," Cook reported. Mistaking the native word for *soil* for that of the place itself, Cook called the volcanic island Tanna. He christened the tropical archipelago into which he had sailed the "New Hebrides," as if so lost he thought he were in Scotland. Over his two-week sojourn, Cook reported that he found the islanders of Tanna "insolent and daring." They seemed indifferent to the technologies of Europe, and scoffed when the Englishmen tried to trade nails for wood, yams, and pigs. The captain attempted to describe their social organization, their grass fig leaves, the architecture of their thatched huts. "We are utter strangers to their religion; and but little acquainted with their government," Cook concluded, and trailed off into the requisite speculations of cannibalism. By 1906, the invaded islands would be colonized by both Britain and France, in a dysfunctional joint administration known as the Condominium. At the capital city of Port Vila, islanders watched as the imperialists obsessively measured to be certain the flags of France and Britain flew at precisely the same height.

It is 1974. Two centuries after Captain Cook's arrival, the same year that sweeps Haile Selassie off his throne, a British monarch vacationing on a yacht stages an inadvertent coup against the old gods in heaven. It was said on Tanna that within the crater of the active volcano, Mount Yasur, dwelled the ancestral god Kalbaben, who had several sons. One of Kalbaben's sons, the story went, incarnated into the body of a man and set forth from the island to marry a powerful woman abroad. A prophecy held that the deity would someday return to Tanna, bringing with Him an end to sickness and death. Life would become eternal; no new babies would need to be born. On the island, prosperity would reign. The harvest would be unending, and fish would jump out of the sea.

With the coronation of Elizabeth II in 1953, islanders on Tanna learned from the British colonizers of Her Majesty, the new queen, and of the athletic, blond naval officer who had won her hand. Coming across photographs of Prince Philip in magazines and newspapers in the 1950s and 1960s, villagers recognized something kindred about his spirit and saved the press clippings. They asked an anthropologist where the prince was from, but he had no good answer: Prince Philip was not actually from Britain, nor from France. He was a prince of Greece, but not Greek; he had Danish, German, and Russian blood, but he was from none of those places. Seeming to originate from nowhere on earth, to the chiefs of Tanna, the answer as to where Philip was from was clear.

As the twilight of the British Empire continued to dim, Prince Philip vacationed in the archipelago with his uncle Lord Mountbatten, on a South Pacific holiday in which he was reportedly sighted sitting on a plastic chair labeled *throne*. In 1974, Philip returned to the New Hebrides with the queen, aboard the Royal Yacht *Britannia*. He stopped on the nearby atoll of Malekula, and participated in a pig-killing ceremony, a ritual to consecrate a chief. Although Their Royal Highnesses didn't land on Tanna, they anchored at the serenc neighboring island of Ane-ityum. Several chiefs paddled out in canoes to get closer to the yacht. "I saw him standing on the deck in his white uniform," recalled the chief of Yaohnanen, Jack Naiva, in a later interview. "I knew then that he was the true messiah." Winding across the dirt tracks, through the yam groves and coconut palms, beneath the shade of the banyan trees, the good news of Philip spread.

✦  ✦  ✦

The *Britannia* had arrived at a hotbed of mythopolitics, an archipelago with a history of particular ideas about the divine. Out of the fertile vol-canic soil burgeoned a host of messianic movements, a response to the ruptures set off by Europe's invasion, which brought microbes, firearms, capitalism, and subjugation. Between 1872 and 1926, the population of Tanna had fallen by half, in part due to a practice in which merchants would lure men onto ships, kidnap them, and take them to work as forced laborers on Australian plantations. The landscape of Tanna was stripped as traders deforested sandalwood trees to sell to the Chinese for incense. Into the chaos and dysfunction of the Anglo-French Condominium, or Pandemonium, as it was known, Christian evangelists stepped in. On an island only twenty-five miles long, several missions competed for native souls, among them the Presbyterians, Roman Catholics, and Seventh-day Adventists, and attempted to ban as "heathen" the islanders' traditional mode of life. Where Tanna men wore *nambas*, penis sheaths made of grass stalks, missionaries imposed trousers. They forbade the natives from drinking kava, a bitter root masticated into a psychoactive brew, which formed an evening ritual. The missionaries condemned as immoral and idle what the islanders regarded as *kastom*, or custom, in the language of Bislama, a creole English that became the lingua franca on an archipelago with over a hundred different tongues. (Its name derived from *bêche-de-mer*, or sea cucumber.) Against the apostles and colonizers, settlers and sea-worm traders, the archipelago began to kindle with mutiny.

Islanders started to gather at secret meetings, where they received messages from an enigmatic deity said to have bleached blond hair. He was called John Frum, possibly a derivation of "John from America." Some said he was *Rusefel*, or Franklin D. Roosevelt; he was also a manifestation of Kalbaben, the volcano god. A British official reported anxiously that Frum was, in effect, a broom, to sweep the colonizers off the island and back into the sea. Tanna would soon be flattened, the islanders said, made into a great obsidian tarmac. With a fleet of airplanes, John Frum would return, bringing eternal life and all the wealth and technology of America for the prosperity of Tanna. An army was coiled inside Mount Yasur, waiting to be let out to fight for Frum. The deity would restore *kastom* and abolish European currency in favor of his own. As they would want for nothing when he arrived, islanders began to throw any money they had saved into the sea, or spend it wildly in the foreign shops. Perhaps if there were no cash, the white traders would be forced to leave. In the jungle interior, the islanders founded new villages, far from the Christian presence, where they returned to *kastom*, sacrificing goats for lavish feasts replete with kava and dancing. It was not long before British and French officials became alarmed and ordered the movement to be suppressed. Policemen arrested John Frum leaders, as well as a series of prophets claiming to be Frum himself, yet the movement only flourished in the prisons.

The cult that foretold the coming of America and its airplanes was powerfully vindicated with the onset of World War II, when hundreds of thousands of American troops actually appeared in the South Pacific. With its masses of military cargo, bulldozers and jeeps, endless quantities of Coca-Cola, cigarettes, and chocolate, the US Army descended on the New Hebrides in March 1942, under the command of General Douglas MacArthur, to thwart the encroachments of Japan. While many islanders were employed to build military bases, airstrips, and roads, others enrolled in militias to fight for the US itself. For the islanders, an unexpected element of the American arrival was that so many of the troops had black skin. Unlike the segregation enforced by the British and French colonial regimes, the Americans appeared, to outsiders at least, to be infused with a spirit of equality: black and white soldiers dined together, wore the same uniforms, and worked on the same tasks.

New prophesies marinated that John Frum was black; that the black American soldiers would soon govern Tanna and liberate the imprisoned. Intercepting the messianic wave, the trading vessel USS *Echo*, captained by a certain Major Samuel Patten, was dispatched to Tanna in 1943 on an unusual theological mission: to convince leaders that America had no link to John Frum, nor was it imbued with any divine nature. But the *Echo*'s mandate went unfulfilled, and with the Allied triumph two years later, the whirlwind of US forces exited the archipelago as abruptly as it had arrived. Instead of donating the leftover cargo to the islanders, and lest the British and French governors acquire it free, American soldiers drove trucks and bulldozers filled with supplies—guns, engines, aircraft parts, bottles of Coke—down a ramp and into the sea off the coast of Espiritu Santo, where it would become, for the barnacles, a home.

In the wake of *Wolwatu*, as it is known in Bislama, the John Frum movement entered a new phase of sacred militancy, drawing upon the influx of information as to American protocol. Bearing wooden rifles and with the letters USA painted across bare chests, Frumist drill sergeants and G.I. Joes marched in military formation. It was said that the return of the American troops was imminent—but unlike its arrival elsewhere across the earth, the US Army would not herald massive casualties but an end to death itself. Islanders built airstrips for the fighter jets and control towers out of bamboo, while boys placed telephone calls to Frum using tin cans and string. In 1952, the cult gained a mythic figure when a recently arrived British administrator, George Bristow, was proclaimed the incarnation of Noah, also an avatar of Frum. The liberal Mr. Bristow had been horrified at the French practice of forcing islanders to labor on the roads and tried to abolish it, an act for which he found himself swept up into Tannese legend.

The story went that Noah and his brother were building a canoe on the shore when a tidal wave crashed over them and carried Noah and the craft away. Ripped apart, with all the science and technology in his possession, Noah left behind his brother, Man Tanna, in ignorance and poverty.

In the form of Mr. Bristow, Noah had finally returned to Tanna, and it was said that he was summoning warships to expel the colonizers. The colonial official had been made into a formidable weapon to be wielded against his own kind. Bristow himself would recount, from his retirement in Lincolnshire in the mid-1990s, how little bureaucratic power he was given, and how he had been forced by French administrators to suppress the Frumists in the end. The elderly pensioner recalled that he eventually departed Tanna with a lingering sense of nihilism.

By the mid-1970s, as the New Hebrides moved toward liberation from Anglo-French rule, the archipelago teemed with political parties. While the cult of John Frum sought to transcend the local factions of Tanna with its worship of a distant power, it was splintering into myriad divisions, among them the Kastom John sect, the Monday Monday group of Frum fundamentalists, and rival wings of Red versus Black Cross. Political tides paired and pitted them against Presbyterian and Catholic groups, "Moderets" and militants in ever-shifting alliances. The scene was further complicated by a cast of opportunistic foreigners, such as Antoine Fornelli, a Corsican plantation owner who proclaimed himself king of Tanna and aligned with Frumists in a new sect called Forcona ("Four Corners"). When Fornelli telegrammed Buckingham Palace to announce Tanna's secession, he was swiftly arrested and later rumored to be a double agent agitating for the French. In the quieter villages of Yaohnanen and Yakel, the chiefs watched from afar as their neighbors fell into dubious liaisons that seemed, most often, to end badly. As everyone aligned under different banners, acronyms, and agendas, a new faction alighted upon a powerful figurehead of its own: a deity that would prove even more compelling because he was alive and clearly active in the world, in his fashion. When they wrote Him, He wrote back.

✦   ✦   ✦

The god was born on a dining room table in Corfu, on June 10, 1921, and named Philip. The infant cosmocrat was the son of Prince Andrew of Greece and Princess Alice of Battenberg, a great-granddaughter of Queen Victoria given to mystical tendencies, and later confined in a

Swiss sanatorium. Eighteen months after Philip's birth, with the Turkish capture of Smyrna, Greek nationalists forced the monarchs into exile. Like a baby Moses in his basket, floating down the Nile, Philip was ferried to safety aboard the HMS *Calypso* inside an orange crate. Raised by relatives in Paris and then England, Philip enrolled as a cadet in the Royal Navy College, Dartmouth. It was there that he met the young Princess Elizabeth, age thirteen, a distant cousin, as she toured the grounds: the charismatic Philip jumped over tennis nets to entertain her, the future queen's nanny, Crawfie, recalled.

In 1947, Elizabeth married him in an opulent and solemn ceremony, despite resistance from Windsor factions who viewed Philip as arrogant, uncultivated, and penniless. Before the birth of their first child the following year, they quarreled with Her Majesty's grandmother and Winston Churchill over whether, as the newlyweds maintained, the royal family should be renamed the House of Mountbatten. "I am the only man in the country not allowed to give his name to his own children," Philip bitterly complained. "I am nothing but a bloody amoeba." When King George VI died of illness, the twenty-five-year-old Elizabeth ascended to the throne, and Philip was forced to relinquish his naval career for the fenced-in life of a consort, required to bow to his wife whenever she entered the room.

There is a natural law governing the British monarchy: as power decreases, pageantry increases, as does the military precision with which it is performed. In the nineteenth century, the actual political influence wielded by the British sovereigns made displays of ostentatious grandeur unpalatable to Parliament and to the people, who satirized them. Compared to other European dynasties, the Hanoverians had the reputation of being inept at ritual; by all accounts Queen Victoria's ascension was an unrehearsed mess. Yet by the early twentieth century, as the monarchy increasingly became marginal to politics with the rise of common suffrage and the Labour Party, the palace began to invent a host of splendid traditions for itself that often looked back to a mythic sixteenth-century past for legitimacy.

Just as on Tanna the rituals of John Frum became a way to find bearings amid political upheaval, so too the jubilees and processions, to the tune of the newly composed "Pomp and Circumstance," became a means to conjure stability, continuity, and control in a kingdom on a decline. At what became the first televised coronation ceremony, a highly crafted spectacle watched by 350 million people worldwide, Queen Elizabeth II was to be crowned at precisely 12:34 p.m., as if time itself were leading up to the act. Her husband was the first to pay homage. "I, Philip, Duke of Edinburgh, do become your liege man of life and limb and of earthly worship," Philip pledged. He bent down on one knee before his wife, who wore a silk dress embroidered with flowers, each symbolizing one of her dominions. They were territories rapidly falling away in a decolonizing world, like petals from a wilting rose of empire. "So help me God," he said.

The word *worship* derives from the Old English *weorðscipe*; broken into syllables, it is *weorð* (*worthy*) + -*scipe* (*ship*). One worships the thing that will carry you safely over the treacherous sea. If worship requires a sense of worthiness, to his critics it may appear strange that Philip, of all possible candidates, should be chosen, a man known for his "gaffes," such as joking about Melanesian peoples as cannibals. The question of whether the British monarchy itself ought to be abolished lingers in the shadows of the junkets and scandals of the royal family. Yet to observers on Tanna, abolition would be convenient, for on an island with a penchant for mystical wordplay, they know the true meaning of Buckingham Palace: "*Back-e-go-home-paradise.*"

✦  ✦  ✦

Although many ages and places have supposed that kings receive their legitimacy directly from the heavens, it was in the British Isles, in particular, in the sixteenth century, that the theory of the divine right of kings was avidly articulated. "For the King has in him two Bodies, *viz.*, a Body natural, and a Body politic," the jurist Edmund Plowden famously declared. While the king's natural body was mortal, "subject to all Infirmities that come by Nature or Accident, to the Imbecility of Infancy or old Age," his political body was immortal, incorruptible, and invisible. It "cannot be seen or handled," Plowden wrote. "The state of monarchy is the supremest thing upon earth," proclaimed King James I in a speech to Parliament in 1610, "for kings are not only God's lieutenants upon earth and sit upon God's throne, but even by God himself they are called gods." In the wake of the Protestant Reformation, English and Scottish jurists and monarchs decreed that only God, and not the Pope, could judge the king. They searched for proof of the king's two bodies in the Old and New Testaments, looking especially to the doubled, divine-human nature of Jesus, king on earth, and the notion, enshrined by Saint Paul, of *corpus Christi*, the body of Christ as the collective of believers. They looked also to the celestials of Greece and Rome, imagining the king ever in close consultation with the classical goddesses, *Ratio*, Reason, and *Iustitia*, Justice. Royal blood was a mysterious fluid, like ichor, the ethereal nectar that flowed through the veins of the Greek gods.

When the head of King Charles I rolled, the divine right of kings stumbled toward an end, first with Oliver Cromwell's regicide, and then the 1688 revolution that decisively established Parliamentary rule. The king would have only one body now, the natural one; it was Parliament that was the true body politic of the realm and the nation that was immortal. With the rise of nationalism and in the aftermath of the two world wars, the vast majority of the earth's dynasties would go crashing into extinction, from Russia to Vienna, Yugoslavia, Italy, and Korea. Yet the British monarchy survived, and the fact that its rituals weathered the convulsions of the twentieth century made them seem archaic, timeless, and eternal. The British royals had lost the divine right of kings, and then lost their right to meddle in political matters at all. But exiled from politics, by the mid-1970s, it was almost as if, in a nation that viewed its government as determinedly secular, it was safe for the royals to become divine again.

It was around the year 1977 that Prince Philip first learned of his godhood. There had been an incident a decade earlier, in which the people of Yaohnanen sent a British commissioner a pig and he never responded nor sent anything in return, insulting the villagers. They still remembered it in 1977, as they told an Australian businessman visiting the area. They spoke of how Prince Philip was a deity, the son of the volcano god Kalbaben, and how a token from Him would set things aright. The Australian promptly reported this to British administrators in the capital of

Port Vila, who passed along word to the palace, who in turn sought the services of an anthropologist, Kirk Huffman, to learn more about the sect. On September 21, 1978, a delegation of British officials arrived in Yaohnanen with a signed portrait of Prince Philip. In thanks, and to test whether the photo had actually arrived from Him, the Tanna politician and philosopher Tuk Noao, formerly aligned with the Frumists, sent back a *nalnal*, a traditional pig-killing stick, to see how He would respond.

In consultation with anthropologists and palace advisors, and after much debate as to the proper way to hold the stick, Philip staged a photoshoot of himself on the lawn of Buckingham Palace, wielding the weapon, and dressed in a sharp charcoal suit. The graven image was dispatched to Tanna, and over the years the correspondence would continue, with letters and photographs passing between the god and his worshippers, though it was deemed unadvisable by the palace for Philip to return to the area in the flesh. As the Condominium powers began to withdraw their administrations from the archipelago now called Vanuatu, the French accused the British of fostering the cult as a means of ensuring continued influence in the region. "The French do not seem to get implicated in similar situations . . ." a French ethnographer on Tanna pointed out.

Philip has two bodies: one mortal, the other divine. One is European, the other Melanesian. The prince was born a Gemini, after all. "He is a god, and when we talk about him and believe in him, it gives us life," Chief Siko Nathuan told Sky News in 2011. It is said that England and Tanna were once connected islands created from the same volcanic explosion, severed halves

that will one day be restored to primeval wholeness, a theory that also explains why the weather on Tanna is often quite bad. It was no coincidence that Vanuatu had once been called the New Hebrides, since Philip is the Duke of Edinburgh—Philip unites the antipodes within Himself, in an alchemy of black and white. According to Tuk Noao, all bodies contain both white and black inside them, harmoniously coexisting. In the Tanna version of the idea of the divine double, each person has another half, existing on the other side of the earth, whose strength they can tap into in a supernatural way. "When I see his photo, I feel like I'm looking at one of my relations," said the villager Kasonipo. "I feel very happy." Some say their white spirit-doppelganger is waiting for them in Britain. To reach their relatives, the villagers conjure a network of metaphorical roads, ropes, and gates, interlacing the earth like a spiderweb, with shimmering, barely perceptible threads.

Of Philip's two bodies, one is relegated to his favorite hobby of carriage racing, but the other is political. On an island with many parties and factions, Philip's cultists are active, spending long evenings debating politics over kava, and the duke himself is occasionally drawn in. When on July 30, 1980, Vanuatu gained independence, and the villagers of Yaohnanen were made to start paying federal taxes, the chiefs wrote a letter to Prince Philip to appeal. Philip responded informing his worshippers that they indeed had to pay, but it was the fact of the letter on palace stationery, and not its contents, that had the power— when tax collectors came to collect, the villagers waved it as proof of their exemption. Like Mr. Bristow before him, Philip has been made alter to Himself, a vessel for a message not quite his own. Other British naval commanders have met a more extreme version of this fate. In 1864, during a Māori uprising against the British led by the prophet Te Ua Haumēne, Captain P. W. J. Lloyd was beheaded. Speared on a pole, his head became the divine conduit through which the angel Gabriel spoke to the liberation fighters, in a religion known as Pai Mārire that deployed the Bible toward the restoration of Māori land (and which, years later, would inspire the Rastas of the Ngāti dread). Captain Lloyd's head told them to drive out the white settlers from New Zealand, and informed them the religion of the Church of England was false. Lloyd's head became a talisman that protected the Māoris against British invaders such as himself. For his own part, Philip's political body spoke of an absolute equality between black and white.

It is said that Philip has several brothers, among them John Frum and also a brother called Jake Raites, or Jack Karaites, another name for Jesus Christ. A story goes that Jake had promised his father Kalbaben that he would work for the betterment of Tanna, but he went off instead to help the Americans, enabling them to build their own empire and even land a man on the moon. Both Jake and John forgot all about Tanna, seeing that there was no money to be made on the rural island. Angered by his two sons' greed, Kalbaben relies on his third son, Philip, to do his work in the world for the improvement of everyday life in Tanna, before he returns home. For villagers in Yaohnanen and Yakel, the act of waiting for Philip's return forms a core of the religion, just like those who wait for Christ, though the Philipists have not been waiting quite so long. "Bilip, Me wantem come," said Jack Naiva, speaking in Bislama a few years before his death in 2009. In the villages, some say prayers to Philip in the evenings, as they sit around drinking kava. "We ask him to increase the production of our crops in the garden, or to give us the sun, or rain," said the villager Nako Nikien. "And it happens."

✦ ✦ ✦

The phrase "cargo cult" was first enshrined in print in a racist screed: a white settler, Norris Mervyn Bird, warned in a 1945 article for *Pacific Islands Monthly* of dangerous fanaticism among New Guineans and urged his readers to protect their own precious cargo, white daughters. For decades, colonial administrators and profiteers had observed strange outbreaks, such as in 1919, when Papuans appeared to cease all normal activities to wait for the arrival of ancestral spirits aboard ships and airplanes loaded with cigarettes, axes and engines, firearms, iceboxes, and meat. Some blamed the Japanese for inflicting the madness: it was said they had arrived first and tried to win over the islanders with messianic and materialistic promises. In 1950, in a bid to demystify "cargo," administrators rounded up cult leaders and flew them to Australian cities for a tour of modern factories and offices. They launched a magazine with a monthly column, "How You Get It," to show how cargo—tinned food, soap, tea bags, printed money and coins—was humanly manufactured and earned by labor, not bestowed by celestial largesse. Born out of racist derision and sensationalism, the phrase "cargo cult" came into widespread use, first by colonizers and then by anthropologists as an empirical object of study. In the discipline of comparative religion, Philipists and Frumists alike have been filed as cargo cults. Yet the category was only ever a figment of the European imagination; a fiction ossified as scientific.

Cargo cult was useful as a term because it masked the actual, economic inequalities of colonized islands. It camouflaged the empty promises of invaders who took what they needed and gave little in return. To call something a cargo cult was to pronounce it the misfiring of irrational, superstitious minds, the tendencies of isolated atolls, rather than a product of the violence of empire and the shackling of peoples to new capitalist machineries of profit. In 1914, in the Torres Strait, annexed by the Australian state of Queensland, a movement known as the German Wislin caught fire, which spoke an invented form of German. Islanders awaited the arrival of Kaiser Wilhelm II to expel the whites who used them as cheap, disposable laborers for pearl fishing and picking sea slugs. Prophets urged the people to leave their work and gather in the cemetery for prayers to summon Wislin, who would usher in an age of freedom and prosperity. The word *Wislin* would persist in the Torres Strait into the 1960s; to Australian and British colonizers, the faulty apotheosis proved advantageous. As movements of emancipation engulfed the earth, the fiction of the cargo cult was evoked as evidence that the Melanesians needed continued paternalist colonial influence. In the tabloids, lurid dreams of free cargo for all were a means of ridiculing efforts by the Australian Labour Party to promote decolonization in Melanesia and welfare subsides at home. Retaining its aura of polemic, "cargo cult" became a pejorative for any social movement in Melanesia that escaped government control, a way to distract from political ideas beneath the sensational visions of fully stocked iceboxes dropping from the sky.

The political purpose of the outside savior was made clear in 1964, when the Australian-occupied territories of Papua and New Guinea had their first elections to create a house of assembly. Rejecting the names on the ballot, half the population of the volcanic island of New Hanover voted for President Lyndon B. Johnson. Only four months before LBJ himself was facing an election at home, the Lavongai people elected him first as their stranger-king, a powerful outsider they invited to rule over them. It was said that, as if divinely planted, everyone on the island had the same idea all at once. The papers reported that thousands of islanders dropped their everyday activities to wait for LBJ on a mountain peak. In a revolt against Australian officials who alternated between oppression and utter neglect, LBJ-ists refused to pay taxes, donating the money instead to campaign financing. *Newsweek* reported that the natives raised $987 to "buy" LBJ and relocate him to New Hanover, "bringing with him, of course, cargoes of Hershey's bars, cigarettes." As many LBJ-ists were arrested, jailed, and beaten by Australian police,

*Newsweek* ran with the racist headline, "Don't Eat the Candidate." When the anthropologist Dorothy Billings sent the president her research on the cult, LBJ blithely replied from his ranch in Texas, "It was nice to know that America had such great support so far away."

The cargo cult was the meeting of two myth-dreams, wrote the liberationist poet-monk Thomas Merton in an essay not long before his sudden death in Bangkok in 1968, four years into LBJ's Papuan term. "The myth-dream of absolute white supremacy brooks no opposition," he wrote. "It is our collective daydream, made up of all kinds of common symbols and beliefs with which we are collectively at ease." It was a dream "tied up in self-admiration over the fact that we know how to make money." It spread the gospel-trap of modern consumption, while ensuring the rest of the world remained in subjection as the wellspring of white profit. "Even when we think we are being nice and fair and just, we are living and acting out a dream that makes fairness and justice impossible," the monk wrote. "Black power, among other things, is trying to tell us so."

The cargo cult was a counter-myth; a dream seeking reciprocity and equality between black and white. Cargo was cigarettes and Coca-Cola and engine parts, but it was also the dream of "a shared standard of living" and equal participation in the larger global order. The cargo was a kind of reparation for what was taken from the South Pacific, the massive debt owed to the islands for their labor, produce, and land, so that time could begin anew. Piecing together mythic figureheads, rituals, and tenets, the cults were an experiment: to try different approaches to discover what would work. On New Hanover, Billings recorded debates among the Lavongai, for and against the movement. "Do you know that America kills all Negroes?" a skeptic named Boski challenged a wandering LBJ apostle called Oliver. "You're clever," Oliver replied. "But you haven't got a good way to save us."

✦ ✦ ✦

The origins of "money" itself are sacred: the word comes from the epithet of Juno, *Moneta*, for it was in her temple in Rome that coins were minted and bestowed with their imaginary value. In order that people would put trust and belief into otherwise quite useless trifles, Juno, the goddess of the hearth, watched over and protected their worth. Different gods guarded different coins, from Apollo and Jupiter to the double-headed Janus; on the US dollar still, "In God We Trust." On the British pound, it is Queen Elizabeth II who occupies the space that once housed pictures of the gods, guarding the currency and watching it rise and fall. It is said the queen herself doesn't carry money; after all, it carries her. Yet for many on Tanna it is clear that the true lord of money is Nakwa, the serpent god.

Though the British speak of the Philipists as a cargo cult, it was they who spread the deification of goods across the globe, replacing local practices of trade with the new religion of capitalism. It was the quest for profit that propelled the British Empire, with the East India Company often held to be the world's first modern multinational corporation. For nearly three hundred years, the company brought loads of cargo back to England from the world, trading salt, silk, and gunpowder, acquiring idols, fetishes, and precious stones, minting its own coins, and wresting political rule. In the footsteps of the merchants came the missionaries, preaching contradiction: that in this life, all was avarice and illusion, but in the afterlife, eternal wealth.

The Christian god was like an economic administrator, with Christ as currency for redemption. *Lay up for yourselves treasures in heaven, where neither moth nor rust will destroy them*, instructed the Son of God. In the fifth century, theologians interpreted the line as revealing that one could build physical mansions in the hereafter, using down payments of daily charitable acts, each one laying a brick made of gold. The rich would claim the best real estate not only on earth, but in the construction site of heaven, villas built beside meadows and sulfuric rivers, near the abodes of celebrity saints. It formed a landscape of gilded, gated wealth that is still a baseline view of what heaven looks like. When colonized people were told by Christian missionaries to endure poverty and servitude and abide for the next life, even the kingdom of heaven that awaited them was still constructed around white wealth. As the sun began to set on the British, the American empire followed, questing for the same viscous substance that has, since Solomon, anointed divine kings. The cargo cult of modern empires reordered the values of our earth.

How do empires sustain themselves after their occupying armies have left? In a parallel, shadow history, Kaiser Wilhelm II, Franklin D. Roosevelt, Lyndon B. Johnson, and Prince Philip once sat together in a celestial boardroom, and drew up plans for the radical betterment of Melanesia. But only Philip arrived, intrepidly traversing the distance of continental drift that separated England and Tanna. Between them, an economy of deification, a cycle of divine exchange, persists. It survives despite the loss of its winged chariot: in 1997, when New Labour came to power, the Royal Yacht *Britannia* was retired amid cries to curtail the crown's expenditure, and never replaced. In the decades since, the British monarchy has cultivated its corporate brand to remain afloat, spreading a cargo of commemorative crockery at every jubilee. In official versions of his biography, Prince Philip's tropical godhood has become a set piece; it is part of his image, an eccentric riposte to the critics who would point out the consort's many spectacularly public flaws. Philip's apotheosis seems to show that the British monarchy, even in its dimmest twilight, are still a people somehow, somewhere, set apart. It looks back to that nostalgic moment, in the sixteenth century, when the heads of British kings were still attached and still divine. It looks to a more recent time when Britain had the world bound and netted, before domestic currents strove to cut it loose and drift it farther into the sea. In many ways, Philip has needed his worshippers more than they need Him.

For the island of Tanna, Philip's divinity brings international recognition, visitors and film crews, and interest in the *kastom* way of life. It has struck up a global conversation about what, and who, matters on this earth; the word *cult*, after all, comes from the Latin conveying a sense of *care*. It doesn't matter whether anyone believes it or not; belief is not the right question to ask. As Merton wrote, "When a myth-dream is constantly in the papers and on TV, it seems pretty real!" The religion of Philip is real because it has been told and retold, by South Pacific priests and BBC storytellers, by journalists and palace press officers, in a continuous, mutual mythmaking over the course of forty years. The myths and sayings are preserved in a palimpsest of video clips and newspaper ink—the *Times*, the *Telegraph*, the *Daily Mail*—ever recycled in new iterations. They are authenticated by how often they are repeated. Some anecdotes are ephemeral and others have become Philip orthodoxy. Some chiefs have become apostles and others are forgotten. Only time will reveal what becomes canon. It may be a modern-day version of how the gospels were formed, although we cannot sail to the distant islands of the archaic past to be certain.

✦  ✦  ✦

In 2005, the BBC producer, novelist, and self-confessed admirer of the duke Matthew Baylis traveled to Tanna to live among the Philip worshippers in Yaohnanen, and recorded his experiences in the memoir *Man Belong Mrs. Queen*. He brought with him some of his research materials, including a few books and a stack of documents from the archives of Buckingham Palace, among them official correspondence from the 1970s and information and press clippings the palace had on file about the Philip cult. Compiled by Philip's former private secretary, Brigadier Sir Miles Hunt-Davis (or, as the Tannese, fond of malapropism, rendered it, Big Ass Dear Summer Lance Daisies), the papers featured retellings of the cult's foundational myths. When the villagers learned that their English visitor was in possession of such a trove, the chief Jack Naiva urged Baylis, as they sat around a fire drinking kava, to read the xeroxed scriptures aloud. Baylis chose the origin myth: how Philip, tall and strong, a hero from *Wolwatu*, once sailed to Aneityum with Queen Elizabeth. As they passed by Tanna, Philip went out on deck in his uniform of gold and silver and gazed sadly over the waters to the shore.

> "*My dear,*" asked the King's wife, "*tell me what is wrong.*"
> "*I have to tell you a secret,*" the King said. He pointed to the rock, Nuaru. "*The name of that rock is Nuaru. In my language, it means, 'I am coming.' . . . I am not a white man. I am from Tanna, and one day I will leave you and return. I am coming back to that rock, and when I put my foot on it, mature kava roots will spring from the ground, the old men will become young again, and there will be no more sickness or death.*"

*When she heard this, his wife knew that it was true, and she began*
*to cry. And the man on the shore heard and saw it all.*

As I finished, the crowd slapped their shins in applause. The Chief waved a finger at them to be quiet.

"This came to you from Prince Philip?"

What Baylis had read aloud was a myth recorded by Kirk Huffman, the anthropologist who advised Philip on the matter of how to wield the pig-killing stick, and Baylis soon realized that no one in the Yaohnanen crowd had heard this particular story before. As the weeks passed on the island—and with a book to write—Baylis became more anxious to locate someone who knew the old, authentic Philip mythology. He at last found a young man who recounted a legend in which Philip begs his father Kalbaben to let him go off to war with his brother John Frum. Baylis recognized the tale from his press packet, and was delighted to know it had been passed on through generations to the Yaohnanen youth. But his elation was soon crushed by the discovery that his guide Nako, who had insisted on keeping the sacred stack of papers in his possession, had been sneaking out of their hut early each morning, while Baylis slept, to visit the surrounding villages and read aloud the stories, in what was perhaps a ploy to boost his own authority on the island. Baylis's young interlocutor had heard the Philip tale in one of Nako's covert liturgies and repeated it. The Buckingham Palace photocopy machine, via Baylis, was planting the myths.

In the scriptures edited by Sir Miles Hunt-Davis, several of the cosmic myths sound much like palace PR describing philanthropic activities in an underdeveloped land. Every night "Kwin Lisbet," as Her Majesty's name was spelled, dreamed of a white building, and the thought of it began to possess her waking life. "Then Philip suggested they hold a competition, and ask all the students of the world to draw the building that Lisbet saw in her dreams," Baylis read aloud around the fire. While pictures poured into the palace mail room, none of them matched the building, until a drawing arrived from a boy from Tanna. In thanks, Lisbet declared they would construct it on Tanna, and the white building became the hospital. On another occasion, Baylis chose to recite a myth not from his sacred photocopies but from a paperback he had with him. As the assembled crowd included a Christian missionary, Loma-kom, who was a nemesis of Chief Jack Naiva, Baylis instinctively had the impulse to protect the secrets of the Philip faith. He read aloud how Kwin Lisbet and Philip first met when she visited the naval academy, and then she sailed off with her father on their yacht. A little dinghy kept following behind them, motoring farther out into the sea. "'Who is that foolish boy in that little boat? He will get himself drowned,'" the king said. The boy stood up and saluted him. "And Kwin Lisbet saw him—he was a young, tall blond man, very handsome, and she fell in love with him. That man was Prince Philip." "This is what they're talking about in Yaohnanen?" the missionary asked with disdain, and spat on the ground.

It was actually a tale from the bestselling book *The Little Princesses*, the 1950 tell-all memoir by Crawfie, or Marion Crawford—Queen Elizabeth II's childhood nanny, who was excommunicated for tell-ing scandalous gossip. Crawfie's account of how Elizabeth and Philip met, however embellished, had become standard myth in England, and Baylis had now seeded it on Tanna. In his weeks on Yaohnanen, Baylis introduced new ideas, practices, and relics into the cult of Philip, often unintentionally. He initiated the ritual celebration of Philip's birthday, and inadvertently put forth the notion, at first met with confusion and slight distaste, that three virgins are promised to the duke. When he used a canceled check as a piece of scrap paper, Baylis created a divinely charged relic, as a villager noticed the bank had the address of Bucking-ham Palace Road. In his travelogue, Baylis wrote with frustration of his inability to locate an authentic Philip tradition, and how, as a fumbling stranger, he kept getting in his own way, creating what he was meant to study. But the Tanna chiefs know better: there is no pure, essential form of their religion, nor of any other. "You don't know how our stories are," Jack Naiva tells Baylis.

> Every one of our stories is like a stone thrown into a pond. It sends out ripples, getting bigger and bigger all the time, so that in the end you can only see the last of the ripples and not the stone or the place where the stone went in. . . . There will always be more stories, so it makes

no sense to take this one or that one and put it on a piece of paper and say this is the story, and it came from here. . . . If you'd understood anything, I don't think you'd have come here with stories on pieces of paper, because you'd have known that our thing isn't like that, it's alive and it's moving.

Fulfilling a prophecy that they would one day meet the god in person, in 2007 Baylis helped organize a face-to-face meeting at Windsor Castle for a delegation of five from Tanna. Before the men left, the aged chief of Yakel village, Johnson Kowia, who at 103 was not up for the odyssey, had instructed them to ask Him a single question, upon which everything hinged. After traveling for three days, the envoys arrived in England on September 27, trailed by a film crew who preserved their impressions on the show *Meet the Natives*. The Philipists were largely underwhelmed by any alleged civilizational prowess; they were distressed to see that, amid the affluence of England, people sleep rough on the streets.

The palace refused to allow the meeting to be televised: when the moment comes for the five apostles to meet the deity, we watch as the doors of Windsor Castle close, furthering the sense that something mysterious is occurring inside the drawing room. Prince Philip reportedly broke the ice with the perfectly appropriate inquiry, "How are your gardens?" The ambassadors hazarded the crucial question: "*Is the pawpaw ripe yet or not?*" It was related that Philip likewise rose to the allegorical in his reply: "Whether the pawpaw is ripe or not, go tell Chief Kowia that now it is cold, but when it is warm, I will send a message." The five took a group photograph with Philip, which they showed to Kowia when they returned from their mission. "He has grown old," the chief said. "Look, my skin is all white!" one of the returning apostles joked.

Some years later, when a cyclone struck the island, bringing winds of 200 miles per hour, the vortex was seen by Philipists as an omen heralding His imminent return. In 2017, just as Philip, aged ninety-five, announced his retirement from public engagements, another cyclone raged, further evidence of his impending move to the South Seas. On Tanna, following the international news has long been a religious practice, a means of continuous, theological searching. For some devotees of John Frum, America's war on Iraq provoked spiritual questioning, as they saw Iraqis as an innocent people simply trying to preserve their own *kastom*. An orthodox Frumist, Chief Isak Wan, argued that the government of *Jojbus*, or George W. Bush, was possessed by the spirit of Tiapolo, or Satan. To liberate America from his grip, John Frum had sided with Osama bin Laden, providing him with sacred stones from Tanna to protect the jihadist from being captured. Struggling to reconcile American neo-imperialism, some Frumists on Tanna converted to Islam.

When bin Laden's hideout was eventually discovered in Abbottabad, Philipists claimed it was due to the prince's powers; and it was Philip, too, who put a black man in the White House. The villagers know that newspapers and magazines, the radio, internet, and mobile phones are just as good tools for expounding theology as the decrees of fourth-century bishops, men who moldered beneath the earth for centuries before turning into dust.

They are not afraid of the news that will arrive telling of the death of a god. Prince Philip has already become haloed with perpetuity. "The movement will always continue," as the villager Nako Nikien said. "And, from my opinion, or from what we believe, the spirit in Prince Philip won't die." Kings, after all, never died: if the infirm body had its demise, it was instantly replaced by the next, and the immortal body politic lived on. But this is an old monarchist fable, and on Tanna, the prophecy is egalitarian: if Philip returns home, he will defeat death for everyone, including himself, as good a reason as any to board a 60-hour flight, with four connections.

✦ ✦ ✦

*This is the way it is. It is revealed to such a person alone, hidden not in darkness and night but hidden in perfect day and holy light.*

The Gospel of Philip, long ago rejected by bishops as heresy, is attributed to Philip the Apostle, one of Christ's twelve, a married man remembered for his impatience at the Last Supper. When Jesus resurrected, Philip went out into Phrygia to preach the word, where, according to the fourth-century *Acts of Philip*, he ended up in a place called

Ophioryma, or "Serpent Town." Ophioryma was known for its temple where a viper lived the lifestyle of a god, drinking libations of wine mixed with human blood. In the year 80 CE, Philip was arrested, imprisoned inside the temple, and crucified upside down, yet still he continued to preach. Raging from the cross against the ophiolaters, Philip conjured an earthquake: the temple, the viper, and seven thousand people were swallowed into the abyss that opened up. Swiftly Jesus appeared and chastised Philip, still hanging upside down, for his vindictive act. God resurrected the men who had been killed, sending down a ladder of light to lift them out of the chasm, but He left the viper languishing below. When Philip gave up the ghost, he was locked out of paradise for forty days in penance, but then the apostle was duly let in.

A story on Tanna goes that when God punished the earth by unleashing the Flood, He warned Noah first, but Kalbaben somehow found out too. Before the rains came down, the god of the volcano rolled up the island of Tanna like a leaf to protect it. He secured the bundle with a pin, as a chief named Yoma recounted in the early 2000s. Kalbaben held the curled island in his fist. The world was drowned, but Tanna was kept safe in the god's giant hand. When the waters subsided, it was Kalbaben's son Nasabl who unrolled the island, but found there were no trees left, nor animals or men. The god's sons began the process of reseeding the island with life, as Kalbaben labored to restart the sun, which had frozen in place in the sky.

Again the sea levels begin an inexorable rise. The archipelago of Vanuatu is among the places most at risk from climate change. It already suffers the effects of the unchecked consumption of fossil fuels by rich nations, the same ones that colonized or occupied it with their armies, or stripped its sandalwood trees for trade. In Vanuatu's northernmost islands, villagers have been forced to flee in the face of storm surges, coastal erosion, and acidifying seas. In 2018, Vanuatu's prime minister, Charlot Salwai Tabimasmas, went before the General Assembly of the UN to seek a clearer road map as to how billions in climate aid promised by the wealthy nations would be collected and mobilized on the archipelago, well acquainted with empty promises. We are only at the beginning of a different kind of imperialism. Into the old structures of domination, inequality, and the white myth-dream come a new set of combatants: seawater, cyclone winds, and fires, leaving the existence of islands such as Tanna at stake.

The yacht, for Prince Philip, is his cross: a vehicle not of suffering but of ascension. Philip will go up laughing, to heaven or wherever he goes, leaving his secrets hidden in perfect daylight. In paradise, Philip will be laughing at himself, and especially at everyone else. But nobody knows for certain that He won't save us. And no one has yet found a better way to save us.

*So ends the gospel according to Philip.*

# MacArthur, Four Ways

*For every part of heaven conspires to the human form.*

—Emanuel Swedenborg, 1756

What follows is a case study of how a singular American male could become divine in four entirely distinct ways. Across three continents and four countries, each episode elevated him to a divinity of a unique species, substance, and shape. Each expressed a prayer for something deeply opposed to the politics and agenda of the man himself. If not the One, he was infinity divided by four: each part of General Douglas MacArthur became a way of imagining a world made anew.

#1

On the island of Ailigandí, to the northeast of the Panama Canal, the uniformed deity was ready for battle. His flesh was made of balsa wood, and he stood seven feet tall. Too powerful to wear any ordinary regalia, the wooden general was dressed in an electric blue jacket with pink pockets, yellow stripes and four stars on the lapels, a black bow tie, and a green army cap.

In October 1941, fearing the canal would be a prime target for German and Japanese submarines, the US military backed a coup to oust Panama's president and replace him with a leader, Ricardo de la Guardia, who would permit the construction of American patrol stations along the coast. Thousands of American soldiers soon descended upon the shores of San Blas, the territory of Panama's Guna people, and began to cut down trees, overturn rocks, and drain ponds to build barracks and landing strips. Hired to work as cleaners and cooks on the bases, Guna villagers from nearby islands such as Ailigandí and Ustupo observed firsthand the machinery of a global war. They also learned for the first time of a legendary American commander, born on a military base in Little Rock, Arkansas, who was fighting on the other side of the earth to free the Philippines from the imperial predations of the Japanese. They saw his picture in piles of magazines in the mess halls: tall, handsome, and photogenic, with a long nose and smooth skin. He was famous for his vanity. "*I shall return*," General MacArthur had recently proclaimed, after he was forced to flee the Philippine island of Corregidor. In San Blas, soldiers told the Guna villagers that MacArthur would protect them.

While the Axis threat never materialized in Panama, the Americans had unwittingly invited a different enemy into that theater of the war. Not long after the arrival of the Americans, an epidemic of fever began to rage across the province of San Blas. When the soldiers cleared land for the runways and bases, they uprooted the *ponikana* spirits from their invisible homes. Some were souls of people who had died in accidents or for unexplained reasons; others were animals of varied species. Sometimes an unsettling sight would alert the Guna to their presence, such as a weeping octopus sitting in a coconut tree. Displaced by the American soldiers, the angered spirits were now roaming in all directions and attacking Guna villagers in revenge. They would startle their victims, kidnapping their souls or *purpas*, and causing their body temperatures to rise dangerously.

To defeat the spirits and force them to retreat, the chiefs of Ailigandí decided to stage an eight-day ritual known as *Apsoged*, or "Conversing." In preparation, the villagers gathered an army of *nudsugana*, divinely charged wooden curing figurines present in many Guna homes. Dressed in fedoras, suit jackets, and ties, or in police uniform, the idols often depicted white men. Pale skin evoked the underworld, illness, and madness: it was thought that in the afterlife, the dead turn white. When white men arrived in San Blas, it was said, they had turned Guna villagers insane, leading them to betray their own people. If whiteness was the agent of sickness, it would need to become the means of the cure.

To lead the army of *nudsugana* into battle, a divine commander was required. His likeness was carved out of balsa, the whitest of woods, a material that is soft but thought to convey superior powers of communication. When the Guna craftsmen had finished, Douglas MacArthur was seven feet tall, with a nose supernatural in size. For eight days, the balsa idol or *uggurwalagana* of General MacArthur led the offensive in the spirit realm, as villagers chanted hymns and imbibed chicha, a drink made from maize, as clouds of smoke rose from the embers of burning cacao seeds. Only the shaman, who entered a dream state, witnessed the battle on the spirit plane. It was said the souls of the *nudsugana* added khaki for camouflage and marched in formation. They cast traps for the evil spirits in the trees, and produced their own tear gas. General MacArthur was tasked with conveying the clear message to the *ponikana* that the islanders were not responsible for the destruction of their homes. In his balsa wood form, the expertise of the four-star general was

invoked to save the villagers from the epidemic and undo the damage
the Americans had wrought.

While the MacArthur who was fighting in the Philippines was known
for being a lone wolf, an egotistical commander with a tendency to take
autonomous decisions, his double in the Panama jungle embodied the
power of the collective. Although the Guna themselves were divided by
factions, the general transcended them, bridging the islands and their
rivalries. With the government of Panama coercing the Guna to assimi-
late, and with both the state and the Americans encroaching upon their
land, the villagers needed to form a united front. In 1945, the chiefs came
together in what would become the first Guna General Congress. Not
long after, an American living in the Canal Zone found the discarded
wooden figure of General MacArthur from the ritual at Ailigandí. At
the end of the eight days, the *nudsugana* had
returned from the front line to their homes
and to their everyday state as curing figurines,
while the gigantic MacArthur was abandoned.
Other icons of the general, used in other
*Absogeds*, were tossed into the sea or left in
the jungle to decay, lest the balsa wood commander become too dangerous, too full of
his own potency and impossible to control.
Having served his function, MacArthur had
to be emptied of his divine soul through the
ravages of nature and time.

On the island of Ustupo, another jettisoned MacArthur was found by an American
ethnographer. The general's body had been
eaten by termites, but the head and shoulders
remained intact. He was shipped to Manhattan, to live in the American Museum of Natural History. The idol from Ailigandí ended
up in Ohio in the collection of the Denison
Museum. In 2016, under the surveillance
of a security guard, against a painted electric

blue backdrop that matched the idol's unlikely jacket, MacArthur stood to attention, the prized specimen in an exhibition titled *The Human Condition*.

## #2

"In the old days we worshiped, morning and evening, before a portrait of the Emperor as if he were a god, but now-a-days we do so before that of General MacArthur," wrote an elderly schoolteacher from a remote Japanese district in Aomori Prefecture in a letter to MacArthur dated January 1, 1950. It was exactly four years to the day since Emperor Hirohito had issued his Declaration of Humanity, or *Ningen Sengen*, an imperial rescript broadcast on the radio and in newspapers across the globe. The emperor had been encouraged to undeify himself by MacArthur, who, in the wake of Japan's surrender at the end of World War II, had been appointed supreme commander of the Allied powers and set about democratizing Japan through his own autocratic rule. For the sake of stability, MacArthur preferred not to abolish the throne, lest that open the gates to communism, but Hirohito's status as "sacred and inviolable" would have to change. A British scholar, Dr. Reginald H. Blyth, and an American officer and ex–Columbia professor, Lieutenant Colonel Harold Henderson, two friends with an interest in Japanese poetry, drafted the first version of Hirohito's speech. Henderson said he had daydreamed it on his lunch break: returning to his hotel room, he lay down in bed with a notepad and pencil and imagined that it was he himself who was resigning as a living god. It was then edited by Hirohito's advisors and, lightly, by MacArthur himself.

Having descended from his clouds, Hirohito set off on a "Humanity" tour across the ruins of his devastated country. If once he rode an immaculate white horse, the emperor now walked the streets, wearing a shabby suit and tie and overcoat. If once he had lived in a state of sheltered transcendence, now he held his own umbrella in the rain. He lifted his hat incessantly to the curious crowds. Hirohito, who was never tried for war crimes, was once believed to be, like the sun, too powerful to look at; now observers pointed to his tiny size, his slumped shoulders, his weak chin, straggly facial hair, and bespectacled squint. Modeling his rebranding on the British royal family, Hirohito tried to feign interest in ordinary lives and make polite conversation. But in his pitiful awkwardness he appeared so ill-suited to the profane, terrestrial world that to many it only reinforced his otherworldliness. As if they felt sorry for him, his Japanese subjects still made an effort to sweep clean the areas before he visited, to protect him from reality, leading the skinny emperor to become known as "the Broom."

If Hirohito had been demoted to deity of defeat, as the ashes of the war were swept away General MacArthur began to fill a certain void. In his aviator sunglasses and iconic corncob pipe dangling insouciantly from his lips, the now five-star general had mastered the stagecraft of authority. As he passed by in his motorcade, Japanese soldiers turned their backs in respect as if he, like the sun, were too incandescent for their gaze. When the general acted swiftly to mobilize food aid to millions of starving people, he quickly won the adoration of the Japanese. The new shogun wrote his "MacArthur Constitution," and set about implementing a series of liberal reforms concerning land, health care, education, and women's rights. Among the bewildering debris of surrender, for many Japanese the enemy commander had become the embodiment of peace, hope, and the power to turn defeat into a moral victory. At his general headquarters at the Dai-Ichi Life Insurance Building in central Tokyo, the mail room was flooded with hundreds of thousands of letters addressed to MacArthur, many telling of hatred transformed into love.

"I have never encountered, as far as I know, a face as infinite in aspect as this," wrote a sculptor in a letter proposing a bronze bust as a gift to the general. The artist saw the universe in MacArthur's face, at once a circular and a square shape, and strove to capture it. "I added some strong active elements of the general in contact with infinity," the sculptor noted. Another correspondent used mystical wordplay to break down the characters in a rendering of *MacArthur* in Japanese, *Makkāsā*, and discerned its meaning: "The everlasting beauty of the glorious pine tree," a name that prophesied immortality for the evergreen general. Envelopes were addressed to "Living Savior," and correspondents suggested MacArthur's portrait should replace that of the emperor in shrines. Many letters likened him to Christ, a comparison that dovetailed with the general's own Christian sense that he was carrying out the white man's burden in the Far East. MacArthur was like Jesus delivering the Sermon on the Mount, a cultural society in a village near Kobe wrote, and sent him a Japanese painting of the biblical scene. Each day brought offerings in the mail: lotus roots and dried persimmons, red beans, rice cakes, bonsai trees, a kimono embroidered by a monk, and numerous walking sticks, for MacArthur was sixty-five. There were samurai swords, deerskins, portraits of Himself, and the first Japanese turkey born from an American egg. Rumors spread that MacArthur had Japanese ancestry; an idea circulated that Christ had died in Japan.

The deluge of ecstatic thanks to an enemy invader had little precedent in modern history. It was reminiscent of Demetrius Poliorcetes's appearance on the Athenian horizon, and the hymn the people sang: *You are here, to you we pray.* Sending letters to MacArthur was cathartic, like casting messages in bottles out to sea to reach remote Greek saints. Occasionally, via his secretaries, the general wrote back. People asked for help with illness, to ferry messages to vanished or imprisoned loved ones, or merely to express the pent-up grief, fear, and guilt that they had been unable to voice under the old regime. "Ordinary men and women confessed their past militarist sins to him as if he were a priest," the historian John W. Dower writes. Some letters, carrying urgent appeals, were written with fine calligraphy brushes dipped in blood. Though some bore only the vague address, "Mr. MacArthur, Tokyo," they reached him nonetheless. The general saved the most worshipful ones among his private papers.

There was much debate as to what exactly was the nature of the godhead that Hirohito vacated and MacArthur apparently filled. While Hirohito maintained that he was never a "god" in any Judeo-Christian sense, the Meiji Restoration of 1868, which enshrined the emperor's divinity within state-enforced Shinto, had in many ways sought to construct a deity that could compete with the Almighty God of European empire. Over the centuries, previous Japanese emperors and empresses had performed various priestly and ceremonial roles, yet real sovereignty and wealth

often lay elsewhere, with the shoguns. With the coup that installed the
Meiji reign, Hirohito's grandfather and his advisors reinvented the collective of traditions known as Shinto and established it not as a religion,
a mere matter of faith, but as a science, unbound by any duties of tolerance or freedom of belief. "The truth of Shinto is no small thing. It
is bound up in the sun, moon, stars and earth . . . everything in Western and Chinese science emerges from it," declared the theorist Ōkuni
Takamasa. Japanese deities had gifted the power and knowledge to make
European technology work, bringing fire to the delicate filaments of a
light bulb. The imperial throne was as ancient as the moment when the
heavens first separated from the earth, according to the Meiji statesman
Itō Hirobumi. Generations of children read in official school textbooks
that it was a scientific fact the emperor was descended, in an unbroken
genealogical line, from the solar goddess Amaterasu.

With the invention of State Shinto in the late nineteenth century,
numerous dissident religions arose that rejected the godhood of the
Meiji emperor and strove for universalist visions of the divine. Among
them was Oomoto, cofounded in the 1890s by Deguchi Nao, an illiterate
priestess who, in a possessed state, penned hundreds of thousands of
pages of revelations that she was unable to read. When her charismatic
son-in-law and cofounder, Deguchi Onisaburo, learned of the existence
of Esperanto, he realized it must be the language spoken in heaven. He
decided to deify its inventor, Ludwig Lazarus Zamenhof, a deceased Jewish ophthalmologist born in Poland, as a *kami*, a Japanese divinity that
takes many forms. For refusing to worship the emperor, Oomoto was
violently suppressed; Onisaburo was imprisoned for seven years, and
Oomoto's assets and shrines were destroyed. Yet after Hirohito abdicated
his godhood, MacArthur imposed reforms that downgraded Shinto to
just one religion among many, prompting what became known as "the
rush hour of the gods."

All the exiled deities and prophets began to return, among them
Oomoto and its *kami* of communication, Zamenhof. With his legendary prophetic powers, Onisaburo had even predicted this turn: when
asked by a disciple to ensure that Japan would win the war, Onisaburo
informed him of its imminent defeat—but assured him that this would

ultimately be beneficial. If the earth was like a house, he said, Japan was its family altar, and it was filthy with dust and blood. It needed to be cleaned, but the Japanese were only making the mess worse. "The *kami* will use a tough guy, MacArthur, to do the job instead," Onisaburo prophesied.

In the strangeness of an American ruling over Japan, people began to refashion old ideas to fit new circumstances, as Dower writes: they were "finding—inventing if need be—something familiar to hold on to." Traditional concepts took on novel interpretations, becoming a bridge for people "to cross from war to peace." A letter in a newspaper claimed that MacArthur was the reincarnation of Japan's first, mythic emperor Jimmu, great-great-grandson of the sun goddess. A businessman in Tokyo later recalled that MacArthur was a *fuku no kami*, a god of happiness or good fortune. But for many Japanese intellectuals on both right and left, the folding of MacArthur into old structures of emperor worship was going too far. In October 1946, the newspaper *Jiji Shimpo* ran an editorial warning against the deification of MacArthur, for it undermined democracy itself. "If the conception that government is something imposed upon the people by an outstanding god, great man, or leader is not rectified, democratic government is likely to be wrecked," the editorial argued. The best way to show gratitude to the general, it continued, was "not to worship him as a god but to cast away the servile spirit and gain the self-respect that would not bow its head to anybody." Although an American in the press censorship office had approved the editorial, MacArthur's hawkish chief of intelligence, Charles Willoughby, was horrified, and confiscated the entire print run of the English translation in the *Nippon Times* before it reached subscribers at dawn.

If MacArthur was there to build democracy, his reign became ever more dictatorial. It was as intolerant of criticism as Hirohito's regime, yet possessed even greater legislative powers. On April 11, 1951, President Truman made the sensational announcement that he was firing MacArthur on grounds of insubordination. Long engaged in a power struggle with the president, MacArthur was accused of publicly contradicting Truman on matters of foreign policy and adopting an aggressive stance toward

China that many feared could lead to a third world war. Like his double, the balsa wood statue in Panama, MacArthur had become too powerful, impossible to control. The *New Yorker* writer E. J. Kahn Jr. reported from an army campsite in Korea that, just as the news of MacArthur's humiliating dismissal came over the radio, a great gust of wind rushed over them, flattening their tents, followed by a hailstorm and then a snowstorm, on what was otherwise a temperate spring day. "Gee, do you suppose he really is God, after all?" one soldier reportedly exclaimed. In Tokyo, people expressed their sorrow at the news by traveling to the American embassy and kneeling in front of the gates.

Returning to Washington, MacArthur testified for three days before Congress on his conduct in the Korean War and gave a melodramatic speech condemning any surrender of Asia to communism. "We heard God speak here today, God in the flesh," Republican congressman Dewey Short announced, a comment he modified in the *Congressional Record* to "a great hunk of God in the flesh." He was "the reincarnation of St. Paul," proclaimed former president Herbert Hoover, whom MacArthur had served as chief of staff. Under Hoover, in the depths of the Great Depression, MacArthur had notoriously suppressed a peaceful protest of unemployed veterans and their families outside the White House with bayonets, tanks, and tear gas, as if they were enemy combatants.

Though he returned to a warm Republican apotheosis, MacArthur was to end up committing his own deicide in Japan. When asked at the congressional hearing if the Japanese would be able to maintain the democracy established under the American occupation, MacArthur's response was deeply racist, likening the Japanese civilizational maturity to "a boy of twelve, compared with our development of 45 years." The phrase, repeated across Japan, was "a stunning slap in the face," wrote the historian Sodei Rinjiro. Outrage turned to shame that the nation had so readily embraced American paternalism, a regime that had no intention of making Japan an equal ally in a future world order. Instantly, MacArthur began to be erased from the collective memory. Plans for tributes in the general's honor, including a statue in Tokyo Bay, were abandoned.

With both Hirohito and MacArthur fallen from their heights, there was once more an absence to be filled. A better choice as deity of hope than MacArthur was Zamenhof, who created Esperanto not only as a global tongue but as a means to promote peace between nations. Zamenhof was the god of a gentler world, with harder consonants—a prospect that doesn't sound bad at all.

#3

*"Why have you failed to attend to me? Have I not appeared to you before?"*

In the darkness of the night, in the depths of her dreams, a woman from Chejudo was being harassed by General MacArthur.

*"Were you not able to find solace with me when you were suffering so much?"*

Chaktu Posalnim was the daughter of a soldier in the South Korean army, who had died two months after she was born, on an unrecorded date in the early 1950s. Her mother, left in poverty, soon remarried and moved the family to the port city of Incheon, but one day she vanished, leaving Chaktu alone with her violent stepfather. Escaping his abuse, as a teenager Chaktu worked on a factory assembly line, folding paper boxes all day. When she lay down to sleep, she would hear voices in her dreams commanding her to go to Chayu Kongwŏn, or Freedom Park. Although she did not know the way, she would sleepwalk for an hour and a half, as if guided by an otherworldly force to the public park by the sea. "It was like I was in some kind of trance where I had fainted, became oblivious to my surroundings, and would suddenly 'wake up' standing in front of MacArthur statue, not having known when I left nor how I got there," Chaktu told the anthropologist Joon Choi in 2006. "I really began to think I was going crazy and started to worry that something was genuinely wrong with me."

On top of a stone pedestal stands the bronze statue of General Douglas MacArthur, ten feet high, the commander who, in dismantling the

Japanese empire, had liberated Korea from colonial rule. In Freedom Park, the towering MacArthur, binoculars in hand, looks out over the site of perhaps his most lauded military feat, when, in September 1950, as Supreme Commander of the UN forces, he led an amphibious landing in the treacherous harbor of Incheon. Although he was warned it was an impossible maneuver in the rough tides of typhoon season, MacArthur led the invasion of thousands of troops over the seawalls, forcing the North Korean army to retreat and leading to the liberation of Seoul. Only six months after his triumph, the general had been dismissed from office. On April 5, 1964, at age eighty-four, General MacArthur died of cirrhosis in a hospital in Washington, DC. But even after his death he carried on giving orders, summoning Chaktu to his bronze seat of power on midnight journeys that continued for an entire year. "This was my first experience with the spirit of General MacArthur," Chaktu recalled to Joon Choi. "However, at this point in my life I had no idea who he even was."

At seventeen Chaktu was married to a fisherman, and in the infinite drudgery of cooking, cleaning, and caring for ill relatives and her children, she forgot all about MacArthur. To support her family, Chaktu gathered clams and sea worms, worked the ginseng fields, and returned to the factory assembly line, but their poverty was insurmountable and her husband grew increasingly abusive. She began to be plagued by nightmares and predictions of tragedies that came true. "I felt like a movie reel was constantly spinning round and round in my head," she recalled. Her eyes would burn with a strange glow. She realized she was possessed by the spirits of the battlefield dead. Action scenes of war surged within her, and her body ached. "Aiooooooo!" she exclaimed. "All day and all night. . . . All these Generals would pester me, over and over again, just hound me!" Her children grew afraid of her, and her horrified Christian in-laws decided she needed an exorcist. When she was twenty-seven, she was instructed in a dream to connect with others suffering from "spirit sickness," and to become initiated in the tradition of Hwanghae-do shamanism, or *musok*. Her husband was appalled: believing shamanism to be heretical, he beat her and demolished her household shrines.

She dreamed she was a spirit called the Blade General, and took the name Chaktu Posalnim, from the words *chaktu*, "straw-cutter," and *posal*, or "diviner." She learned the shamanic art of walking barefoot on a razor's edge. In the trance of the *kut*, or ritual ceremony, possessed of the gods' inviolable power, Chaktu was able to dance gracefully on sharpened blades, her feet unscathed. One day her husband was out at sea when his fellow fishermen began to perform a ritual to appease the maritime spirits. Enraged, he destroyed their offerings of rice cakes, and immediately dropped dead. Chaktu was now freely able to devote herself to shamanic practice, although her woes persisted, as money remained scarce and her son fell gravely ill. It was at this time, in the quiet of the night, that MacArthur began to appear to her once again.

*Why have you ignored me? Do you not know that if you worship me I will help you?*

Every night he arrived, again and again, although he had never spent a single night in the country when he had been commander of the war in Korea, preferring to return to Tokyo to sleep. In Chaktu's dreams, MacArthur became ever more admonishing, his reproaches verging on divine blackmail: if she didn't include him in her rituals, the consequences would be dire. "I finally realized that it was my duty to incorporate him into my pantheon of spirits," Chaktu recalled to Joon Choi. "I described this dream vision of General MacArthur to a shaman painter who created a portrait of the General for me, and now I include it in all of my *kut*." In Chaktu's *musindo*, or shamanic portrait, the deified MacArthur looks uncharacteristically jovial. The likeness presided over Chaktu's altar, alongside other gods such as her guardian Chaktu Sinryŏng, the spirit of blade dancing, and Yŏ Changun, a female warrior. Chaktu did not choose MacArthur: he chose her. But the general gave her strength to persevere in the face of constant adversity. "My life has improved significantly since General MacArthur returned and I introduced him into my pantheon," she said. Her children married and gave her grandchildren; her financial situation improved; she was even able to locate her disappeared mother and rebuild their relationship. With her own life on track, the woman who danced on razors was now able to use her shamanic powers to help others in need.

Hwanghae-do shamanism came to the South through refugees from North Korea, escaping the regime's persecution of religion and superstition. Fleeing their homes in the coastal province of Hwanghae, prominent *mansin* or shamans such as Madame Chung Hak-Bong and Kim Kum-Hwa ended up in Incheon. The women became teachers of the new Hwanghae practitioners in the South. Sometime in the early 1960s, they began to incorporate MacArthur as an amphibious god into their practice, a shamanism infused with seawater spirits and fish fertility rituals. For the northern shamans in exile, MacArthur was a deity of resistance, not to a foreign conqueror but to the foreign ideas of Marx, Lenin, and Mao. A warrior god who moved between land and sea, MacArthur led the struggle over rival visions of how we should live.

He sometimes appeared in a trinity of historic officer-gods, with the seventeenth-century general Im Kyongup and the naval commander Yi Sunsin, who presided over different seas. In the *kut*, just as in the Guna ritual in Panama, the commanders move on the spirit plane against deities who cause misfortune and illness. They also appease the spirits of the *kunung*, a hungry crowd of anonymous war dead, forgotten soldiers from different ages and killing fields. When the shaman is possessed by the *kunung*, she is known to devour raw meat; the spirits fill her with their delight and messages of thanks. "The Spirits are history," says the shaman Lee Jong-Ja, whose guardian deity is MacArthur, and who makes pilgrimages to his statue in Freedom Park. "No spirits exist without history, and we may not understand them without history."

The shamans themselves are sometimes inhabited by General MacArthur; they wear GI uniforms in their trance state. Chain-smoking and drinking whiskey libations, some *mansin* who have no knowledge of English have been heard delivering fluent prophecies in the general's tongue. In the 1980s, the shaman Hyun Myungboon was arrested for possessing a contraband carton of Marlboro cigarettes, which she had placed on her altar before her spirit portrait of MacArthur, but she was released after convincing Incheon police that the cigarettes were for the general and not for her. In the shamanic practice of Kim Kye-Sun, "the spirit of MacArthur likes to give divinations using South Korea's national flag," the anthropologists Heonik Kwon and Jun Hwan Park report. The global order imagined by the amphibian god MacArthur is profoundly egalitarian, one of mutual respect between nations, and in many ways, as the scholars write, "is quite un-American." For the shamans, MacArthur is a means of claiming a power that is life-affirming and regenerating, peaceful and nondestructive. As a divinity, he is at odds with his earthly legacy in Korea, where he presided over hundreds of thousands of military and civilian deaths, dropped ninety-three napalm bombs onto the small island of Wolmido, next to Incheon, and, in threatening the North with atomic weapons, unleashed the peninsula's nuclear arms race.

From time to time, protesters gather to call for the removal of the bronze statue of Douglas MacArthur from Freedom Park. Occasionally clashes erupt at his feet. Policemen are sent to watch over the commander, who gazes idly out to sea. Late in the night MacArthur came to Chaktu, haunting her with his voice. Perhaps a demon had haunted him, with a question. What if you could live as a god, again and again, in every different possible way? What if you could try on every outfit and size of divinity? Would you want to?

#4

*"I shall return,"* he said.

On the islands of Biak, to the west of the coast of New Guinea, General MacArthur entered a myth. It told of an old man with a terrible skin disease. Manarmakeri lived alone in the jungle as an outcast, despised for his sores and scabs. One day, when he caught the Morning Star stealing his palm wine, the thief promised him a wish. With the star's help, he managed to impregnate the most beautiful woman in the nearby village, Insoraki, in a virgin birth. When it was discovered that the "Itchy Old Man" was the father, her furious family abandoned her, and Insoraki was sent off to live with her husband, bitterly making cruel jokes about his skin. Offended by her contempt, Manarmakeri decided to transform himself. He constructed a giant pyre not far from their dwelling on the atoll of Wundi. Setting the wood alight, he leapt into the flames, whirling in the fire as his old skin peeled off and was changed into porcelain and jewels. He stepped out from the fire young and naked, his skin burnished and radiant. Some versions say Manarmakeri emerged with white skin, others that he reentered the flames "to roast it to an attractive brown." In his baptism by fire, he was transformed into Manseren Mangundi, the Lord Himself.

The newly hatched god collected his treasures from the smoldering ashes and walked to the seashore, where he built a steamship by drawing with a stick in the sand. He then returned to collect Insoraki and his son. But the deity changed back into the Itchy Old Man again, to test his in-laws, and still they rejected him. No one on Biak believed in his powers, and so he disappeared and took his prosperity to Europe. He authored the Holy Bible, instructed Gutenberg to print it, and showed the people the way toward eternal life. He bestowed upon the tribes of Europe his scientific prowess, and he introduced to them what became known as "Western clothes."

It is said that one day Manarmakeri will return on a ship bound for New Guinea, bringing all his wealth and knowledge and inaugurating a utopian state. His arrival will herald the age of heaven, *Koreri*, from the Biak root meaning, "We Change Our Skin." "The dead will rise, and there will be no more planting and harvesting, for everyone will dine richly on Mangundi's magical fare," an account of the prophecy, recorded in 1889, relates. "The old will become young, and a golden age of end-less eating and drinking, and dancing and leaping will dawn, for there will be no more death." All people will change their skins. But who will recognize the Lord when he comes? He stays in the collective memory, for he wrote epic songs about himself that he would sing as he paddled a canoe. People on the shore heard them, and passed down the hymns through the generations.

*Yado yamasasi yo mare piryar yano fawi yo, fawi aya bva*, Manar-makeri sang.

I descended and bathed at my spring, they did not recognize, did
not recognize me.

Since the mid-nineteenth century, the islands of Biak had been under
a fragile, dysfunctional Dutch rule. Staking their claim to western New
Guinea, Dutch missionaries, officers, and traders had landed with
instructions to pacify the allegedly lawless Papuans and turn them into
productive labor. To instill Protestant values, the Dutch tried to ban the
evenings spent drinking palm wine, the dances, singing, and drumming
that gave joy to daily life. The colonizers offered little in return in terms
of material progress, education, or infrastructure, and the people looked
askance at their claims to authority. A series of Papuan prophets arose,
announcing the news that Manarmakeri would imminently return
and *Koreri* was near, overturning the colonial order and reversing
all hierarchies of race. As all their needs would be fulfilled, villagers
destroyed their crops and sat together on the beach awaiting the ship's
arrival, enacting a myth-dream that would inevitably be branded as a
"cargo cult."

In early 1942, the strategic islands were captured by the Imperial Japanese Navy, and a famine soon spread. Although they had no desire to
help the latest conquerors, thousands of starving islanders were recruited
to work on the Japanese naval base at Manokwari. There the Biaks heard
about a general who was leading a series of American victories against
Japan, and seemed to be everywhere at once. The press was reporting
that he moved between Brisbane and New Guinea so swiftly "that often
two luncheon tables were set for him, fifteen hundred miles apart." He
possessed nuclear weapons and ships loaded with inexhaustible supplies. All the signs indicated that MacArthur must be Manarmakeri, or
Manseren Mangundi, the Lord Himself returning in a new skin.

Among the most powerful prophets of *Koreri* was a woman, Angganeta Menufandu, who was imprisoned, first by the Dutch and then by
the Japanese, for preaching the imminent arrival of a new world order.
Born in the village of Sowek, she had contracted a virulent skin disease
when her husband and child died, and went into seclusion on an unin-
habited island. A strange old man appeared to her; he brought medicine

and cured her, and anointed her his messenger. Manarmakeri revealed to her the flag of *Koreri*—blue, white, and red, with stripes and stars—and said: "If thy right and thy flag are not recognized, if again thou art oppressed, then a third world war shall destroy the whole world," as one of her followers later recounted. The prophetess became a radio, picking up messages from the gods and the dead and transmitting them to the trusted disciple she called her "wire." Other prophets arose to challenge her: when a man from Numfor claimed he himself was the Living God, Angganeta's general, Stephanus, tried to humiliate him by calling him *Koki*, or the cook. Sent back to his village, the pretender promptly changed it to *Kapten Koki*—Captain Cook—and built his own rival legion of followers.

Angganeta warned that if *Koreri* was not attained, all would end in *Korore*, a word that meant, simultaneously, progress and bloodshed. Either way, all would be changed. Stephanus laid out plans for their new state in a *Koreri* charter that would come to serve as foundational text for generations of Papuan separatists. The *Koreri* army was to be named AB, or *America Babo*, "New America." Japanese bullets would be turned into water. In a letter from prison in June 1942, not long before she was executed, Angganeta prophesied the Allied victory: "*After these dark times the Morning Star will rise in the east, Japan will be defeated, and we shall rise again.*" The Morning Star, her followers knew, meant MacArthur.

In one of Manarmakeri's songs, he imagined the dead stacked in layers above the clouds, like the thatching on a roof. In 1943, as the Japanese attempted to clear land to build airstrips on Biak, soldiers killed scores of unarmed islanders who had gathered in protest on the beach. The following year, in May 1944, Biak became the front line of the war, as MacArthur's stepping-stone for his much-vaunted return to the Philippines. For two months, Allied soldiers fought viciously in the Biak jungles, firebombing Japanese soldiers camped out in caves and leaving thousands of dismembered corpses. "After the carnage came the cargo," the historian Danilyn Rutherford writes; the victorious US troops unloaded masses of supplies and tons of canned food, which they distributed to the famished islanders. The unreal quantities of goods that descended on an island that now resembled a landscape in hell furthered the sense that *Koreri* must be near.

For many residents, it was not a coincidence that MacArthur's army chose to use as its storehouse the atoll, Wundi, where Manarmakeri had been baptized by fire. As the globe was divided up in the wake of the Allied victory, the islands grouped as Indonesia gained independence, but western New Guinea returned to being a Dutch colony. While the Dutch promised they would "prepare" the Papuans for self-rule, in 1962, the United Nations ceded the territory to Indonesia, without consulting the Papuans at all. The messianic myth-dream of *Koreri* grew ever more urgent, fueling the separatists of the Free Papua Movement, who fought for liberation under a flag striped white, blue, and red, with a single Morning Star, the celestial body that could be MacArthur and is also said to be the angel Gabriel.

In the 1990s, Danilyn Rutherford traveled to Wundi, to visit a prophet whom she calls, to protect his identity, Uncle Bert. The atoll was still covered in detritus from the war. There were burnt-out shells of vehicles, resembling the brittle bodies of dead insects, and the rusting metal helmets of the dead. The people of Wundi had made their homes out of the relics of combat. Uncle Bert, a fisherman who had encountered Manarmakeri himself, lived, she writes, "in the husks of history." In Bert's house, "one of the tables was an old refrigerator, one of the chairs, a fighter-pilot seat; a shining airplane wing provided a bench." The prophet had a collection of talismans given to him by Manarmakeri, among them a green flashlight, from when he came to announce his Second Coming, and an iron plate with the words *White Freightliner*, which the deity told him was a passport to travel the earth.

Bert took out a copy of the book Manarmakeri wrote; inside the Holy Bible was a laminated card. It was a drawing of not one Douglas, but two: MacArthur, and the British field marshal Douglas Haig. Standing behind them was Christ, with the image of the *Koreri* flag; on the back were the words *Independence Day 1943*. For Bert, the card was imbued with forces of protection and, like the tarot, of divination. It was laced with the contagious power of the foreign, distant figures it depicted, but also the ancestral core deep within them, indigenous to Biak. It prophesied the return, of both people and property, to a place deemed a marginal backwater by the hierarchs who drew up the borders of the globe.

What sort of person might be God? This was the question posed by the myth of Manarmakeri, as Rutherford writes. The answer it gives is someone who ached and itched and aged, someone who faced rejection and sought acceptance and love. In the 1990s, the Indonesian government strove to turn the tropical Biak islands into the new Bali, a lucrative tourist haven, and repackage Papuan tradition as a "regional" culture. The ministers spoke of Biak "taking off"; developers razed Biak family lands to build hotels, although few of the projects ever got off the ground. Uncle Bert took the Indonesian state rhetoric and subverted it, folding it into his prophecies. The world itself would "leave the launching pad" soon, he predicted. The fact that the tourism initiatives were bankrolled by American loans was further proof of Manarmakeri's hand. Not only on Wundi, but across the archipelago, sightings of the Itchy Old Man were frequent. He would be seen lingering along a road, or sinking his toes into the sand, and then he would vanish. Fires that destroyed construction sites and tourist shops revealed he was at work in the world. According to Bert, on one occasion the Lord disclosed to him the secret meanings of the letters *B-I-A-K*: *Bila lngat Akan Kembali*, "If Remembered, Will Return."

It was said that when Manarmakeri was a young man, he once chased after a pig who was uprooting the taro plants in his garden. He hurled his spear, but the impaled creature disappeared, leaving a trail of blood and human footprints. The young man followed it, and found himself at the mouth of a deep cave; when he entered, it was radiant with the light of the sun. Inside was a vast paradise, a village of thatched roofs knotted together, teeming with inhabitants, rejoicing and laughing, all untouched by signs of age. They said to him, "Your time has not come yet, you are still in the husk . . . This is a *Koreri* place." They told him he would enter it someday, but he must exit the cave by walking backward. When he bent down to retrieve his spear, he saw the writhing, iridescent scales of a snake coiled alongside it. Startled, he spun around and ran out of the cave. Returning home, he found his crops had withered. He lost all joy in life and grew depressed, for everything around him seemed meaningless and empty. This was the prehistory of the man who became god. When people asked about the change that had come over him like a rash, few believed him when he recounted his tale. In his despair at losing heaven, he began to itch.

The lingering impression left by the testimonies of those who fought alongside Douglas MacArthur when he was a young soldier in the trenches of the first global war was that he had no fear of death. Like changing dressings on a wound that keeps reopening, again and again the general found and lost and found divinity. MacArthur was as though quadrisected, each quarter experiencing a different way to become fleetingly, precariously divine. If the general sought glory, immortality, and fame, he found it in ways and places he could never have foreseen. He was a balsa-wood idol, a Shinto *kami*, a needy amphibious spirit, and the Lord Himself, a hunk of god covered in scabs. Like a snake, he kept shedding his skin. General MacArthur was American destruction incarnate, and he was four ways of imagining the earth renewed. When he returns, finally, to wherever it may be, the vain general will not recognize himself.

4

———

# Gods in Uniform

Of all possible situations in which one might find oneself suddenly divine, the most physically uncomfortable is that of spirit possession, which can happen in one of two ways. It may be that *you* are the rogue, roving power: your spirit has left you to enter the cramped innards of another human and move them, acting in the world through their unfamiliar limbs. In the case of Douglas MacArthur, the general was nonchalantly dead by the time his spirit began to animate shamans in South

Korea who danced on knives. Others have found their spirits deserting them while still alive: an unlucky French officer in Niger, as we will see, watched as his spirit double ran riot in the bodies of other men, against his will and his best intentions. You may become the possessor, or the possessed. You may find yourself the receptacle of an invading spirit; when it enters and controls you, often at terribly inconvenient times, there is nothing you can do until it passes.

You are, for a moment, like a strange, soft ore, in which spirit and flesh, self and stranger, have alchemized and become briefly, unstably, divine. It may be nauseating and painful to have a spirit enter your body, but it imbues you, temporarily, with a superhuman might, as if you contain a force never meant to fit into human size. "He described the way his body ached after he caught power," recounted an anthropologist of a man living in Trinidad who suffered reoccurring bouts of possession. "He then pointed towards a large police building that we were passing. 'It's like trying to fit that police station in your body,' he said."

What if there were a way to harness this power, to organize and deploy it? What if the possessed could form an institution, an army, a nation of their own? In 1925, a French dossier from the capital of Niamey in Niger reported "a kind of crazy wind" that had blown through the city's districts that summer. At a dance in the village of Chikal, a woman named Zibo had suddenly fallen into a trance. A spirit had entered her body. "Who are you?" the crowd around her demanded to know. The spirit answered through Zibo that he was the governor of the Red Sea. Speaking through his mesmerized vessel, the spirit commanded the people to make rifles, which they fashioned out of wood. Soon other spirits began to speak: sergeants, soldiers, secretaries, chief justices, and generals of the French empire who had invaded and occupied Niger in 1900. Ventriloquizing the bodies of spellbound villagers, the spirits demanded pith helmets and libations of gin. They moved in a gruesome subversion of imperial protocol, marching stiffly in formation, doing backflips, foaming at the mouth. They cast flaming torches across their borrowed bodies without being burned, to show they were not human. The spirits soon revealed their name: *Hauka*, or "madness." They vomited black ink, the quotidian liquid of bureaucracy.

Within months, the crazy wind had blown north across the region of Filingué, where seemingly all the youth were becoming possessed. "Serious trouble in Kourfey," according to a French official. Zibo and her father, Gandji, had "created a sect that copies our administration and wants to supplant our authority." Zibo, or the spirit of the Red Sea governor, was preaching insurgency. The villagers were refusing to pay taxes or to perform corvée labor, the unpaid, exhausting work of building the infrastructure of the French empire from the ground up—slavery by another name. Rejecting French subjugation, they left the colonialists' world and went into the bush, where they conjured a deific, dissident double of the French regime: a spirit army of over a hundred soldiers, majors, lieutenants, governors, doctors, and technicians. In the arid wilderness, the *Hauka*'s mediums established a counter-society and began to train for war.

Bewildered by these strange uprisings, the chief of Filingué wrote to the district commissioner of Niamey, Major Horace Valentin Crocicchia, who ordered him to round up the *Hauka* mediums. The chief arrested sixty people, Zibo among them, and brought them in chains to Niamey, where they were imprisoned for three nights without food. On the fourth day, Crocicchia summoned the prisoners and ordered them to perform the ritual dance that was known to attract the spirits. By the sudden, zombified changes in their faces, their unearthly groans, and odd, disjointed movements, Major Crocicchia could tell when the spirits had allegedly descended. Taunting them, the Corsican officer commanded the spirits to cry—an insulting request that caused the trance state to grind to a halt and the spirits to promptly exit their vessels. "You see, there are no more *Hauka*, I am stronger than the *Hauka*," Crocicchia gloated. Turning to Zibo, he jeered, "Where are the *Hauka*?"—and began to beat her until she said that there were none.

He repeated his brutal torment on the other prisoners and then locked them back up in their cells. Yet inside the prison, a new god suddenly appeared: the deified spirit of Crocicchia himself. "I am a new *Hauka*, I am Corsasi," he declared, a name meaning "the Corsican." "I'm stronger than all the other *Hauka*," Corsasi announced. "We have to break out of jail." Led by the divine spirit of Crocicchia himself, the prisoners broke through the mudbrick walls of the jail, before the human Crocicchia had them recaptured and locked up. Zibo was exiled to the Ivory Coast, but the movement continued to grow, spreading across cities like a virus. As he passed through a series of new, warm bodies, Crocicchia became known by several names, among them Krosisya, Kommandan, Major Mugu, and the Wicked Major: a god capable of many aggressions.

✦ ✦ ✦

What physically occurs when a divine spirit enters a man? It was said in Niger that the human being is threefold, consisting of the body, the energy, and the *bia*, or double, whose reflection can be seen on the calm surface of a lake or who appears as a shadow on the noonday sand. At night, the restless *bia* leaves the body, rising up to roam the world on travels we call dreams. According to the ethnographer Jean Rouch, a witness to hundreds of possession rituals in the 1950s, the medium can see the invading spirit or *bia* coming toward him, invisible to everyone else. The spirit is attracted by the smells of incense and the sounds of drumming, as the people start to dance. "The spirit holds in its hands the skin of a freshly slaughtered animal and presents the bloody side of it to the dancer three times," Rouch recounted. "The first time, tears flow from the dancer's eyes; the second time, mucus flows from the dancer's nose; the third time, the dancer cries out . . . On its fourth pass, the spirit places the bloody skin over the dancer's head."

This is how it ensnares the *bia* of the host's body, securing it as if inside a sack, rendering it inert, before the attacking spirit enters the body and takes its place. In the state of possession, the subjugated body, yoked to the invading spirit, attains a transient divinity. The spirit speaks and moves through its new skeletal frame, endowing it with unearthly strength and utter disregard for mortal norms and making it impervious to pain. When the invading spirit decides to leave the body, it lifts off the animal skin, freeing the captured *bia*. The vessel opens his eyes. "They always cough as if they had just left an airless vault," Rouch related. Although the possessed never remembered what had unfolded, exhaustion followed in the wake of the trance. For his own part, around 1976, Rouch met Horace Crocicchia himself, at the very end of the infamous major's life, after he had risen to become governor-general of the Ivory Coast. Rouch reported that Crocicchia, by now an old man in his late eighties, wasn't entirely coherent, but he still remembered the incident in the Niamey jail.

Possession was involuntary: a person couldn't choose a particular spirit, and if he found himself chosen by one, that spirit might keep deciding to return for life. It was impossible to turn them away. This could be unwelcomed and embarrassing: a man who worked as a government official, with a salaried job he hoped to keep, might suddenly find himself inhabited by Krosisya, frothing at the mouth and hurling insults at his colleagues, a spirit so violent he sometimes killed his cushiony receptacle in a fit of rage. But through the format of the ritual ceremony, the *Hauka* spirits could be invited in, to a safe, prepared space in the wilderness or a private compound, far from the horrified eyes of society. Here this strange power could be experienced in a structured way, imbuing the adepts with a voltage that far outlasted the few minutes or hours of their possessed state. Entering the trance, the mediums performed drills and marches, goose-steps and right-handed salutes, to the military beat of a drum. The adepts summoned the colonial spirits to roundtable discussions and issued new policies and declarations. In the absence of a pith helmet, they could fashion one out of a gourd.

Ever-increasing in strength and numbers, the spirit movement of the *Hauka* was a way of occupying the French just as the French had occupied Niger. Deification was a means of dissidence and resistance, on a plane too high for the mechanisms of European imperial authority to reach. It was painful and unwilled—but it was precisely in the fact of its unwantedness that its power lay. The forces of accident, error, and chance formed a vortex of possibility. As Frantz Fanon wrote in *The Wretched of the Earth*, "It is to this zone of occult instability where the people dwell that we must come."

✦  ✦  ✦

The idea of "possession" was born at the crossroads of enslavement and enlightenment, at a juncture where early modern notions of property rights, demonism, and the nature of the self converged. Although there were archaic precedents for it, spirit possession attended the savagery of modernity, beginning with the kidnapping of men and women into the Atlantic slave trade and the onslaught of European imperialism. The reports of "uproar," "wild gesticulation," "frenzies," and "madness" that filtered into Europe from the invaded peripheries of the map were inter-preted through the Christian lens of demons requiring an exorcism. A vast array of meta-human occurrences and rituals became labeled with the same word used to describe ownership of bodies and land: *possession*, from the Latin *potis* + *sedere*, meaning "the power to sit in, or occupy, a particular place." "Mad Men are said to be Possessed With A Spirit," Hobbes wrote in *Leviathan*.

For Enlightenment philosophers, spirit possession was a way to think about the nature of the human. Modern man was made by exorcising his spirits and mastering his demons, to become a rational, *self-possessed* individual who could participate in economic contracts and exchanges. This self-possessed man, "proprietor of his own person," as John Locke wrote, was the foundation upon which the modern state was to be con-structed. His shadow counterpart was the person possessed or dispos-sessed, enslaved by propertied white males or other deities. Against the backdrop of the slave plantation, possessed men and women served as the negative foil for the European thinkers who theorized the abstract, transcendent ideas of what the modern human being was or should be.

In the late nineteenth century, the abolition of the Atlantic slave trade unleashed the "scramble for Africa." European rulers looked to profit from the interior of the continent once feared as the sepulcher of the white man, felled by a single mosquito's bite. In 1899, the Voulet-Chanoine mission stormed through Niger on a trail of destruction, leaving ashes and famine in its wake. French soldiers pillaged and set fire to villages and granaries, raped women, and massacred villagers. Instituting a politics of terror, the French violently crushed any revolt, and in 1922 Niger was formally transformed from an illegally occupied military territory to a colony, administered by the governor-general in

Dakar. French colonialism imported a new language, clothes, habits, rules and regulations, and schools to train young men to become useful civil servants. In the name of humanist ideals, Nigeriens who had served as domestic slaves before the French arrival were ostensibly freed, then enslaved to the French instead in *villages de liberté*, where they were made to labor on public projects such as building roads. As taxes to the French had to be paid in francs, farmers switched the crops they planted from sustenance grains to cash crops such as cotton, making the population more vulnerable to famines. The village chiefs, who once held communities together and possessed a sacral power, were conscripted as tax collectors and became loathed and profaned.

"However pressing may be the need for economic change and development of natural resources, our mission in Africa is to bring about a cultural renaissance, a piece of creative work in human material," declared the governor-general Jules Brévié, describing France's liberal, civilizing mission. As if in response to the hypocrisy of the entire colonial project, which was fueled by profiteering and racism only ever loosely masked by lofty ideals, the madness that arrived was a highly creative piece of work too. While European imperialists tried to impose their definitions of who was human or what "human material" should become, the *Hauka* turned colonialists like Horace Crocicchia into nonhumans. Their Major Crocicchia was no longer "self-possessed": unable to control his own actions, he released his prisoners from jail. The *Hauka* forced the colonizers to examine their selves and their violent actions as if in a mirror. Among the *Hauka* pantheon was a spirit not human in nature: the deified form of the locomotive. Possessed by it, a medium would incessantly churn, motoring back-and-forth until he collapsed from exhaustion. He was a testament to how modernity in all its wealth was built upon the bodies of black laborers, as they laid the tracks across European colonies and could still be seen in the forced labor crews toiling along Nigerien roads. The *Hauka* sometimes plunged their hands into cauldrons of boiling water, as if to say, power should involve a great deal of pain.

✦ ✦ ✦

By 1927, the gods of madness had begun to get directly involved in politics. When the elderly chief of Filingué, Gado Namalaya, died, the French administration wanted to appoint his son, Chekou Seyni, but the *Hauka* spirits and their mediums threw their weight behind a rival candidate, Maïnassara, and refused to recognize Seyni's authority. With the migration of Songhay workers to the Gold Coast, the *Hauka* reach now extended to Accra, where it was centered around a new high priest, Ousmane Fodie, who had served with the British army in the First World War. When in 1935 the British district commissioner attempted to jail the *Hauka* mediums, fires broke out across Accra and the department of public works was destroyed. New deities continued to incarnate, from Minis de Ger, or the minister of war, to the lawyer Wasiri, to Lokotoro, a doctor who wore a white lab coat and a pith helmet and was seen injecting a patient with a mysterious white fluid. A god called King Zouri was likely the spirit of the reigning British monarch, the stammering George VI. In 1948, Prazidan di la Republik descended into the body of a Niamey laborer, at the very time that the actual president of the republic, Vincent Auriol, was in Paris dealing with a series of massive workers' strikes. Auriol would not have known of his Nigerien spirit double, but he wrote in his diary of "madness."

In 1954, in a rural compound outside Accra, Jean Rouch filmed his notorious documentary, *Les maîtres fous*, or "The Mad Masters." At the invitation of Mountyeba, a cacao planter and high priest, Rouch used an old 16 mm Bell and Howell to record the colonial deities as they began to descend into their human vessels, men who worked as market sellers, truck drivers, irrigation crew. In a clearing near the termite mound that is the *Hauka* governor's "palace," with an ersatz Union Jack fluttering above, Capral Gardi, the corporal of the guard, is the first spirit to arrive. Sentries keep a lookout along the perimeter, aiming wooden rifles at those who will become possessed. We watch the eerily disjointed march of an army of possessed bodies—the governor, captain, lieutenant, and the locomotive, who cannot stand still. The Wicked Major, or Krosisya, appears, inhabiting a man who suffers from impotence. The governor challenges Krosisya to burn himself, and the major "chooses such a small torch that the governor insults him," Rouch narrates. In reply, Krosisya sets his own shirt on fire.

A smashed sacrificial egg runs down the head of an effigy of the governor. *Les maîtres fous* cuts to footage of the "real" governor of the Gold Coast, Sir Charles Arden-Clarke, inspecting his troops in a gigantic pith helmet cascading with white ostrich plumes. Then comes Madame Salma, the African wife of the first district commissioner of Niamey, who appears in the body of another woman. The colonial gods gather to sacrifice a dog and drink its blood, an act of absolute transgression that proves they have become utterly nonhuman. The governor and the general hold a roundtable, the "Conference of the Dog," to decide whether to eat the dog raw or cooked. The administrators boil it and plunge their hands into the scalding pot to fish out the meat; Krosisya eats the head. When *Les maîtres fous* had its first screening at the Musée de l'Homme in Paris, it was swiftly condemned. For viewers such as the Senegalese director Blaise Senghor, the film reinforced primitivist stereotypes and provided ammunition for the racism he contended with in Paris each day. The British and French authorities, who were appalled at the sinister mirror image reflected back at themselves, banned it in the colonies. Some called for the reels to be destroyed and wondered whether it should have been filmed at all. Rouch would only say that having witnessed a dialogue between humans and an otherworld for the first time in his life, all he could do was instinctively reach for his camera.

On display at the *Hauka* summit meetings, transcending the grotesque pyrotechnics, was the power of language: how words possess strength beyond their meanings. In Songhay villages, sorcerers were known to transmit words from their mouths, to mix them with roots, resins and water, and grind them into paste that could be ingested or applied to the body as a potent cure. The *Hauka* were powerful not only because they possessed bodies, but because they took over words too; they ground up the rhetoric of politicians, of colonial "discourse," and applied it, almost literally, as a balm to heal everyday life. Before the ritual began, the men would describe the issues they hoped to cure, from sickness and infertility, to unemployment, daily injustices, romantic rivalries, and personal dilemmas. The morning after, they would sometimes report their problems had been solved, as the vessel of Krosisya noted of his impotence. The *Hauka* refused to detach the machinations of power from people's quotidian concerns. Whether marching in formation, swigging blood at cabinet meetings, or performing cures, the *Hauka* took on issues of poverty, oppression, and health care in a way that was more literal and effectual than that of the inept statesmen. Taking the words right out of the politicians' mouths, the spirits fulfilled their promises. This was the power of the gods in uniform, electrifying a circuit of policy and obscenity, majesty and fear.

✦ ✦ ✦

From the azure blue of the Red Sea, over the Sahara dunes and into the basin of Lake Chad, moving west toward the Atlantic coast, a network of anti-colonial uniformed spirits crisscrossed Africa. They traveled in the bellies of airplanes and inside the tire treads of British tanks. One might catch them in the marketplace or on the pilgrimage to Mecca, where spirit-carrying worshippers from all terrestrial directions convened. Among this constellation of cults were the *kizungu* from Tanzania, autocratic Swahili spirits of British and German colonizers, who desired toast made from white bread. The *kizungu* were said to wear their pith helmets with black coattails, and needed flashlights to be able to see when night fell. The *varungu* spirits from Mashonaland, part of the territory appropriated by the British as the Colony of Southern Rhodesia, were famous for complaining a great deal. They were the deified, dead spirits of Europeans who, in search of wildlife and gold, had fallen prey to fatal greed. In the 1950s, the anthropologist Michael Gelfand noted that the *varungu* insisted on dining at a table set with knives, forks, spoons, white porcelain cups, and plates, and craved eggs and libations of beer. They demanded that their mediums sleep on pristine white bedsheets and wear white shirts, constantly lamenting that their linen was dirty and worn. The *varungu* were afraid of microbes and washed their hands incessantly. For phantasms, their standards of material living were impossibly

high. They often forgot their hats or walking sticks. When they exited their medium, they said stiffly, "Goodbye."

The *ntambwe bwanga* cult, which began in the Congolese town of Kabinda in the early 1920s and spread across the Kasai region, claimed to have created deified duplicates of all the colonial Belgians. The spirits descended into the Luba traders and foremen who worked in the mines, as the anthropologist W. F. P. Burton recorded. Every adept who joined the society took the name of an individual Belgian resident, and, in a trance state, appropriated their power. The *ntambwe bwanga* possessed the spirits of Belgians of all social ranks, from *Son Excellence le Gouverneur Général* to military officers, bureaucrats, and clerks, in a kind of occult class system. The wives of Luba adepts, meanwhile, possessed the corresponding Belgian wife, creating meta-human doubles of colonial marriages. A woman would chalk her face, put on a special dress, and carry brown feathers under her arm, possibly to represent a purse. She screeched in a shrill voice, demanding bananas and hens, according to

Burton, and was addressed as "Mandamo So-and-So." With the Belgian spirits ensconced in their human vessels, the deities had the power to heal and protect, and avert calamities, natural disasters, and theft. The spirit colonizers were able to liberate Luba men wrongfully imprisoned by the brutal regime. Presiding over the hierarchy was Le Roi Albert himself, Belgium's devoutly Catholic sovereign Albert I, who died in 1934 after falling sixty feet off the side of a mountain. It was said Le Roi Albert had a snake who followed him wherever he went, always one village behind him, to gather gossip as to the people's loyalties and treasons.

By the late 1950s, the *Hauka* gods had manifested as part of the *bori* cult among the Hausa-speaking people of Northern Nigeria, then under British colonial rule. Descending into the bodies of their mediums, the *iskokin turawa*, or European soldier spirits, performed military drills in green-and-beige uniforms and pith helmets, and set their bodies on fire with kerosene. Their ranks of officers, lieutenants, infantrymen included *Hauka* deities such as Komanda Mugu, another manifestation of Crocicchia, and Kafaran Salma, or Captain Victor Salaman, husband of Madame Salama of Niamey. The *turawa* demanded offerings of cigarettes, soft drinks, sunglasses, whistles, whips, sacrificial animals, notebooks, and pens. Their spirit-tongue was "a glossolaliac mélange" of Hausa, English, and French, with observers reporting that the spirits often spoke in languages their human vessels did not know. When the *turawa* exited their fleshly vehicles, the mediums would sneeze precisely three times.

Like the Italian propaganda that helped foment a branch of Rastafari, the British propaganda of World War II was incarnated in a new *turawa* spirit. The deity was named Jamus, Bata K'asa, or "Germany, Destroyer of Land," a phrase taken from an anti-Nazi slogan circulated by the British administration and apotheosized into a new soldier god. The divinity had an epithet in Hausa: *Jamus 'bata k'asa—bindiga cike da mugunta— wuta gasa baya.* "Jamus, destroyer of land—gun full of wickedness—fire that roasts the back." Like many gods of creative destruction, Jamus had to annihilate before he could build, razing the land with a Caterpillar. It was said Jamus flew to Rome every Sunday to pray, duplicating wartime alliances in the spirit realm. Jamus might have been a god in Hitler's army, but he was also the deified spirit of the German road-construction companies in Nigeria that paved the country's highways. When Jamus took his Nigerian mediums, they became filled with Germany's military might, technology, diplomatic alliances, and armies of philosophers and poets. But for those who caught Jamus it was painful, like trying to fit a whole nation inside your chest.

Some say it all began in Ethiopia, the cradle of divinity, where parchment scrolls date an early network of spirits known as the *zar* to the sixteenth century. Like the theogony of the *Hauka*, the *zar* spirits were birthed in a moment of rapid social change and upheaval, as the Oromo people found themselves under subjugation by Amhara imperialists, the minority ruling caste whose power Haile Selassie would perpetuate. According to some historians, *Zar* was originally a name for the Cushitic sky god worshipped by the Oromo, but in their forced conversion to Christianity, *zar* was recategorized as a malevolent demon, a Supreme Being "reduced to a minor rank." *Zar* spirits were fallen gods, made of air and fire, who began to seek out human mediums: unlike the *Hauka*, their preferred vessels were women rather than men. From Ethiopia, the *zar* moved along the slave trading routes, traveling west across the Sahel to the Gold Coast, and east into Arabia and Iran. It radiated into the vast skyscape of spirit cults, weaving a network of solidarity that breached the boundaries of colonies and nations and religions as quickly as they were drawn up.

The *zar* became particularly active in the Sudan, arriving in the 1820s during the Ottoman occupation. The spirits were a way to contend with the invasion of a foreign force, much like the French in Niger, that had brought with it heavy taxes, famine, and oppression. The cult spread through villages and cities across northern Sudan, becoming increasingly present with each subsequent wave of domination, from British and Egyptian troops to the arrival of capitalism, Sharia law, and new codes of behavior that relegated women more strictly to the home. Under the British regime, the *zar* developed a taste for fervently Protestant British rulers. In 1884, when the messianic leader Muhammad Ahmad, known as the Mahdi, led a revolt against the colonizers, a prominent general, the hot-tempered, deeply religious Charles George Gordon, was sent to Khartoum to observe the situation. He soon took on the Mahdi's revolt as his personal crusade, seeing it as a battle between good and evil, Christianity versus Islam. Against the wishes of the British government, Gordon refused to leave Khartoum and continued the war against the Mahdi's troops, who had besieged the British inside the city. (British public opinion was divided, some hailing him as a hero and others a "loose cannon," but Gordon's eccentricity was never interpreted as fanaticism inherent to Protestantism itself, though that was how the British understood the Mahdi's Islam.)

As the people of Khartoum began to starve, the chain-smoking general, who kept an inchoate, prophetic diary during the siege, descended deeper into madness. While waiting desperately in his office in his tattered uniform for British reinforcements to arrive, Gordon held a council of war with a mouse. It was said that when the enemy forces reached his doorstep, Gordon changed into the pristine ceremonial garb of governor-general, navy blue with braided links of gold, put on a red fez, and stepped outside to be martyred, Christlike, in a sacrificial death. Little did Gordon know that he would be resurrected—and Islamicized as a *zar* called Gordel, a spirit seen manifesting in Khartoum and surrounding villages, taking over mediums clad in khaki, highly polished boots, and a fez. Gordel was the ghoul who had needlessly escalated the violence, leading to the deaths of thousands of Khartoum's residents. Gordon himself had left no suggestions for how to repair the inordinate damage he had wrought. In his last diary entry, of December 14, 1884, much like an indignant *varungu* spirit, Gordon signed off with a curt "Good-bye."

A contemporary of Gordon's, Sir Evelyn Baring, 1st Earl of Cromer, was a staunch Anglo-Saxon supremacist who ruled over Egypt and the Sudan for twenty-five years and controlled the coffers of both countries. Lord Cromer thought he saw "Mohammedan fanaticism" everywhere: to him, Muslim subjects were no more than "political ciphers," incapable of conducting politics but filled instead with a fiery lava of religious anger that threatened to erupt at any moment. A people without politics, only religious fervor, were incapable of self-rule, Cromer claimed, and justified the British occupation as vital for protecting the region's native Christians from Muslim rage. But first as tragedy, then as farce: after his death in 1917, like Gordon, Cromer was Islamicized, supernaturalized, and turned into a jinn, who went by the name Al-Wardi Karoma. It would have appalled his so-called Western mind. Karoma kept appearing in the cities of Khartoum and Omdurman well into the 1970s, thirsting for liquor and cigars. Rather than occupying someone else's territory or bank accounts, the earl now occupied the intestines of spirit mediums, dressed in khaki for the occasion. An ethnographer witnessed Karoma descending into his human vessel and recorded a song used to welcome him:

> Greetings for Lord Cromer,
> Be generous to us, Lord Cromer,
> Oh bottle rum, you are over-indulged.

The *zar* were most energetic at night. Consigned to lurk in latrines, piles of garbage, and grimy hovels that would have had Cromer turning in his grave, jinn such as Karoma sought out fragrant oils and soap, gold jewelry, and diaphanous shawls. Like amoebas of fire, the *zar* would invade the female body through its orifices when her, or society's, defenses were down: in times of political upheaval and conflict, during childbirth, at the sight of blood, or simply from working too hard. The spirits would often cause them persistent headaches, nausea, insomnia, anxiety, and mysterious pains, symptoms not unlike those of pregnancy. At ceremonies, it was essential to coax the invading *zar* to identify itself, to communicate with it, reduce it to the sphere of comprehension, and thus render it able to be controlled. Other Anglo spirits who revealed themselves, recorded by the anthropologist Janice Boddy in the late 1970s, included Basha Birdon, probably the fire form of the orientalist polymath Sir Richard Burton, translator of *The Thousand and One Nights*. If the budget permitted, *zar* priestesses would hold a *mayz* or mess, featuring a long table laid in European style, with offerings of *towst* and jam, tinned meat, cheese, Pepsi, whiskey, and beer. (In later years, the British *zar* expressed deep unhappiness with Sudan's 1983 liquor ban.)

Janice Boddy met Sadiya, a woman possessed by the spirits of two European boys who wanted her to dye the soles of her feet with stripes of henna, to look like the bottoms of sneakers. The demands of the colonial spirits were often exorbitant, but if properly appeased they could cure a rash of illnesses where nothing else had succeeded, from blindness and infertility to ailments triggered by the evil eye. Boddy encountered another woman, named Bakheita, who had suffered a freak accident: the ceiling of a house had fallen on her, pinning her beneath a heavy beam and leaving her paralyzed for six months. Bakheita recounted,

> They did a *zar* for me and I walked! I stood up tall, I arose to descend while standing erect. And I made requests. I asked for liquor and a cap and a khaki suit and a walking cane like those used by Europeans. I am possessed by Westerners, the Christians. No other spirit species is above me.

*Zar* was a kind of alchemy of the personal and the political: the spirits cured infirmities and simultaneously enacted geopolitical conflicts and diplomacies on the spirit plane, forming alliances and animosities among flickering tongues of fire. Included in the taxonomy of the *zar* were the Habash, or Abyssinian spirits, and among them none other than Haile Selassie himself. His spirit was said to be small in size, and often seen riding a horse; an image perhaps dating to time spent in exile in Khartoum in 1940 during the Italian occupation. The emperor wore a pith helmet, its circumference too wide for his narrow, delicate head. Years later, Janice Boddy interviewed Sittalbenat, a portly woman who was possessed by a spirit called Romani, Ya Wazir Galla ("Roman, Vizier of the Galla"). This was the jinn of an Italian who forged diplomatic relations with Oromo leaders, when they saw an opportunity to wrest back sovereignty from the Amhara elite during Haile Selassie's exile. The spirits of Oromo activists manifested as well, capturing the original, sixteenth-century conflict that may have first given birth to the *zar*. At the same time, Sittalbenat revealed she was also possessed by a wealthy Westerner who simply smoked Benson & Hedges in bed all day. Histories, politics, alliances churned within her: Sittalbenat was reportedly by turns irascible and jolly.

The gods in uniform were not only etheric spirits but made of heavier substances, able to be carved in wood and stone. Their material manifestations joined a long lineage of objects saturated with divinity, and labeled by European invaders as "fetishes." When Portuguese traders landed on the coast of Guinea in the late fifteenth century, everywhere they saw what they called *feitiços*, amulets or charms: wooden idols, bundles, pebbles, nuts, nails, and seashells, which seemed to enjoy sacrifices and to be appeased by them. The word derived from the Latin *factitius*, meaning something manufactured, artificial, or man-made. In 1757, the French Enlightenment thinker Charles de Brosses coined the word *fétichisme*, to describe in polemical terms "African" practices of worship. According to de Brosses, the origins of fetishism were based on a primordial mistake: of consecrating as divine whatever object or creature a person had seen or encountered first.

"In their fit of superstition they choose a rock, a piece of wood, indeed the first object that flatters their caprice," he wrote. Fetishism endowed objects indiscriminately with supernatural agency, imbuing things terrestrial and finite with the qualities of infinity. Fetishism saw god in an animal tail. A fetish was always incidental, a trifle a person latched on to in violation of the Enlightenment phrase "common sense." To worship a walnut as a deity was a fundamental misunderstanding of the value of the thing; the fetish was the apotheosis of error. Within de Brosses's category of fetishism were included not only easily portable sacred objects, but also practices such as spirit possession; in 1937, a colonial observer in the region of Filingué denounced the *Hauka* movement as "a fetishist agitation."

In what would become an authoritative image of "Africa" for generations of Europeans, a disgruntled Dutch Protestant merchant, Willem Bosman, described in 1702 the "fetish problem" of the Guinea coast, taking as his paradigm the fanaticism of a serpent-worshipping cult at Whydah. For European traders, the fetish was maddening: the Guineans imposed their own, often mysterious values onto objects, didn't always cooperate with the Europeans' intentions, and often refused them access to things they wanted. The hostile travelogues and treatises of men such as Bosman and de Brosses were widely read, including by Enlightenment luminaries such as Hume, Hegel, Kant, and Auguste Comte, who saw fetishism as the dark counterpart of reason. If Africans allegedly deified objects, Enlightenment theorists deified concepts, forging abstract ideas such as race, religion, politics, sovereignty, and freedom, turning them into disembodied truths that transcended place or history.

"The peculiarly African character is difficult to comprehend," wrote Hegel in his *Philosophy of History* (1832), for it lacked "the principle which naturally accompanies all *our* ideas—the category of Universality." Hegel pointed to reports of fetishism and spirit possession to argue that the enslavement of Africans was part of the natural order, since they were not yet capable of abstract thought. The fetish proved that Africa "is no historical part of the World," Hegel wrote, misunderstanding that the fetish, as a concept inscribed by Europe to denigrate a vast array of old and ancient traditions, was entirely historical, the product of a specific encounter. What philosophers derided as error and unreason was actually a disagreement between certain Europeans and Africans about the proper worth, not of things, but of people. It revealed how correct knowledge about divinity is never a matter of the best doctrine but of who possesses the more powerful army.

If the fetish, Europe's fiction, was a weapon wielded against Africans, sanctioning their subjugation, it could also be subverted, by turning the colonizers into fetishes themselves. After the French invasion of the Ivory Coast in the late nineteenth century, Baule artisans reimagined an old art form, to carve statues of colonial officers, or *colons*, elongated men often wearing pith helmets. The Europeans joined the *waka snan*, "people of wood," figures that served as stools for spirits to perch on and receive offerings. For the Baule, there existed the idea, present in many times and places, that every person has a divine double or twin. This double was of the opposite sex: they lived in the spirit world and could become jealous, causing maladies unless they were appeased. Interpretations of the *colon* figures varied: some said they were representations of European spirit doubles, or they were a means of transferring the power of the colonizer to one's own Baule spirit self. Others said they were made to be placed along the side of the road to warn people of the presence of French soldiers nearby. Sacrifices were offered to them to ward off Europeans or drive them away. Turned into fetishes, the colonizers became tools to exorcise themselves. They stood as warnings that the world of surfaces is seldom what it seems. Another spirit world lay beneath it, a vast circuit of networks over which their earthly empire had no dominion.

Breaking through the crust of the earth like a worm, an Englishman emerges, wearing eyeglasses and a pith helmet. In 1967, the scholar Herbert Cole photographed the *mbari* spirit houses, built by the Owerri Igbo people in southeast Nigeria. When British settlers in the mid-nineteenth century introduced the architectural style of the windowed two-story home, "they were quickly appropriated as houses for the gods, who must have the first and best of everything," Cole wrote. The *mbari* were full-size houses, erected as forest shrines, that featured scenes of Igbo goddesses and gods, leopards, lions, colonists, and police officers. "Their bones are sticks, their fat and muscles sun-dried mud," reported Cole. The shrines were a means of propitiating the gods so they would bring rain clouds and yam harvests, and expel the imperialists. They were a way to try to control the otherwise inscrutable forces that govern daily life. The sculpture of the colonizer-worm, widely reproduced in anthropological texts, was said to represent the unceremonious origins of the white man: he had crawled out of a hole in the ground.

"He frightens me, this African white man," wrote the anthropologist Michael Taussig in *Mimesis and Alterity*. The figurine's expression is unsettling: arrogant and undead. "Why are they Other, and why are they the Colonial Other?" Taussig asked as he self-consciously observed his own white maleness in similar figures made by the Guna people in the San Blas archipelago of Panama, who had staged the curing ritual with the seven-foot-tall MacArthur.

> This question leads to still more of a very particular and particularizing sort, because in asking it I am, as a "European type," brought to confront my cultured self in the form of an Indian figurine! What magic lies in this, my wooden self, sung to power in a language I cannot understand? Who is this self, objectified without my knowledge, that I am hell-bent on analyzing as object-over-there fanned by sea breezes and the smoke of burning cocoa nibs enchanting the shaman's singing? . . . The Indians have made me alter to my self.

The existence of the European idols meant that the spirit of Taussig, a Columbia University professor, or Cole, or men resembling them, possessing a secular, scientific authority, had been removed from its fleshly shell, appropriated, and was now animating wood or sun-dried clay. This was unnerving, for after all, Taussig writes, "The image is more powerful than what it is an image of." In the intricate tableau of the *mbari* forest shrine, the idol was a means to rid the land of British presence by summoning other deities to attack. It was thought that by depicting the scene of the white man protruding from the earth, the Igbo gods would be angered by it and decide to intervene. Captured in its own likeness, European power could be controlled.

No object was more fetishistic than the pith helmet: even glimpsing one, people fell into a trance, according to reports from what was then the Eastern Province of Kenya, seized as a British protectorate in 1895. The Swedish ethnographer Gerhard Lindblom reported that several Kamba villagers would become possessed at the mere sight of a European. When missionaries attempted to convert the Kamba to the word of Christ, villagers caught the spirit of Jesus or *Kijesu* like an unwanted, contagious illness, entirely subverting the evangelists' endeavors. Possessed by Jesus, they cut themselves with knives without losing blood, burned themselves without feeling pain. They acted more like Christian saints than an obedient colonized labor force. The dove of the Holy Spirit burst into feathers in the zone of occult instability. After the foreign militants had seized the Kamba's land, proclaiming European supremacy, they were followed by European missionaries bearing the message: *In the eyes of our LORD all men are equal.* Convulsions were, in a way, almost the only appropriate response.

The fetish became a mirror, in which Europe could see itself. Transported north by sea, whether in wood or exoticizing prose, it was integrated into some of the foremost theories of Western modernity itself. What began as a polemic against other people's divinities was taken up as a basis for understanding capitalism and articulating the nature of the darkest recesses of the human mind. In *Capital*, drawing on his readings of Charles de Brosses, Karl Marx formulated his theory of commodity fetishism, how inanimate goods become deified with a value far greater than the materials from which they are made. A piece of wood transformed into a table "not only stands with its feet on the ground, but, in relation to all other commodities, it stands on its head, and evolves out of its wooden brain grotesque ideas, far more wonderful than if it were to begin dancing of its own free will." Taking on an animated life of its own, the fetish comes to exert a supernatural power over its creators. Though we may demystify other people's gods and deface their idols, our critical capacity to demystify the commodity fetish still cannot break the spell it wields over us, for its power is rooted in deep structures of social practice rather than simple belief. While fetishes made by African priests were denigrated as irrational, the fetish of the capitalist marketplace has long been viewed as the epitome of rationalism.

The fetish was the animating heart of capitalism, and it was also

inside the body and the mind, in the theories of sexual fetishism first articulated by Alfred Binet and then by Sigmund Freud. Africa, the "heart of
darkness," was for Freud a key to the unconscious self, the shadowy entity
known as the id that was concealed by the facade of European civilization,
but which could be unearthed by studying neurotics, children, and imagined "savages." As he smoked cigars and probed the innermost Africa of
his patients, the doctor would lean back from a desk crowded with an army
of his own fetishes, from a marble baboon of Thoth to a bronze cat-headed
goddess, jade sages, Tang spirit figurines, and an ivory Vishnu. The followers of Freud and Marx promoted their ideas as "transcendent, omniscient,
panoramic, and socially neutral distillations of the truth about all societies, all social statuses, and all historical periods," as the scholar J. Lorand
Matory writes in *The Fetish Revisited*. And yet, "abstract European social
theories are no more universal, eternal 'truths' than African gods are." This
was something the *Hauka* understood when they vomited francs.

◆  ◆  ◆

In 1974, the same year that saw Haile Selassie deposed and Prince Philip
stage his unintentional coup aboard the royal yacht, Lieutenant Colonel
Seyni Kountché led a midnight mutiny in Niger. He ousted President
Hamani Diori, the first president of Niger since its independence in
1960, who ruled in alliance with the country's former colonizers, commanding a repressive, one-party regime that relied on the French army
and police. At the time, Niger was in the grip of a devastating famine.
As waves of dissent and unrest simmered, the government was accused
of ignoring the mass starvation and misappropriating aid. It may be that
at one a.m. on April 15, 1974, the spirits of madness, of wind, fire, and
dust, rushed into the presidential palace in Niamey. Although he would
neither confirm nor deny the rumors himself, it was said by many that
Kountché had been initiated as a teenager as a *Hauka* medium, and his
wife was filmed by Jean Rouch in a trance. Perhaps once, or more than
once, *Hauka* spirits such as Krosisya had entered, rioted, and passed
through the vessel of the lieutenant; perhaps their power had stayed.
Kountché and his officers charged the palace, arrested Diori, killed his

wife, and suspended the constitution. A month later, Kountché demanded
the removal of the French military from Niger, thus accomplishing what
no other Nigerien politician had ever been able to do. As the myriad
generals, officers, and soldiers of the French army began to withdraw,
Kountché's coup marked a new independence.

Kountché moved swiftly to legitimize his power along lines that derived
from the French yet also seemed to have been filtered through the *Hauka*:
a combination of military ceremony, anodyne bureaucracy, and terror.
Physically, Kountché himself was said to be unimposing. An interviewer
in *Jeune Afrique* remarked upon "his frail body and his under-average
height. . . . His physique, in any case, contributes to making him an invisible man." To maintain his grasp on power, Kountché cultivated a theatrical
aura of fear, punishing any traces of disloyalty. "Because I am neither tall
or fat, it's a thing with me, to scare Nigeriens . . ." he said. The autocrat
wore fatigues, highly polished boots, and a green military beret, pairing
his khaki jacket and epaulettes with a white shirt and black tie. He reor-
ganized the government and appointed a cabinet that allegedly included
several other *Hauka* mediums. Kountché's political opponents accused
him of taking orders from Satan. Yet the dictator soon gained the approval
of many villagers as he coordinated the successful delivery of aid. The next
year, the rains arrived in Niger, quelling the famine and bringing to an end
six years of drought. As if summoned by Kountché himself, the clouds that
hovered over his reign furthered the sense that the dictator was connected
to the instrument panel of an otherworldly plane.

Who is possessing whom? To summon the spirits of the gods in uniform is a ritualized revolt, or as the scholar I. M. Lewis wrote, "a strategy
of mystical attack." Perhaps for any revolt to succeed, it has to tap into
the mythopoetics of mutiny. Deification was a form of defiance, and in
many ways, it worked. The divine doubling of colonizers like Crocicchia
or Cromer was not only a response to displays of imperialist power but
a political tool in itself, a means of resistance in the face of oppression. It
was a way to reclaim sovereignty, by spiritually and physically participat-
ing in the sanctity of the state and its representatives. Catching power,
the general rumored to be a *Hauka* was able to expel the French troops

from Niger. Subversively turning the imperialists divine, the *Hauka* showed that the deified copy could have an impact on the original, even rising in power above it. Over the decade of Kountché's reign, the militant deities became increasingly popular in Nigerien villages, and new spirits continued to manifest. "Possession is in our blood," a Nigerien official told the anthropologist Paul Stoller in the mideighties. "All of us are touched by it in one way or another. . . . Soldiers are mediums. Government ministers are mediums. Professors and researchers are mediums. That is our experience." In 1984, during a second famine caused by drought, Nigerien officials asked *Hauka* adepts to help bring the rain, and down it came, seeping into the cracks of the fissured earth.

As Seyni Kountché's regime grew ever more repressive and his health deteriorated, the dictator found himself increasingly alone. In 1987, he died in Paris of a brain tumor, having survived numerous assassination attempts. Over the years, every member of his original inner circle had deserted or betrayed him, including his right-hand man Bonkano, a *Hauka* priest and fortune-teller who became the head of Niger's secret police. In 1983, Bonkano made a failed attempt to seize power, before fleeing the country with millions of dollars embezzled from the national treasury.

Power tends to corrupt, and the corrupt so often lapse into paranoia and madness. Near the termite's nest that is the *Hauka* governor-general's "palace," one of the *Hauka* generals, caught by Rouch's camera, is fuming: "Always the same thing, they never listen to me." During the heated discussions that take place during the Conference of the Dog, another officer, wearing a pith helmet, repeats the bitter complaint, "Nobody listens to me, it's always the same." Absolute power tends to sink into absolute instability, revealing what was always there, beneath the uniform, beneath the mask of authority, beneath the decorations, the helmet, the khaki carapace of the general who can see his shadow in the air.

5

---

# The Apotheosis of Nathaniel Tarn

It had not occurred to me that the accidental god might be someone you know, perhaps even a friend, until a cryptic message arrived out of the blue. I had just published an essay in the *London Review of Books* about Prince Philip and his worshippers in Vanuatu, when an email lit up my screen from the octogenarian poet, anthropologist, and translator Nathaniel Tarn:

> Incidentally too you may recall—from my book Scandals
> in the House of Birds, that I was taken for a god in Atitlán
> during my first visit

The missive had arrived from a remote compound in the desert out-side Santa Fe, where Tarn and his wife, the poet Janet Rodney, lived in retirement above a concrete bunker with eighty thousand books. Protected by steel doors, bronze Buddhas, and a collection of Indonesian daggers, Tarn surrounded himself with the artifacts of decades of fieldwork and of his long career as a poet, editor, and author of over thirty titles. Meticulous photo albums, relics of his earlier life in London and Paris, documented friendships and encounters with midcentury luminaries, from André Breton, Octavio Paz, and Alberto Giacometti to Pablo Neruda and Susan Sontag. Swarms of toy fighter planes, taxidermied butterflies, and headshots of ballerinas testified to a lifelong fixation with flight. Though I hadn't seen him in several years, we began a correspondence. I was living in Marrakesh at the time, as writer-in-residence at an artists' colony. Although Nathaniel had once alighted upon every continent, including Antarctica, he had never seen Morocco. At five p.m. on a November afternoon in 2014, I was there waiting in the arrivals lounge of Menara Airport, when the silver jet carrying Tarn glided down from the heavens, landing gear out like a set of claws.

I can still picture him, emerging from the gate: at eighty-six years old, he towered over the rush of passengers, with no luggage and a nearly empty backpack on his shoulders. He has blue eyes and silver-gray hair; his bearing is regal and his nose aquiline. He informed me straight away that he was wearing all his clothes on his back: a khaki jacket, olive pants, baseball cap, plaid scarf, plus a walking stick and reading glasses on a chain. For someone who had apparently been a god once, he had made his travel logistics as complicated as possible. He had left London at five a.m., caught a connecting flight in Lisbon, and had now planned for us to take a night train to Fez, a seven-and-a-half-hour journey. He had carried with him two tuna sandwiches and one falafel burrito all the way from Gatwick Airport, which he offered to me. We made a date to consume them at eight p.m. sharp. On our arrival in Fez at two-thirty a.m., heavy rain fell in the darkness as we navigated the labyrinth of the old medina, guided by stray cats. Nathaniel, who had been in transit for twenty-three hours straight, remarked that he felt he had walked straight into the Old Testament.

✦  ✦  ✦

His name is theophoric: it "bears or carries a god" within it, for power
or talismanic protection, or simply the beauty of the syllables. Nathaniel
means "Gift of God" in Hebrew. (Other such names are Michael, "Who
is like God"; Eliot, "The Lord is my God"; and Ismael, "He Whom God
Hears.") Born in Paris in 1928, Nathaniel lived in Belgium until the age
of eleven, when his family was evacuated to England just before the German occupation. They moved to London, only to find themselves right
next to the Marble Arch station bombing during the Blitz. As a child,
Nathaniel became obsessed with reading about the life of Abraham
Lincoln and imagined escaping the broken Old World for the New. He
went on to study history at Cambridge University and then discovered
anthropology with Jean Rouch, Marcel Griaule, and Claude Lévi-Strauss
at the Musée de l'Homme. A Fulbright grant sent him to the University
of Chicago to pursue his doctorate, setting in motion a series of events

that would gain him admission into a peculiar club. He would join a strange breed of divinities in the twentieth century who, following in the footsteps of the military officers, generals, and soldiers, crisscrossed the earth. This was the race of deified anthropologists, with their cameras and tape recorders, their notepads and pens. On a terrace café in Fez, after a day of sightseeing, Nathaniel began to recount the story of his unexpected divinity.

In 1952, he was sent by his doctoral supervisor to the highlands of Guatemala to live among the Tz'utujil Maya in Santiago Atitlán. "I'd never done any fieldwork before," Nathaniel told me, recalling how daunting it was to arrive into an utterly foreign land, tasked with getting strangers to talk to him about their lives and culture. "I walked for days before anyone spoke to me. . . . So I thought, okay, how do I start a conversation? One of the things I did was embroider a yellow sun on my trousers," he related. "I felt protected by it—and I saw the sun as a symbol of authority, the anthropologist's authority, to do the job I was here to do."

He soon learned that the village was in the midst of a conflict: between the *catequistas*, the orthodox Catholics, and those who worshipped the indigenous god Maximón, or the *Mam*, a word meaning "grandfather." Often categorized as a trickster, Maximón was said to keep the world in motion. God of travel, sexuality, and the flow of the seasons, He is Lord over everything and its opposite, embodying the power of creative destruction. In His physical form, the Mam is a four-foot-tall bundle of wood, iron, and cloth who lives in the rafters of the *cofradía*, the house where his worshippers convene. For ceremonies, the Mam is dressed in a carved mask, a hat, and boots, and draped in multicolored scarves. He receives offerings of tobacco, liquor, incense, and clothes, while listening to prayers that He may or may not feel like answering. Among the Mam's prophets, Nathaniel learned, was a figure called Francisco Sojuel, an ancestor said to have founded the religion in its present form, dictating the rituals and carving the Mam's wooden mask with his own hands. Imprisoned by the government, Sojuel was allegedly rescued by the Mam himself, who switched places with him and sat in his jail cell, coolly smoking a cigar. After Sojuel died, he ascended to the heavens and became a deity with control over the rain clouds. It was said Francisco Sojuel would return to earth in times of dire need.

In the year he spent in Santiago Atitlán, Tarn became a confidant of the village's foremost *aj'kun*, or shaman, Nicolás Chiviliu. During Holy Week, Tarn took part in the washing of the Mam's clothes in the lake, a ritual that occurs at midnight, the hour when this world and the Other World of gods and spirits are thought to be in closest alignment. Some drink the water the laundry has been washed in, believing it possesses curative powers. Tarn helped lay the clothes out to dry, but when it was time to recite the prayers, everyone was too intoxicated. "It seemed to me that we could all fall on the ground and go to sleep, but I thought, maybe I should step in," Nathaniel remembered. "I knelt down and I conducted a whole service in broken Latin from Nicolás's Catholic prayer book, with great dramatic gestures and crosses." One afternoon not long after, Nathaniel was working in his room when a villager entered, and perched on the corner of his desk. "You know, a lot of people here think you're a god," the man said.

Even before Nathaniel arrived in Atitlán, the village's climate was turning messianic. The battle between the orthodox Catholics and the followers of the Mam had reached a point of crisis. Local laws were passed that forbade the worship of Maximón and imposed heavy fines on those who refused. The situation had deteriorated to such an extent that Nicolás Chiviliu, after fortifying himself with a drink, had telegraphed the president of Guatemala to ask him to intervene and defend their freedom of worship. Condemning the Mam as diabolical, a group of priests was bent on destroying the idol. First they tried to set it on fire, then they shot at it with a gun; on the third attempt, the priests decapitated the Mam and kidnapped two of his three wooden masks, relics said in Atitlán to be as ancient as the universe itself. An article in *Time* magazine described the priests dashing away from the scene of the deicide with the god's head and a machete, "robes aflutter." In the wake of the holy crime, gloom settled over the villagers of Atitlán. There was a pervasive sense that the world had turned upside down, that they were living through the end of days, and some sort of cosmic judgment was imminent.

Nathaniel was curious to see if he could track down the masks, and after some investigation at the French embassy, he learned that one of them was in the possession of a French priest, a certain Father Teste. He paid him a visit to try and convince the priest to donate the mask, "in the name of science," to a European museum. The priest agreed, perhaps thinking the best way to kill something blasphemous might be to turn it into an object of empirical study. During the mask's captivity, Tarn discovered, it had become infested with worms and the face was beginning to disintegrate. He took it to a representative of the Musée de l'Homme in Guatemala City, who transported it to Paris, where it was fumigated and restored. Not long after, Nathaniel left Guatemala and returned to London. The mask remained in Paris, where it may have eavesdropped on the screening of *Les maîtres fous* the following year.

◆ ◆ ◆

In his London study, Tarn toiled for several years to produce a six-hundred-page dissertation—by all accounts too long—on his fieldwork. In 1958, a fraction of the material was published in Spanish by a press in Guatemala City, under the title *Los escándalos de Maximón*. On its cover, against a subtly psychedelic, faux-bois swirl, is a floating cutout photo of the mask of the Mam. The chiseled face looks pained: the Mam's eyes are shut as if bracing himself against the battles of this world, but his lips are pursed, creating an indent deep enough to receive a sacrificial cigar. In the late 1970s, a young American, Martín Prechtel, was living in Santiago Atitlán, where he was a musician and disciple of Chiviliu. He happened to own a copy of the book. One day when Chiviliu was over at Prechtel's house, the shaman caught sight of the cover of the book and the image of the mask, whose return he had been prophesying for nearly three decades. Seeing the mask triggered dreams of its advent that became contagious. Prechtel had not met Tarn, and no one knew that he had anything to do with the mask's whereabouts, but Prechtel decided to write to the Musée de l'Homme, mentioned in the book, on the villagers' behalf.

Around the same time, Nathaniel had also begun discussions with the museum to determine whether the time was ripe to return the mask

to Atitlán. He worked with curators and lawyers to settle the question of the relic's legal status, as letters and petitions from Atitlán poured in, all serving to convince the museum's board that the mask had been intended as a loan, not a gift, and should be given back. An agreement was reached, and a date was set for the repatriation of the relic, March 1, 1979. To celebrate, a ceremony that was both bureaucratic and shamanistic was organized in the village, a day of dancing, singing, feasting, and speeches, in which villagers, local politicians, and representatives from the museum took part. Nathaniel, in keeping with his penchant for complex travel logistics, had decided to drive to Guatemala from New Hope, Pennsylvania, in a van with his wife, Janet, and arrived just in the nick of time.

After the passage of three decades, people were astonished to see Nathaniel. As he sat on a bench during the ceremony, villagers came up to him to kiss his face, to ask why he had been dead or sleeping for twenty-seven years, and inquire about news of the other deities in the Holy World. Janet, who was sitting next to Nathaniel, wrote a poem about what she saw and heard, lines that capture something of what it is like to watch your husband being received as divine.

A heavy solemnity hung in the air, Nathaniel recalled, as the French curator finally pulled out the package containing the mask from a bag. Everyone began to cross themselves and to kiss the parcel, still in its bubble wrap. When the mask was unwrapped, Chiviliu scrutinized it from all angles, as though facing it off, before lighting a cigarette and placing it in the mask's mouth. Then he announced that the mask was ancient, that it must be starving; cradling the mask in his arms, he began to rub it with a cloth soaked in alcohol, letting the liquor flow into its wrinkles. When the mask was placed onto the trunk of the Mam's body, and the deity stood in its full glory, the musicians began to play. Chiviliu danced and fell to his knees in prayers, and Tarn, not known to be much of a dancer, was amazed to find himself moving too. With the mask's return, it was said that the world could now begin anew. Tarn wrote in *Scandals*: "And all the next days, people coming up to each of us, individually, in small groups, sliding, slithering, sidling up: Is it true, is it fact that the Lord of the World is among us again? And leaving with smiles on their lips."

It was only then that he began to understand more about what "the *god* business" from his earlier visit had meant, Nathaniel told me. It was thought, by Chiviliu and other villagers, that he was an incarnation of Francisco Sojuel, or Aplas in his Tz'utujil name, the shaman, political radical, and religious founder who would return to Atitlán in times of upheaval. Tarn hadn't realized when he performed the washing of the clothes, and gave his spontaneous liturgy, that it had taken place in the same house said to have been inhabited by Sojuel. After he died, Sojuel became a *nuwal*, or a rain angel, a powerful divinity responsible for thunder, lightning, and storms. Rain angels live at the point of connection between heaven and earth, atop the highest trees, which they use as an office or throne. Other anthropologists who came to Atitlán after Tarn recounted legends—that Sojuel never needed to eat, that he possessed books with talismanic words inside them that he didn't have to read in order to know what they said. According to one story, when Sojuel was crucified, he summoned the rain and hail from his heights on the cross, along with hundreds of baskets of tropical fruit, a sign that he was not dead. He was cut into pieces and sprinkled with lemon juice and salt, but still he resurrected, and kept appearing to government officials. When he sent the rains crashing down, he never got wet. At the time of the mask's return to Atitlán, stories circulated that Nathaniel had reached into a fire and pulled out the mask of the Mam, unscathed.

"A lot of the *aj'kuna* who became rain angels were a little bit, or more than a little bit, *weird*," Nathaniel recalled, laughing, "They were strange people. Often they were mute, never saying a word. That's how you get chosen, by whatever spiritual forces are out there." It was said that when Francisco Sojuel appeared to people in the village, the divinity was reluctant to reveal his name, or would claim not to remember it. Although he could understand the Tz'utujil language, Tarn wasn't able to speak it. With the exception of the night of the washing of the sacred laundry, Tarn had followed Nicolás Chiviliu around silently, and his taciturnity had probably encouraged the recognition of him as a rain angel. So, too, the yellow sun emblazoned on his trousers was interpreted as a sign: Tarn hadn't known when he chose it that the Mam was also known as "the Old Sun." Lord of the last five days of the Maya calendar, the Mam was said to move across the sky from west to east, and went in search of the Young Sun in a myth of cosmic renewal.

With the mask's repatriation, the shaman Nicolás Chiviliu divined that the time had come for him to make his earthly exit. Now in his mid-eighties, Chiviliu began to seem as if he were living in another world, as though he had already crossed over into the hereafter. The shaman would stand at the window of the house where Tarn was staying during his return visit and stare in, silently. He was, Tarn wrote in *Scandals*, "full of mood swings, visions, battles with demons visible to him alone, and prophecies . . . Dogs, the radio, telegraph poles, clouds: everything will seem to have been talking to him or at him." Several months after Tarn

left Guatemala, a letter from Martín Prechtel dated April 1980 brought
the news that Chiviliu had died. He wrote that Chiviliu had remembered
Tarn as Sojuel and kept a photograph of him above his altar. "All the
people at the wake kept waiting for you and Janet to walk in: at one point
I was wishing like hell that you would," Prechtel wrote. "There was a certain amount of excruciating pain I didn't know where to put."

There is a story from Atitlán about how the wood was chosen for the
Mam, which Tarn recounts in *Scandals*. The ancestors approached
eleven different types of trees, including cypress, guava, hornillo, and
pine, to ask whether they would be willing to give their body, but they all
refused. Each one claimed it was too busy doing other things—glowing

at night as firewood, or being made into bed frames or musical instruments. As the villager Juan Ajcot told the story, they came across a *tz'ajtel*, or coral tree, "but it has bad wood, is dumb-looking, and soft," like balsa. Instead, they started chatting up the smooth alder tree nearby. "They begin to hear the coral tree panting uneasily: its heart is almost jumping out of its body, it is so anxious to talk to them." The alder refused to be chopped down, but the coral tree, known by its botanical name as *Erythrina corallodendron*, was more than willing to make the sacrifice. "Are you the chosen one?" the ancestors asked, according to another villager's account. One version has it that the Mam was already formed inside the tree: "He is peering out. They cut around his outline and haul him out whole." According to Ajcot, with each stroke of the machete, they heard the tree crying out, "A! E! O! Oh! Ay! Ou! A! E!" "You feel that?" they asked. When they were finished, they stood the idol upright and said, "He looks pretty good this man made of pain."

I asked Nathaniel about something I thought I'd read in his book, about how an idea circulated that the wooden mask of the Mam physically looked like Sojuel, and thus, like him. Tarn laughed and shook his head. "I think you imagined it," he said. I had my copy of *Scandals* with me in the hotel, bristling with Post-its. I searched through it, and through my notes, but I still couldn't find where I got this from, that the mask resembled Nathaniel's face. But later on, Nathaniel says, yes, that actually rings a bell, although he cannot locate it either. "Maybe we both dreamed it," he says. The idea lingers and adheres: mythmaking in real time.

✦  ✦  ✦

It would happen on several occasions in Fez that we noticed people at the next table listening to our unusual conversations, trying to decipher who we were and how we had ended up there. We settled on the alibi that we were grandfather and granddaughter. Each morning we set out at a slow pace through the maze of the medina, past the stalls of antique carpets, the piles of chickpeas and spices, butchers quivering with tripe, down the landmark that we called Snail Street, where cauldrons of snails bubbled away for soup. If Europe's military officers and imperialists had cut pathways across the globe for the ethnographers to follow, they in turn had opened the gates for the characters we were now: the tourists. We went in search of medieval mosques, craft museums, and libations of mint tea. After prolonged negotiations, we acquired two camel hair blankets, one large and one small. Over the course of five evenings, we would return to the terraced café, where Tarn unfolded new installments of his story, a little as if Scheherazade had been an anthropologist in the *Thousand and One Nights*. On one evening, we realized two American ladies from our hotel, a bit like characters from a Paul Bowles novel, were seated next to us, with their ears perked. "Can I ask you a question?" one of them hazarded to Nathaniel. "Who are you?" He effortlessly dodged the question, as if well practiced, never revealing his name.

Decades earlier, having lived a dual existence as poet and anthropologist for some time, Nathaniel had decided to break with academic anthropology, and resigned his professorship in London to devote himself to poetry. He often speaks of his lifelong dilemma between the two disciplines as the battle between two angels: the angel of Creation, and the angel of the Record. While the angel of Creation is autonomous, the angel of the Record requires "data donors" to go about its work. Of the two, the Record lives a more frustrating existence, for so often the scientist becomes caught up in his or her own empirical data, muddying the waters. We spoke about how the angel of the Record must be a great curmudgeon, having to contend with a pantheon of anthropologists who have found themselves elevated to the sky.

Among the earliest of them was Nikolai Nikolaevich Miklouho-Maclay, a Russian scientist who was interested in sea sponges before turning his microscope to comparative human brains. From 1871, he lived for three years in Papua New Guinea, where the inhabitants of the coast of Astrolabe Bay received him as a celestial being. "They asked me about the stars and tried to find out on which I had been," Maclay wrote in his diaries. It was thought that he could set fire to water, that he could cure illness or injury with a glance. The scientist was asked to put a stop to the incessant pouring rain. Once his divinity had been decided on, everything he said or did only served to confirm it, Maclay reported. The word *Maclay* or *magarai* became a Melanesian word for *deity*, still in use at least into the 1950s.

In 1909, decades before MacArthur came on the scene, the German doctor and ethnographer Max Moszkowski was taken for the Papuan deity Manseren Mangundi, heralding the overthrow of all existing power structures and the resurrection of the dead. Some sixty years later, in the 1970s, Maria Lepowsky was doing fieldwork in the nearby Louisiade Archipelago. She reported that she was seen as supernatural, an undead ancestor glowing white. Studying the *zar* cult in northern Sudan, Janice Boddy was mistaken for a *khawajaya zar*, the powerful, deified spirits of dead Europeans. Her presence startled one of the women in the village where she worked, but when she noticed Boddy's Dr. Scholl's sandals and realized that she had toes not hooves, the woman laughed and exclaimed, "This *khawajaya* has human feet! I thought she was a *zar*!" For Boddy, it was jarring to suddenly morph into the object of her own study, as if encountering a divine, spirit double of herself. "Something trembles in the whole enterprise of analysis and knowledge-making here: the whole anthropological trip starts to eviscerate," wrote the anthropologist Michael Taussig, staring down the white male Guna curing figures that looked like him. The angel of the Record recoils.

Not long after I published the *LRB* piece about Prince Philip and Tarn's message glowed across my screen, another email arrived, from Matthew Baylis, the author of the book I had reviewed, *Man Belong Mrs. Queen.*

> There were a few things that didn't make the final edit so I
> wondered if they might be of interest to you with your book . . .
> Firstly, my visit to Tanna led to me being turned into a god
> myself.

Baylis wrote of how he had noticed "a general weirdness in the way [he] was treated," with endless questions and a sense of urgent expectation. But he "just put it down to being a stranger, on Tanna, with an assumed connection to Prince Philip because of the letters in [his] bag." He had an unsettling feeling of becoming too implicated; there is a scene in his book where he realizes he leads a double existence at night, appearing to people in dreams. In his email, Baylis told me how, after he left Tanna, he had been in touch with a missionary, who informed him that in the more remote villages legends were circulating "about a tall man who'd come from Philip." A baby girl who had been named Masyu after him was growing taller each day. Baylis had become "not quite a god," he wrote to me, but "more what they call a 'tabu man', someone so sacred and dangerous that they occupy a space somewhere between the living and the dead."

For the deified anthropologists, the vertiginous heights of divinity thrust upon them often stood in contrast to the realities and real dangers of fieldwork. Ethnographers such as Maclay left plaintive accounts of their anxieties and fears, their insomnia and intense sleep deprivation, of the boredom of days staring at a motionless tropical sea, and their defenselessness against insects. A fellow doctoral student at Chicago, Robert Pehrson, who studied with Tarn's mentor Robert Redfield, died of malaria at the age of twenty-nine while conducting research among the Marri of Baluchistan in the early 1950s. It was reported that the site of his tomb became a shrine, where Marri pilgrims made sacrifices and the anthropologist could continue his fieldwork in the afterlife.

In the wilderness of western Brazil, Tarn's former professor Claude Lévi-Strauss sank into a state of extreme loneliness and depression as he lived among the Nambikwara people, unwelcoming of his presence. When the tedium of fieldwork, coupled with the weight of scholarly expectation and ambition, nearly drove him to madness, he started to contemplate deification: that of the Emperor Augustus. In the field notes that would become his 1955 classic *Tristes Tropiques*, Lévi-Strauss began to write a play on the reverse side of each page, titled "The Apotheosis of Augustus." In one scene, Augustus finds himself alone with a feral eagle, the bird that carried Roman emperors to the heavens on its back, talons out:

> The eagle explained to the incredulous Augustus that the divine nature he was about to acquire would consist precisely in no longer experiencing the feeling of revulsion by which he was now overwhelmed while still a man. Augustus would realize that he had become a god, not by some radi-

ant sensation or the power to work miracles, but by his ability to tolerate the proximity of a wild beast without a sensation of disgust, to put up with its stench and the excrement with which it would cover him. Carrion, decay and organic secretions would appear familiar to him.

This was the silver lining of godhood: Augustus was now able to sleep on the ground and tolerate butterflies copulating on his neck, Lévi-Strauss writes. Godhood was supposed to provide a kind of buffer against the world, like a hazmat suit. Yet for Nathaniel, the notion that he might embody some kind of divinity contrasts with his experiences of the quotidian travails of this world, its bruises and scrapes and frequent quarrels. At breakfast in Fez, he poured sugar over his hard-boiled egg, mistaking it for salt. His eyesight was fading and the nerve endings in his feet had gone numb. We talked about his fear of the Other, when the Other is absolutely everyone who isn't you. Some days the shield between oneself and the enormity of the world, its avalanche of details and sorrows, is more resilient than others. For a person prone to depression and dark moods, what could the intrusion of godhood possibly mean? Did it point the way to any transcendence at all?

Nathaniel's lifelong project has been the writing of an auto-anthropology, which studies the self as if it were a foreign tribe. What he finds difficult, he told me, is the way that society always wants to fix you in a certain human identity, comprising nationality, race, religion, occupation; a single name. He spoke of the tyranny of his Wikipedia page. Yet to find oneself unexpectedly a god of some kind is to confirm Tarn's suspicion, that the self will never be the perfectly bounded, neatly encapsulated, single entity that we think it is. The deified anthropologist may meet his divine double on the street, in the field, on the page. In 1970, Tarn published a poem about the two angels, of Creation and of the Record, and the battleground where they converge. It is composed of fragments of prayers that Nicolás Chiviliu offered on Nathaniel's behalf in Atitlán. The words are translations of those of Chiviliu, but they also sound like Tarn's, lines in which the refrain of the inadvertent deity is embedded.

*I alone      I am people      I am people who live on a basis of food and*
*drink      I am not God      I am not Angel before the World and the*
*Face of the Earth      You Angels are of God . . .*
*perhaps you keep me here      in the mountains in the valleys      perhaps*
*you detain me in your hands in your feet*

Later, going through my own field notes of our travels, I will have to
balance the angels too.

It was said in Atitlán that the Mam ferries the dead to the afterlife, heading east toward the sun but not too close—not as close as the Christian heaven—for that would be absurd: "souls would fry." Although it is
impossible to say when the god was born, it is often supposed that the
Mam in his present form came on the scene the year the earth died, in
1524, when the Spanish invaded Atitlán. One of the Mam's many forms
is Don Pedro, the deified Pedro de Alvarado, who commanded the Spanish forces in Guatemala. Infamous for his fiery temper and his searing
cruelty toward the people of Mexico when he was second-in-command
to Hernán Cortés, the blond-haired, red-bearded Alvarado was called
by the name of the Aztec sun god Tonatiuh. In Atitlán, the conquistador
allied with the Tz'utujil's rivals, the neighboring Kaqchikels, and forced
the Tz'utujil to surrender. Francisco Sojuel is said to have lived at the

time of the conquest, and could still remember the old Maya kingdoms. Appropriating the violence of Alvarado, the Mam became the vortex of the conquerors' power. The deity harnessed their destructive force to restore order in the face of indescribable loss, and rebuild. Around Lake Atitlán, thousands of Maya villagers were killed, their ancient capitals razed to the ground, and illness spread. But for the most part, the Tz'utujil people were spared the worse devastation that befell their neighbors.

After the conquest came the Catholic missionaries, polemical friars such as Diego de Landa, who noted the presence of the wooden Mam in a 1566 report. One story goes that when the priests arrived, they informed the old stone gods that they would need to take new jobs as *santos*, or saints, and reinvent themselves in wood. And so the Mam helped himself to the power of Christianity. He is Maximón, and he is also known as San Simon, or Simon Peter, holding the keys to heaven in his pocket. As a trickster, the Mam is also Judas Iscariot, who sold Jesus for thirty pieces of silver. He is the traitor who set the gears of the crucifixion in motion—but also the one who made it possible for Christ to live out his destiny. Stalking the events of the New Testament, the Mam is a liminal, ambiguous character; in Atitlán, his idol presides over the Easter processions, embodying the power of death as rebirth.

So it is that myths stay immortal, through their ability to adapt, encompass, and absorb, accruing layers and branches. Myths refuse to fossilize, to be killed. The Mam, the old, pre-Columbian grandfather god, became a powerful ally for the Tz'utujil to contend with their oppressors, first the conquistadors and missionaries, and then the Guatemalan Army, backed by American imperial might. The year after Nathaniel first left Atitlán, in 1954, a CIA-organized coup, authorized by President Eisenhower, overthrew Guatemala's democratically elected leftist government and installed a military dictatorship. By the time Nathaniel returned, Atitlán had in many ways been transformed: the government had seized villagers' ancestral land, leaving them destitute, while the population had exponentially grown. Tourism and industry had arrived in the region, as well as a new crop of Protestant missionaries, who preached individual salvation above communal bonds. Meanwhile the conflict between the military and the guerrilla groups fighting for justice had spiraled into terrifying violence.

Not long after Chiviliu's death in 1980, the civil war that had been raging across the country descended upon Santiago Atitlán with brutal force. Two army bases were built near the town, and the soldiers began to persecute the Tz'utujil on suspicion of being subversives. Over the course of a decade, thousands of villagers were executed, disappeared, or tortured, women were raped, and homes were ransacked by soldiers. The army created a program of terror for the purpose of "counterinsurgency," in what amounted to an ethnic cleansing of the Maya and indigenous ways of life. The forced recruitment of Maya people into the military became common: army trucks would arrive in the night and drive off with boys as young as thirteen, treating them as disposable ammunition. It was said that a mysterious guardian would give the army recruiters photographs of the boys instead, and the images would go off to fight, leaving the boys behind in safety—the ingenious Francisco Sojuel.

On December 1, 1990, an unarmed crowd of several thousand villagers, holding white nylon banners, gathered to protest the abuses of the military. Soldiers fired on them, killing eleven, in an incident that provoked international outrage and led to the relocation of the army bases. A few weeks earlier, soldiers had stormed a meeting of the Mam's followers in Santiago Atitlán, walking into the house of worship and executing one of the Mam's priests, who was sitting next to the god. It was said the Mam's nose was blown off by gunfire, but it swiftly grew back, and the army suffered casualties in revenge.

Throughout the genocide, the Mam was a force that held people together, in face of the deepest suffering. Sojuel and other rain angels would be remembered as active participants in the war effort, conjuring thunderstorms to thwart military operations, causing firearms to jam, directing worms to invade the soldiers' food. The three volcanoes that encircle Santiago Atitlán huddled closer together, protecting the villagers like a shield.

✦   ✦   ✦

In the first rays of the dawn, we left Fez. We made our last pass down Snail Street as the shopkeepers were setting up their wares, and set off on the drive back to Marrakesh. We had decided to take the scenic route through the Atlas Mountains, a trip that would take us eleven hours. (Later we would argue over whose idea that was.) As the landscape grew more beautiful, we noticed it less, for we fell into a debate about the nature of belief. It started when Nathaniel said he thinks the world is essentially divided into two kinds of people: those who believe in some sort of transcendent, divine power, something that exists above us, and those who don't. But I'm not sure about this. What he describes sounds to me like a light switch either on or off inside our brains. Perhaps belief is just as much a set of relationships between people as it is an absolute state of mind. Rather than someplace unlocatable, unfathomably high above us, perhaps transcendence is all around us, and so the sacred stays within reach for us to grasp when we need it. What else could it mean to say that, for a moment, people believed in *him*?

Whatever the myths and stories that adhered around Nathaniel, he never became a "religion," like other incidental deities have become. Other strangers have arrived in Santiago Atitlán and been recognized as Francisco Sojuel too. It may be that his divinity meant more to Nathaniel than to anyone in Atitlán, electrifying that contradiction—between the desire to live forever, and the desire to end it—that we all feel. "Early on I acquired the habit of looking for the eternal side of things," he wrote in 1964 on the first page of his first book of poems, *Old Savage/Young City*. Whatever it was that coalesced around him probably vanished with Nicolás Chiviliu's death, and the deaths of many others he had known, in the violence of the civil war. But for a period of time, all the power that is Nathaniel, which I can see in him too—his kindness and intrepid spirit, his humor and erudition, his physical stature, many languages, and worldly connections—was deployed on the mythic plane of Atitlán for a higher cause. His divinity was a means of restoring the rightful order of things, in a place that has contended, again and again, with loss—and somehow, in a way, it worked. The mask of the Mam was returned to the village. And with the carved god made of coralwood back in Santiago

Atitlán, the rain clouds would arrive on schedule, the harvest would be fruitful, and the universe would keep ticking, like a clock.

On Nathaniel's last morning in Morocco, it was still pouring with rain, appropriately enough for a former rain god. In as many days as it took God to create the world, we had walked only one of its labyrinths. I had wanted to give Nathaniel a daylight tour of my Marrakesh surroundings, but the oceanic puddles and slippery streets were treacherous for an octogenarian. I dropped him off at the airport, the tarmac of inadvertent divinity, and I was sad to see him go. If the world we inhabit is disenchanted, perhaps no place is more so than the high-security, fluorescent glare of the airport terminal. Yet still we find enchantment in one another, in often unexpected ways. We are what Tarn calls "a relatively late-appearing animal," and a disappearing species on this terrestrial stage. In this brief corridor, we need a sense of the eternal in order to live. As he turned to leave, Nathaniel's backpack was heavy with the camel hair blanket. And I could see them now, one sitting on each shoulder: the angel of Creation and the angel of the Record. His flight took off, and on the seventh day, I rested.

II

# THE RAGGED EDGES OF RELIGION

A is for AUGUSTUS who came back in an urn,
B is for BECKWITH whose temperature burned.
C is for CARDEN, dead in Gujarat,
D is for DIXON whom no one forgot.
E is for EARL CORNWALLIS, entombed in Ghazipur,
H is for HENCKELL, mourned in Jessore.
J is for JOHN JACOB who convulsed and thrashed,
M is for MAXWELL, killed in a clash.
N is for NICHOLSON, gunned down in combat,
O is for OUTRAM, mauled by a cat.
P is for POLE who thirsted for a cigar,
R is for REVELL who perished in Bihar.
T is for TAYLOR who couldn't be saved,
W is for WALLACE who gets bored in the grave.

6

## The Mystical Germ

Far from the cradle of his birth, an Englishman died on a hill. His sun-burnt face had been just one among many in the East India Company regiment when it attempted, in February 1809, to capture the kingdom of Travancore, at the southernmost point of the Indian subcontinent. His name was Pole, Powell, or Poole; missing from the official registers of British casualties, he is thought to have deserted or fled in fear. Fatally wounded in a surprise attack at the Arambooly Pass, Pole staggered away from the site of the battle and was found by a group of Shanars, a Tamil caste of palm sugar cultivators, who tried to carry him to safety. An account passed down through generations of Shanars told of how, when

Pole died in their arms, they buried him in a desolate spot outside the city of Tinnevelly, under a banyan tree. They searched through the dead officer's meager possessions and found brandy and cigars in his bag.

Thirty years later, when the young Anglican missionary Robert Caldwell arrived in Tinnevelly, he noticed a strange phenomenon. In the village of Illamulley, the Shanars had erected a shrine they called *Pole Pettai* or *Poolypettai* where they worshipped a certain Captain Pole. The Englishman had undergone some type of demonification, Caldwell reported in his 1849 study *The Tinnevelly Shanars: A Sketch of Their Religion, and Their Moral Condition and Characteristics*, and in several later dispatches. "An ordinary Indian demon would have preferred blood, but the offerings made to this English officer consisted in ardent spirits and cigars," Caldwell noted, along with chickens and occasional sacrifices of rare beef. In a report from 1876, not long before the reverend was consecrated bishop of Tinnevelly, Caldwell related that "the simple rustics" had built several obelisks near the Pole altar, for it was believed the captain walked on air, never touching the ground. The obelisks served as a resting perch for the spirit, who could stand on them to watch the dances in his honor, "and see, with a grin of infernal satisfaction, the fowls which are being sacrificed . . . flapping and tumbling about comically in their death throes!" The bishop sounds as if he grew rather hungry as he watched.

Illamulley was "an inveterately heathen town," grumbled another cleric, the Reverend Thomas Ragland, in a letter mailed from Tinnevelly in 1846. A certain *Pooley Sahib* was "the most dreaded deity of the place," a malign entity who needed to be appeased with offerings "of mutton, arrack, and cheroots," Ragland reported. "And whom do you imagine this mysterious personage to be? You will be as much astonished as I was to learn that he is nothing more nor less than the spirit of an English officer, of the name of Pole, or Powell, or some other similar name." It was alleged that *Pooley Sahib* was the cause of all sickness and death in the village—the revenge of a deity who had died an unpleasant death. "A man could not get a headache in a walk past the grave, but the Englishman's spirit was taxed as the author of it," the reverend wrote. A hymn, written by a Shanar poet, sang of Pole's powers, his ability to strike men with madness, to slay herds of cattle, and even how his wife—"a second

Andromache"—tried "to dissuade him from the fatal fight." It began with an invocation of the Virgin Mary, and what followed next was "intolerable . . . mangled members of our own noble confession of faith," Ragland exclaimed. "Alas! The death and resurrection of our blessed Lord and Saviour . . . are dragged in to ornament the abominable rites of devilworship." If Pole was on a cross, we will never know, for Ragland refused to transcribe the blasphemous hymn.

Like Ragland, Caldwell had come to Tinnevelly to save souls, a task he found exasperating at times. ("To every . . . argument they mutter in reply; 'Who has seen heaven? Who has seen hell?'") In an 1886 report, he wrote that he wouldn't have mentioned Captain Pole at all, would not have devoted space to such idolatry, had it not been for "the unfair use" of the story that had recently been made. He related that an English "globe-trotter," returning from the colonies, had given a speech before Parliament. "In the course of a tirade against the English Government in India," the man asserted that "this worship of an English officer as a devil was an illustration of the horror in which the English were held by the natives." For the nameless, anti-imperialist dissenter, the deification of a British officer was proof of the daily terrors of colonial life. It was evidence of the fact that colonialism was so inhumane it could only be understood by the colonized as something supernatural. Reverend Caldwell, however, would not entertain any such criticism. "The fact is, that the motive of the people of the neighborhood was not horror or dislike," Caldwell related, "but pity for his melancholy end, dying as he did in a desert, far away from friends."

◆  ◆  ◆

In the same year that Captain Pole fell at Travancore, a certain Colonel William Wallace died in Siroor, an army cantonment near Poona. He was buried beneath a fifteen-foot-tall fluted column, with an inscription exalting his "Ardent Honourable Rectitude" and "Devoted Public Zeal." When the melancholic East India Company officer John Howison was dispatched to Siroor a decade after Wallace's death, he found that the once-bustling military base, housing a combined forty thousand British troops and natives, had become a ghost town. The regiments had moved on, leaving a small Indian population living among the decaying messrooms and the remains of a tennis court where jackals prowled by night. Howison soon grew irritable with the boredom of life in the colonies, the oppressive climate, the nights of insomnia tormented by mosquitoes. Writing in his 1825 travelogue, he longed "for a fate similar to that of the Seven Sleepers," who slumbered for three hundred years in the chill of a cave. To fill the hours, Howison went on walks, and daydreamed of the rousing military bands that had paraded down the same streets. After the rows of derelict houses, he reached the small, unsheltered Siroor cemetery, bleaching in the sun. The graveyard was crying out for shady trees, and "the hallowing influence of a church," Howison reported. But what was worse, he observed, it contained something "repulsive to British feelings."

At the moldering tomb of William Wallace, a cult had begun to germinate. Twice a week, the inhabitants of the desolate town would pile offerings of coconuts, rice, and sweetmeats upon his grave in a display of *bhakti*: the Sanskrit idea of devotional love and participation in the divine. They burned incense and sacrificed goats to the dead commander, whom they worshipped as *Sat Purush*, or "Holy Man." It was said that Wallace could cure illness and infertility; newlyweds would visit his monument to touch it. Some said Sat Purush possessed oracular powers; a voice was heard to rise from the tomb, dictating prophecies. Buttoned up in a white uniform, the colonel would walk the cantonment on the nights of the full moon. His former sepoys, or Indian soldiers, Howison noticed, were in the habit of lining up in formation and presenting arms at the time they expected the deity to pass before them. In 1883, when the villagers appeared to become less generous with their offerings, Wallace Sahib sent a plague to sicken three hundred cats, as a warning. The historian H. G. Rawlison noted that an American missionary in Siroor who attempted to suppress the idolatry died of cholera not long after, "which, of course, greatly enhanced Wallace's posthumous reputation."

One must not think of incidents such as these as "miracles"—acts that alter or transcend "unvarying natural laws"—explained Sir Alfred Lyall, Chief Commissioner of Oudh, in his *Asiatic Studies*. "For in India, no such laws have been definitely ascertained." From the arrival of the East India Company in the early seventeenth century until India's independence in 1947, British imperialists attempted to transform what they saw as an enchanted and disorderly subcontinent into profitable, well-administered districts. Yet as they went about their bureaucratic duties, the colonialists repeatedly found themselves caught up in the spiritual proclivities of their subjects. When the British erected the first statue to honor themselves in Bombay, depicting Richard, 1st Marquess of Wellesley, an observer lamented that "Maratha simpletons" supposed the East India Company "had very kindly imported an English god for their worship." Pilgrims came to perform rituals or *pujas* and take "vows" at the foot of the pedestal upon which the marble Wellesley sat, reading a book that rested on the hunted head of an elephant.

Nearby, an idol of Wellesley's successor as governor-general, Charles Cornwallis, would receive similar excesses of devotion. Known for his surrender in the American Revolution, Cornwallis rose to power in India but then succumbed to fever and was immortalized in marble, shaded by a neoclassical dome. James Douglas, the Bombay sheriff, recorded that the monument "was thought by the natives to be a place of religious worship, and they called it *Chota Dewal*," or "small temple." Villagers would make pilgrimages to the portly Cornwallis, in his tailcoat and breeches, for *darshan*, from the Sanskrit meaning "view": the powerful, auspicious act of seeing and being seen by the god, who was physically present inside his images and likenesses. Face-to-face with the deity, visitors heaped garlands upon Cornwallis and received blessings from him in turn. "Government tried to stop this, and issued some vernacular notices that it was a mistake. But it was of no use, for when these feelings take possession of the natives they are not easily eradicated," Sheriff Douglas reported. At the base of the statue, an iron fence was constructed and a watchman appointed to shoo any adorers away.

The British understood these religious tendencies to be like a rash: inflammable, irrational, and liable to erupt at any moment, under the slightest provocation. There was Sir Thomas Sydney Beckwith, deceased commander in chief of Bombay, who was worshipped at his tomb in Mahabaleshwar, where a clay doll resembling him imbibed plates of warm rice. There was Tilman Henckell, an efficient and kindly judge given the verdict of godhood by workers on the salt flats of the Sundarbans. There was Patrick Maxwell, once a fallen colonel of the Light Dragoons and now a demigod, venerated at his grave near Aurangabad. The colonizers maintained they had done nothing to provoke such worship: their deification was as accidental as the British Raj itself. "The British went to India not to conquer but to trade. Events, not intention, created the British Raj," the *Manchester Guardian* newspaper would claim. Lyall theorized that the British apotheoses arose out of two emotions: wonder, at colonial power and prowess, and pity, for the imperialists' frequent sorry ends, whether by microbe, suicide, or wild beast.

✦  ✦  ✦

Though the British were captivated by their own presence in Indian pantheons, the apotheosis of the dead predated the colonizers' arrival by several millennia: the British were only parvenus. From the veneration of cattle herders in Rajasthan, who perished protecting their flocks, to the *vettuppatta vatai*, or "cut-up spirits" in the bow-song tradition of Tamil Nadu, the practice of deifying humans who had died in premature or tragic ways was age-old. It shared similarities with rituals of ancestor worship, but while the average ancestor would reincarnate, the violently departed could not, remaining instead as unsettled spirits unable to enjoy new births. The slain had become the violence they encountered, embodying death itself in raw form, as if its power were forcibly driven inside them with the turn of a knife. Killed in battle or by sudden illness, by grisly accident or natural disaster, the deceased gained abilities to rain misfortune onto the living, or to save them. While some Hindu traditions held that the supreme gods such as Shiva might authorize or rubber-stamp a deification, as if granting an ill-starred man a boon, it was the agency of living people that turned the dead into divinities. It happened through acts of *bhakti* or devotion, by laying offerings above their remains, singing their life stories into hymns, or simply bearing witness to the new deity and being seen. Slowly, his or her human history might be forgotten, obscured into legends sized for a god.

The dead were not necessarily righteous, virtuous, or prized as heroes: apotheosis was not a moral judgment. More often, they were cruel, nefarious, or far-from-innocent characters, but they had suffered too. Deification was not a mode of honoring them, but a way to mediate with their power, a means for worshippers to try and shift the tides of individual and collective fates. To deify death was to reverse our universal defeat and turn it into victory. The collective rites of coming together, to build an altar, perform a song or a dance, was also a way to create something beautiful from the precarity, to forge meaning and routine from the violence and purposeless destruction that became ever more prevalent with the arrival of the East India Company. With boots on the ground, advancing across the subcontinent by the hundreds of thousands, the Englishmen were only the latest to prodigiously, conspicuously expire. They imposed their own meanings onto what happened next.

"Hinduism lies in urgent need of a Pope," declared William Crooke in his bestselling compendium, *The Popular Religion and Folk-Lore of Northern India*, published in 1896. According to Crooke, who served as a magistrate in the North-Western Provinces, Hinduism desperately required an "acknowledged orthodox head . . . to keep up the standard of deities and saints." Crooke collected numerous accounts of new celestials, among them a deceased official in Muzaffarnagar, an alcoholic in life who quaffed whiskey and beer into the hereafter. Even a Frenchman, an industrialist by the name of M. Raymond who had built a gun factory in Hyderabad, was worshipped at his tomb with offerings of sweetmeats. "The worst part of the matter is that there is no official controller of the right to deification," Crooke complained. The British deities were at least always "benevolent," which, in Crooke's opinion, formed "a remarkable and unconscious *tribute* to the foreign ruler." Apotheosis was a kind of class mobility, Sir Alfred Lyall supposed. "The saint or hero is admitted into the upper circles of divinity, much as a successful soldier or millionaire is recognised by fashionable society," in a heaven that was "judiciously liberal." A first-rate god might start out "exceedingly obscure," Lyall noted, "but if he or his shrine makes a few good cures at the outset (especially among women and valuable cattle), his reputation goes rolling up like a snowball."

Outside the British cantonment in Mairwara was a sign warning car-
avans to "Be Aware." The region was famous for its dangerous bandits,
"marauding Mairs," who robbed wedding parties and penniless pilgrims
alike. They were experts in blackmail: villagers were obliged to purchase
immunity from the Mairs to protect their property from plunder. In
Beawar, as the town became known, the British observed with horror
"pernicious customs" that included infanticide, slavery, and the practice
of sons selling their widowed mothers. Yet under the leadership of Colonel Charles Dixon, the Mairs were "converted to Honesty and Industry,"
as Dixon himself reported in *Sketch of Mairwara: A Brief Account of the
Origin and Habits of the Mairs; Their Subjugation by a British Force; Their
Civilization, and Conversion into an Industrious Peasantry*, published in
1850. Dixon told of how he formed a Mair Corps to channel their "wild
ferocity" into military discipline, and modeled little Beawar after the elegant avenues of Jaipur. The colonel instituted prohibitions against the
pernicious customs, but in such a noncoercive way that the Mair leaders supposed they had thought of them themselves. Peace, prosperity,
and civilization soon settled over the hilly district, as Dixon wrote in his
*Sketch*, in which he claimed the "Preference of the Tribes for British Rule."

After Dixon's death, the British commander Sir Walter Lawrence visited Beawar, and discovered that, each day, the Mairs went to worship
at the site where the colonel had been laid to eternal rest. He had transformed the Mairs from "a criminal tribe" into "fine, picturesque men,"
Sir Walter wrote in *The India We Served*, and so it was not surprising
Dixon had been raised up to the heavens. The seemingly omniscient
colonel was renowned for his awareness of every detail of village life; it
was said Dixon knew each inhabitant by name, and was always ready to
address their grievances and settle their disputes, acting as arbiter of justice. Sir Walter concluded his memoirs with a tribute to the "sun-dried
bureaucrats" such as Dixon, "the good, keen men who scorned the fierce
Indian sun when there was duty to be done," who fanned out over India's
countryside like an army of raisins. "The white man must carry on the
burden under the pitiless iron sky," Sir Walter declared.

✦  ✦  ✦

It was through the exertions of the men in the colonies, laboring under a burning sun sometimes as gods but more often as men, that the modern concept of religion was forged. The age of imperialism brought not only an influx of new wealth to Europe but also a flood of documentation around the spiritual proclivities of different peoples in all corners of the globe. The travelogues and missionary reports by men such as Robert Caldwell among the Shanars, as well as the old, sacred manuscripts colonists plundered or purchased, became the raw data that a new generation of European scholars in the mid-nineteenth century would analyze, classify, and study, from the safe and temperate confines of a preferred armchair.

For the German philologist Friedrich Max Müller, the much-vaunted founder of comparative religion, and an expert on India who never stepped foot there or in any other colony, the reports written by weathered civil servants served as his eyes and ears, allowing him to adventure beyond the tedium of Oxford life. Diving into the jungle of myths, rituals, and creeds contained within these accounts, he sought to understand how humankind had spun such a vast web of belief and to find the patterns in the data. Even Queen Victoria, rarely seen at a scholarly lecture, went to hear Müller speak. Her Majesty, Müller recalled in a letter to his wife, "listened very attentively, and did not knit at all, though the work was brought."

According to the new science, man was *homo religiosus*: religion was a universal and eternal fact of all human life. Müller defined "religion" as, at its core, the human faculty *to perceive the Infinite*, in a way that transcends reason. For Müller, religion was born when men noticed infinity in nature: an ocean seemingly without an opposite shore, the limitless sky. Not all men could immediately grasp the highest concepts of God by gazing skyward, but rather, humans contain within themselves "a germ," Müller contended, "a living germ . . . without which no religion would have been possible." From this seed, human thought had grown to attain the most sophisticated ideas of divinity through a lengthy process of evolution, he supposed, in a theory influenced by Darwin's recent *On the Origin of Species* (1859). Religion began with the perception of the Infinite, and gradually took on "a more and more definite shape through similes, names, myths, and legends," passing through a stage when words became deities, until at last it was "divested again of all names, and lives within us as the invisible, inconceivable, unnameable—the infinite God," who was, as it were, the Christian god. The earlier stages of evolution were still ongoing in certain corners of the earth, Müller maintained, and visible in the primitive thought of "uncivilized races" such as the Shanars.

Often thought to be the oldest surviving religious text continuously in use, the ancient Sanskrit *Rig Veda*, Müller argued, was our earliest testament to how this process of evolution occurred. Operating on the principle that the better one understood one's exotic subjects, the better one could rule over them, in the 1840s the East India Company commissioned the young Müller to prepare the first published edition of the scripture. Müller hypothesized that the *Rig Veda*, said to date as far back as the eighteenth century BCE, contained the history and beliefs of the Aryan race, from the Sanskrit *arya*, meaning "noble one." These pale-skinned, valiant warriors on horseback, shared ancestors of Europeans and high-caste Indians alike, had traveled from north to south, taking civilization with them to the darker-skinned aboriginal peoples, the forebears of tribes such as the Shanars, whom Caldwell classified as "Dravidians." According to Müller, it was possible, through reading the *Vedas*, to pinpoint "the first roots and germs" of what would evolve into the faiths of Bristol clergymen and Bombay brahmins alike. For the *Vedas'* Aryan authors, manifestations of infinity in nature, such as the inexhaustible sun, became "their Devas, their 'Brights', the same word which, after passing through many changes, still breathes in our *Divinity*," Müller claimed.

In comparing religions, many nineteenth-century scholars observed similarities between the Christian idea of incarnation and the Hindu *avatar*, the Sanskrit word for a "descent": the notion of a god, most frequently the pale-blue Vishnu, coming down from the heavens to inhabit a terrestrial form for a period of time. It was said that on Vishnu's eighth visit, he took the form of Krishna, the handsome, mischievous son of cow herders, who would famously act as charioteer for a prince fighting a war against his own brothers in the *Bhagavad Gita*. "O Arjuna," the avatar tells him, "*I am born again and again, age after age.*" In 1836, a Yorkshire antiquarian named Godfrey Higgins claimed that *Christ* was derived from *Christna*, or *Krishna*, and that both were incarnations of the same solar god. Jezeus Christna piously performed his ablutions in the Ganges, according to the Frenchman Louis Jacolliot. Both the Christian and Hindu faiths, scholars noted, believed in life beyond death and the incarnations of man-gods, and recognized an innate divinity in all mankind.

Yet Hinduism, Müller theorized, as it presently existed in the world had become "decrepit," a degeneration of the original Aryan faith—the memory of which seemed only to be preserved by European, Christian scholars. "If we want to tell the Hindus what they are worshipping—mere names of natural phenomena, gradually obscured, personified, and deified—we must make them read the Veda," Müller wrote. Now, in a later, modern cycle of Aryan migration, the British had come to India to restore its lost noblesse, bringing back the spiritual knowledge the subcontinent had forgotten, or that had been jealously guarded by corrupt Brahmin priests. The Christian colonizers were, quite literally, returning the *Vedas* to India: when the Prince of Wales toured India in 1875, he brought with him as gifts several volumes of Müller's edited *Rig Veda*.

If the roots of religion were found in the human perception of the Infinite, there were people living on earth at the time, Müller acknowledged, who still located it in their fellow men. It was not surprising, he contended in his lectures, that in the field notes of colonial administrators we should find a teeming ecology of apotheosis, not only in India but across the globe. "In Africa, in America, in the Polynesian islands, everywhere we catch glimpses of the process of deification." The idea of apotheosis might seem a contradiction in terms: "Nay, if there are two *genera*, which seem completely to exclude one another, they are those of gods and men. Gods might well have been defined as beings who, whatever else they may be, are not men; men as beings who, whatever else they may be, are not gods." For the professor, however, instances of mistaken deification clearly illustrated the process by which religion evolved, and provided valuable proofs for his theories. These episodes revealed "the primitive theogony that takes place in the human mind," which unfolds, slowly and inevitably, from the germ to God Himself,

occasionally encountering, along the way, the presence of the Infinite
in one of our own, mortal kind. "The people construct for themselves
Jacob's ladders between earth and heaven," Sir Alfred Lyall reported in
his *Asiatic Studies*. "The men are seen ascending until they become gods;
they then descend again as embodiments of the divinities," he observed.
"The Nature god sometimes condenses into a man, and is precipitated
upon earth, a hero or saint often refines and evaporates into a deity up
in the skies." Apotheosis was as natural as the formation of clouds and
the fall of rain.

Under his microscope, Max Müller studied religion in both the singular and the plural, "that marvelous harvest which we call the *religions*
of the world," which sprouted from the same germ. In 1864, the Dutch
theorist Cornelis Tiele used the phrase *wereld-godsdiensten*, or "world
religions," and Müller elaborated upon the concept to argue that there
were eight: "the *Vedic*, with its modern offshoots in India, the *Avestic* of
Zoroaster in Persia, the religion of *Buddha* . . . the *Jewish*, the *Christian*,
and the *Mohammedan* . . . that of *Confucius* and that of *Lao-tse*." These
different religions, reified and discrete entities with clear boundaries,
were all alike in form and structure. A "religion" was essentially anything that sufficiently resembled Christianity: it had a God, or several,
scriptures or sacred texts, a set of tenets and rituals, and houses of worship. Each religion was similarly corrupted by actual human practice:
"Every religion . . . suffers from its contact with the world, as the purest
air suffers from the mere fact of its being breathed." The fanciful myths
and legends that accrued around them, Müller argued, were "the parasites, not the marrow, of religion." It was in the scriptures that the pure
forms of each religion were enshrined, such as the Bible or the Qur'an.
In his magisterial, fifty-volume series Sacred Books of the East, Müller
set about creating authoritative editions of sacred texts, first published
in 1879. Yet the decision as to which books were to count as "sacred"
was left entirely up to Müller and his collaborators at Oxford University
Press.

In many ways, the nineteenth-century "science of religion" invented
what it purported to describe. According to its theorists, religion was
an ancient, eternal fact of human existence, and the study of it was as

old as the philosophical schools of Greece, enshrined by Socrates, Plato, and Aristotle. The word *religion*, derived from the Latin *religio*, "rose to the surface thousands of years ago," Müller remarked. However, the original term did not have anything like its modern meaning, nor was the concept it described as archaic, or natural, or universal as Müller made it out to be. In presenting the study of comparative religion as a classical pursuit, and religions as timeless, unchanging entities, Müller erased the contemporary context of colonialism in which his science was forged. Looking to 1700 BCE for confirmation of his theories, the professor elided the soldiers, missionaries, and bureaucrats, men like Caldwell among the worshippers of Captain Pole, who wrote the reports from which Müller mined his evidence. Glossing over the conditions in which his data was collected, the professor erased the mosquitoes, and the sleepless nights, and the violence of an army coming over a hill.

❖ ❖ ❖

The word *religio* conveyed the action of binding; a sense of scruples, obligations, or restraint. In works by Roman authors such as Cicero, *religio* appeared as a set of proscribed actions, or *religiones* in the plural: rules, rites, or prohibitions dictated by either gods or men. The earliest way of classifying these practices was through a binary: ours versus theirs. In the work of early Christian thinkers such as Augustine, *vera religio*, or "true religion," was contrasted with myriad false dogmas and heresies. It was thought that the entire world was innately Christian, yet many groups had become fallen or "wayward Christians," who practiced corrupted versions of the true creed. In early English, the plural "religions" at first meant different Christian monastic orders: monks were "religious," while the "secular" were those who lived in the tumult beyond the abbey walls.

Long before Müller's eight world religions, the world's population, from medieval Europe's perspective, was divided only into four: Christians, Jews, Mohammedans, and a category variously known as "Pagans," "Heathens," "Idolaters," or "the Rest." With Columbus's landing on an uncharted shore, a new age of exploration began, and with it the drive to learn more about the predilections of peoples everywhere. As the East

India Company knew, the better knowledge one possessed of the exotic Other, the better one could trade with him, surmount him, and control him. As Müller put it, "Let us take the old saying, *Divide et impera*, and translate it somewhat freely by 'Classify and conquer.'"

If the modern concept of "religion" came to the rest of the world by conquest, its genesis in Europe itself was violent, born out of disunity and polemic. "The world is pestered with too many Sects and Heresies," lamented Alexander Ross in his 1653 compendium *Pansebeia, Or, A View of All the Religions in the World*. Catholicism and Protestantism were considered to be different religions, as the English theologian Richard Hooker attested. But in the wake of Europe's Reformation, it became ever more urgent that people with differing approaches toward the divine learn to live together in peace. Writing a few years after the Treaty of Westphalia brought a shaky truce to sparring Europe, Ross argued that since religion was "the pillar on which every Common-wealth is built," only one must be permitted in each state. Philosophers such as John Locke countered that what was needed was tolerance; stability could only be attained not by determining which Christian creed was correct, but by relegating spiritual beliefs to a private sphere, while public loyalty must belong to the state. The meaning of "religion" began to shift from an outward display of rituals and practices to an inner state of mind, in the sense of belief. In 1851, the British newspaper editor George Holyoake coined the term *secularism*. He was imprisoned for suggesting not that God was nonexistent, but that it was time for Him to retire: to retreat from the realm of law to that of feelings.

If world religions were all alike in structure, after the template dictated by Christianity, the distinctiveness of a particular religion would become defined most clearly by the content of its beliefs. A religion, as a kind of modular form, could, ominously or sometimes comically, be founded around anything as its object of belief. In *The Varieties of Religious Experience*, the philosopher William James defined religion as "the feelings, acts, and experiences of individual men in their solitude, so far as they apprehend themselves to stand in relation to *whatever they may consider the divine*." While James confessed that he himself had "no living sense of commerce with a God," he still felt that "*there is something in me,*" an interior place within himself that stirred at the thought of anything divine. "Call this, if you like, my mystical germ," James wrote in a letter to a friend. "It is a very common germ. It creates the rank and file of believers." The human experience of believing was supposed to be everywhere alike, even though the objects of belief would differ. Located deep within the heart or the head, where it could not be seen, belief took on the quality of a natural and universal aspect of human life. It became part of our physiognomy; yet belief itself, like religion, was still a profoundly modern concept.

"As the wave of colonization advances, the world fills up with believers," writes the contemporary philosopher Bruno Latour. "A Modern is someone who believes that others believe." Although belief has come to be seen as a private conviction of the isolated self, for Latour it is ultimately a web of relationships among peoples, constructed by modern society. In the colonial age, it was exported across the globe by explorers and missionaries, spreading belief like a germ to peoples who did not have a word for it, nor any clear equivalent in their languages. It was, however, highly problematic to universalize belief as the same in form in every part of the world. Doing so meant that when colonialists saw the cigars left behind on a tombstone, the detritus of a *puja* made to Captain Pole or the idol of Charles Cornwallis, they also saw belief. It perpetuated the assumption that the people who performed these rituals must also *believe* in the colonial demigods in the same way as the colonizers understood their own religious convictions.

Searching the dark skies of BCE, Max Müller supposed he had found evidence of "belief" even in the *Rig Veda.* "The Latin word *credo,* 'I believe,' is the same as the Sanskrit *sraddha*," the philologist claimed. Translating several of its appearances in the three-thousand-year-old text, he used that term: "When Indra hurls again and again his thunderbolt, then they believe in the brilliant god." Yet as later scholars would argue, in its Vedic context, the word *sraddha* didn't capture some interior conviction, but rather was an empirically observable exchange. It conveyed a sacrificial contract between men and gods, and a confidence or trust in the efficacy of the ritual act. Alongside *belief,* Müller also found the word *religion*, in the Sanskrit *dharma*. But again, in its original Vedic setting, dharma encompassed a wide array of performed actions, social behaviors, and habits well outside the English sphere of religion. Mistaking his own parochial experience for something universal, the Protestant professor insisted that belief and religion, as we understand them now, were ancient and timeless concepts, so primordial and essential that tracing them back would tell us the entire story of humankind itself. "The real history of man is the history of religion," he wrote.

✦ ✦ ✦

For the sun-dried bureaucrats, more crucial than the question of how to define religion was the problem of how to manage it—whatever it was. Unlike Portuguese colonizers in the seventeenth century, who were known to have converted temples into churches and desecrated shrines, the directors of the East India Company swiftly realized that religious tolerance was in the best interests of commerce and trade. When they seized control over local districts, Company officers often found themselves in charge of temples previously administered by the local rulers, whether Hindu or Muslim. The British took over the management of the endowments and upkeep of holy sites, gave patronage to festivals, and, where useful, tried to harness their administrative role in Indian worship to their own advantage.

In one incident, the British officially instituted the worship of an inadvertent god. A cholera epidemic had broken out in the military camp run by Governor-General Francis Rawdon-Hastings in Bundelkhand. The villagers blamed the outbreak on the fact that British troops had slaughtered a cow for beef in a grove where the ashes of a dead nobleman called Lala Hardaul rested. Originating in the grove, the epidemic was "generally understood to have spread all over India," William Sleeman recounted in his *Rambles and Recollections of an Indian Official*. "The spirit of Hardaul was everywhere supposed to be riding in the whirlwind, and *directing the storm*."

Hardaul, the son of the Raja of Orccha, had been murdered in 1627 at the hands of his own brother, who suspected he was sleeping with his wife. The slain prince was canonized as a minor deity, though by the nineteenth century his worship had fallen out of fashion. Yet in the grip of the cholera plague, as farmers fearing the disease fled, leaving no one to cultivate the fields, the British attempted a highly unusual strategy. District officers were told to order the villagers to construct altars to Lala Hardaul as the "Cholera Godling," and present offerings to appease him. According to Sleeman, the epidemic was cured by Hardaul, who enjoyed the well-ordered processions and sacrifices the British had arranged in his honor and forgave their transgression. Sleeman's native informant remarked that he "had himself never seen a *puja* so entirely and imme-diately efficacious as this, and much of its success was, no doubt, attrib-utable to the science of its planning." In a mere six years, Hardaul priests had spread to villages as far north as Lahore, and the god's microbial domain had expanded to also include viral epidemics, influenza among them. If religious fanaticism was a contagion, it could also be a cure, British administrators supposed, as they efficiently manufactured a god.

At home, such British entanglements in "Hindoo idolatry" were not well received. General Peregrine Maitland, who had been tasked with overseeing Muslim and Hindu sites of worship as former commander in chief of Madras, had returned to London appalled at his assignment and launched the Anti-Idolatry Connexion League. The league staged pro-tests and printed off blistering pamphlets calling for the East India Com-pany to dissociate itself from any participation in "Heathen" worship. Activists spun tales of Christian soldiers forced to participate in ungodly customs against their better conscience, their bodies bent beneath the weight of the heavy idols they were required to carry on their backs at fes-tive processions, not to mention the contaminating presence of "dancing temple girls." Under pressure from evangelicals, the East India Company reluctantly began to cede control over religious endowments to Indian management, and the government of Madras adopted a new policy of "non-interference." The company began to conform to the growing idea that a government must be seen as secular and dispassionate while reli-gion belonged to the private sphere.

The East India Company had initially banned British Christian mis-sionaries from proselytizing in India, fearing that they would inflame local sensibilities. Yet under mounting calls for Britain to carry the cargo of Christ alongside goods for trade, the company conceded and allowed evangelists into India to preach the Word. Unleashed, the apostles' work was, in many lower-caste communities, prodigious: under the Reverend Caldwell, eighteen thousand Shanars in Tinnevelly were converted to Christianity in only four years. But once again the intrepid foreigners found themselves enmeshed in the spiritual proclivities of those they tried to convert. In 1819, the newly constructed Scots Kirk of Saint Andrew's in Bombay opened for public worship, presided over by a Scottish-born Presbyterian chaplain called James Clow. Increasingly unable to tolerate the Bombay heat, Clow returned to Scotland, eventually dying in Australia. Long after he left, his portrait continued to hang in the vestry of Saint Andrew's Church, where the sheriff of Bombay, James Douglas, recorded, "The native servants were beginning to hold it in such veneration as to do *pooja* to it, a proceeding, of course, most abhorrent to the feelings of the then *padre* . . ." Much to the Presbyterian congregation's horror, Clow's worshippers tried to cut pieces from the canvas of his portrait to carry as talismans. A white sheet was draped over the oil painting, Douglas reported, "which exorcised the evil spirit, and put an end to the worship of the dead."

With the secularization campaigns in Britain in the mid-nineteenth century, the tide of apostles flowing to India changed from British to American. Dr. John E. Clough was born in upstate New York. Known as the "Apostle to the Telegus," Clough spent forty years working as a Baptist minister in the district of Nellore, north of Madras. During a famine in 1878, he oversaw the mass conversion of thousands of starving villagers to Christianity, which he described in biblical tones. In the town of Ongole, Clough cut down a large tamarind tree, where a shrine to an unnamed god had stood, to become the site of his baptistery. "Just at sunrise, we began to baptize," Clough recounted in his memoir, *Social Christianity in the Orient*, published after his death. "When in the evening we put the lists together, we found that we had baptized that day 2,222. . . . In six weeks—39 days—we had baptized 8,691." Many of the new converts were Madigas, a group vilified as untouchables, seeking to escape the caste system. But Clough preferred to see them as propelled by the Holy Spirit alone. It was, Clough's wife Emma reflected, "strangely like the early centuries of the Christian era. Men marveled at it, and felt their faith refreshed."

Feeling a deep connection to Ongole, Clough determined to live out his days there, and selected a plot in the Christian cemetery for his final resting place. However, he soon realized "that almost any other place, even the ocean, would be a better place for my grave." Clough learned from fellow missionaries that certain Telegu people "were not even waiting till I was dead; they had already begun to use my name in the various rites and incantations." Stories circulated of how the invocation of the holy syllable *Clough* sent water gushing up from dry wells or brought fruitful harvests to barren fields. News of his pagan miracles left the reverend dismayed. "I can only say, I am sorry they are doing that," he wrote. He knew of another minister, "who had really loved the people as I had," whose grave had become pockmarked with the traces of idol worship—remnants of leftover sacrifices, knotted rags that carried prayers. When a high wall was built around the hapless apostle's plot, the adoration persisted outside the wall. "I had held to it, that *no one would interfere with my grave*," Clough announced, now determined *not* to die in India. He and Mrs. Clough returned to the United States, where the reverend expired on the suitably American date of Thanksgiving 1910. He was buried, according to his revised instructions, in a cemetery in the Boston suburb of Newton. Yet on Clough's gravestone, confusingly, was inscribed the following verse:

BE STILL AND KNOW THAT I AM GOD.

✦   ✦   ✦

One of the first recorded appearances of the word *Hindooism* was preceded by the word *renounce*. It was found in a 1787 letter from the East India Company director Charles Grant, who, following the death of his two daughters from smallpox, had converted to evangelical Christianity. He became convinced that the company must allow missionaries to proselytize in India. "In case of converting any of the Natives, as soon as they renounce Hindooism, they must suffer a dreadful excommunication in civil life," Grant wrote, "unless they are under the immediate protection of the English." Over the next century, *Hindooism* gradually replaced earlier terms such as *Bramanismo*, *Gentooism* (from *gentile*), and *Banian Religion*.

While *Hinduism* slowly caught on in common use, and became an object of study, other colonists noted that no such thing actually existed. "The term 'Hinduism,' like the geographical term 'India,' is an European generalization unknown to the Hindus," the Reverend Caldwell reported in 1849. "The Hindus themselves call their religions by the name of the particular deity they worship," such as Shiva or Vishnu, apart from the Shanars, Caldwell noted, who, "though they hold a different faith, have not philosophy enough to invent a distinctive name for it." Even the word *Hindu* itself was first a regional identifier, referring to the Indus River; there were Hindu Christians and Hindu Muslims alike. Whatever it was, no light was shed on anything by calling it Hinduism, Caldwell maintained, for the religions of India had few ideas or practices in common. Worse, devotees would be "indignant" at the assumption "that their own religion, and the detested heresy of their opponents, are after all one and the same."

The British regime increasingly portrayed itself as the "transcendent arbiter" in a country fractured by -isms—Hinduism, Buddhism, Sikhism, Jainism, and Islam—protecting each from the other. Yet these were first enshrined as incompatible, clearly demarcated "religions" by European scholars. (Buddhism, or *Budoism*, would first appear around 1800, in the *Lectures on History* by the French orientalist Constantin François de Chassebœuf de Volney, as an umbrella term bearing little connection to the lived ideas or self-definitions of people at the time.) The year the East India Company was founded, in 1600, a great expanse of the northern subcontinent was ruled over by the Mughal emperor Jalaluddin Akbar, who exemplified other ways of approaching the many streams of the sacred. Akbar sought to bring together all peoples, Muslim and "non-Muslim," under a new movement of *Tawhīd-i-Ilāhī*, or "the Oneness of God," and attempted, in his own daily life, to blend the rituals and practices of the empire, from Hindu vegetarianism and yoga to Buddhist tonsure, Parsi fire rituals, and even celibacy inspired by the roving Jesuit apostles. Like the British, the Mughal empire sponsored vast initiatives to collect knowledge, deploying troops of scribes to translate scriptures between Sanskrit, Arabic, Persian, Urdu, and other languages. Yet the spirit of the project was ecumenical, driven more by the aesthete's love of the sublime than what Max Müller had captured as "classify and conquer."

It was Müller's great rival in the study of Sanskrit, Sir Monier Monier-Williams, who, despite acknowledging its limitations, popularized *Hinduism* in common use. "Hinduism is like a huge irregular structure which has no single architect," Monier-Williams declared, reifying the term in his 1879 text, *Modern India and the Indians*. It was a structure soon to be flattened: "A mighty stir and upheaving of thought is shaking the foundations of ancient creeds," the evangelical professor declared; "and those not reared on the living Rock are tottering and ready to fall." He undertook the laborious task of creating what is still the authoritative Sanskrit-English dictionary, believing it would facilitate the conversion of India to Christianity. For Monier-Williams, Sanskrit, in its "exuberance and flexibility," was the best vehicle for Christian truth. He was irritated by Hindus he met who told him that, as pantheists, they were already Christian "and more." Hinduism encouraged "hideous idolatry," the scholar countered; its followers "degrade their deities to the level of sinful creatures." In his chapter on "Devil-Worship," in a book that authoritatively defined the concept of Hinduism for audiences in Europe and beyond, an uncanny figure, craving spirits and cigars, appeared once again. Monier-Williams recounted a pair of anecdotes, stripped of names or place:

> When a certain European, who was a terror to the district in which he lived, died in the South of India, the natives were in the constant habit of depositing brandy and cigars on his tomb to propitiate his spirit, which was believed to roam about the neighbourhood in a restless manner and with evil proclivities. The very same was done to secure the good offices of the philanthropic spirit of a great European sportsman who, when he was alive, delivered his district from the ravages of tigers.

Whatever this strange worship was, the vast, unstable canopy of Hinduism could encompass it. Most important of all for European theorists, the borders of Hinduism were drawn in opposition to Islam, which was, in their narrative, so fanatical in its monotheism as to reject even the divinity of Christ. On the map of the world religions, there was no place for practices such as those that coalesced around the dead lieutenant William Carden, remembered as Colonel-Shah Pir, an Irishman who died outside Ahmedabad in 1817 and was worshipped by Hindus and Muslims alike with offerings of hard-boiled eggs—unless it was as a category error of primitive peoples who couldn't keep their religions straight. Monier-Williams concluded, "The moral conquest of India remains to be achieved."

A fellow professor at Oxford, Edward Burnett Tylor, offered the brandy and cigars yet again in his landmark tomes *Primitive Culture* (1871) and *Anthropology* (1881), foundational texts of the modern study of religion. "Not long ago, in South India, where the natives are demon-worshippers, it was found that they had lately built a shrine of which the deity was the ghost of a British officer, a mighty hunter, whose votaries, mindful of his tastes in life, were laying on his altar offerings of cheroots and brandy," Tylor recounted. The deified Englishman was grist for Tylor's theory of animism, for which he would later become renowned. For Tylor, religion was defined simply as "the belief in spiritual beings," and he viewed animism as its most primitive stage.

*Animism* was the "savage belief" that the world is "swarming with intelligent and powerful disembodied beings": invisible spirits that were in the air, or lodged in animals, alive inside objects, and infesting flowers. This first phase of religion was the awareness "that *life is full of accidents which do not happen of themselves*," and formed a "rude" attempt to find the causes. Tylor argued that, over time, animism evolves through any number of "isms"—fetishism, totemism, polytheism, shamanism—to reach the highest of them all, *monotheism*, defined as a rational belief in a Supreme Being, ideally resembling Tylor's own Quaker faith. If all men had not yet reached this stage, it was because they possessed what Tylor called *survivals* or *remnants*, obsolete spiritual fancies with no place in civilized religion. It was the purpose of ethnography "to expose the remains of crude old culture which have passed into harmful superstition, and to mark these out for destruction."

In constructing his theory of animism, Tylor sifted the heaps of colonial memoirs, district gazetteers, and evangelical reports from all crevices of empire to find the patterns within the chaos of data. Every few years, his friend Max Müller would lodge appeals to the Colonial Office to initiate a more organized, centralized plan for collecting materials relating to "wild-grown" religion, although his petitions largely went unanswered. Tylor was well aware that his data was scattershot and his informants—travelers in strange lands, unable to speak the languages of the peoples they described—often unreliable. To distill a scientific theory of primitive religion from the maelstrom of sources, Tylor, like Müller, adopted the method of erasing the specific contexts in which the information was gathered, whether military cantonments or hastily erected missionary classrooms. In order to unearth "the religious systems of the lower races," Tylor wrote, "careful examination is necessary to separate the genuine developments of native theology from the effects of intercourse with civilized foreigners." For Tylor, the presence among "savage" peoples of higher ideas such as God, heaven, or good and evil, was a modern, colonial contamination, and had to be put aside. Like extracting a pure ore, his method sought to dig up the animism of what he called the lower races, "untouched." The technique would leave the beliefs of natives visible and exposed, able to be studied, and ultimately corrected through civilizing British rule.

As the authoritative professor in his field, Tylor and his theories of animism appeared in the 1889 edition of the *Encyclopedia Britannica*, in the definition of *apotheosis*, "the enrolment of a mortal among the gods." Citing Tylor, the entry stated, "In its most rudimentary form, this practice may be regarded as an offshoot of the universal belief of primitive mankind in the existence of disembodied spirits, and their continued agency in human affairs." Apotheosis constitutes "a large part of the religion of most negro nations," the *Encyclopedia* entry continued. It warned that in India, due to the widespread belief in reincarnation, deification was never considered "absolute." In a land in which souls were constantly reincarnating, "admitting of no fixity of condition," one might be God one day, and not-God the next. "Discredited saints and shrines are always passing into contempt and oblivion; new worthies are being constantly canonized," William Crooke recounted in *Popular Religion*. Nevertheless, India's ephemeral colonial gods, deities as transient as dead soldiers, had their own entries in specialized encyclopedias, and soon became part of Europe's canon of verifiable information. In the Scottish Orientalist Edward Balfour's 1885 *Cyclopædia of India and of Eastern and Southern Asia*, the entry for *Pole, Captain* ("His worship . . . consists in offering to his manes spirituous liquors and cheroots") appears directly above *Pole-Cat*, a species found in Tibet: "the length from snout to vent is 14 inches, and the tail is 7 more."

What the British Empire's theorists of religion achieved was a science that presented Christianity as the only "rational" faith, contrasted with the irrational, misfired devotions of locals left to their own devices. "The Hindu's ruling passion and preoccupation—*worship*," declared Sir Walter Lawrence in Beawar. "He will worship anything or anybody, and as he saunters through life there is much to interest him . . . beasts and birds to be observed; stones and rocks and trees to be propitiated." From railway trains to anthills, Indians appeared prepared to see all manner of things as divine. It was reported that in Sindh province, the natives of Jacobabad would prostrate themselves at the grave not only of General John Jacob, but also that of his favorite horse, Messenger, to whom they made suitably equestrian offerings. The *Central Provinces Gazetteer* recorded that the Halba tribe in Bastar worshipped "a pantheon of glorified distillers," alcohol-fermenting gods. In *Omens and Superstitions* (1912), Edgar Thurston wrote that when a British official in the district of Vizagapatam tried to tear up some old liquor licenses, a man implored him not to. It turned out that the man collected the certificates to dip into water, which he then drank as medicine; "they had brought him life for a year, and were therefore worshipped." Indians were even known to deify silence. The district gazetteer for Tanjore noted that a man who was unable to speak was worshipped as a god and "was fêted wherever he went."

Such apotheoses became an arsenal of evidence that Christianity alone grasped the cosmos with the lucidity of reason. "The Science of Religion will for the first time assign to Christianity its right place among the religions of the world," Müller declared, calling it "infinitely superior." History was truly an "unconscious progress towards Christianity," the professor surmised. With the invention of the modern concept of religion, as a private mystical germ, stripped away from any political or economic context, the worship of a deific bureaucrat or a government-issued liquor license was taken as proof of an innate backwardness. (Later, in the early 1950s, castes such as the Shanars were officially labeled by the Indian government as "Other Backward Classes.") If partitioning the world into autonomous spheres, with religion, politics, and economics existing in self-contained realms, was a key mark of the modernity envisioned by Western Europe, the persistent category errors of colonized peoples were wielded as evidence that they were neither ready to be modern nor to rule themselves.

At the birth of religion as we recognize it today, the accidental godlings were there. At the moment of conceptualizing what "Hinduism" is, those same, upright deities hovered nearby, hankering for cigars. The act of defining religion was also an act of justifying colonialism: as they generated "empirically" grounded theories about belief, scholars dictated that the East should play a game of evolutionary catch-up on the path to civilized self-rule. The anecdotes of Indians mistaking men for gods formed a picture of an irrational, spiritual East that contrasted with the rational, Christian West, and marked the East as in need of further colonial tutelage. The righteousness of empire was validated by collecting and classifying deities, by quoting, footnoting, and repeating. It was legitimized through shards of proof, the detritus of worship: feathers and bones left behind after a sacrifice, an empty glass of brandy on a tombstone. The evidence was immortalized in encyclopedias, or embalmed and displayed in a new institution, the ethnographic museum, such as the Pitt Rivers in Oxford. Like an unwitting Atlas, holding the globe on his shoulders, the deified British officer propped up an empire.

✦  ✦  ✦

What constitutes a religion, and what shall be considered worthy of that name? Is there a primeval germ that has given birth to all the great religious institutions of the world? And if so, how shall we recognise it?

In an 1877 lecture to the Anthropological Institute in London, William L. Distant, an expert on insects who also weighed in on human affairs, concluded it would be best for scholars "to discard the use of the term Religion" altogether. It was an "undefined term," he asserted, "and as such not admissible in science." The word should be left to the theologians, Distant argued, articulating a view with which many of his colleagues in the audience agreed. The term *religion* was innately incoherent, burdened with Protestant theology, and heavy with history. When a psychologist compiled a list of all the various definitions of *religion* that were circulating, he came up with over fifty, many of which contradicted one another. Some scholars suggested terms to replace *religion*, such as the more neutral, if cumbersome, "cosmographic formation." A century later, the American historian of religion J. Z. Smith would write, "Religion is solely the creation of the scholar's study." In a later essay, he observes, "'Religion' is not a native term; it is a term created by scholars for their intellectual purposes and therefore is theirs to define." To study religion is still to possess this power: to define it, transform it, discard it.

Perhaps most problematic of all was the question of what to do with God Himself, for the earliest definitions of "religion" had Him in them. "The foundation of all religion is that there is a God who has dealings with his creatures and who requires them to worship him," the entry for *religion* in Diderot's eighteenth-century *Encyclopédie* stated. To accommodate newly enshrined "world religions" such as Buddhism, later theorists eliminated God from their definitions, replacing Him with more encompassing terms. While Max Müller preferred the *Infinite*, other scholars proposed the *Sacred*, the *Transcendent*, the *Unknowable*, the *Absolute*. Yet their new definitions left behind an absence, a shadow where God had been. "We find ourselves in a discipline organized around a core that no longer exists and we cannot in good conscience reconstruct," observes the contemporary scholar Jason Josephson Storm. "In excluding God," he writes, "'religion' remains as a category structured around a hole or fissure." The act of making the Christian notion of religion into something universal left a vacancy at its center where God was once enthroned. And in trying to find meaning in the "encounter" of one religion with another, in the act of comparison, there was, inescapably, an emptiness.

It was an emptiness most keenly perceived by a novelist's eye. In E. M. Forster's novel *A Passage to India*, a group of British colonists observe the rituals of a faith that is not their own. They watch, from rowboats, an evening *puja* to Krishna taking place by the side of a lake. There are flowers and chants, an idol carried on a palanquin, and little figurines of Vishnu's avatar set afloat in baskets. Suddenly the rains arrive, pelting down upon the worshippers, putting out the torches, ruining the streamers, and washing the scene in confusion, as the colonists' boats collide. "The singing went on," Forster writes,

> Ragged edges of religion . . .
> unsatisfactory and undramatic tangles . . .

Looking back at what the colonists had seen, Forster reflects, "no man could say where was the emotional centre of it, any more than he could locate the heart of a cloud."

✦　✦　✦

Trawling back over his memories, Sir Walter Lawrence, the officer who first discovered the Colonel Dixon shrine, recalled a moment during the monsoon season in Mairwara when there was a pause in the rain. He decided to venture out by himself in the evening to go shooting. Although he had walked along this particular stretch of countryside a thousand times before, somehow everything seemed changed. Where once there was land, there was now an enormous, shimmering lake. On the surface of the water floated an empty boat, waiting with its paddle. Sir Walter got in and rowed to a promontory he spied in the distance. "On it, by the edge of the lake, sat a most lovely girl," he marveled. "I asked her what the name of the lake was, and where her village was. But she laughed and shook her head and said nothing." Sir Walter continued rowing until he reached the other bank, where he left the boat and walked home. A few days later, he decided to return. Yet when he made his way to the same spot, he found no lake, no girl, and no boat, although he could remember every detail so clearly. No one else in the district had ever heard of a lake in the area. It was all an illusion, Sir Walter concluded, a strange, unsettling occurrence that prompted him to plunge into an uneasy meditation over what, if anything, was real:

> Our life in India, our very work more or less, rests on illusion. I had the illusion, wherever I was, that I was infallible and invulnerable in my dealings with Indians. How else could I have dealt with angry mobs, with cholera-stricken masses, and with processions of religious fanatics?

In Mairwara, Sir Walter reflected, Colonel Dixon was "the hallowed name." Yet Dixon was ultimately just an avatar, one of a myriad offshoots of a single, unseen godhead: the British Empire itself. Many of the "primitive and simple Mairs," Sir Walter mused, had never even seen an English soldier, but "they saw the head of the Queen-Empress on the rupee, and worshipped it." The empire was "a power, omnipotent, all-pervading, benevolent for the most part, but capricious, a deity of many shapes and many moods." Its avatars were always changing: an endless stream of administrators, magistrates, collectors, who would serve their terms and leave, or wilt in the heat and die of fever. The Mairs would grow accustomed to "a certain shape," but then, "the agent of the deity would be transferred, and wearily and anxiously they would start again to learn the nature of the new shape and the new mood."

It was a divinity that was, like the mirage of the lake, entirely an illusion. Sir Walter had brushed against the Indian notion of *maya*, the force that casts the spell all of us are under in assuming the world as it appears to us is real. "They called us the 'Heaven-born,'" he wrote. "The idea is really make-believe—mutual make-believe. They, the millions, made us believe that we had a divine mission. We made them believe that they were right."

7

## A Tumescent Trinity

Religion must not be all damp tears and sacred texts, declared the ex-army officer Robert Baden-Powell in his 1908 manual *Scouting for Boys*, which would become the bestselling book in English for nearly fifty years, second only to the Bible. The lieutenant told of two frogs, who were leaping through an undiscovered land when they came across a bowl of milk. Looking over the edge of the bowl, both frogs fell in. "How can a fellow swim in stuff like this? It is no use trying," the first frog despaired, and he sank to the bottom and drowned. The second, how-ever, was "a more manly frog," and worked hard to stay afloat, paddling with arms and legs as forcefully as he was able. Hours later, on the verge of succumbing to exhaustion, the frog had a triumphant realization. He had churned the milk so violently with his frog legs that he found him-self standing safely on a lily pad of butter.

In the wake of a fraught war with South Africa, and with Germany gaining power in Europe, a sense of doom had begun to pervade Brit-ain. Worried that the British Empire was about to meet the fate of the Roman one—which, Baden-Powell conjectured, had fallen because "young Romans gave up soldiering and manliness altogether," becom-ing instead "wishy-washy slackers"—the former army officer founded the Boy Scouts movement. As its official handbook, *Scouting* was meant to drill values of masculinity, leadership, and perseverance into generations of young men, through adventure tales and first-aid tips, imperial geog-raphy lessons and Zulu ritual how-to. Following the fable of the frogs came a section on RELIGION, in which Baden-Powell declared: "Religion can and ought to be taught to the boy, but not in a milk-and-watery way, or in a mysterious and lugubrious manner; he is very ready to receive it if it is shown in its heroic side."

"Muscular Christianity" was the spirit of the age, a phrase coined in the London papers in 1857, the same year an uprising across India had shaken imperial officials to the core. A new sense of invincibility was needed to hold together a world that seemed on the verge of slipping away. By the mid-nineteenth century, notions of male honor and chiv-alry, tied to aristocracy and noble blood, had given way to a more ath-letic and aggressive ideal of masculinity. It championed a strong, healthy body as a steeled, reflective surface for the robust Christian morals con-tained within. It took its aesthetic from the chiseled torsos of ancient Greek boy-gods like Antinous, catapulted to Olympus long ago. Even the Holy Trinity was a tumescence of the male: in 1868, the surgeon Thomas Inman noted that the male sexual organs, unlike the female, were conspicuously three.

Against currents of religious skepticism and doubt, the new mascu-linity exalted conviction—in one's faith, and in the right to dominate and steer the globe. Christ no longer turned the other cheek. As the Scottish philosopher Thomas Carlyle asked in his famous lecture, "The Hero as Divinity," "Hero-worship, heartfelt prostrate admiration, submission, burning, boundless, for a noblest godlike Form of Man,—is not that the germ of Christianity itself?" Muscular Christianity was Protestant; it scorned the *Mariolatreia* or "Mary-worship" of Catholics. At a moment when the demands for women's suffrage were beginning to gather force, masculinity defined itself in opposition to all that was "feminine," passive, and weak, sharpening the imaginary lines between the genders to a razor edge. It ignored the proverb that warns one must never leave a knife with the blade upward, for God or an angel might step on it.

In the first edition of *Scouting*, Baden-Powell included a play for boys to perform, featuring an exemplar of Christian manliness, the celebrated brigadier John Nicholson. The tales of the colonial Englishmen, dead of germs, fevers, and the heat, who decomposed and thirsted for spirits and cigars, paled beside the legend of the formidable Irish Protestant hero. "He was a man cast in a giant mould, with massive chest, powerful limbs, and an expression ardent and commanding, with a touch of roughness; features of stern beauty," an infantry captain remarked. It was always his powerful physique that fellow officers, and later biographers, would comment upon first. As the scholar George Mosse notes, by the nineteenth century, "a messianic element was introduced into the formation of the male body, never to leave it entirely." If the female body existed solely for the sake of childbirth, the male was to serve a higher, transcendent cause. Nicholson "was of a commanding presence, some six feet two inches in height," a soldier recalled, while another estimated him at six foot four. He had "a colorless face, over which no smile ever passed," and a heavy beard. With "strong hands" and "cool brains," in the words of one hagiographer, Nicholson was the very embodiment of the "sceptered race." An icon of muscular Christianity and British character, Nicholson came to epitomize the modern notion of masculinity that arose alongside a new national consciousness. It was a manhood that might, at its most perfected, be mistaken for godhood.

In Baden-Powell's play, the lucky boy chosen to be Nicholson is surrounded by "adoring" Indian soldiers, who have taken off their shoes in his presence as a sign of respect. One Indian refuses, a mutinous chief named Mehtab Singh. The scout playing him was to wear blackface— "*Dark rouge, not black*"—and a "*Big turban, coloured dressing-gown and girdle, white socks, and black shoes.*" If the British were the epitome of masculinity, the scene taught that the people they colonized were effeminate, degenerate, and childlike—less than "real men." Nicholson chastises Singh, and in the stage directions, the Indian's humiliation as he takes off his shoes is drawn out in an excruciatingly slow step-by-step. "A Briton, even though alone among a thousand of your kind, shall be respected," the boy playing Nicholson thunders, "though it brought about his death. That's how we hold the world." A few pages later, a diagram depicts a series of disembodied, increasingly muscular white legs clad in sandals and socks, to show the budding Boy Scout how calf muscles are made.

A religion, the concept with a hole at its center, might coalesce around anything, even a blistered, ill-tempered brigadier. Born in Dublin in 1821 into an evangelical Protestant family, the young major John Nicholson began his military career fighting in the British invasion of Afghanistan of 1839, also known as the "Disaster," and was imprisoned in Kabul for several months. After his release, he went to search for his younger brother, who had enrolled with him as a cadet, and found his body in the Khyber Pass; he had been grotesquely tortured, castrated, and chopped into pieces. Those who knew Nicholson heard him say he could never transcend the immense hatred he felt for the entire subcontinent. Nonetheless, he remained there, fighting in the Second Anglo-Sikh War and rising to the position of deputy commissioner of Peshawar, and then Rawalpindi in the Punjab. As their new ruler, Nicholson was welcomed, according to one of his early biographers, Lionel Trotter, by the mass of his Sikh subjects, "who had already learned to note the contrast between a grinding Sikh tyranny and the strong yet upright, even-handed sway of an English sahib." For his bravery in the war, Nicholson was heaped with honors, among them one that even the British Crown "had not the power to confer," another hagiographer noted: "the unique distinction of deification by his enemies."

The story, which has been eagerly retold by British war historians, novelists, and the BBC, went that Nicholson found himself surrounded by a devout band of 250 Sikh sepoys who followed him everywhere he was stationed, took no government salary, and recognized no authority but his own. The Sikhs' devotion, it was soon determined, was more than mere military loyalty. "Their religion admits of repeated incarnations, and this noble, sad-faced man was thought by them to be their god veiled in human flesh," the soldier Reginald Wilberforce recounted in his memoirs, published in 1894. Their adoration was seen as a particularly notable testament to Nicholson's power, for the British supposed that, among India's supposedly effeminate peoples, the men hailing from the Punjab were the most "martial race." On the evenings he spent encamped with the Sikh column, the captivated sepoys would venture inside Nicholson's tent. "They seated themselves on the ground and fixed their eyes upon the object of their adoration," Wilberforce related. Their eyes watched god as he shuffled paperwork and ignored them. Every now and then, a sepoy, murmuring prayers, would prostrate himself at Nicholson's feet, overcome with "feelings he could not control."

In his 1917 treatise *The Idea of the Holy*, German theologian Rudolf Otto attempted to taxonomize such human emotions in the presence of the divine. He described the feeling of drowning in your own nothingness, in face of a supreme being "of some kind," the creeping sense that your fate was entirely dependent on the whims and character of this absolute might. Otto named this emotion *creature-feeling*. To be understood, it had to be experienced firsthand, the philosopher noted.

Not long after the Sikh apotheosis, the worship of Nicholson entered "a still more remarkable phase," Trotter recorded. In 1849, a wandering Hindu ascetic from the Gosain sect declared the deputy commissioner to be an avatar of Brahma. He "began to preach at Hasan Abdal the worship of this new god *Nikalsain*"; other Gosains embraced the new creed, and the religion of Nikalsain "became a historical fact." The Nikalsainis would be spotted in swaying processions, chanting hymns to the deity, wearing robes "the color of faded leaves." Nicholson, according to the historian Charles Allen—who happened also to be his descendant— "was revolted and enormously irritated by the whole business." The chief Nikalsaini *faqir*, or ascetic, "after experiencing several rebuffs from his adopted deity, determined to try his luck with the Deity's old comrade," as James Abbott, the comrade in question, recalled. Abbott would hear the "Nicholsynie Priest" crouched in front of his bungalow, chanting prayers "with all the power of his lungs," so precisely at daybreak that Abbott theorized Nicholson must be a sun god. At first, Abbott was amused that his friend's name had been enrolled "upon the scroll of the Hindoo Olympus." Yet soon he tired of the cacophony that roused him too early in the dawn. Driven away by Abbott, the *faqir* returned to Nikalsain, who kicked him into the dirt.

"'Dread' becomes worship," Rudolf Otto wrote; "out of a confusion of inchoate emotions and bewildered palpitations of feeling grows '*religio*', and out of 'shudder' a holy awe." For Otto, there is "an almost gristly horror," a trembling and fear, at the heart of all religion, the feeling "of standing aghast," something beyond ordinary fear—a terror that is, ultimately, God's own. *I will send out my fear before thee*, the Lord Himself says to his followers in Exodus 23:27.

Each time Nicholson caught his worshippers bent over in prayer, or chanting hymns, the stern, bearded deity unfurled his riding whip. "The penalty never varied," wrote Wilberforce: "three dozen lashes with the cat-o'-nine tails on the bare back." Nikalsain would imprison them in chains, thrash them, and rain curses and blows upon them, yet, Trotter wrote, "they took their punishment like martyrs." Anglican interpretations painted the Nikalsainis in the image of Catholic penitents, or Old Testament Jews submitting to Yahweh's rage. "Their only persecutor was the divinity whom they adored," Trotter recounted. The worshippers, whether Hindu or Sikh, "rejoiced in the punishment," according to Wilberforce, "for they used to say: 'Our god knew that we had been doing wrong, and therefore punished us.'" The violence was purifying. Their torments redeemed them of their sinfulness, their fallenness, and so they "appreciated," as another of Nicholson's many biographers wrote, "their god's righteous chastisement."

In styling Nikalsain as a wrathful god, his storytellers edited out any responsibility or wrongdoing on the part of the aggressive brigadier. If Indian devotion to Nikalsain was fanatical, the riding crop was framed as the rational response, a way of instilling British civility and order. In this perverse view, Nikalsain's whippings, done for the Indians' own good, were a kind of love too. As the early Christian theologian Lactantius declared, "a God who cannot be angry cannot love." One account held that some of Nicholson's fellow administrators found the entire situation uncomfortable, and tried to negotiate: Nicholson would stop beating his worshippers on the condition that they transfer their adoration to a hapless officer named John Becher. But it was to no avail; the Nikalsaini faith allegedly grew as new devotees flocked to the raging god.

Nicholson was, a fellow officer wrote, "the very incarnation of violence"; he performed it as a spectacle. It was reported that with a single stroke of his sword, Nicholson once sliced a man cleanly in two. He kept a severed head on his desk, though not for literary inspiration, as he disliked writing. Keen to punish Indians whom he suspected of rebellion, in one of his few correspondences, Nicholson appealed to higher British authorities for "a Bill for flaying alive, impalement. . . . The idea of simply hanging the perpetrators of such atrocities is maddening." In another rare missive, Nicholson noted, "When an Empire is at stake, women and children cease to be of any consideration whatever." Yet it was said that when a would-be assassin burst into the cantonment and demanded to know, "Where is Nicholson?" his Indian attendants replied, "We are all Nikal Seyn here." It was not just a means to protect him—for to worship Nicholson, as the British schoolboy would learn, was in some sense *to become him*, imbued with his might. If the empire aimed to strike its subjects with abjection, inert before its power, to become Nikal Seyn was to appropriate this force for themselves. By partaking in His divinity, they were no longer simply creatures, but creators of fear.

✦ ✦ ✦

On September 14, 1857, at the height of the Indian Mutiny, when sepoys and civilians alike across the subcontinent rose up against their oppressors, British troops undertook a destruction of Delhi so complete that the poet Ghalib would write, "there was once a city of that name." Under siege for weeks, the citizens of Delhi were dying of starvation when British troops invaded the city, led by none other than John Nicholson. The night before the attack, at the British camp, a priest led a final church service and read from the letter of Saint Paul to Timothy. *I am ready to be offered*, it went, from the Greek verb σπένδομαι: *I am made a libation*, poured out like a sacrificial drink. Nicholson led the charge at sunrise, and early on was shot below the armpit. For eight days, he lay dying inside a hospital tent, occasionally firing bullets through the curtains to encourage the people outside to cease their irritating chatter. He stayed alive long enough to be certain the siege had been a success by his own measure, with thousands slaughtered, the last Mughal ruler, Bahadur Shah, exiled from his palace, and huge amounts of Indian wealth seized. On September 22, the god died of his wounds and was buried outside Delhi's Kashmere Gate.

The accounts of Nicholson's funeral are conflicting. While some reported it was a small and "sober" affair, others related that, after the coffin was lowered into the earth, the brigadier's formidable Sikh sepoys gave themselves over to floods of tears. "Throwing themselves on the ground, they sobbed and wept as if their very hearts were breaking," Wilberforce recalled. They had believed that no sword or bullet could harm the immortal brigadier. Now, in their grief, "they threw their traditions of manhood to the winds, and over John Nicholson's grave poured out the flood of their pent-back love." The news was carried to the Nikalsaini *faqirs*, who also had to face the difficult challenge of what to do when the living god is dead. Several reportedly committed suicide. According to the commissioner of Peshawar, Sir Donald Macnabb, one Nikalsaini proclaimed, "There was no gain from living in a world that no longer held Nikalsain," before slitting his throat. Another dug his own grave and was found dead inside it. But a third Nikalsaini leader, Wilberforce noted, chose instead to address his congregation, saying: "Nickelseyn always said that he was a man like as we are, and that he worshipped a God whom we could not see, but who was always near us." If they hoped to please him, and to see him again "in a future state," he went on, "let us learn to worship Nickelseyn's God." The remaining Nikalsainis traveled to Peshawar, where they were baptized.

Each new theogony poses the question: what did His mother think? The widowed Mrs. Clara Nicholson had four sons who served as East India Company officers, all of whom died on the subcontinent. According to Trotter, John's apotheosis was a source of solace to her as she grieved his death. "Her heart was gladdened by such a revelation of her dead son's influence for good," he wrote. Yet Mrs. Nicholson, who lived in Lisburn, in Northern Ireland, stopped short of embracing her role as the mother of a god, for her son's divinity did not sit easily with her evangelical faith. When she commissioned a monument for him, she deemed it best to avoid idol-like images, and had the artist create a frieze depicting an action scene instead. In the decade after John's death, several British officers told of "a Punjabi ballad" heard in the streets of Delhi, which sang of how the queen herself wept in sympathy with John's mother. The viceroy of India, Sir John Lawrence, took it upon himself to make sure Mrs. Nicholson was forwarded a copy of the translation, thinking it would cheer her:

> Oh, Nicholson was bravest brave that English Chief could be;
> My brother, such a gallant man seems very God to me.

✦  ✦  ✦

He became an answer to the question: How should a man be? Two years
after his death, Nicholson was canonized in Samuel Smiles's bestselling treatise *Self-Help*, hailed as the foundational text of the self-help genre. The Scottish reformer preached a gospel of industry, self-improvement, and upward
mobility to a captive Victorian audience that bought copies by the hundreds of thousands. *Self-Help* championed a capitalist work ethic, conveyed
in pithy if inaccurate maxims such as, "Accident does very little towards the
production of any great result in life." Translated into many languages, the
book impressed even the Khedive of Egypt, who had the sayings of *Smeelis*
carved onto his palace walls, and claimed to prefer it to the Qur'an. The
dead brigadier made his appearance in chapter 8, "Energy and Courage,"
wherein Smiles declared, "John Nicolson was one of the finest, manliest,
and noblest of men." He was "a tower of strength," the apex of masculinity;
his energy was "titanic," and "in whatever capacity he acted he was great."
A "nucleus of national character," Nicholson could endure hours beneath
the burning Indian sun. In the highest testament to his greatness, Smiles
recounted, "A brotherhood of fakeers—borne away by their enthusiastic
admiration of the man—even began the worship of Nikkil Seyn. He had
some of them punished for their folly, but they continued their worship."
To the question of how a person should shape himself, *Self-Help* seemed to
say: act like a man who might be mistaken for a god.

For wasn't it the case that British divinity worked in everyone's favor?
Wouldn't beatitude trickle down from the overlords onto the flock? This
was the message of several tales by Rudyard Kipling, the storyteller who,
for generations of young readers, painted the Orient as a kind of fantasy
training ground where boys went to become "real men." Nicholson himself appeared in several stories and inspired more; for Kipling's fictional
boy-heroes, it is a rite of passage to be unwittingly taken for a god, as if
the transition from boy to manhood entailed a stop on Mount Olympus
along the way. In "The Tomb of His Ancestors" (1897), Kipling tells of
young John Chinn, sent to serve as an officer among the Bhils, the very
same "pre-Aryan" jungle tribe that had once apotheosized his grandfather. When the young Chinn arrives at the Bhil camp, those who knew

his grandfather, among them the devoted servant "Old Bukta," are stunned at the resemblance. "Bukta propounded a theory which to a white mind would have seemed raving insanity," writes Kipling, but the Bhils consider it quite sensible, and soon young Chinn finds himself caught up in a wild, orgiastic *puja* to himself and lavished with offerings, "not all of them seemly."

In Kipling's tale, young Chinn is irritated at first by his godhood and by all the extra tasks it means he must perform. The Bhils lay their conflicts before him, and ask him to determine punishments for sundry crimes. When Chinn protests that he is a soldier and not a lawyer, Bukta replies with biblical gravitas: "*Thou art their law.*" Soon enough, the young Englishman learns to take on the divine mantle of authority that, in Kipling's telling, is rightly his. He begins to act godlike; his way of speaking changes as he issues commandments. His words, as if they were *Vedas* or Qur'an, are carried by messengers, careful never to alter a single syllable. Chinn takes up his white man's burden, which Kipling enshrined in his 1899 poem, published in the final year of a century in which there was not a single day in which Britain wasn't at war. The English boy uses his authority as a god to impose civility and modern medicine upon the Bhils. Frightened of needles, the Bhils were famous for slaying the vaccinators who made their rounds. Chinn commands the Bhils not only to get the shots, but to treasure the scars as marks of god's favor. "*Ye did not believe; and so came I here to save you, first from Small-pox, next from a great folly of fear,*" Chinn godsplains. With the Bhil population now immunized, British godhood—the moral of the story seems to say—ultimately works for the greater good.

Over a century later, Kipling is still read and invoked, conjuring an invincible past that, if it had existed at all, is now irrevocably lost. For some, it has proved difficult to stop reciting Kipling. In 2017, Boris Johnson struck a bell in a temple in Yangon and intoned,

*The temple bells they say, Come you back, you British soldier.*

✦ ✦ ✦

In the spirit of science, John Nicholson's biographers sought to compare and contrast the several species of Nikalsain-worship. It was problematic,

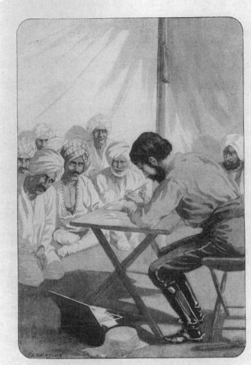

"THEY SEATED THEMSELVES AND FIXED THEIR EYES
UPON THE OBJECT OF THEIR ADORATION."

for Nikalsainism seemed to cut across the divisions of "religions" at the same mid-nineteenth-century moment that they were becoming solidified: *Hinduism, Sikhism*—James Abbott noted there were even "Muhammadan Races" "crouching" at the divine Nicholson's feet. "Whereas the Sikhs were never able to reconcile Nicholson's religion with their own, which prevented their absolute recognition of his godhead," one scholar theologized, "the Nikalseyn fakirs did not bother much about his beliefs, contenting themselves with a belief in him." The sect continued to exist after the Irish brigadier's death, undergoing a series of transformations over the following decades in the Hazara region of what is now Pakistan. In Abbottabad, the city founded by Abbott, and later the site of Osama bin Laden's capture and extrajudicial killing, Nicholson's divinity took on new forms. Among a small, mystic-minded segment of the Shia Muslim community, Nicholson was seen as a chivalric incarnation of the sainted Imam Hussayn, the martyred grandson of the Prophet

Muhammad. As the Sufi shaykh and scholar Omer Tarin recorded, the words *Nicholson/Nikalsayn* converged with *Hussayn* and *Nikka-Sain*, meaning "a smaller or lesser Hussayn."

"In time, stories relating to Nicholson's fairness, justice, and stern retribution merged with Islamic stories and concepts," Tarin related, along with the colonial concepts of masculinity that the British soldier embodied. As Nikkasayn, or little Hussayn, he was "no longer a Hindu deity," but "a sort of folk hero, a semi-legendary Islamic personality—not quite divine, but still mystical, possessed of superhuman qualities." With an Islamic revival and the rise of education that strove to banish local "superstitions," the Nikkasayn sect dwindled in numbers, but did not completely die out. It was preserved into the twenty-first century by at least one family, who lived as the caretakers of a quiet, crumbling Christian graveyard on the site of the old military cantonment in Abbottabad. In the 1990s, Tarin interviewed Ali Akbar, who worked as the cemetery's chowkidar, or watchman, a position his family had held for three generations. Though outsiders assumed the impoverished family must be Christian, Ali Akbar's grandfather had been a Nikkasayni, and passed down its myths and tenets. Yet Ali was the last in his family to hold on to such ideas, for his son converted to orthodox Sunni Islam and eschewed all mention of "Nikkasayn."

Whatever it was that coalesced around the irate brigadier, it breached the borders of the world religions, hinting at how artificial, and porous, these distinctions are. One might call the muscular Christian-Hindu-Sikh deity and Muslim saint an instance of *syncretism*, defined as the blending of elements of one religion with another. Like "religion," the notion of syncretism had its roots in intra-Christian polemic, in the conflicts between the Protestant faith of Luther and the Reformed version dictated by Calvin. From the Greek, meaning a "joining of Cretans," who were famous for their quarrelling, *syncretism* became a pejorative conveying the mixing of incompatible things. It was adopted by missionaries to describe peoples that had converted to Christianity but still retained traces of their old, exotic faith. *Syncretism* would take on a more positive valence in contemporary efforts to study how people make religions their own, embracing a plurality of traditions in often idiosyncratic ways. Yet the term rests on the pernicious assumption that religions actually exist in pure, self-contained forms, such that they can be mixed at all, and which suggests there are more or less "true" versions of each one. While the idea of a Hindu-Muslim sect might seem a glaring contradiction, "mixed" practices in India, later sifted out as Hindu or Muslim, were common prior to the watertight world religions. The convergence around Nikalsain revealed the very inventedness of the concept. In an eroding cemetery in Abbottabad, Nikalsainism stalked the margins of religions and then vanished among the graves.

✦  ✦  ✦

Where others had gazed upward to the heavens, the psychoanalyst looked inward, and concluded that "the root of every form of religion" is, at base, "a longing for the father." In *Totem and Taboo*, published a year before the First World War broke out, Sigmund Freud drew upon Müller's science, Darwin's evolution, and Tylor's animism in order to understand the dank recesses of the human psyche. The doctor, inspired by the army of fetishes on his desk, drew on the vast storehouse of "primitive" beliefs collected by missionaries, colonial officers, and travelers to forge the language of psychoanalysis. He was untroubled by his own footnote warning that the data was unreliable, collected as it had been across language barriers and interpreted by scholars at an even further remove. Among his sources, Freud leaned heavily on the Scottish anthropologist James Frazer, who in 1890 published the first volumes of *The Golden Bough*, his compendium of religious beliefs and practices that sought to reveal how Christianity was derived from ancient, primal streams of myth. It was, Freud wrote, a gold mine "of valuable facts and opinions."

The fourth volume, *The Dying God*, told of deities, from Osiris to Quetzalcoatl, who die and resurrect, and of sacred kings killed and deified, in ritual cycles that parallel the harvest seasons. In his chapter "Eating the God," Frazer wrote how, anticipating the Eucharist, the Aztecs would, in a "solemn communion," kill and devour their deity and refuse to eat any other food: "They feared no doubt to defile the portion of God in their stomachs by contact with common things." In his section "On Incarnation," Frazer focused on India. "Nowhere has the divine grace been poured out in a more liberal measure on all classes of society," he wrote, and told of the Toda tribe in the hills of Tamil Nadu that worshipped the milkman as god. Frazer continued:

> To this day in India all living persons remarkable for great strength or valor or for supposed miraculous powers run the risk of being worshipped as gods. Thus a sect in the Punjab worshipped a deity whom they called Nikkal Sen. This Nikkal Sen was no other than the redoubted General Nicholson, and nothing that the general could do or say damped the ardor of his adorers. The more he punished them, the greater grew the religious awe with which they worshipped him.

Clipping myths and branches from *The Golden Bough*, Freud theorized that at the heart of religion was "emotional ambivalence"—the simultaneous feeling of love and hate toward the same object, of which the Nikalsainis seemed to present a classic case. *They named him Nikal Seyn*, the American poet Louis O. Coxe would write in a 1966 poem. *And worshipped him, a straight-out kind of faith / Mixing hate and love.*

Building upon Frazer's dying god, in *Totem and Taboo* the doctor created a theology entirely of his own. Deep in the hunter-gatherer past, religion was born out of the primal love and hate for a father felt by his own sons, who killed and deified him. "They hated their father, who presented such a formidable obstacle to their craving for power and their sexual desires; but they loved and admired him too," and wanted to *be* him, Freud wrote, recalling what he had earlier christened "the Oedipus Complex." After the band of brothers slew their father, remorse soon set in. Magnified by their guilt, "the dead father became stronger than the living one had been." In turning their father into God, they brought about the reorganization of primitive society itself. "God Himself had become so far exalted above mankind that He could only be approached through an intermediary—the priest. At the same time divine kings made their appearance in the social structure and introduced the patriarchal system into the state," Freud wrote. "Society was now based on complicity in the common crime." Out of the corpse of the slain father rose a god, and from the root of all love and hate grew the patriarchy.

Freud was rather dismissive about making room for "mother-goddesses" in his new myth. "I cannot suggest at what point in this process of development a place is to be found for the great mother-goddesses, who may perhaps in general have preceded the father-gods," he wrote. There may have existed some primordial fertility goddesses; in Austria, the voluptuous Venus of Willendorf had been dug up only a few years earlier, her grandeur preserved intact. Nonetheless, in the wake of the great patricide, "with the introduction of father-deities, a father-less society gradually changed into one organized on a patriarchal basis." Ever since, the cycle of "religious craving" has, Freud argued, continued through the generations, "the persistence of an unappeased longing for the father." So it was that Freud, a self-proclaimed atheist, made divinity an ever more patriarchal space. Not only the mother-goddess, but also the sister deity and divine wife were denied a place in heaven or on earth. "The psychoanalysis of individual human beings," Freud wrote, "teaches us with quite special insistence that the god of each of them is formed in the likeness of his father, that his personal relation to God depends on his relation to his father in the flesh and oscillates and changes along with that relation."

Of all the world religions, Christianity offered the "most undisguised" acknowledgment of "the guilty primeval deed," Freud wrote. The murder of the father was the true original sin for which Christ would atone. Ever since Jesus replaced his father as the new God, the weekly Eucharist has served as "a fresh elimination of the father," Freud supposed, the crime reenacted with wine and bread. The guilty deed was embedded in Juda-ism too: in *Moses and Monotheism*, Freud theorized that Moses himself had been murdered and deified by his sons and followers. Published in 1939, a year after Freud moved from Vienna to London to escape the Nazi regime, the book coincided with the apex of the cult of militarized masculinity. The Reich's veneration of the supreme Aryan man, modeled after chiseled Greek idols, stood counter to the trope of the effeminate and scholarly Jew, with his soft hands and delicate fingers, only fit to turn pages filled with prayers. Haunted by a childhood memory in which he recalled seeing his own father humiliated as a Jew, Freud turned to myth as a weapon of defense. All men, he argued, have the innate, violent impulse to kill their fathers and turn them into gods. Masculinity, like divinity, describes an embodiment of power, and in the deification of Moses, Freud sought to wrest it back for himself and his fellow Jews.

Delving into the psychoanalytic depths of Nicholson's story, new generations of biographers influenced by Freud began to see the sadistic brigadier as the epitome of repressed desire. There was a danger, of which Baden-Powell was keenly aware, that adulation of the perfect male body could easily slide into homoeroticism, transforming idealized manhood into its "degenerate" countertype. In the late nineteenth century, what had previously been regarded only as erotic proclivities and practices became reified into "sexualities," thought to express some innate identity—much in the same way that sacred practices, rituals, and tenets were consolidated into distinct world religions. Along with modern ideals of masculinity, new laws were brought into effect in Britain, and later imposed by the Raj in India, that criminalized "homosexuals," a word that first appeared in English only in 1891. While earlier hagiographers had occasionally noted Nicholson's lack of interest in "the fairer sex," his mid-twentieth-century biographers found Nicholson's "homosexuality"—a term that didn't even exist when he was alive—a fruitful avenue of investigation.

Using the insights of psychoanalysis, historians now explained Nicholson's divine rage as the eruption of sexual repression. "Nicholson was a homosexual, a repressed homosexual, disgusted by his own inclination and one who translated his disgust into a violence manic in its manifestation," Michael Edwardes claimed in a 1969 study. Nicholson was "tortured by homosexual desires that shamed and horrified him," wrote the English author Christopher Hibbert. In 1981, a retired US Army doctor, Major-General Frank M. Richardson, included Nicholson in his *Mars Without Venus: A Study of Some Homosexual Generals*, a manual that aimed to help young American soldiers correct their "deviation" for the sake of "happiness." Nicholson was "well to the right of center on the Kinsey scale." To his homosexuality "was added sadomasochism, as is often the case," the general wrote, in a book that expressed gratitude to the "common sense" of his wife several more times than was necessary.

"No doubt his dedication to soldiering was fired by sublimation of his repressed sexual feelings," Richardson theorized; Nicholson was a fine example "of the contribution which sublimation of sexual instincts made to our Empire-building activities." To see Nicholson's violence as the product of his private psychosexual drama was to justify it and explain it away, once again erasing the context—of the imperialism that enabled and rewarded his rage. The story became just one man-god's struggle against himself.

◆  ◆  ◆

*So I will make*
*In uttermost truth a new god, since the old*
*Are dead, or drunk with wine, and soma-juice*

These were the words of a man before he killed and deified his own sister, as imagined by Aleister Crowley in his 1903 play *The God-Eater*. Sometimes described as the wickedest man on earth, the English occultist and poet-prophet had read too much of the science of religion. He had overdosed on Max Müller, gorged on Edward Burnett Tylor and most of all James Frazer's *Golden Bough*, of which the chapter "Killing the God" was his favorite. Born into a Christian family in Warwickshire, of the Plymouth Brethren ilk, Crowley was sent to an evangelical boarding school at the tender age of eight. For Crowley, reading the classics of comparative religion became a means of revolt against his fundamentalist childhood, and an inspiration for the black magic for which he later became infamous. If the science of religion had propped up the British Empire's civilizing mission across the earth, perhaps it also held keys to the total subversion of Britain's social and spiritual conventions, which Crowley viewed as entirely parochial. If British boys were raised to aspire to accidental godhood in the colonies, perhaps they could create and worship sacrilegious new gods too.

In the summer of 1916, Crowley went into occultation in the forests of New Hampshire. He hid inside a cottage by the side of a placid lake, where he would fall into reveries contemplating the night sky he called "Nothingness with twinkles." One evening, he decided to enact a ritual that would serve as an ending to the entire era of Christian hegemony, using Frazer's *Golden Bough* as his spell-book. It was "a Magical Operation to banish the 'Dying God,'" he later wrote in *The Confessions of Aleister Crowley: An Autohagiography*. In the shadows of a New England night, the magician hunted in silence until he caught a frog, and locked it inside a chest. Like a subversive *Scouting* manual or a dark *Self-Help*, Crowley reprinted his steps as a how-to:

> Dawn being come, thou shalt approach the chest with an offering of gold, and if available, of frankincense and of myrrh.

> Thou shalt then release the frog . . . with many acts of homage and place it in apparent liberty. He may, for example, be placed on a quilt of many colours . . .

> Now take a vessel of water and approach the frog, saying: *In the Name of the Father + and of the Son + and of the Holy Ghost +* (here sprinkle water on its head) *I baptize thee, O creature of frogs, with water, by the name of Jesus of Nazareth.*

Crowley recorded that he spent the day worshipping the frog and asking it to perform miracles, which were duly fulfilled. When night fell again, he arrested the amphibian, accused him of sedition, and put him on trial. "Lo, Jesus of Nazareth, how thou art taken in my snare. All my life long thou hast plagued me and affronted me. In thy name—with all other free souls in Christendom—I have been tortured in my boyhood . . . Thine hour is come." Crowley stabbed the frog with something pointed and sharp. As the professor of religion E. D. Starbuck remarked in 1899, "Theology takes the adolescent tendencies and builds upon them."

Constructing a miniature cross, Crowley crucified the creature that Baden-Powell had once deployed to teach imperial fortitude in his fable of the manly frog. Crowley sacrificed the amphibian and dismembered it. And as if, in a blasphemous Eucharist, he could bring about an end to the muscular Christian age, with its sinews of the spirit, its smug supremacy and civilizing raids, as if he could bring about redemption for its wars and cadet-heroes and divisive myths, the magician sautéed the frog's legs and ate them.

8

———

# Passage

In 1833, a brigade of eighty Europeans set sail for Egypt on an unlikely quest: to locate the female messiah. Ever since Eve had succumbed to the serpent's temptation—*Ye shall be as gods*—it had become the lot of woman that no one would ever mistake her for one. She didn't look like a god: the lines in Genesis suggest that only Adam was created in *Imago Dei*, provoking millennia of debate among theologians as to the extent to which women could share in god-likeness. At the Temple in Jerusalem, even the animals worthy of sacrifice were male: young bulls, rams, he-goats. When in 1547 Guillaume Postel, a French linguist, announced he had found the female messiah—an Italian woman named Joanna who worked as a nurse in a Venice hospital—he was swiftly declared insane.

Christ had descended into Joanna, he believed, precisely because she was a woman: she was something other than the powers that be, and thus better suited to criticize them. Postel called her the New Eve. After preaching the divinity of Joanna for several years, Postel was imprisoned for heresy. Some claimed he was merely in love, or that Joanna was a witch.

There was little likelihood that anyone was going to accidentally stumble upon a female messiah—it would require a deliberate quest to locate her. In Paris, a group of Saint-Simonians, followers of the late French utopian industrialist Claude-Henri de Saint-Simon, energetically debated the question of where she might be found. Some said she lived in the Himalayas, others that she resided in the new world of the United States. According to the sect's romantic ideologue, Barthélemy Prosper Enfantin, she was most probably in Egypt, "the nuptial bed of East and West"—the fertile basin where a carnal, feminine Orient met a rational, masculine Occident. Enfantin liked to call himself "the Father," or occasionally the *Père Suprême*. At meetings at their temple east of Paris, he would leave the chair next to him empty, waiting to be filled by the Mother—*la femme messie*, the next chosen vessel of an androgynous God. Condemning marriage as tyranny, Enfantin strove to subvert the norms of bourgeois family life emerging across Europe, and soon found himself imprisoned for endangering public morality. According to Enfantin, *la femme messie* would formulate a new moral code, in which the sexes would live in sacrosanct equality. But until she was located, no changes could be made to the rights of women, in society at large or within his sect. Until they found Her, the women who joined the expedition had no say in anything at all.

Enfantin, like many of the Saint-Simonians, had studied engineering at the École Polytechnique, and arriving in Egypt, pursued a double obsession. On their quest to find, and fertilize, *la femme messie*—many supposed they were looking for "a Jewess"—the Saint-Simonians had also set their sights on constructing a new route between Europe and the Orient, rendering their project both sacred and scientific. They focused "on 'piercing' a canal through the thin 'membrane' of virgin desert, which alone blocked the consummation of East-West commerce," as the historian James Billington wrote. The canal was to be "very long and deep." It would vastly cut down the time it took to reach India, initiating a global age that would link distant civilizations. In Egypt, the engineers drew up detailed blueprints. As Enfantin wrote years earlier from prison, in a feverish poem:

> *SUEZ*
> *Is the focus of our Life*
> *This will show the world*
> *That we are*
> *Male*

Three years later, the Mother was nowhere to be found, many of the Saint-Simonians had caught the plague and died, and the mission was declared a disaster. Enfantin went into the more opportune business of railroad management. Nonetheless, through the failed search for the female messiah, an eccentric group of pilgrim-engineers had initiated the first stages of what Walt Whitman would celebrate as the "Passage to India," the Suez Canal. When it opened in 1869, it unleashed the race for Europe to colonize the rest of the East, ushering in the high imperialist age.

*O we can wait no longer!* Whitman exclaimed, as he circumnavigated the globe in his poem. He set sail on waves of ecstasy, over seas *inlaid with eloquent, gentle wires*, and through Suez, in a hymn to the engineers. *The earth to be spann'd, connected by net-work*, the poet intoned. Whitman, who was familiar with Saint-Simonian ideas, exalted the canal and the rolling waves of progress not only as the product of modern science but also as inseparably intertwined with the work that myths and legends do, although he made no reference to the female messiah that had inspired Suez. Modernity was made by sea captains and architects, and it was also the creation of "the elder religions," *ye aged fierce enigmas*, in a poem that linked the material and the spiritual, and captured the god in the machine. Aboard a steamship heading East, Whitman cruised on a metaphysical ascent. *Bathe me O God in thee*, he beseeches, as he gets closer and closer to the divine.

✦ ✦ ✦

Sailing through the passage and on to India, British colonizers found an ecology teeming with what they translated, from the many Indian languages, as "goddesses"—not quite gods, something less. From the sanguinary Kali, garlanded with skulls, to the bejeweled Lakshmi, to what Sir Arthur Lyall called "the fresh blood . . . the swarm of earth-born deifications," theorists of Hinduism attempted to list them. Very occasionally, colonial officers and missionaries noted the worship, at tomb shrines, of British women, most of whom had died in the treacherous passage of childbirth—the bequest of Eve for eating the fruit. There was a certain Mrs. Clare Watson, whose grave in the Bhandara region of the Central Provinces was "smeared with turmeric and lime," though nothing else about her was known. Near the altar to Captain Pole in Travancore, there was said to be a shrine to the nameless "wife of a certain German missionary," who, a villager explained, had been "a most charitable lady and so is very dangerous now."

There was the wife of an administrator in the Cuddapah district of Madras, who died in premature labor inside a police station. She became a demon with backward-facing feet; no one could remember her name. Another officer's wife, Mary Rebecca Weston, died in childbirth in 1909 and was buried in a cemetery in Dagshai near Shimla. Her husband erected a white marble tombstone, depicting mother and child watched over by an angel. When the news spread that pieces of her grave were imbued with the power to bless women with sons, Mary's monument began to shrink as it was chipped away.

The stories are scarce; what the British chose to record about their deified wives is much less detailed than what they wrote about their male counterparts—the myriad bureaucrats, dead but still heroically panting for cigars. Many of the imperial chroniclers were emissaries of a Christianity deeply uncomfortable with the idea that God could arrive on earth in the belly of a woman—let alone be a woman Herself. Her domain was supposed to be that of piety, cloistered in the home: the worshipper and not the worshipped.

The Englishwoman best known for being unwittingly hailed as

divine was, as it were, only a fiction. She was the aging mother of Ronny Heaslop, the colonial magistrate in E. M. Forster's novel *A Passage to India*. After visiting him in Chandrapore, Mrs. Moore dies on board the ship heading home to England; somewhere around Suez, in the transition between Europe and Asia, the matronly ghost is "shaken off." At the same time, in the Indian village she had only recently left, Mrs. Moore undergoes an apotheosis, redeeming, if only in the novel, Enfantin's quest. She is hailed as the messiah, defending an Indian falsely accused of assaulting a white woman in the Marabar Caves. Though Ronny decides to ship his mother home, at Aziz's trial Mrs. Moore's sacred name "burst on the court like a whirlwind" and villagers chant it in the streets. Soon tomb shrines spring up, with offerings befitting a British mum—"earthenware saucers and so on." Ronny, whose own religion is of the "sterilized Public School brand," is appalled. "It was revolting to hear his mother travestied into Esmiss Esmoor, a Hindu goddess," Forster writes.

> *Esmiss Esmoor*
> *Esmiss Esmoor*
> *Esmiss Esmoor* . . .

In the novel, which remains the classic portrait, or critique, of British India, Forster captures the double valence of the colonial gods. Mrs. Moore's apotheosis could be interpreted, by a prejudiced reader, as confirmation of the fanaticism and irrationality of a people liable to worship anything—even somebody's oft-muddled mother. Yet the story also hints at her deification's power: in a world in which Indians could expect little justice, at the trial Aziz's innocence is properly recognized and he is acquitted of what was seen as the worst of crimes—proving that Her Name works. Just as with the Nikalsainis, deification could be a means of harnessing colonial imperium for oneself, to bathe in its divinity. But Esmiss Esmoor's godhead also stands apart from that of the men of empire. Forster intimates that it is she alone, as a wise, older woman, who sees many layers of truth: of what happened in the cave, the hollowness of Britain's imperial position, and deeper illusions of the human condition. Overwhelmed by his burdens as a cog in the government machine, Ronny considers her divinity yet another annoyance he must bear. "What does happen to one's mother when she dies?" he grumbles. "Presumably she goes to heaven; anyhow she clears out."

✦ ✦ ✦

One exception to the dearth of stories of women inadvertently turned divine was an occurrence that warranted several articles in the London papers, and was later retold in Frazer's *The Golden Bough*. Arriving in India in 1879, Sir Walter Lawrence had found villagers worshipping "the head" on the rupee, which belonged, as it happened, to Queen Victoria. In March 1883, the *Spectator* reported "a striking incident" in the seaside province of Orissa, where a certain Sergeant Atkinson had come across a sect that consecrated Queen Victoria as its god. "We have no details either as to worship or creed," the paper noted. "Such an elevation for the Queen is in entire accordance with all that is known of the operation of religious feeling among the lower castes and wilder tribes," the author wrote, and quoted Lyall on his theory of the Hindu Jacob's ladder, the superhighway between heaven and earth.

"To India she was divine and sacrosanct," Sir Walter recalled, and recounted the sorry fate of a pandit in Kashmir who was exiled for claiming Victoria "was human like himself." It was "spontaneous," "simple" love that the millions felt for Her Majesty; in their sparse huts, her image was often "the only ornament." According to the *Spectator*, reverence was not limited to the queen or her effigy but even extended to an ornate silver centerpiece dish presented by Victoria to a regiment of Gurkhas. The native cavalry, in "their hunger for belief," would respectfully dismount their horses whenever they passed the opulent platter. The *Spectator* speculated as to whether the new religion would spread: "Temples may yet rise over Orissa, or farther . . . thousands will bow, and march, and dance in an ecstasy of adoration, and hundreds of thousands, as they pay or receive coin, will put it to their foreheads, because it bears the effigy of the new goddess." But, the paper concluded, "Little of all this will probably happen," for Orissa was not far from the more skeptical climes of Calcutta, and moreover, "the English officials, fearing ridicule, will stamp out the new faith, if they can." Even in a reign as unusual as Victoria's, it was, the magazine noted, "a most weird incident." Just as Britain was attempting to use India as a laboratory for imposing Victorian morals on the masses, Victoria's jungle apotheosis seemed a misfiring of their mission. "We suppose some official note of the occurrence will one day reach the Queen, and we wonder how she will feel," the *Spectator* added.

It was an apt point, for Victoria, despite her inherited omnipotence, didn't believe in women's political rights, though she would become an icon of female power in spite of herself. In 1870, at a moment when equal voting rights were being debated in Britain, Her Royal Highness wrote, "The Queen is most anxious to enlist everyone who can speak or write to join in checking this mad, wicked folly of 'Woman's Rights,' with all its attendant horrors, on which her poor feeble sex is bent. . . ." Reflecting upon Victoria's Orissan godhood, the *Spectator* compared it to what befell John Nicholson and his followers: "Perhaps Queen Victoria will be angry, too, though she will hardly order whippings for the poor Ooreyas." Yet when it came to the blasphemy of feminism, Her Majesty could rage just like Nikalsain. A leading suffragist, Viscountess Amberley, "ought to get a good whipping," Victoria seethed. "It is a subject which makes the Queen so furious that she cannot contain herself," she wrote. "God created men and women different—then let them remain each in their own position."

Military Cemetery Dagshai, India. One of the monuments.

To India's colonizers, divinity—the kind that strikes you down in awe and dread, with such a feeling of nothingness you cannot but worship it—was supposed to be male, and so British observers made little attempt to understand India's own traditions of female deification. Rather than the heroic splitting open of the heavens in a brigadier's ascent, tales of women worshipped as gods, in the British accounts, were tragicomic. (Writes the magistrate William Crooke: "Genda Bir, a woman who was tired of life, and, instead of burning herself, threw herself down from a tree, is worshipped at Nagpur.")

Several incidents of the apotheosis of women, as recorded by the British, appeared to involve strange family dynamics. In a report from Travancore, Reverend Samuel Mateer recounted the case of a man named Vallavan, who had become convinced that his long-dead mother had morphed into a nagging demigod. In her old bedroom, Vallavan would leave offerings of her favorite things: expensive saris, cakes, plantains. When his wife Patmasuri entered the room, she would dress herself in the cloth and become possessed by the spirit of her mother-in-law. In an entranced state, the wife would begin to dance, calling out to her husband: "*My son, am I not your mother? Be assured that I shall make you happy.*" Vallavan would beseech the goddess for blessings and began to proselytize worship of his mother to all who would listen. Reverend Mateer noted with relief how the family had, under the influence of his missionary, *surrendered* their "demonolatry" and accepted Christ.

In his 1817 report *The Hindoos*, the Baptist minister William Ward included several traditions of female deification amid chapters such as "Worship of Beings in Strange Shapes," "Log of Wood Worshipped," and "Inferior Celestial Beings." Ward noted that the daughters of *bramhûns*, up to the age of eight, were reverenced in elaborate ceremonies as avatars of the goddess Bhagavati. He may have been describing the ritual of Kumari, famously practiced in Nepal, in which prepubescent girls are selected to be the vessels of the goddess, if only for a day. It was said that if a mother dreamed of a red serpent, her daughter would ascend to divinity. In his observations from Travancore, the Reverend Mateer noted a cult of mothers who worshipped daughters who had met tragic and untimely deaths, perishing before they were old enough to marry. Mateer reprinted an account by a fellow missionary of his encounter with a group of mothers, turned mystical by grief, who would present offerings of "milk, fruit and cakes, silk, and coloured cloth" before their filial deities:

*Are not these virgin demons your own unmarried daughters, who are now dead?*

They acknowledged that it was so.

*How silly and degrading a thing it is to bow down and express your sorrows, with the hope of obtaining relief, <u>before your own children</u>, whom you reared, who were subject to you and afraid of you, and who even when alive were unable to afford you comfort when they saw you weeping! Can you think for a moment that such children have power over your lives now that they are dead, any more than when they were living?*

They assented to his reasoning, and acknowledged their folly.

Inside modest houses, behind diaphanous curtains and closed doors, new gods were being made in profane ways. Ward, in his *Hindoos*, noted "a most extraordinary and shocking mode of worship," prescribed in certain tantric scriptures. "A person who wishes to perform this ceremony must first, in the night, choose a woman as the object of worship," the minister related, either his wife, a mistress, or a prostitute. "Place her on a seat, or mat: and then bring broiled fish, flesh, fried peas, rice, spirituous liquors, sweetmeats, flowers, and other offerings," and repeat incantations, Ward instructed, recalling the ritual as he had learned it from an erudite pandit. "The female . . . sits naked," Ward narrated, and "* * * * * * * * * * * * * * * * *Here things too abominable to enter the ears of man, and impossible to be revealed to a Christian public,* are contained in the directions of the shastrû." To his easily scandalized audience in Britain, Ward would only divulge that "the persons committing such abominations" were fast increasing in number, and the rituals becoming "more and more indecent."

There was one pathway to heaven that horrified the British, as well as many Indians, above all: *sati*, the divine suicide of the Hindu widow who immolates herself on her husband's funeral pyre. As she makes the supreme sacrifice of *sahamarana*, or "dying with," the mortal woman incandesced into a goddess in the flames. Through her act, the *sati* attains salvation, not only for herself but for her family, her lineage, and everyone who watches. The cremations often took place on the riverbanks, so that boats passing by would see and pass on the news of what had transpired in villages now imbued with a new sanctity. For some, the act of watching the gruesome spectacle was itself a form of *darshan*: seeing the deity and being seen by her. The widow would dress in a new sari; the sides of her feet were painted red. As she circumambulated the pyre seven times, she scattered coins and rice, which the crowd hastened to gather, as they were said to possess healing powers. Calling upon the sun and moon as her witnesses, the widow would recite the *sankalp*, a ritual vow, which Ward, an eyewitness to two immolations in Bengal, reprinted in his *Hindoos*:

> *As long as fourteen Indras reign, or as many years as*
> *there are hairs on her head,*
> [said to be three million and a half]
> *may she abide in heaven with her husband:*
> *that the heavenly dancers during this time may wait upon him,*
> *and that by this act of merit, all the ancestors of her*
> *father, mother, and husband*
> *may proceed to heaven.*

In Bengali, she was called an *agunkhaki*, a "fire-eater": the devourer and not the devoured. Some said it was her virtue itself that kindled; the fire and smoke were only a shield. In this baptism by fire she would wash away the sins of her relatives and ancestors, and emerge divine. Her name was soon forgotten as she dissolved into a collective deity, a many-armed goddess on a bed of flames worshipped at *sati* shrines that dotted the subcontinent. Sometimes her last handprints were preserved in ochre on temple walls.

If *sati* was a ladder between earth and heaven, the first rung was the accident of fate that the husband had died before his wife. The second

rung was the wife's resolution to go through with the intensely controversial act; the third was its spectacular violence. There was something
mysterious and holy about the passage through fire; the *sati* followed
a route like the women who died in childbirth, only to emerge, on the
other side, as a god. In her theatrical, public display of will, the *sati*
seemed to turn all structures governing the roles of men and women
upside down, "the rules of deference and submission, the injunctions
of silence, modesty, and invisibility," as the scholar Tanika Sarkar writes.
At the moment the torch was lit, the *sati*'s divinity could turn either
benevolent or evil. If she maintained her resolve and went through with
the act, she would become a revered, exalted figure. But if she changed
her mind and desperately tried to escape, she would curse her family's
honor with infamy. If the widow nonetheless died, hurled back into the
pyre by an outraged crowd, she would become a malevolent demon of
the worst kind. In Poona in 1786, a European official watched as Toolseboy, a widow of nineteen, joined the body of her husband on the pyre,
leaving her four-year-old child behind. "Her face was discoloured with
turmeric, her hair dishevelled and wildly ornamented with flowers," he
wrote; her eyes "in a gaze of total abstraction," like one "whose soul
was already fleeting and in a state of half-separation from the body."
"The Hindoos," Ward concluded, "treat the idea of death with comparative indifference, as being only changing one body for another, as the
snake changes his skin."

Observing "suttee" with revulsion and incomprehension, British colonizers did not interpret it as divine suicide, even though, as followers of
Christ, they too worshipped a deity who had come to earth in order to
be killed. It was an idea present in the Gospels that God, incarnating in
the body of Jesus, had arrived to bring about his own death and triumph
above mortality. John 19:30 relates that on the cross, Jesus said, *"It is
fulfilled,"* and, *bowing his head, gave up his spirit,* capturing his intention at the very moment he passed. In 1608, John Donne wrote his
controversial *Biathanatos,* a treatise in defense of suicide that cited Jesus
as its exemplar. Yet in Britain suicide remained a criminal act, and the
colonists tended not to see any similarities between *sati* and Christian
notions of holy and ecstatic, self-inflicted pain, nor with the early Chris-

tian, often female, martyrs who were, in Clement of Alexandria's phrase, "athletes of death." Rather, the burning women were seen as the victims of crude societal pressure: in villages where widows were forbidden to remarry, they became useless and unwanted, facing a future in which no one would take them in. For British bureaucrats and missionaries, as well as for many Indian critics, the custom represented the nadir of backwardness. Each new fire was used by the colonizers to justify the British regime: for Indian men who were unable to care for their own women properly were surely not ready for self-rule.

Although government staff and the public condemned the ritual, official British policy was not to interfere with religious practices. In 1789, Governor-General Charles Cornwallis, whose own marble statue after his death became the site of a "small temple," had refused to prohibit *sati*, "a ceremony authorized by the tenets of the religion of the Hindoos and from which they have never been restricted by the ruling power." If something was enshrined in scripture it was considered religious, and *sati* was present in numerous verses in the *Vedas*. In 1795, the Orientalist H. T. Colebrooke compiled a painstaking list of archaic citations for the journal *Asiatic Researches* to prove its scriptural authorization. He translated a hymn from the *Rig Veda*:

> *Om! let these women, not to be widowed,*
> > *good wives adorned with collyrium, holding clarified butter,*
> *consign themselves to the fire!*

Rather than ban *sati*, instead British officials attempted to correctly administer what many of them interpreted as the widow's excessive display of romantic love and grief. The first step was to gather data: on how many women had gone ablaze each year, their identities, the regions, such as Bengal, where the rite was most prevalent. Before an immolation, the police needed to be informed, and officials were sent to supervise the act. The police documented the widow's name in their ledgers: *Rassoo, Binde, Panchee, Rollo, Ullungo, Dassee*. Observers recorded descriptions of her expressions, her last words and gestures, and published them, imbuing her sacrifice with a new kind of immortality. Relying on the testimony of Brahmin priests and the work of Orientalists such as Cole-brooke, the British legislated when *sati* could lawfully be performed and when it could not. Vedic verses upheld an unlikely hierarchy, in which colonial law, rather than supplanting the Hindu sacred, reinforced it with all its bureaucratic might. After laws restricted *sati* to the upper castes, the widows' ascent to divinity became a powerful means of social mobility for lower orders. With an illicit, holy suicide, a woman could elevate her entire caste. Women burned their hands to demonstrate their resolve.

At the cremation ground, women began to voice dissent against the colonial regime. In 1816, when the widow Digambari learned she could not legally immolate herself because she was only fourteen, she set out with her husband's corpse on a palanquin, on a protest march to the government in Calcutta. When she was turned back along the way, Digambari staged a hunger strike next to the pyre. Under pressure from the widow's community, which feared she would otherwise die a ritu-ally polluted death, British officials permitted the illegal *sati* to proceed, allowing the sacred to surmount colonial law.

"Controversially but recognisably, she became the bearer of some-thing like rights rather than of sacred prescriptions and injunctions alone," Tanika Sarkar writes. Through the British attempt to control the fire-eaters, and the debates that raged over whether the ritual should be banned, *sati* paradoxically became a channel through which women won basic rights and legal recognition for themselves in colonial India. "This was a development," Sarkar argues, "that neither the state nor its Brah-man ritual specialists had actually intended." To distinguish consent from coercion, the widow was set apart, for the first time, from the male family members who had hitherto spoken for her, and defined her identity to authorities. She was interrogated alone, on her own terms. She had to declare, in public, before police officers and crowds of spectators, that it was her will to die. She had to prove she was of legal age, over sixteen, of sound mind, uninfluenced by any drugs or intoxicants. In the eyes of the law, women had inadvertently attained a new autonomy. Through a ritual conferring godhood, women gained legal personhood, something perhaps more, or perhaps less, powerful.

Understanding the ways the colonial state needed scripture as its script, in the 1820s, the Bengali reformist Rammohan Roy turned to the Sanskrit hymns to argue that *sati*, as it was being practiced, was a modern misconstrual. Roy, often said to have been the first Hindu to use the word "Hinduism," rebutted conservative Hindus who decried any state restriction of ritual, using a scene that all would know well: the battlefield of the *Bhagavad Gita*. In the midst of the war against his own brothers, the distraught Arjuna pauses to seek council from his charioteer, the god Krishna, as to whether he should continue fighting such a senseless conflict. Krishna urges him to go on and to sacrifice his desires, because only action performed out of duty alone is holy. Referring to the *Gita*, Roy argued that the widow who chooses to die on the funeral pyre *desires* heaven—making *sati* at best a lesser religious act. And in practice, Roy contended, the widow's consent was often nebulous. In shocking detail, he described how some women, rather than walking freely into the flames, were tied with ropes to their husbands' corpses, transforming *sati* from sanctified suicide into murder. As debate erupted over the ritual, it sparked a new, vernacular print sphere in India: newspapers and presses were founded and a culture of petitioning took hold, drawing people into a world of modern campaign politics. While various regional edicts against *sati* were introduced, it was not until 1861 that the Orissan goddess Queen Victoria issued a decisive, all-India ban, closing off the violent, female passage to divinity, at least in law.

"I am still inclined to think," wrote Max Müller not long before his death in 1900, "that in its origin it was voluntary and arose from blind, passionate love, and a strong belief in an immediate meeting again in a better world." Even so, Müller, who had studied the work of Rammohan Roy, theorized that *sati* was all a mistake: the falsification of the *Vedas* by corrupt Brahmins, who were likened by Protestant observers to nefarious Catholic priests. Diving deep into the Sanskrit that sanctioned holy suicide, Müller concluded that the passages in the *Rig Veda* had been "mangled, mistranslated, and misapplied," ending thousands of lives in the process. According to Müller's interpretation, the grieving widow was not supposed to kill herself, but after accompanying the corpse of her husband to the pyre, she was commanded to:

> Rise, woman.
> Come to the world of life;
> thou sleepest nigh unto him whose life is gone.
>     Come to us.

It all hinged, according to Müller, on a distortion of the phrase *yonim agre* to *yonim agneh* in the preceding verse. What originally conveyed a sense of "go up first to the altar" became "go to the womb of fire"—a small, linguistical error, yet one that condemned many lives to the pyre. The mangled syllable had sent women to their deaths and made goddesses in their place.

◆   ◆   ◆

One of the best-known hymns in the *Rig Veda* sings of a figure called Purusha, sometimes translated as "Person" and more often as "Man." The universe itself was created when this cosmic being, infinite in size, was torn into pieces, limb by limb, in an act of sacrifice greater than any white man's burden. From his body parts grew the structures governing both planetary bodies and human society, though Müller and other scholars would argue that the lines were another modern interpolation by Brahmin priests—to sanctify the caste system.

> When they divided the Man, how many portions did they make?
> What did they call his mouth, his two arms, his thighs and feet?
>
> His mouth became the brahmin, his arms were made into the warrior.
> His thighs were the people, and from his feet the servants were born.
>
> The moon was born from his mind; from his eye the sun was born.
> Indra and Agni came from his lips, and from his breath the wind was born.

*From his navel came mid-air; the sky was fashioned from his head.*
*From his toes came the earth, and the four directions from his ear.*

The feminine sacrifice of *sati* offered a different version of the creation myth. Beyond the individual widow-goddesses, there was the supreme Sati, wife of Shiva, who was said to have once entered the fire herself. Her body was pulled from the flames, dismembered, and the pieces scattered across the landscape of the subcontinent, just like those of the Sacred Man. At the places where the pieces of Sati fell to earth, each blossomed into new shrines, becoming centers of female power that traced the shape of *Bharat Mata*, the idea of India herself deified as a mother goddess that was frequently invoked from the late nineteenth century. Long after the passage to heaven had been sealed by law, the widows would remain vivid in collective memory. For some, the *sati* was an icon of anti-colonial resistance; her immolation a brave sacrifice to Mother India. Indian women were seen as mothers of the nascent nation: to die to that end, whether in childbirth or widowhood, was to ascend new heights of beatitude. The courage of the fire-eaters was exalted in newspaper editorials and theater plays, conjured by Rabindranath Tagore in his early poems, and in paintings by artists such as Nandalal Bose. At the cremation grounds, worshippers continued to perform rituals in their honor, such as the *chunari mahotsav*, in which wedding veils are unfurled as offerings.

Yet for the most part, the *sati* goddesses were eschewed by new generations of Hindu modernizers, revivalists, and mystics, viewing the ritual as an emblem of all that was wrong with Hinduism and in need of change. Fighting back against the British claim that India could never constitute a nation because its inhabitants were so disparate in their deities, castes, and creeds, many reformers sought to create a coherent Hinduism that would unite all Hindus, and could compete on the global stage of the world religions. While the British maintained that India would never be ready for independence as long as it practiced barbaric customs such as *sati*, Hindu activists aimed to purify Hinduism of what they argued were latter-day corruptions that left India vulnerable to foreign interventions.

Conjuring an ancient golden age, the eminent Gujarati ascetic Dayananda Saraswati called for a return to an authentic Aryan religion, as enshrined in the *Vedas*. As a child, Dayananda had been horrified to catch sight of mice scurrying over his family's Shiva lingam, the phallic icon of the god's power, devouring the offerings meant for Shiva himself. The grotesque scene threw Dayananda into a crisis of doubt as to how such a helpless god could have any real potency in the world. Yet he began to see such aspects of Hindu worship as mistaken, human impositions, "the parasites, not the marrow," of true religion, as Max Müller had remarked. In 1875, the swami founded the Arya Samaj, a movement that sought to cleanse Hindu practices of idolatry and superstition, to create a rational, universalist Hinduism that would fit the image of a world religion. Powered by its revitalized faith, India would take its place among the independent nations. Dayananda was said to have been the first to issue the call for India's *swaraj*, or "self-rule," before his 1883 assassination by milk laced with shards of glass.

"Ladies, excuse me, but through centuries of slavery we have become like a nation of women," the charismatic Bengali monk Vivekananda declared in one of his fiery trademark speeches, given at Madras in 1897. The iconic, turbaned swami in saffron had represented Hinduism at the World's Parliament of Religions in Chicago in 1893, the first ever gathering of world religions, as they had only recently solidified. He had electrified the delegates with eloquent talks on how the East was superior in spirituality to the West. The swami had first become known as the disciple of Sri Ramakrishna, the famous Kali-adoring, ragged holy man from Kamarpukur often found in an ecstatic trance. Devoted to the divine feminine, Ramakrishna deified his chaste bride Sarada Devi, hailed as *Sri Sri Maa*, or the "Holy Mother." In his *Hindoos*, Ward had sensationalized such wifely deification rituals as "diabolical business," yet for the celibate Ramakrishna the *pujas* were a way to neutralize the erotic, to transcend any human urges by reaching the metaphysical plane. Moving away from the ideas of his teacher, Vivekananda turned to male divinity in soaring lectures that galvanized Indian audiences to rise and fight, as if entering a sacred boxing ring.

"First of all, our young men must be strong," Vivekananda declared in another speech from 1897, eleven years before Baden-Powell established the Boy Scouts. "You will be nearer to Heaven through football than through the study of the Gita," he instructed. The swami strove to forge a faith that could match muscular Christianity, wrestle with it, and win. He dreamed of organizations for training men, in body and spirit, to preach Hinduism at home and abroad. "You will understand the Gita better with your biceps, your muscles, a little stronger." In this vision there was no place for the goddesses of *sati*, whom Vivekananda counted among the backward superstitions that kept India shackled to an emasculated past. Instead, the guru urged Hindu men upward and godward in the struggle for India's freedom. "Make your nerves strong. What we want: muscles of iron and nerves of steel, inside which dwells a mind of the same material as that of which the thunderbolt is made," declared the swami, who could never reconcile himself to the ill health that plagued him. Three years before his death in 1902, at only thirty-nine, Vivekananda wrote a con-flicted hymn—almost a continuation of the prayer began by "the Father," Barthélemy Prosper Enfantin, in a jail cell long before:

> *O Thou, Mother of the Universe, vouchsafe manliness unto me!*
> *O Thou, Mother of Strength, take away my weakness,*
> *Take away my unmanliness and make me a Man!*

As he bodybuilt the divine male, Vivekananda dreamed not only of equality with the British but of domination. He imagined no less than India's future conquest of Victoria's empire. Political liberation, when it came, would be like religious salvation. In his Madras speech, which he titled "The Future of India," and which was given exactly fifty years before India gained its independence, Vivekananda invoked the Sacred Man from the *Rig Veda*:

> For the next fifty years let all other vain Gods disappear from our minds.
> This is the only God that is awake: our own race—everywhere His
> hands, everywhere His feet, everywhere His ears, He covers everything.

All other Gods are sleeping. Why should we vainly go after them, when
we can worship the God that we see all around us . . . ?

The first Gods we have to worship are our own countrymen.

✦  ✦  ✦

As the century rolled over, weeds were beginning to grow over the
graves of the colonists. The cold slabs of white marble would wait: for
libations of gin and cigars befitting a sahib, the offerings of candles more
appropriate for a reverend, or the earthenware saucers ideal for dead
ladies who take tea. But in the stillness, the pine trees bristled and the
distant peaks of the Himalayas refused. The placid lakes demurred, and
the earth itself, the ferns and the lichen, the myna birds and the bulbuls,
they laughed and said in their hundred voices, *No, not here*, and the sky
said, *Sorry*.

*It could be, after all, that God is not sleeping but hiding from us out of fear.*

—Elias Canetti, 1973

*I beg for haven: Prisons, let open your gates—*
*A refugee from Belief seeks a cell tonight.*

—Agha Shahid Ali, 2003

# 9

# The Tyranny of Love

In 1878, a court in London ruled that a woman was unfit to be a mother because she did not believe in God. Thirty-one-year-old Annie Wood had been, by her own account, a devout Anglican when she married the dour clergyman Frank Besant, a man so cold he noted in his diary he charged *No fee* to baptize their newborn son. Trapped in a life of endless housework and childcare, in face of Frank's increasing autocracy and physical abuse, Annie began to undertake a systematic questioning of everything she believed in. If God is good and all-powerful, and Christ in his sacrifice atoned for our sins, why does faith seem to do nothing to relieve our suffering and pain? If religion was *religio*, the ties that bind, it was also a rope that could fray.

On the verge of killing herself with the chloroform prescribed to treat her infant daughter's illness, Annie was stopped by a mysterious voice that seemed to come not from heaven but somewhere else. Now determined to live, and convinced that the root of her unhappiness lay in the inequalities and oppressions of the earthly world, she befriended a circle of freethinkers and dissident preachers, studied Darwinian science, and took up the twin causes of socialism and women's rights. To fill her empty hours at home, she began to write a series of atheist pamphlets arguing that Jesus had merely been a great man, and signed them, devilishly, "By the Wife of a Beneficed Clergyman." In church one Sunday, as her husband dispensed pale slivers of the body of Christ, Mrs. Annie Besant stood up and walked out.

When Frank and Annie separated, it was agreed that Frank would take custody of their son, Arthur, while Annie would care for their daughter, Mabel, with a one-month swap each year. Yet as Annie became increasingly prominent as an atheist writer and orator, Rev. Besant grew more and more outraged by the activities of the "Mrs." who tarnished his name. At a lecture on the similarities between Krishna and Christ, Annie met Charles Bradlaugh, the founder of the National Secular Society, dedicated to disentangling church from state. Together, they shocked England by printing a notorious, if innocuously titled, tract, the physician Charles Knowlton's *The Fruits of Philosophy*, which argued in favor of birth control. Swiftly prosecuted for obscenity, when the police destroyed the treatise, Mrs. Besant wrote her own, and would be remembered by history as the first woman to ever make a public statement advocating contraception.

Mrs. Besant's *The Law of Population* became a bestseller, with hundreds of thousands of copies sold across the English-speaking world. Arrested on charges of endangering public morality, she gave a stirring, two-day-long speech on birth control, in a sensational trial that even attempted to subpoena Darwin. The indictments of Besant and Bradlaugh were eventually nullified, and the following year the world's first birth-control clinic opened in Holland. Yet the triumph for reproductive rights would cost Annie her own children.

Soon after the verdict, Frank filed a lawsuit charging that her "indecent and obscene pamphlet" and other works, such as *The Gospel of Atheism*, rendered Annie dangerously unsuitable to mother a child. For the sake of their "morals and happiness," the vicar demanded the children be removed from their mother's influence until they reached adulthood. In response, Annie wrote her history *Marriage. As It Was, As It Is, and*

*As It Should Be*, which demonstrated how married women in Britain amounted to chattel slaves in the eyes of the law. At the trial, the judge was horrified to see Annie Besant defending herself, an act unbecoming in a lady, and he ruled that Mabel, if raised by her firebrand mother, would become "outcaste in this life and damned in the next." In addition, the verdict forbade Annie from visiting her son, though she was granted two weeks a year to see both children if under the constant watch of two supervisors, appointed by Frank. Faced with this humiliating prospect, Annie determined it was best not to see the children at all until they were old enough to return to her by their free will. As eight-year-old Mabel was carried away shrieking, the highly publicized case would lead to a change in English law, for Besant had exposed how even a mistress had greater legal right to care for her own offspring than a wife did.

Deprived of her children, Annie renewed her assault on religion with a barrage of pamphlets, among them *Is Christianity a Success?*, *The Natural History of the Christian Devil*, and *The World and Its Gods*, which had a corresponding "special exhibit of specimens" on display in London's Hall of Science, founded by Bradlaugh. Of Irish descent, Annie took up the cause of Irish home rule, and became close friends with George Bernard Shaw, whose Fabian Society she joined. She soon became a leading labor activist: in November 1887 she led tens of thousands of unemployed workers in what became known as the Bloody Sunday protests in Trafalgar Square, violently suppressed by the police. The next year, she organized a thousand London matchgirls to strike against their dangerous working conditions and meager wages, calling attention to their plight in her fiery editorial "White Slavery in London."

Caught up in the whirl of her work as secularist, socialist, feminist, trade unionist, and reformer, Annie Besant wasn't aware that, on another plane of existence, there were efforts underway to make contact with her. Cryptic letters, written on rice paper in blue crayon, were circulating among a global network of correspondents. The missives were delivered not by postal service but by "precipitation," dropping out of thin air. One read:

> *Meanwhile use every effort to develop such relations with A. Besant*
> *that your work may run on parallel lines and in full sympathy; an*

*easier request than some of mine with which you have ever loyally*
*complied. . . .*

*Yours ever truly,*
*K. H.*

✦ ✦ ✦

When Mrs. Besant was asked by a newspaper to review a monumental treatise, *The Secret Doctrine* by Madame Helena Blavatsky, she found it spoke to her in a way that moved far beyond literary criticism. The book laid out the tenets of Theosophy, a movement that seemed able to solve problems of human suffering "which Atheism leaves untouched," as Besant later wrote in her *Autobiography*. Madame Blavatsky, an aristocratic, clairvoyant, mystic divorcée, had founded the Theosophical Society with the ex–Civil War colonel Henry Steel Olcott, whom she met at a séance in Vermont. Born during the period when the academic science of comparative religion was being established, at the same time as Max Müller and Edward Burnett Tylor were bent over their data, Theosophy undertook its own comparative study of world religions and determined that all were valid paths to the same eternal truth.

Viewing itself not as faith but as science, Theosophy united all religions into a single aspiration: the divine perfectibility of man. All prophets, messiahs, and avatars were part of the same forward march of spiritual evolution, through karmic cycles of reincarnation. Blavatsky and Olcott's Theosophical Society aimed to establish a universal brotherhood of man that would transcend all creeds and races, and seemed to reject the prejudices of the Victorian age. Taking a pantheistic view, it formed an attack on Christian supremacy—Jesus was just another avatar, like Krishna—and looked toward the East for enlightenment. In India, Theosophy was at first embraced by many Hindu reformers, pleased with its exaltation of Sanskrit scriptures and Vedic rituals and its dismissiveness of Christianity, after the humiliations of a century of invasive missionaries. In 1879, Madame Blavatsky sailed to the subcontinent, in search of a location for the society's headquarters. She established a first home for the Theosophical Society at Tinnevelly, before acquiring a large estate in the palm groves of Adyar, outside Madras. It served as the base for a movement that rapidly grew branches, tendrils, and offshoots, reaching over a hundred thousand acolytes worldwide.

On her travels in Tamil Nadu, Blavatsky, often rumored to be a Russian spy, would gather intelligence on the activities of the British godlings of empire. One night she found herself on a journey by elephant through the Tinnevelly jungle, on a mission to meet a Shanar priestess rumored to be three hundred years old. As the madame and her entourage waited for the ancient Kangalim to emerge from the ruins of a temple, their Indian guide told Blavatsky of a deified Englishman, as she related in *From the Caves and Jungles of Hindostan*, a collection of reports written for Moscow newspapers. The guide had a friend who was plagued by a demon that poisoned his crops and brought illness to his family. When he beseeched his tormentor to reveal his identity, the next night, Captain Pole drew a self-portrait on the blank surface of a whitewashed stupa. The guide described to Blavatsky the sacrificial Pole rituals he had himself witnessed, songs and dances accompanied by a fiddle strung with human veins. He watched as a priest was possessed by the spirit of Pole; he leapt in the air, slew an ox, sipped its hot blood, and started to dance. The possessed Pole-priest began "to inflict deep wounds all over his body with the bloody sacrificial knife," as a crowd cheered him on. "To see him bathing in the blood of the sacrificed animal, mixing it with his own, was more than I could bear," the guide recounted. Yet his story was interrupted, Blavatsky recalled, by the sudden appearance of the skeletal priestess. She stood there, towering before them, holding burning camphor in her palm.

Not long after she finished her book review, Annie Besant decided to pay a visit to the aging Blavatsky, who had returned to London on account of ill health. The madame said little but stared penetratingly, with liquid blue eyes and an interstellar gaze, at her visitor and exclaimed, "Oh, my dear Mrs. Besant, if you would only come among us!" Soon Besant shocked her secularist comrades and horrified Bernard Shaw with a new pamphlet: *Why I Became a Theosophist*. Though Blavatsky was dogged by scandals and allegations of fraud persisting beyond her corporeal exit in 1891, Theosophy was becoming increasingly prominent as a charged, compelling means of resisting the powers that be. Besant joined a crowd of illustrious converts that grew to include Oscar Wilde, W. B. Yeats, Piet Mondrian, Paul Gauguin, and Thomas Edison. Even Albert Einstein was said to have heavily annotated a copy of the *Secret Doctrine*. Besant was admitted to the Esoteric Section, Blavatsky's innermost circle of initiates who had attained the highest occult powers; eventually she rose to the position of president of the Theosophical Society. In a dramatic farewell speech to the National Secular Society, Besant revealed that she, too, had been receiving enigmatic rice paper missives, signed by a cryptic "K.H."—letters that fell like raindrops from the ceiling.

Scattered across the earth, there existed a committee of ancient, supernormal men, the Theosophists contended, deific elders who had survived long beyond ordinary life spans, in order to pass along their knowledge to future generations. Called the Mahatmas, or "great souls," their physical bodies were so frail they were unable to journey long distances, but they could leave their wrinkled shells to travel on the astral plane to meet their pupils. As rulers of a "spiritual empire," they lent their personalities to the unseen power structures that controlled modern earthly life. Blavatsky spoke of them as the Great White Brotherhood, a celestial bureaucracy that in many ways paralleled that of the British colonial administration itself. The Mahatmas were known for sending rather bossy letters, often offering unsought-for advice.

Among them was Master "K.H.", or Koot Hoomi, and the Master Morya, whose fragile bodies were said to dwell in Tibet. Theosophists carried talismanic portraits of the bearded, turbaned K.H. and M., and Blavatsky claimed to have visited them in Shigatse. Prolific correspondence from Koot Hoomi and Morya was preserved by the Theosophist A. P. Sinnett and collected in the book *The Mahatma Letters*. One thousand three hundred pages of letters are held in the archives of the British Library, and have been examined by handwriting experts. (Morya prophesied it: "*Ah Sahibs, Sahibs! if you could only catalogue and label us and set us up in the British Museum, then indeed might your world have the absolute, the desiccated truth.*")

In the mid-1990s, a historian asserted that the Masters bore uncanny resemblances to actual public figures—various politicians, reformers, and

*With the exception of few—too exaggerated—his views are quite correct. Such is the impression produced upon the native mind. I trust, my dear friend, that you add a paragraph showing the Society in its true light. Listen to your inner voice, and oblige once more your's Ever faithfully*

*K. H.*

activists—and that Blavatsky had based them on real men. Master Morya (said to have taken a special interest in Edison and his light bulbs) was modeled on Ranbir Singh, an erudite Kashmiri philanthropist, and Koot Hoomi was based on the Sikh revivalist leader Thakar Singh Sandhanwalia, the scholar K. Paul Johnson argued. Blavatsky had, in fact, met both men on a trip to the Punjab in 1880; they were said to be extremely handsome and elegant, with highly refined senses of style. Other Masters also appeared to be modeled on people Blavatsky had known. It was as if she had taken all the illustrious men she had encountered in her lifetime—friends, former lovers, statesmen who had impressed her deeply—given them code names, and turned them into deities in a complex pantheon, active in the terrestrial world. Soon, the rice paper messages began manifesting. If it was all a dream, conjured in the depths of a single mind, once it became shared, it became real. Whoever the Mahatmas were, Annie Besant suddenly awoke to find one, in his radiant astral form, scented with sandalwood, standing at the foot of her bed.

✦ ✦ ✦

MASTER KOOT HUMI                    MASTER MORYA

The Mahatmas had heard about Besant's activism on birth control; in the words of Koot Hoomi, they found it "highly pernicious." The issue was that if contraception became widespread, there would be fewer bodies for souls to reincarnate into. "*The sooner we leave the subject— the better,*" K.H. wrote. He knew about the tract she had published, and condemned "its unclean spirit, its brutal aura." In response, Besant publicly renounced her earlier stance, bought up all surviving copies of her pamphlet *Law of Population*, and saw to it that the printer's plates were destroyed. She decided to give up politics entirely and turn instead to the spiritual East. When, in 1893, Besant first set foot in India, the place she knew was her true "motherland," among her first stops was Pole's dominion of Tinnevelly, where she visited temples and delivered her inaugural Indian address.

Meanwhile on the astral plane, a wayward and energetic Anglican priest named Charles Webster Leadbeater had also been hearing from Master Koot Hoomi. The Mahatma directed him to sail to India, where he eventually took up residence in peaceful Adyar and worked on refining his clairvoyance in the wing built for him, "Leadbeater Chambers." A charismatic, towering presence with mesmerizing eyes and vampiric teeth, Leadbeater's occult allure was infectious. He liked to wear a cassock with a heavy amethyst cross, and projected a merriment that seemed to tumble in from another world. His prime interest was in the education of boys; he had founded a school in Ceylon with Colonel Olcott, though his intentions as headmaster had been the subject of frequent scrutiny. Among his Sinhalese pupils, Leadbeater had grown devoted to a thirteen-year-old boy called Jinarajadasa, whom he took away from his parents to live with him, claiming he was the reincarnation of his murdered (and invented) younger brother Gerald. Surrounded by adolescent boys, Leadbeater organized a junior society for them, the Lotus Circle, and numerous Theosophists entrusted their sons to his care.

Oblivious to allegations of deviancy, Mrs. Besant soon became Leadbeater's close friend and collaborator. Having been stymied in her attempts to gain a degree in science from London universities that didn't admit women, with Leadbeater she pursued the new science they called occult chemistry, which involved shrinking your perception to the level of the atom itself. Turning their gaze to the solar system, they discovered four new planets. The pair also began to deepen and develop paradoxical ideas, first appearing in Blavatsky's *Secret Doctrine*, of racial hierarchy, seemingly so at odds with Theosophy's egalitarian oneness of humankind. Drawing upon theories of Aryan migration advanced by Max Müller, they argued that evolution would eventually produce a racial type of superhuman men, with the ability to lead the world into a utopian age. Humankind had evolved through a series of root-races, beginning with the First Race, which was sexless and self-generating, and which formed in the North Pole at the same time as oceans and landmasses. By the Third Race, which arose in the lost continent of Lemuria, sex and gender were differentiated—Adam and Eve were Lemurians. The Fifth and current Race, the Aryan, inaugurated the world in its current geopolitical form.

Each race had subraces, and in the present age the Teutonic was dominant, displaying the highest mental aptitude and empire-building abilities. Through British imperialism, the Teutonic race was bringing cultural renewal to an India that had fallen into decay after its golden Aryan past. On the verge of appearing was the Sixth Race, which would arise in California and usher in an age of harmony—a theory supported by American ethnologists who claimed they had found skulls of this new racial type. With the dawning of the new race, a messiah would arrive to lead mankind out of the claustrophobic nineteenth century and into the light.

The coming messiah would be the Director of Religion, Leadbeater proclaimed, a figure who descends into the world periodically in different human vessels and under various names. "Remember that all these great religions are alike expecting that some one should come," he wrote. While Muslims await the Mahdi, "among the Red Indians, Quetzalcoatl, the Great White Teacher, Who shall come from over the sea, is looked for." Leadbeater continued, "As Lord of Religions He is Lord of all and not of one only."

Among Theosophists, he was often spoken of as the Maitreya, or "the World Teacher"; his previous vessels included a Hindu cowherd and a Jewish carpenter. "Call Him Christ, or Buddha, or what you will," Mrs. Besant declared in lectures across Europe, India, and the United States, "but do not quarrel over the name, lest the dust raised by the quarrel should cloud the sunlight of the Ideal." He would come to help mankind realize the latent perfection within, "for in each of us lives the same Divinity, in germ in us, unfolded splendidly in Him," wrote Besant, adding, "You all know that myth is much more important than history." In the British and Indian newspapers, critics relished satirizing the Theosophists—their messianic fervor, their letters falling from on high, their "Mahatmosphere" ("too foggy"). "Laugh at us, scorn and insult us, but do not insult this grand ideal," came Mrs. Besant's stern response.

It was thought that the messiah would appear on earth by taking possession of a body specially chosen and groomed to be his vehicle. God would wait for the Body to be ready—He wouldn't want to waste His power on the travails of adolescence, in all its awkward phases, from braces to wet dreams. "It was at what is called the baptism that He entered the body of the disciple Jesus," Leadbeater wrote, espousing the theory known as adoptionism—that Jesus was *adopted* by God after a certain age—a notion as old as the second century CE, though declared blasphemous. When, after his long absence of millennia, the messiah returned, Theosophists foretold that the railroads would act as modern science's "offering" to Him, enabling him to reach many million more people this time. "You may meet Him in the train . . . You may hear Him speak on the hill-side or in the hall. You may touch His garment," wrote the eminent Theosophist George Arundale. Mrs.

Besant would say, "The welcome that the earth shall give Him shall not again be a cross."

✦ ✦ ✦

Convinced the messiah would descend in the American Midwest, in 1906 Leadbeater alighted upon a handsome and precocious eleven-year-old boy called Hubert Van Hook, who attended the University of Chicago laboratory school. Young Hubert's parents were enthralled by the idea of their son's chosenness, and ignored the hint of scandal that pursued Leadbeater wherever he went, accusations that ranged from pedophilia to sodomy to encouraging masturbation as a fast track to enlightenment. Even the Masters themselves had ordered Leadbeater to reform his behavior: as the dying Colonel Olcott wrote to him, "They have told both Annie and myself that your teaching young boys to * * * * is wrong. I do implore you from my death bed to bow to Their judgment in the matter." Informed that he was to be the vessel for the Maitreya, a mystified little Hubert and his excited mother set out for Adyar, where he was to receive the proper training for a messiah-to-be. Yet the passage from Chicago to India was long, and by the time Hubert and Mrs. Van Hook arrived, they found that his celestial seat had been taken.

On a stretch of beach in Adyar, where the river meets the sea, Leadbeater had watched from the shadows of the palm groves as an Indian boy bathed. The boy possessed the most unusual aura he had ever seen, Leadbeater recalled, "without a particle of selfishness in it." The boy was the eighth son of Jiddu Narayaniah, an impoverished Brahmin who had recently been hired by the Theosophical Society as a secretary for the Esoteric Section. Born in the town of Madanapalle, the child was named Jiddu Krishnamurti—"image of Krishna"—after the eighth avatar of Vishnu. While his father took a series of civil servant jobs, including one for the East India Company, his pious mother, Sanjeevamma, raised Krishnamurti and his siblings. Alongside the Hindu deities in the family puja room, she hung a portrait of *Sri Vasanta*, or Annie Besant, sitting cross-legged on a tiger skin. When they moved to malaria-stricken Cuddapah, where the colonial demoness with backward feet had roamed, Sanjeevamma died, but Krishnamurti continued to follow her ghost around the house as she went about her chores. While his younger brother Nityananda was hailed as the clever extrovert, Krishnamurti was considered dim and vacant, prone to nosebleeds. Yet catching sight of the eleven-year-old boy on the shore, the lapsed Anglican priest was godstruck.

Leadbeater soon learned from other Adyar residents that the boy was the secretary Narayaniah's son, and asked that he be brought to his bungalow. He placed his hand on Krishnamurti's head and began to unspool memories of his past lives. Master K.H. confirmed Leadbeater's enthusiasm, writing, *"There is a purpose for that family to be here . . ."* Mrs. Besant was away from Adyar at the time of Krishnamurti's discovery, though she was apparently kept informed of it telepathically. Leadbeater arranged to tutor both brothers, who spoke not a word of English, and after a few months found accommodation for them inside the Theosophical compound, allegedly to relieve their widowed father of the burdens of their care. Each night, Leadbeater pursued his investigations into the many lives of this being, whom he renamed Alcyone, after the brightest star in the Pleiades. His brother Nitya was Mizar, the first double star, and Leadbeater called himself Sirius. On an August night in 1909, Sirius decided the boys were ready to travel, in their astral bodies, to meet Koot Hoomi. A few months later, they met Mrs. Besant at the railway station in her physical body when she returned to Madras. When Besant stepped off the train, the boy timidly threw a garland around her neck, and Leadbeater announced, "This is our Krishna."

Soon it was determined that Krishnamurti was ready to undergo a ceremony of initiation with the Masters themselves. Though Mrs. Besant was away again, in Benares on her busy lecture circuit, it took place in her bedroom, and she said she was there supporting him on the astral plane. Krishnamurti and Leadbeater entered the room while Nitya and other Theosophists stood outside the door, keeping watch. Leadbeater lay down on the floor, and Krishnamurti left his body on the bed to fly alone to the celestial empire, where he met the Masters and successfully answered their exam questions. For the group assembled outside the door, there was an unearthly quiet to the night, though they began to worry when the profane chattering of squirrels broke the stillness at

dawn. After his meeting with K.H. and others, Krishna traveled onward
to Shamballa, in the Gobi Desert, to meet the sovereign of the occult
government, the Lord of the World himself, who turned out to be a boy
of his same age. "He is strong like the sea, so that nothing could stand
against Him for a moment, and yet He is nothing but love," Krishnamurti
later recalled. "When He smiles it is like sunlight." When the initiate
returned to his spindly body and regained consciousness, Leadbeater
brushed his hair and swathed him in white silk.

Thirty-six hours after he had entered the chamber, Krishnamurti
emerged, and Nitya fell to his knees in front of his divine brother. Even
Narayaniah allegedly prostrated himself before his son, though he later
denied it. To those who witnessed it, the boy seemed utterly transfigured,
radiating an opalescent majesty not of this world. As the party walked in
slow procession toward the sea, it was noticed there were precisely twelve
apostles accompanying Krishna. "Out of the deified man is visibly spun the
whole myth, which envelops him as a silk-worm in its cocoon," Sir Alfred
Lyall had written of the Hindu Jacob's ladder, the busy highway between
heaven and earth. If Indians had once apotheosized Englishmen, it was a
history that now played in reverse. A few weeks before the initiation, Mrs.
Besant managed to convince Narayaniah to sign a legal document granting
custody of his sons to her, a demand he would have found difficult to refuse
given that he was her employee. Deprived of her own children, Mrs. Besant
would raise those of somebody else, and transform one of them into a god.

The boys took to calling Annie "Mother," and with Leadbeater, the
two formed an odd pair of adoptive parents. In the gated, lush compound of the society, as they awaited the descent of the Maitreya, "the
vehicle" settled into a daily regimen of schooling, exercise, and a wholesome diet, in a routine that fused British and Brahmin habits. For the
grooming of a god, the strict schedule began at five a.m. with ablutions
at the well, followed by enforced meditation with Mother. The boys then
met Leadbeater for their morning meal in the Octagon Bungalow, at
which they were served warm milk, which Krishna had little taste for,
and prunes, which he liked even less. Leadbeater would ask them what
they had dreamed the night before, and related in turn his own version of
the adventures with the Mahatmas they had experienced together on the

astral plane. This was followed by a bicycle ride, and afterward, hot baths with a great deal of soap. Then their schoolwork would commence, in English and Sanskrit, as their native Telegu faded away. The afternoons included tennis or swimming, followed by "a thorough and efficient evening bath," their British tutor recalled. At bedtime, Leadbeater would read Krishna sufficiently terrifying ghost stories, in order to eliminate all fear unbefitting a deity. Then the netted door to his room was bolted from the outside. It was a highly regimented existence, but as Besant would say, "Occultism is the most orderly thing in the world."

The vessel was protected by an adult bodyguard of Theosophists known as the Lieutenants of the Lord, who wore purple sashes and emblems of a yellow rising sun. The only other child the boys would see was Hubert, who, much to everyone's embarrassment, had arrived with his mother at Adyar just at the moment when Krishnamurti appeared as the One. Hubert, or Orion, as he was renamed, remained in the compound for five years, continuing his studies with Leadbeater, alongside the Indian brothers. Yet Hubert felt bitter about his demotion, and was forbidden to touch any of Krishna's possessions, "for fear of infecting them with imperfect magnetism," as Krishnamurti's biographer Roland Vernon noted. The humiliated boy would end up at the center of a swirl of allegations of sexual impropriety surrounding Leadbeater. In his later life, as a straitlaced Chicago lawyer, Hubert refused ever to speak of Theosophy again.

As months passed, Krishnamurti grew taller and his face began to change as he settled into the holiness that was his station. He received a new, Christlike haircut, shoulder length and parted in the middle. His nose turned aquiline and his eyebrows dark and heavy; only his most important attribute reportedly remained unchanged—his vacant, beatific stare, a divine emptiness to be filled. There was something aloof and detached about the groomed Krishnamurti. It was as if he were moving through the actions of a dream, a perfect tool of someone else's ideas, playing some other Director's script. As his exterior surface became ever more perfect, several observers began to express concern. Sir Edwin Lutyens, the architect who built New Delhi, wrote disapprovingly to his captivated, theosophical wife, "I do not believe any Christ was ever brought up to be a Christ—as a profession—as one might call it."

On certain evenings, the entire colony of Adyar, around fifty people, would climb up to a rooftop terrace. Under the glow of the constellations, they would sit cross-legged to listen to Leadbeater and Besant tell the history of their past lives. They learned that their egos had been bound together by love over the millennia; each person was given a code name purely to keep track of their movements, as they changed identity with each new birth. Seventy thousand years ago, Alcyone, or the ego of Krishnamurti, had taken his first birth on the misty shores of the prehistoric Gobi Sea. Everyone was eager to hear how their lives had intersected with his. The stories were full of intrigue and romance—innumerable marriages, children, scandals—plus invasions, occasional genocides, destroyed cities, and mundane details such as what time they had lunch circa 30,000 BCE.

The Theosophists would jealously compete as to who featured most heroically—"*Who were you in the Lives?*"—and a craze caught on to speculate who had been whose husband or grandmother. For her part, "Herakles" Besant (on account of "my many labours") had lived six hundred existences, including one as sixteenth-century martyr Giordano Bruno. Herakles had been born as Alcyone's baby sister in Manoa, then as his father, then his mother at least twice, eventually reappearing as his son in Mexico. Leadbeater, or Sirius, frequently appeared as Alcyone's spouse—in Zimbabwe in the sixth life, Persia in the tenth, and even Mississippi in 22,662 BCE. As Besant wrote in her preface to the published version of *The Lives of Alcyone*, "The troubles of the present lose their seriousness when seen in the light of immortality."

At night, after everyone had retired from the Lives, Krishnamurti would lie down in his bed, only to take off again on an astral commute to his lessons with the Masters. In the morning, he would dutifully write down what he had learned, and Leadbeater would type out his notes. After several months, Koot Hoomi took over correcting the manuscript, and showed it to the Lord of the World in Shamballa, who, much to everyone's surprise, suggested, "You should make a nice little book of this to introduce Alcyone to the world." As Leadbeater noted, "In the occult world we do what we are told," and so the text, titled *At the Feet of the Master*, was published. When he received finished copies, bound in blue leather, Krishna sent one to Koot Hoomi by transmitting it under his pillow while he slept.

Within a few years, the little book, dedicated "To Those That Knock," had sold hundreds of thousands of copies in forty editions, and been translated into twenty-seven languages, Esperanto among them. Letters to the fourteen-year-old Krishnamurti began to flood in from readers thanking him for transforming their lives with his divine teachings of the Path. An organization was formed around the young messiah, the Order of the Star in the East, and it soon grew to fifteen thousand members. In late December 1911, Krishna traveled to Benares to initiate several hundred new acolytes into the Order. As he handed out certificates in a solemn ceremony, attendees began to surge forward in a wave of passion, weeping as they spontaneously prostrated themselves before the young messiah. It was a scene that could only be described as biblical, Leadbeater wrote, "the outpouring of the Holy Ghost at Pentecost." A phosphorescent blue halo appeared a foot above Krishna's head "and then stretched down into a funnel," Leadbeater reported; through it "a torrent of blue fire tinged with rose" began to flow. Annie Besant was exhilarated and deeply moved to see that the Lord was beginning to use her adopted child as His vessel. She wrote in a letter to her ward,

> *I love you, my own dear Krishna . . . I have loved you for so many years.*
> *How many? I do not know. Since we were leaping animals, and guarded*
> *our Masters' hut? Perhaps longer still; perhaps when we were plants, we*
> *put out delicate tendrils to each other in the sunshine and the storm;*
> *and perhaps when we were minerals—oh! So very long ago—I was a bit*
> *of crystal and you a bit of gold in me.*

✦ ✦ ✦

In 1913, just before the earth's factions hurtled into war, the Indian ambassador to the occult empire invited Annie Besant to visit him in Shamballa. The astral diplomat, the Rishi Agastya, urged her to bring home rule to India, a phrase that was being used everywhere in the context of Irish liberation. "*Claim India's place among the Nations,*" the "Regent of India in the Inner Government" commanded her, perhaps the same ancient Agastya said to have been born out of a pitcher into which several gods had ejaculated, and who authored some of the hymns in the *Rig Veda*. "*The end will be a great triumph*," the Rishi concluded, as Besant later recalled in an article for the *Theosophist* magazine. Although Annie, when she converted to Theosophy twenty years previously, had sworn off "politics," she could not ignore the Rishi's directive. She penned a fiery editorial, "Wake Up India!" sent off a volley of pamphlets, started a newspaper, the *New India*, and so began Besant's next incarnation as a major figure in the movement for Indian independence. She joined the Indian National Congress, met with the viceroy of the Raj to persuade him that India was ready for self-rule, and presented him with detailed schemes for how best this should be achieved.

Yet just as her career in Indian politics was beginning, Mrs. Besant found herself embroiled in her second custody battle, charged with an unlikely crime for a liberationist: that of stealing someone else's child and turning him into a god. Narayaniah had finally decided to take her to court for the devastation she had wrought on his own home. Ever since he had signed the document granting custody of his sons, Narayaniah (or "Antares," as the Theosophists had named his ego) had become alarmed by rumors of Leadbeater's intimacy with his sons—from the frequent baths, to the milk-drinking and other habits that broke caste, to reports from a servant who had seen them naked in each other's presence. He was horrified by what Leadbeater had christened the "Pentecostal" incident, and by the swelling tide of Krishnamurti worship.

In January 1912, Narayaniah had written to Besant threatening legal action, demanding that Leadbeater be kept away from his sons. Assuring him she would comply, Besant arranged for the boys to be whisked off to England, ostensibly to study for their Oxford entrance examinations. However, the boys, attended by bodyguards lest their father try to kidnap them, were soon reunited with Leadbeater for occult training in Taormina in Sicily, where Master Koot Hoomi was said to have lived a previous life as the philosopher Pythagoras. Narayaniah wrote to Besant: "Surely none can feel and understand the pangs of a parent better than you, who are an embodiment of love to all?" When his courteous pleas went unfulfilled, the father changed his tone: "I therefore request you to produce and hand over my two sons to me at No. 118, Big Street, Triplicane, Madras. S. at your earliest possible convenience." Besant responded by firing Narayaniah from his job as Esoteric secretary, ordering him to hand over his papers and leave the Adyar premises.

The case that began at the High Court of Madras on March 20, 1913, was not only about the fate of a captured boy-god, but that of a captured nation. To the side of Narayaniah rallied the growing network of Hindu fundamentalists, such as the politician Dr. T. M. Nair, who considered Mrs. Besant to be appropriating and corrupting Hinduism for her own, imperialist aims. For Hindu observers, it was impossible to ignore the connections between India's struggle for liberation and a father's struggle to liberate his son from English predators, rapacious in ways sacred and profane. While both sides of *Narayaniah v. Besant* were invested in the fight for India's self-rule, the trial exposed profound differences of opinion as to how India, or any conquered land, should reclaim its sovereignty, and what independence should look like.

While Annie was highly critical of the British government, she did not seek to abolish the empire itself: home rule was "a cry for freedom without separation," Besant would say. India ought to be allowed to govern itself, Mrs. Besant contended, but still preserve its allegiance to the Crown, gaining the same dominion status as Canada. More radical nationalists, their numbers ever increasing, countered that India must fight for nothing less than complete independence. In a subcontinent that had been divided by European scholars into an "Aryan" north and a "Dravidian" south, activists from the latter were becoming disenchanted with Besant's privileging of Aryan Hinduism, and her nationalist politics only seemed to engage the upper castes.

At the heart of Mrs. Besant's politics was the strange, romantic view that it was *love*, and not profiteering, that held the British Empire together. "This mighty British Empire has been formed and has been welded together by bonds of close affection in a way in which no Empire has ever been united before," she declared. "There was a huge Roman Empire; but it was self-interest, the Roman peace, and the power of Rome which held that together. . . . But what else than love holds *this* Empire together? England, the little Mother State, has no wish to coerce it." Bound together by the tyranny of love, the empire was, above all, a family—in a theory that perhaps exposed Mrs. Besant's history of belonging to especially dysfunctional, broken ones. She wrote, "The genius of the Empire is to make every nation that you conquer feel that you bring them into the Imperial Family, that they and you from that time forward are brothers."

Accordingly, Besant discouraged militant rebellion as a means to bring about self-rule, for family members must not violently attack one another. She held fast to the idealistic notion of a "commonwealth," a unity of Occident and Orient under the Crown that was theosophical in nature, with Krishnamurti groomed to embody it. Though Besant had adopted Hindu customs—she wore saris, did *pujas*, and even learned enough Sanskrit to translate the *Bhagavad Gita*—under her watch, the Indian boy-messiah was becoming Anglicized, hinting that "the little Mother State" still knew best.

The battle that waged for over a year, in the courtroom and on the front pages of newspapers across the empire, would become infamous in legal history. "Deified and Defiled. Two Boys and a Beast," ran the headline in the London paper *John Bull*. Even Aleister Crowley, himself "no prude," drew the line "when a senile sex maniac like Leadbeater proclaims his catamites as Coming Christs." As plaintiff, Narayaniah charged that his son had been the victim of "improper and dangerous practices" with a known pedophile who deified him and pretended that the barely literate boy had written a scripture, *At the Feet of the Master*. His son's apotheosis was not only a malicious deception, but would be deeply "injurious" to his future, or any chance of living an ordinary life. The transcript of the trial noted:

```
The plaintiff submits that the conduct of the
defendant as aforesaid renders her totally unfit
to be in charge of the boys. The plaintiff further
submits that the defendant has been stating
that the first boy, who is named Alcyone by the
defendant, is or is going to be Lord Christ,
and sometimes that he is or is going to be Lord
```

```
Maitreya, and she has induced a number of persons
to believe in this theory, with the result
that the boy is deified and that a number of
respectable persons prostrate before him and show
other signs of worship.
```

The arrow of deification, however, had not simply been fired in one direction, the plaintiff revealed. Narayaniah himself had long considered Annie Besant, or *Sri Vasanta*, to be divine. "The plaintiff believed the defendant to be superhuman, and was completely under her influence and control," the proceedings recorded. Narayaniah had been induced by Besant's spiritual power to hand over his sons, and it was only when he began to lose faith in Her that he sought legal action. In reply to Narayaniah's pleas for the boys' return, Besant had threatened, "I am prepared to prove that when the children were taken over, they were half-starved, beaten, dirty, their lives made a veritable hell, they lived in terror of you," in a letter in which she cruelly reminded her penniless former employee that of his thirteen children, only five had survived, "an eloquent testimony as to their home surroundings." Narayaniah testified that when he read the letter, he was left without words.

At the trial, Mrs. Besant once again forcefully conducted her own defense, and highlighted the educational opportunities both boys were receiving in her care. She led the courtroom in an esoteric, theological discussion of what precisely the nature of Krishna's role was as "vehicle," careful to avoid any overt statements regarding his divinity. She cautioned that if a court of law upheld Narayaniah's sexual allegations, in an empire still under punitive sodomy laws, the stigma would ruin Krishnamurti for life—a warning reminiscent of the charge by her husband Frank years earlier that her daughter Mabel would become an "outcaste in this life and damned in the next."

In his verdict, Justice James Herbert Bakewell ruled that, while there was not enough concrete evidence to prove Leadbeater guilty of the crimes of * * * *, the decision was in favor of Narayaniah. Bakewell maintained that the plaintiff was not aware when he signed the document granting custody to Mrs. Besant that his son would be raised as the "'vehicle' . . . of supernatural powers," and therefore had the right to rescind. Further, Mrs. Besant had failed in her promise to keep the boys away from Leadbeater. Pronouncing the children wards of the court, the judge ordered Mrs. Besant to deliver them from England and hand them over to Narayaniah, or else face imprisonment. The outraged Besant swiftly lodged an appeal, but the court, a few months later, upheld the original verdict.

"Bristling with indignation," as a biographer recounted, Besant decided to take it to the highest court of appeals in the British Empire, the Judicial Committee of the Privy Council in London. Several of its overlords, including the lord chancellor, were friends from her previous life, and in Downing Street her case was followed in an amicable, if bemused way. In May 1914, the justices ruled that the original verdict had not considered the boys' own wishes, which were to remain with Mrs. Besant—although the boys themselves had never been permitted to speak. Narayaniah's lawsuit was thrown out, and the woman who had once lost her own children now had custody over somebody else's. It was a triumph of one version of love over another; a victory for the idea of empire as family.

Throughout the proceedings, later published in the volume *Mrs. Besant and the Alcyone Case*, an unlikely set of witnesses were brought in from the astral plane. It was, the defendant argued, direct messages from the Mahatmas that had justified the decision to remove Krishna from the profane influence of his father. The Masters had been concerned that "the nominal father by his angry jealousy" was being used as an instrument of "the darker powers." *"I want you to civilise them,"* Koot Hoomi had allegedly written to Leadbeater of the boys, *"to teach them to use spoons and forks, nail brushes and tooth brushes, to sit at ease upon chairs."* The transmissions, received as rice paper letters or as ethereal, telepathic commands, were invoked at the trial to sanction the daily routine established for Krishnamurti. In the courtroom, under cross-examination by Besant, Narayaniah was asked whether he believed in the Masters or not, and she brought in evidence that he once said he had encountered one on a night train. The judge interrupted that *beliefs* were not relevant to the suit.

By dragging nonearthly Mahatmas into the tense, heated courtroom in Madras, Besant had imbued them with a new dimension of reality, and they helped her win the case. But it was a profound paradox to invoke them not as anti-colonialists but rather in favor of British tutelage and its "civilising" influence, as supporters of the rights of the British over Indian subjects. In creating her spiritual empire, Madame Helena Blavatsky had subverted the discourse of the British Empire that painted the Orient as backward, irrational, and fanatical by locating the true source of enlightenment and authority in India. The historical men who allegedly inspired her Mahatmas, in particular Thakar Singh Sandhanwalia (Koot Hoomi) and Ranbir Singh (Morya), had pursued anti-colonial politics, as reformers and activists promoting agendas that sought to expel the British from India. Ranbir Singh, who died in 1885, had gone on missions to Tashkent to solicit Russian military support. Sandhanwalia was the first president of the Sikh reform movement, Singh Sabha, and was killed in 1887, in a rumored assassination by the British.

Ever since Blavatsky first revealed the existence of Mahatmas to her followers, they had long served as a beacon of guidance for the politics of Indian independence. Allan Octavian Hume, a retired British civil servant who founded the Indian National Congress in 1885, had for a period of time depended on K.H. and Morya, as occult practices were seen as a means to gain political insight. Hume learned of the nature of Indian dissent, plans for uprisings, and what reforms were needed from the rice paper letters that appeared before his eyes, wherever he was, transmitted at the speed of electricity. For their own part, the Masters grew unhappy with Hume's tendency to treat them as "native clerks"; despite his liberal politics, he seemed unable to transcend a deep-seated racism. Eventually, Hume substituted his own masters for K.H. and Morya, basing his activism on information gleaned from a mysterious, seven-volume set of thousands of reports detailing Indian discontent and nationalist networks, said to have been collected by an astral authority, and which only Hume had ever seen.

The men behind the Mahatmas had become omniscient, suprahuman authorities, in spite of themselves and even in spite of Helena Blavatsky's own intentions. As undying, ethereal figments, they had become so real they could be summoned to a British court of law. Toward the end of her life, Blavatsky would reveal her regret at the myths she had created. In

a private letter written in 1886 to the occult doctor Franz Hartmann—
who only three years earlier reported he had seen Morya himself in
astral form—she claimed the reason was that her cofounder, Colonel
Olcott, and their followers were so desperately hungry to believe. The
myths that sprouted from anecdotes of "mortal men" she had known,
and been impressed by, had spiraled out of control, misleading an "army
of the deluded," she wrote. But in the end, it was "no one's fault," Blavatsky concluded. "Human nature alone, and the failure of modern society
and religions to furnish people with something higher and nobler than
craving after money and honors—is at the bottom of it."

◆  ◆  ◆

When in 1914, a few months after the trial ended, the cataclysmic war
foreseen by the Theosophists broke out, the Mahatmas invited Besant
and Leadbeater to attend a special film screening on the celestial plane.
They lay down in their beds and left their bodies to watch, in flickering
moving pictures, a reel of the war's battles to come and the future triumph of the Allies. World War I would lead to a surge in Theosophy's
membership, among men returning from the trenches or their grieving families, as they searched for an answer to the question, of whence
suffering, which Christianity's benevolent God seemed unwilling to
explain. For Theosophists, the masses of the dead were merely souls lining up to reincarnate in California as the next, more perfect root-race.
"A special new department of astral work has been organized to train
them," Leadbeater announced. "Death himself is no cruel reaper, but a
tender gardener, choosing the fairest blooms for transplantation, not to
a far-off heaven, but to the gardens of the new Earth."

During the war, Krishnamurti and Besant were separated for five years.
While he remained in England, Annie was in India, where she continued
to work for her two causes, the coming of the messiah and Indian home
rule. After she helped launch the All-India Home Rule League, Besant was
imprisoned in a hill station by the British government for her seditious
activities, the Raj having failed to deport her. Upon her release several
months later, the seventy-year-old Besant was elected to the most pow-

erful leadership role in the Indian nationalist movement, president of the Indian National Congress party. All the while, Krishnamurti and Nitya floated among the luxurious homes of wealthy Theosophist patrons. Krishna's caretakers, believing that the Body must remain properly groomed and anointed to become the vessel, saw to it that he was always scrubbed and coiffed, dressed in the finest suits from Savile Row, silk ties from Liberty of London, and brogues polished to an otherworldly sheen. Entirely insulated from political debate, the would-be messiah would occasionally horrify those around him by voicing his support for the Germans.

With his brother, Krishnamurti enjoyed going to the cinema, perfecting his golf, playing practical jokes, and riding around the countryside on his motorcycle. Yet beneath his styled surface was a growing despondency, an apathy impossible to ignore regarding his divine mission. As would-be messiah, he was bored; his quotidian work was dreary, mainly involving answering endless letters from members of the Order of the Star. While the Theosophists jealously bickered over their proximity to him, the rest of England spurned him for the color of his skin. When the brothers tried to contribute to the war effort by working in a military hospital, they found many of the wounded soldiers refused to be treated by Indian nurses.

While Annie had dreamed of her adoptive children studying at Oxford, none of the colleges wanted to admit them, tainted as they were by the scandal of the custody battle. Balliol College rejected Krishnamurti on grounds that it wanted nothing to do with "a brown Messiah." Nitya secured a place at Cambridge, but Krishnamurti kept failing his entrance exams, sometimes leaving the piece of paper entirely blank. "Who can teach Christ anything?" remarked P. G. Wodehouse's Theosophist brother Armine, who became the boy's tutor. An ever-apologetic Krishnamurti would wonder aloud, "Why did they pick me?" Though he tried to shield his mother from his disaffection, he wrote letters to Leadbeater remorsefully expressing his doubts and received in return admonishments for his selfishness. Severed from their birth family and with no money of their own, Krishna and his brother knew that if they left the Theosophical Society, they would have nowhere to go and no prospects.

Krishna felt overwhelming guilt at his ingratitude. The future god incarnate spoke to his younger brother of suicide. In Sir Edwin Lutyens's wife, Lady Emily, Krishna found another mother-substitute and devoted confidante. He began to send her confessional letters, venting his teen-god anguish. "I am a lusus naturae," or freak of nature, he wrote, "and nature enjoys its freak while the freak suffers." Yet still, sometimes, Krish-namurti felt he had "spiritual moments," and the Mahatmas continued to appear in their astral forms. When Koot Hoomi informed him that he needed to develop a larger vocabulary, Krishna and Nitya set about memorizing several lines of Shakespeare each day.

> What kind of god art thou, that suffer'st more
> Of mortal griefs than do thy worshippers?

the bard had written, lines that spoke too clearly to a wartime deity, shivering in his woolens in the bleak English rain.

✦ ✦ ✦

"I did not feel at all sea-sick," recalled Mohandas Karamchand Gandhi of his voyage in 1888 from Bombay to England, where he was to study law. The journey was otherwise miserable; Mohandas spoke little English, "was innocent of the use of knives and forks," too embarrassed to ask which dishes contained meat, and in shyness confined himself to his cabin down below. Arriving in London, it was in his quest to find vege-tarian food that he fell in with a group of Theosophists, who invited him to the Blavatsky Lodge and introduced him to the formidable Madame and Mrs. Besant. The Gujarati student read Besant's *Why I Became a Theosophist*, attended her lectures, and applied for membership. As Gandhi later recounted in his autobiography, it was after reading Blavat-sky's *Key to Theosophy* that his desire to learn more about Hinduism was sparked. Ashamed by what he called "my meagre knowledge of my own religion" and unable to read Sanskrit, Gandhi recalled that it was two Theosophist friends who compelled him to read the *Bhagavad Gita*, in Edwin Arnold's translation. Set on the eve of the final, apocalyptic battle that ushered in the dark present age, the *Gita* would become Gandhi's lifelong scripture and the inspiration for his ethics of sacrifice.

The young law student also turned to Max Müller's *India—What Can It Teach Us?* and his series Sacred Books of the East for guidance as to what "Hinduism" entailed. Later, as a lawyer and political activist in South Africa, Gandhi would cite Müller on Aryan theory, as he pressed British colonial officials to recognize that both the British and Indians belong to the same racial stock. Lecturing on religion at a Masonic temple in 1905, Gandhi drew upon the Indian nationalist B. G. Tilak's *The Arctic Home of the Vedas*, which argued that the scriptures were written by the descendants of a people who dwelled in the Arctic Circle around 10,000 BCE. All progeny of the same sacred and dismembered Man, the British and the Indians were brothers. But then again, the *Bhagavad Gita* sang of fratricide among a hundred brothers all born together at once. It could not but speak to the growing tensions, not only between the British and Indians but Hindus and Muslims, who saw themselves as relatives, friends, and neighbors headed perilously for war.

It is often said that Annie Besant was the first to call Gandhi "Mahatma." In 1915, Mrs. Besant threw a garden party for the Great Soul in Adyar, and at some point bestowed on him the epithet he would grow to loathe. The following year, Besant founded her Home Rule League and drafted the first bill, the Commonwealth of India Act, for the establishment of self-government. As Gandhi rose to fame, he and Besant began to disagree with increasing vehemence as to how independence should be attained, and famously argued onstage in 1916 in an incident known as the "Benares affair." While Besant insisted that self-rule could only be achieved through law-abiding, constitutional reforms, Gandhi was formulating and testing his experiments in non-cooperation and civil disobedience. Drawing on a Hinduism he had in part learned from Theosophy, Gandhi sought to mobilize the masses, while Mrs. Besant, primarily engaged with the Hindu and British elite, worried that the people would not understand Gandhi's principles of passive resistance, or *satyagraha*, leading only to disorder and violence. For Gandhi, the way Theosophy plucked elements from world religions was a violation of *swadeshi*, or self-sufficiency, the same principle that propelled his movement to boycott British goods. "I must restrict myself to my ancestral religion," declared the Mahatma, who let his Theosophy membership lapse soon after he joined.

It was difficult for Gandhi and other Indian nationalists to collaborate with Besant, for she would travel at night to Shamballa to receive her "Marching Orders" from the Rishi Agastya, or even the Lord of the World himself. She would ask the occult empire for guidance on matters such as how to run her nationalist paper. Besant argued that winning India's political freedom was "necessary to prepare her for that *greater* work, when she shall arise and shine, and the Glory of the Lord shall be revealed in the Sacred Land," and planned for her adopted boy-god to take the helm in the campaign for home rule. The students of the university she founded, Central Hindu College in Benares, an institution that trained many young Indian politicians, began to revolt against the Krishnamurti worship that formed part of their curriculum. Occultism, the realm of hidden, elite mysteries, seemed to contradict the spirit of democracy. As Tilak declared, "Congress recognizes no Mahatma to rule over it except the Mahatma of the majority." While he was subtly becoming folded into the concept himself, Gandhi was suspicious of the Mahatmas, and of any astral bureaucracy. "I long to belong to the masses. Any secrecy hinders the real spirit of democracy." Nonetheless, it was thanks to Besant, as Gandhi himself said in 1918, that "'Home Rule' has become a household word all over India."

Beneath the momentum of nationalist politics was a deep, powerful current of the sacred, propelling it forward. The question was, what kind of sacredness. If religion is a concept with a hole at its center, Gandhi dwelled precisely in that emptiness, in the space of renunciation, offering himself in sacrifice. Besant, much like Freud, placed family at its center, making her adopted son her god—while Gandhi, in his commentaries on the *Gita*, seemed to contemplate fratricide. While Gandhi fought for *swaraj*, or "self-rule," Besant used the term *home rule*, a phrase that portrayed the state as a household, a space governed not by any constitution but by love. Unless India settled for being "mistress in her own household," while still a part of the British Crown, Mrs. Besant maintained, it would take decades and violent conflict before independence would be attained. Worse, the Mahatma's noncooperation was interfering with the process of spiritual evolution that had brought Britain and India together, working toward the divine perfectibility of man. In a pamphlet, *Apart or Together?*, Besant conjured the domestic in the union of colonizer and colonized: "Can the relationship be symbolised by a wedding ring rather than by handcuffs?" she asked. Her image suggested an imperialism that was almost erotic. After all, as Sappho first taught, Eros is the ceaseless striving for something that you cannot have and can never fully possess.

✦ ✦ ✦

In early 1921, in the sky above the village of Chauri Chaura, in the region of Gorakhpur, a gigantic serpent slithered upward and coiled itself into a celestial ring, or a noose. A woman, Naujadi Pasin, still vividly remembered the omen sixty-seven years later, as she recalled in a conversation with the scholar Shahid Amin:

> Har-har-har-har, everyone is grinding and splitting daal. And then Babu! From this very corner—I am not lying, I tell you—from this very side it arose, and then went round and round and round . . . Like ash, like smoke in the sky it was. People said it's a python, a python has descended from the hills.

People of all castes climbed to the rooftops for a closer look. The next day, in the sky, a broom appeared, as if to sweep away a desiccated age. A plow followed, to clear out the clouds. Soon, the floodgates opened and the miracles poured in. A field of wheat was transformed overnight into sesame. Two dead trees that had fallen in the garden of an eminent lawyer, Mr. Kishore, replanted themselves and came back to life. Smoke was seen rising from five different wells, perfumed with the fragrance of the pandanus flower. The Indian newspaper the *Pioneer* reported that a girl took a grain of maize in her palm, "and lo! the one grain became four," after she had blown upon it invoking Mohandas Gandhi's name. When a servant in Basantpur, a town named after Annie, said he would believe in the Mahatma if the roof of his house was raised, it lifted itself fifteen feet and then fell down again. A pandit who displayed his contempt for Gandhiji by eating seafood found every meal crawling with worms.

In the weeks before and after Gandhi arrived in Gorakhpur to meet with local organizers and deliver a speech, stories of his miracles began to circulate, appearing in the nationalist papers and later collected and classified by Amin. For all his rejection of capitalism, Gandhi's divine name was surprisingly efficient at restoring lost property and increasing wealth, as cows multiplied and stolen wallets reappeared. Despite his belief in sacrifice, renunciation, and non-harm, the Mahatma became a wrathful, vengeful god in the tales of his acts, raining feces on a lawyer who defied his call for noncooperation. When a villager in Ghazipur slandered the Mahatma, his wife, sons, and brothers all dropped dead. Another man who dared insult Gandhi found his eyelids became stuck: it is not recorded whether open or closed. At sites such as Mr. Kishore's garden, thousands gathered each day, leaving coins as offerings. The rupees were transferred to the nationalist fund, like a miraculous bounty of campaign financing.

India's colonizers had justified their presence by their own inadvertent deification; now India's liberation would proceed along the fault lines of apotheosis, redefining who is a man and who is a god and reclaiming the territory of divinity. Everywhere Gandhi was invoked as the latest, perhaps the final, avatar of Vishnu. He had opposed Besant's occult Mahatmas and her Anglicized boy-god as elitist; now his own divinization would prove deeply democratic. Hundreds of thousands of peasants set off on a pilgrimage to meet the Mahatma, lining the route of his railway journey to Gorakhpur. The ecstatic crowds hailed him at every station, from Nunkhar to Chauri Chaura, with estimated throngs of fifteen to forty thousand people in each town. Gandhi was treated like a temple statue, positioned on top of the train carriage so that the people could have *darshan*: the privilege of seeing the god and being seen by him. His personal secretary Mahadev Desai recounted in his diary that the rail officers would wait to give the green signal permitting the train to move, to allow the masses sufficient minutes of *darshan*. "Some people, overcome with their love, were seen to be crying," the newspaper *Swadesh* reported, as the crowd pressed against the hot metal of the train. "Wherever he went," the biographer D. G. Tendulkar recalled, "he had to endure the tyranny of love."

On his return from Gorakhpur that evening, the Gandhi devotion had become ever more extreme; according to Desai, "*darshan* was now demanded almost as a right." The Mahatma was exhausted from the day's activities, yet his worshippers wouldn't let him sleep. "Hordes and hordes of people began to rush upon our compartment," Desai remembered. "At every station peasants with long long lathis"—bludgeoning sticks—"and torches in their hands would come to us and raise cries loud enough to split the very drums of our ears." Exasperated, the loyal assistant pretended to be Gandhi himself, and the devotees, not knowing what the Mahatma looked like, would prostrate themselves before him, try to brush against him, to touch his clothes, and leave. At every stop, the chaos was repeated. "At last even Gandhiji's endurance and tolerance was exhausted," Desai recorded. "He began to entreat the people, 'Please go away. Why do you harass us at this dark hour?' He was answered only by sky-rending shouts of victory to him! . . . That was the height of the people's love-mad insolence." "What was I to do?" Gandhi later recalled. "Should I jump from the window? Should I cry? Should I beat any of them?" At Salempur, the sleep-deprived Mahatma began to hit himself on his forehead until the people cried out to him for forgiveness, "and requested me to go to sleep."

When addressing the huge crowds at Gorakhpur, Gandhi preached *ahimsa*, or nonviolence, and condemned a recent outbreak of riots. "We cannot get *swaraj* by pitting our own devilishness against the Satanic government," he declared. "This is a peaceful struggle." In his speech, Gandhi outlined his code of ethics and maintained that if the people followed it, *swaraj* would be realized within a year. The people must not use *lathis*, nor loot or steal, Gandhi warned; they ought to uphold the boycott and take up spinning their own cloth, purify themselves, stop drinking and gambling—advice that was instantly enshrined as divine commandment, if not precisely followed. Leaving Gorakhpur on the night train, the Mahatma had been in the area for less than a day. Yet for the hundreds of thousands who had seen him, heard him, brushed against him or his secretary, Gandhi's divine presence among them seemed to subvert the power structures of their everyday lives. The Mahatma had presented the people with an alternative authority, one that seemed to overturn every sacrosanct hierarchy—between India and its British rulers, peasants and landlords, high caste and low—and to usher in a new age.

For many of the Mahatma's devotees, his secular promise of *swaraj* was understood as a kind of *moksha,* or the ultimate salvation of the soul: the release from the worldly cycle of reincarnation. At first, India's congressmen made little attempt to quell the masses' ardent belief in Gandhi's divinity. An editorial in *Swadesh* encouraged readers to help channel the energy of the peasants' worship to the nationalists' cause. "For Mahatma Gandhi to avatar before us in these difficult times is a tremendous boon, for us, our society and our country . . . *Blow the conch-shell of Swaraj* . . . This movement is an elixir for you. Mahatma Gandhi is offering it to you." The editorial urged party activists to harness this power and use it for concrete, political gains. Yet when Gandhi-worship began to shade into what they viewed as dangerous demands, contradicting the agenda of the Congress party, the Indian papers began to issue "prompt disclaimers."

Capturing a different sense of salvation, *swaraj* was interpreted as a coming millennium in which steep taxation would no longer condemn peasants to eternal poverty. Farmers would be able to thrive from their hard labor, no longer exploited by landlords. The receipts for donations to the movement became prized as an alternative currency, the Gandhi Note. When the notes were rejected as legal tender, it was considered a gross violation of the Mahatma's will. In Bihar, a rumor spread that Gandhi had ordered prices to be reduced to only what was reasonable, a fraction of current costs, and shopkeepers were beaten for refusing to comply. In March 1921, a tale began to circulate that Gandhi had made a bet with the British: if he could walk through fire without being burned, India would gain its independence. When the news spread that the Mahatma had taken hold of a calf's tail and emerged from the flames unhurt, huge crowds assembled in triumph, believing that India was free. The journal *Gyan Shakti* reported that hundreds of villagers led a procession through the streets at night, beating cymbals and shouting,

*"This is the drum of swaraj. Swaraj has been attained."* Toward the end of that year, in a newspaper editorial for *Navjivan*, Gandhi wrote the sentence, possibly for the first time, that he would find himself saying, again and again, for the rest of his mortal life.

*I am not God.*

He would repeat it when asked why some people are condemned to die in earthquakes and others are not:

*My answer is: I am not God.*

And in a speech to mill workers in Ahmedabad,

*I am not God. I am a labourer like you.*

And in a speech reprinted in a Bengali newspaper:

*Do not ask for my darshan or want to touch my feet. I am not God; I am a human being. I am an old man and my capacity to stand the strain is limited.*

And in a letter to a friend, G. D. Birla, in the last year of Gandhi's life,

*For after all I am not God. I can commit mistakes . . . I am dictating this with a mud-pack over my eyes and abdomen.*

His believers did not believe Him.

In the village of Chauri Chaura, Gandhians who attempted to enforce his will by halting the sale of meat, fish, and alcohol, and reducing other prices found themselves brutally beaten by the police. A few days later, on February 5, 1922, a furious crowd gathered at the police station in protest. When officers fired into the air to disperse them, people cried, "Bullets have turned into water by the grace of Gandhiji!" and rushed at the police, who shot at the protesters, killing three. The officers were attacked in turn with a volley of stones and bricks. When the policemen retreated inside the station, the enraged crowd barricaded them in and set the building on fire with kerosene, shouting, "Gandhiji's *swaraj* has come. Burn it down!" Officers who tried to escape the flames were pushed back inside, or hacked to pieces and the body parts thrown onto the fire. In the gruesome violence sparked by the god of nonviolence, twenty-three policemen were killed. As word spread to the neighboring villages, the destruction of the police station was seen as the decisive act inaugurating what was now known everywhere as Gandhi Raj. Villagers from all directions poured in to witness the smoldering ruins at Chauri Chaura, including a militia from Gorakhpur led by a sadhu carrying a flag. Declaring martial law, the British arrested hundreds of people, nineteen of whom were convicted and hanged. Among the incarcerated was the husband of Naujadi, who had seen the python in the sky and knew at the time it foretold disaster.

As an avatar, Gandhi had become a dark double of himself, a divine twin who undermined his own message of nonviolence by igniting an incendiary love. In an editorial in *Young India* on February 6, he decried the events of the previous day as a "national sin," and announced he was suspending the campaign of civil disobedience that had, until now, met with remarkable success. Yet even this was "not enough penance," Gandhi wrote, for his having been the instrument of raw bloodshed. "I must undergo personal cleansing," the Mahatma vowed, and began a five-day fast. "I lay no claim to superhuman powers. I want none. I wear the same corruptible flesh that the weakest of my fellow beings wears," he added. A month later, he confessed to inciting violence in court and was sentenced to six years in Yerwada prison. Locked in a concrete cell with a cow-dung floor, Gandhi began writing his autobiography and passed the hours reading the *Bhagavad Gita*. When he was released two years later, Gandhi would reflect upon the events of 1922 as "the death of non-violence."

He had come to realize the paradoxes that were always coiled within his principles: nonviolence was only a negation, after all, and without violence as its counterpart it had no meaning. Nonviolence contained just as much reality as a non-truth. Through noncooperation, he initiated situations he knew very well would lead to physical conflict and harm, yet he prized them as the opportunities for nonviolence's display. His politics, as historian Faisal Devji writes, "consisted of tempting violence in order to convert it by the force of suffering into something quite unexpected." Nonviolence was supposed to work by being a kind of miraculous intervention in history—as if freezing a bullet in midair— but Gandhi failed to anticipate he would become a supernatural interference of his own. He claimed he felt nauseated and suicidal whenever anyone called him Mahatma. Trapped in his own holiness, he declared in 1924: "The word 'Mahatma' stinks in my nostrils."

✦ ✦ ✦

The deity sat beneath a pepper tree and emitted a feeble sound, a cross between a mantra and a moan. In July 1922, Krishnamurti and his brother were invited by a Theosophist patron to come to Ojai, California, in the hope that the warm climate would cure Nityananda's tuberculosis. His brother was dangerously ill, and Krishna had nearly reached a breaking point beneath the weight of the divine burden foisted upon him. The demands were incessant, from astral diplomacy to requests for locks of his hair, to bury in order to magnetize farmland. ("I shall be bald," he complained.) "What a life & is it worth it? This striving striving. For what I don't know," he wrote to his confidante, Lady Emily Lutyens, "... there is a rebellion within me, surging quietly but surely." The twenty-six-year-old had also experienced his first taste of profane love, with a crush on a Theosophist named Helen, from New Jersey, although he was obliged to keep the vessel pure at all costs.

In public, he continued to perform as the groomed messiah; in 1921, his Order of the Star had its first congress in Paris, and Mrs. Besant was thrilled at how well Krishna presided. While Besant was convinced the Maitreya had finally begun to descend into His vehicle, Krishna's private turmoil persisted. "You don't know how I abhor the whole thing ... the meetings & the devotional stuff," he wrote to Emily. "I am not fit for this job." Arriving in California, Krishnamurti was smitten by its "air of equality," the Hollywood stars keen to meet him, America's optimism and its soft drinks "fit for the very gods." He felt exuberantly happy and a deep sense of peace as he wandered in the apricot groves of idyllic Ojai. Yet on a midsummer day in August 1922, Krishnamurti began to feel very strange.

The symptoms were a lump in the neck, a coil at the base of the spine, intense fevers and chills, swelling, fainting spells, revulsion to touch, and an agonizing sensitivity to light, as if trapped under a desert sun "with one's eyelids cut off." Day after day, Krishna's condition worsened. He writhed on a mattress as Nitya, his nurse Rosalind, and a Theosophist neighbor looked on in fear. On the third day, Krishna crawled under the pepper tree in the garden and began an unearthly chant as the sky shaded to dusk. "Now there was perfect silence," Nitya recorded, "and as we looked I saw suddenly for a moment a great Star shining above the tree, and I knew that Krishna's body was being prepared for the Great One." Etheric strains of music began to play. Nitya watched as Rosalind's face flickered with rapture. "Do you see Him, do you see Him?" she cried, pointing to a Presence above the tree, and swore a vow to it— "I will, I will"—before fainting. Transfixed by his older brother, "a great longing came upon me to go on my knees and adore," Nitya wrote in a letter to Besant. Later, Krishnamurti described how, in that instant, he had felt physically broken, yet in a state of absolute union with everything around him. In his testimony, he sounded as if he were the Sacred Man from the *Rig Veda*, reanimated for a modern world:

> *There was a man mending the road; that man was myself; the pickaxe he held was myself; the very stone which he was breaking up was a part of me; the tender blade of grass was my very being, and the tree beside the man was myself . . . Just then there was a car passing by at some distance; I was the driver, the engine, and the tires; as the car went further away from me, I was going away from myself. I was in everything, or rather everything was in me, inanimate and animate, the mountain, the worm, and all breathing thing.*

It seemed as if the Lord had finally taken up His vessel, but what became known as the Process was not finished yet. Each evening, the violent symptoms would begin anew, revving up like a merciless machine at six-thirty p.m. and lasting until eight p.m., as if directed by some invisible, inexorable overseer. It was a process of cleansing; a baptism by flame. One day in October, Krishna informed Nitya and Rosalind that a visitor would be coming that evening, and they should remain outside the cottage. As Nitya listened outside the door, he heard, in the words of the biographer Roland Vernon, "screams, snippets of his one-sided conversations, promises of secrecy, apologies for the clumsiness of his body, assurances that he would remain absolutely still for the momentous presentation that was about to begin." When, after several hours, Krishnamurti opened the door and emerged from the cottage, he appeared transfigured, radiant, as if in a replay of his initiation ceremony with Leadbeater twelve years earlier. He seemed to be surrounded by an audience of invisible beings giving him a rousing ovation. "There's nothing to congratulate me about," Krishna remarked, "you'd have done the same yourself." That year, he wrote his lyric treatise, *The Path*:

> *I am the lover and the very love itself. I am the saint, the adorer, the worshipper and the follower. I am God.*

He had, on the beach in Adyar in 1909, been in the wrong place at the wrong time and found god-training thrust upon him. But now the accidental deity had his own experience of divinity, unmediated by Leadbeater or Besant, or even the Masters, though letters from them continued to arrive. "*We are sorry for the pain. . . .*" His adoptive parents felt they could not understand the process and questioned Krishna as to why his "Brahmin body" needed such violent purification rituals. For his own part, Krishnamurti felt relief, for the heavy contradiction between his public image and his inner self seemed to have melted into air. He became reinvigorated to take up his mantle as divine teacher, and to lead his Order of the Star. He went on speaking tours, filled with an energy that seemed only to grow in the immediate wake of Nitya's untimely death in November 1925. Krishnamurti would tell his audiences that his dead brother was now inside him. "Sorrow is wonderful if you can taste it in the Divine cup," he wrote, intoxicated with grief.

Returning to Adyar in late December that year for Theosophy's Jubilee Convention, Krishnamurti experienced a sudden pronoun shift while he was giving a speech beneath a banyan tree. He was midsentence when the clouds parted in a gloomy sky, the sunlight poured in, and his voice swerved in pitch. "He comes only to those who want, who desire, who long, and I COME FOR THOSE WHO WANT SYMPATHY, WHO WANT HAPPINESS, WHO ARE LONGING TO BE RELEASED, WHO ARE LONGING TO FIND HAPPINESS IN ALL THINGS. I COME TO REFORM AND NOT TO TEAR DOWN, I COME NOT TO DESTROY BUT TO BUILD." Then he stopped, as the audience sat in stunned silence. "The coming has begun," Mrs. Besant proclaimed, and spoke of how "the Voice," not heard on earth for two thousand years, had sounded again in human ears. In her fervor, she announced the creation of the World Religion, and began plans to build on the site a Hindu temple, a church, a mosque, a Buddhist shrine, a Sikh shrine, a Jain shrine, a Parsi fire temple, and a synagogue, as if the coming were an apotheosis of comparative religion itself. In January 1927, Besant broadcast the good news across the world with a statement to the Associated Press: "The Divine Spirit has descended once more on a man, Krishnamurti, one who in his life is literally perfect, as those who know him can testify."

"Krishnamurti as such no longer exists," the vessel declared to reporters clamoring for an interview. In the throes of what he saw as his own experience of genuine divinity, a union beyond all language and thought, K., as he began to call Himself, embarked on a lifelong career to transcend the entire category of religion itself, revealing the inventedness that was always its nature. If, as Theosophy held, all religions are paths to the same truth, then, having found that truth, that thing at the center that might be emptiness or God, one should be able to eliminate the modular template: the dogmas and creeds, houses of worship, rituals, even the sacred texts. Rejecting the edifices Theosophy had constructed, and all spiritual authorities—Koot Hoomi and Morya prime among them—and all trifling deities and especially that explosive word, *beliefs*, Krishnamurti's theme became liberation. By stripping away the template, peeling back the layers of received knowledge, anyone could attain the same state of unity as K.—for, he preached, God already exists within us all. Having passed through the fire, his words were water "that shall wash away your sorrows, your petty tyrannies, your limitations, so that you will be free." "Because I have been held in bondage, I urge you to escape into freedom," the caged messiah proclaimed to a gathering of his followers.

Across the Theosophical Society, Krishnamurti's message was received with shock, most acutely by his adoptive mother, though she tried hard to understand the new teachings that undermined her own. She turned to psychology for theories of what was happening to her ward and supposed it was a split personality, "a blending of the consciousness of the Christ with the consciousness of His Disciple." Another possibility was that Krishna had become possessed by one of the "Blacks," the Dark Brotherhood that ever tries to thwart the spiritual empire of the Masters. As if in a subtle protest against her rogue son, in March 1928, Mrs. Besant announced that a new celestial teacher had come down to earth: the World Mother, who had last appeared as the Virgin Mary. Mrs. Besant had finally located the female messiah—she was Rukmini, the young, beautiful Indian wife of George Arundale, who had frequently tried to compete with Krishnamurti for influence in the society. Rukmini was chosen, like Krishna, for a certain vacant quality, her otherworldly blank stare. ("I have wondered at the absence of all that we know as personality in her," Mrs. Besant marveled.) Yet the press ridiculed the World Mother, and Rukmini later claimed it was all an embarrassing error, joining Hubert Van Hook in Theosophy's pantheon of mistakes.

When Krishnamurti first hinted to his adoptive mother of his intentions to renounce his divine status as vessel and disband the Order of the Star, the organization of forty-five thousand she had constellated around him, Annie Besant collapsed. The eighty-one-year-old lay in bed for several days, slipping in and out of consciousness, unable to speak or to recognize faces. After she recovered from the news, she called an emergency council at which it was decided to frame Theosophy and K.'s new teachings as, still, two paths to the same truth. She was present at Ommen in the Netherlands on the morning of August 3, 1929, when Krishnamurti, in front of a crowd of thousands of followers, dissolved the Order of the Star in the speech that led Leadbeater to remark: "The Coming has gone wrong."

I maintain that Truth is a pathless land . . . Truth, being limitless, unconditioned, unapproachable by any path whatsoever, cannot be organized; nor should any organization be formed to lead or to coerce people along any particular path. If you first understand that, then you will see how impossible it is to organize a belief . . . If you do, it becomes dead, crystallised; it becomes a creed, a sect, a religion, to be imposed on others. . . . I do not want followers, and I mean this. The moment you follow someone you cease to follow Truth . . . I desire those who seek to understand me to be free; not to follow me, not to make out of me a cage which will become a religion, a sect. Rather should they be free from all fears—

from the fear of religion,
from the fear of salvation,
from the fear of spirituality,
from the fear of love,
from the fear of death,
from the fear of life itself.

✦  ✦  ✦

On September 20, 1933, the day Annie Besant died, the Bombay Stock Exchange stopped trading in mourning for her, and universities, schools, and offices closed for the afternoon, as eulogies poured in from Gandhi and other luminaries, even those who had disagreed with her. A man who had, as a twelve-year-old boy, attended her lectures and felt compelled to join the Theosophical Society at a precocious age interrupted a speech to pay her tribute: he was Jawaharlal Nehru, now one of India's foremost politicians.

Besant, the once-formidable *Sri Vasanta*, never recovered from her disappointment at Krishnamurti's betrayal. After he disbanded the Order of the Star, Krishna did not visit her for two years; when he went to pay his final respects, he found Besant in a deep delirium. Leadbeater was at her side when she died, having traveled from Sydney to be there in his physical body. Dressed in his white bishop's cassock and heavy cross, Leadbeater put the light to her funeral pyre by the banks of the Adyar River, as the crowd looked on. They chanted verses from the *Gita* as the flames leapt up and searched, as if for something missing in the heavens. Sometime around that moment, Krishnamurti lost, or said he lost, his memory of everything that had happened to him in his life thus far. When he was asked about the events of his childhood or his god-hood, he would say he could remember nothing at all.

*India a nation! What an apotheosis! Last comer to the drab nineteenth-century sisterhood! Waddling in at this hour of the world to take her seat! She, whose only peer was the Holy Roman Empire, she shall rank with Guatemala and Belgium perhaps!*

—E. M. Forster, *A Passage to India*

# 10

## Mythopolitics

It is said that Vishnu reclined on a gigantic serpent, as the sleeping god dreamed the universe into existence. Through the ages, the pale-blue deity would descend to his terrestrial creation, taking the forms of different species: a fish, a tortoise, a boar, a frail Gujarati ascetic. In the mid-1930s, according to a group of Brahmin activists in Calcutta, a new shape revealed itself, perhaps Vishnu's worst, with a dark, clipped mustache, sleek hair parted to the side, pale skin, and an angry face. The Brahmins, eager to see Britain defeated by a greater power, had decided that Adolf Hitler was the final avatar of Vishnu. The deification of Hitler was the logical end point of the idea of the Aryan, a scholarly concept for Max Müller and a spiritual one for the Theosophists. The Führer had come to restore Aryan blood, which flowed alike in Hindu and European veins, to its former consistency of pure, divine light, inaugurating a new golden age. In household shrines, photographs and idols of Hitler could be spotted next to Vishnu and Shiva (flanked, occasionally, by Stalin), awaiting *bhakti*. It marked a particular subtype of apotheosis: to turn your enemy's enemy into your god.

The religious adoration of German strongmen, linked inextricably to hatred of the British, had a history. During the First World War, a league of Oraon tea plantation workers in Chota Nagpur were arrested for worshipping Kaiser Wilhelm II as a god. He had last been identified as Wislin in the Melanesian skies. At clandestine midnight services they passed around his portrait, his waxed mustache upturned like a pair of angel's wings, and sang hymns to the "German Baba," calling upon him to drive out the British demons and establish the Oraon Raj. At their trial for sedition, a song was brought in as evidence:

*German Baba is coming,*
*Is slowly slowly coming,*
*Drive away the devils:*
*Cast them adrift in the sea.*
*Suraj Baba (the Sun) is coming,*
*The Devils of the Oven will be driven away*
*And cast adrift in the sea.*

In the hymn, said to have been sent down to earth by God himself, Wilhelm II was the sun and stars, while the Devils of the Oven were fellow Oraons who denied His divinity. In a 1916 report on the movement, in which it was claimed the cult had spread to over sixty thousand Oraons, a retired British Army surgeon wrote of how Wilhelm II prevented bad harvests and rising food prices, and was acting as a figurehead to elevate the tea workers from the lowest rung of society. Believing their old gods to have lost their efficacy, "they were on a look out for a fresh powerful personality . . . The proverb says, that '*distance adds to enchantment*,'" the lieutenant wrote.

"In order to prepare unhindered access to their houses for the 'Spirit from Above', many Oraons removed several rows of tiles from the roofs of their huts, for when the god descended," according to another source. It was said the Kaiser was going to expel the British during a period of darkness lasting seven days and seven nights, followed by a week of blinding light, during which Oraon *swaraj* would come to pass. A single grain of rice would be sufficient to feed hundreds. The British newspaper the *Times of India* declared that the Oraons worshipped Wilhelm as an evil spirit, comparable to the goddesses of Cholera or Smallpox: "It would be nothing surprising, if some hints of the Kaiser's exploits in Belgium had penetrated even to the haunts of the Oraon, suggesting to his untutored intelligence the existence of a more sinister deity than any in his pantheon, needing propitiation." The Oraon faithful were said to face toward the west for just this purpose.

More sinister still was the worship of Hitler as avatar, an idea that spread across both India and the white supremacist Occident through the efforts of a French-born fascist-mystic who called herself Savitri Devi, or "solar goddess" in Sanskrit. Born Maximiani Portas in Lyon in 1905, as a young woman she developed a hatred of Christianity, Judaism, and Enlightenment reason. A self-proclaimed pagan with a PhD in philosophy, in the early 1930s Portas sailed through the Suez Canal and on to Calcutta, where she fell in with a loose network of Nazi Brahmins, RSS freedom fighters, and Hindu missionaries. Portas studied B. G. Tilak's theories on the Aryan origins of the Vedas in the North Pole, and was delighted to find, in homes that prayed for the vanquishing of the British Raj, Hitler resting next to Indian deities on the altars.

Stuck in India during the war, Savitri Devi spied for the Germans; in the wake of defeat, her stealth missions rose to the level of the astral plane. She claimed she traveled in her celestial body to visit Hermann Göring in his Nuremberg jail cell one night, to deliver the poison he used to commit suicide. In 1948, as soon as she could physically enter Allied-occupied Germany, she arrived to distribute leaflets encouraging the Nazis not to accept subjugation, and ended up imprisoned with female former concentration camp wardens in Westphalia, where she decorated her cell with an icon of her ersatz god. Later, posing as a journalist, Savitri Devi undertook a pilgrimage to various Hitler holy sites, including his birthplace in Braunau am Inn and his parents' grave, where she had an encounter with a spectral Führer himself. In the unearthly rock formations of the Externsteine, believed to be a prehistoric sacred site, she performed a midnight ritual to resurrect the Reich.

In India, Hitler incarnated as a deity who, like so many in the pantheon of accidental gods, despised his devotees. He considered Indians to be racially inferior and believed that if they did have any Aryan blood, it had long been polluted by race mixing. Though worshipped as the supreme enemy of the British, the Führer in fact rather admired the organizational prowess of the Raj and thought it imperative that India remain under white rule. He spurned attempts by anti-colonial activists to make alliances with him, including the militant freedom fighter Subhas Chandra Bose, dismissing such Indian liberationists as "Asiatic jugglers." Hitler would never have wished to become an avatar of a brown, blue, or occasionally lavender god such as Vishnu. But, as the *Bhagavad Gita* makes clear, the only divinity that ascends to heaven's highest rings is the one who does not desire it. His acolyte Savitri Devi had some contact with Bose—who was himself deified after his death in a mysterious plane crash in Taipei in 1945—and frequently cited verses from what she called her "Book of Books." She read the *Gita* as the secret Sanskrit wellspring of Nazi strength, which she claimed had prophesied the rise of Hitler: *When justice is crushed, when evil is triumphant, then I come back*, Lord Vishnu, avataring as Krishna, intones. *For the establishment of the Reign of Righteousness, I am born again and again, age after age.*

✦ ✦ ✦

According to the German philosopher Carl Schmitt, the political is born when we distinguish between friends and enemies: the division between those we love and those we hate is the original antagonism to which all politics can be reduced. In 1922, the year that Gandhi's worshippers set a police station on fire in Chauri Chaura, Schmitt published a treatise titled *Political Theology*, in which he argued that politics is the transfiguration of the sacred into secular forms. "All significant concepts of the modern theory of the state are secularized theological concepts," he declared. For Schmitt, who joined the Nazi party in 1933, the power to determine who was friend and who was enemy was the prerogative of the godhead of state. To Schmitt's maxim, I would add that the political comes into being when we distinguish between men and gods, a line as primordial as that between friend and foe, and as old as Adam's fall. Who decides who is a deity, and who is a man? Political power is the ability to create something out of nothing, just as God once labored to bring light and dry earth from the void.

We need a word that will capture how politics takes place in the dreamworlds of the popular. Though it is little used, and not in any dictionary, the word *mythopolitics* speaks to how power is so often rooted in myth. It is not merely a description but a call to action. Though the mid-ninteenth-century invention of "religion" would strive to partition the concept from "politics," sifting out all that was mythical, ritualized, and holy in the name of secularism, modern politics can still be understood as a metamorphosis of the sacred into new forms. Political power is always mythological: drawing on the divine, it travels the fault line that separates gods from men. This does not mean it stands outside of or violates reason, as the Enlightenment, promoting its own myth of rationality, would convey. Myth *is* enlightenment. And it summons us to the work of transformation. It seeks to find the origin, the cause, the reasons why things are the way they are, and thus to shape the future. Different ideas of divinity determine what form political rule should take.

"Political theology is polytheistic as every myth is polytheistic," Schmitt concluded, seeing its potentiality as always multiple. For many Indian nationalists, perceiving how Hindu polytheism had long been used as a weapon against India, liberation would have to be won through a politics so singular it went even beyond monotheism. It was so *one* it required fewer syllables, not monotheistic but monistic: the Vedantic idea, preached by gurus such as Vivekananda, that all dualities—God and the world, matter and spirit, friends and enemies—do not exist. Staring down the long history of allegations that Indians worshipped British officers and monarchs as gods, in the struggle for a democratic future for India, liberationists would have to dissolve any distinction between man and deity. The unity of the future independent India would have to resemble the unity of the divine, with every citizen a part of the godhead. Yet it required quite a sleight of hand, as the scholar Milinda Banerjee has written, to establish the highly particular, well-armed, and strictly bordered nation of India on a universalist idea of divine oneness, transcending boundaries between people and place. It required mythical thinking—and so the Sacred Man from the *Rig Veda* stepped in.

The dismembered divinity of the Sacred Man was a perfect parable for democracy. The millions of workers in the factories and fields represented his legs and feet; the businessmen were his torso, soldiers his arms, and academics his head. Politicians, of course, were his mouth, as the Bengali intellectual Bhudev Mukhopadhyay had imagined in his "History of India as Seen in a Dream" (1875). The ancient Vedic myth of the Sacred Man transformed the vast multitudes of India into a unified body, with a single will and a common cause, divided into parts yet still one. If the godhead is equally present in, and indistinguishable from, each individual soul, then every human being has an equal right to representation. Democracy is the cosmic state of man, at once natural and supernatural. "The King or Sovereign is no doubt a part and parcel of the God-head," remarked B. G. Tilak in a 1907 speech, alluding simultaneously to the charge that Indians were deifying the British and to the European notion of the divine right of kings:

> But according to the Vedanta, so is every member of the subject people. . . . The King may himself be a sort of deity, but the conflict between him and his subjects begets another deity only superior to him. And if the cause of the people be just, the second deity quietly absorbs the first. . . . The divine King as soon as he ceases to be just ceases also to be divine.

Like the fire-eater who could turn from benevolent to evil, the unjust king morphed into an *asura*, or a demon. He must be replaced, according to Tilak, by the greater god: that of the people, in a theology of revolution. In the aftermath of World War I, the British had introduced elections into India, not to prepare the groundwork for independence but to consolidate colonial rule, in part by the division of Hindus and Muslims into separate electorates. While many Indian leaders boycotted the first elections, arguing that it was, in effect, a vivisection of India, the idea of voting, with its ritual of the secret ballot, was powerful. Invocations of divine democracy roused the people, as India fought to liberate itself from the demon kings, a series of Edwards and Georges. Politicians spoke in the idiom of the sacred in a way that was not just metaphor.

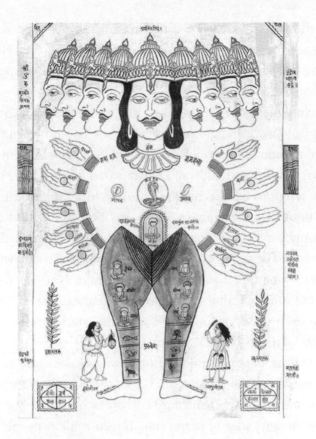

"Nationalism is a religion that has come from God," the freedom fighter
and mystic Sri Aurobindo Ghose declared in a Bombay speech. "Nationalism is immortal; Nationalism cannot die; because it is no human
thing." In the struggle, a space opened up, for hope. "God cannot be sent
to jail," the yogi advised.

✦  ✦  ✦

Like shapes in the clouds, nations are imagined into existence. The
politicians who conjure them are needed also to sanctify them in order
that they become real. When, at the stroke of midnight on August 15,
1947, the Republic of India was born, the frail and sacred human body
that embodied it was far from the festivities. As Jawaharlal Nehru was
being inaugurated in Delhi as the first prime minister of India, and power
was transferred from the British viceroy, Lord Mountbatten, the Mahatma

was in the slums of Calcutta, encamped in a squalid, abandoned mansion, fasting, in a grim mood. He refused to participate in the celebrations, seeing them only as stirring conflict with India's twin, Pakistan, born in the same hour.

The arrangement of Partition was, in its way, the dark end point of the concept of "world religions," forged in the late nineteenth century. The idea of a population transfer based on religion—Muslims in India swapped for Hindus and Sikhs in Pakistan—could only have come into being once religions had been reified, turned into impermeable entities with firm borders to be policed. There was no place within this modern taxonomy for the hundreds of thousands who labeled themselves "Mohammedan Hindus" on a 1911 census, or for those who worshipped the prophet Muhammad as an avatar of Vishnu. Nor was there room for a certain group of Rajputs who gave two names, one Hindu and one Muslim, to each child, or for the Nikalsainis, whose faith haunted the most remote outposts of the religions.

The Mahatma slept past midnight but was awake again at two a.m., reciting verses from the *Bhagavad Gita*, as the subcontinent was swept by violence and chaos that ended up costing two million lives. In a bitter twist on Besant's idea of home rule, fifteen million people lost their homes in the British-negotiated population transfers that the Raj deemed a requirement for independence. The people would not recover until they got their homes back, Gandhi prophesied, and most never did. For the horrors of Partition, the Mahatma was blamed on all sides. Hindu nationalists condemned him as too conciliatory and tolerant of Muslims, while Muslim leaders saw him as responsible for creating an Indian politics of liberation in a Hindu idiom that made it all but impossible for Muslims to be part of a Hindu nation-state. Still, in Calcutta, thousands of Hindus and Muslims alike came to the dilapidated villa, acrid with powdered bleach, for *darshan*—to see the divinity and be seen by him. When riots broke out across the city, Gandhi began a hunger fast, ransoming his life for several days until a group of thirty-five Hindus who had been involved in the slaughter of Muslims agreed, in what became known as the Miracle of Calcutta, to surrender their weapons to Bapu, the Father, and protect Muslims instead.

"If I seem to take part in politics, it is only because politics encircle us today like the coil of a snake from which one cannot get out, no matter how much one tries," Gandhi once said. "I wish therefore to wrestle with the snake." This is a problem that is true of any king or autocrat, at any time or place. In order to rule, the sovereign must stand both within society and outside of it—he must be simultaneously above the law, and subject to it. He must be at once present and absent. To be legitimate, an earthly ruler must relate to his kingdom like a god: he must be both immanent and transcendent, at work in the world and above it, as if he had two bodies, one mortal and human, one political and divine. How can a single individual achieve this? Even in a democracy the paradox persists: how can the people rule *over* themselves from within? In a way, accidental divinity resolves the conundrum of sovereignty. Hailed as a god against his will, having no desire to rule, nor any official role or title in the state, Gandhi reconciled the contradiction of existing both within and above society in his slender frame.

He was present but he was absent, with his hunger fasts and his severe, otherworldly asceticism. Unintentionality was the message of the *Bhagavad Gita*, the sacred scripture that guided India's liberation at every turn. It taught that only action performed without desire is sacred—and accidental gods do not aspire to godhood. "*I am of the earth, earthy*," Gandhi protested. The Mahatma's repeated avowal of his lack of interest in becoming a god made his will divine and sovereign over India, in a way that many Indians would consider dangerously omnipotent.

✦  ✦  ✦

A deep pit formed as people rushed for handfuls of soil—"sacred souvenirs," a newspaper reported—from the place where the Mahatma fell. Only five months after India's midnight birth, the Father was slain on the grounds of Birla House in Delhi at the hand of an ultraright Hindu assassin, who claimed both to love and hate him. Raised in infancy as a girl due to his parents' fear of a curse against their male sons, Nathuram Godse saw Gandhi as emasculating Hindus with his tolerance of Muslims. He was enraged by Partition, believing it to represent the dissection of the goddess India, and Godse despaired of the Mahatma's hold over India's government. At his trial, defending the murder as a religious duty, Godse spoke of how, in the *Gita*, Arjuna must kill even his own family and friends. For the good of millions, Gandhi had to be removed, and yet there was no legal way to remove him; the Mahatma was above the law.

"There was no legal machinery by which such an offender could be brought to book and for this reason I fired those fatal shots," Godse declared. He had been inspired by the ideologue V. D. Savarkar, who in 1923 drew upon Aryan theory to write his famous treatise *Hindutva*, or *Hindu-ness*, from his prison cell. Savarkar had been president of the ultraright political party Hindu Mahasabha, which Godse joined. Both men had been members of the RSS, the fascist-inspired paramilitary organization, recognizable in its uniform of colonial khaki shorts, which sought to promote Hindu supremacy and create an ethnically Hindu nation-state. Godse was sentenced to death and hanged, as if fulfilling the prophecy that had begun with a python that snaked, like a noose, in the sky.

In *Gandhiji's Journey to Heaven*, a painting by the artist Narottam Narayan Sharma, the Mahatma commands a celestial chariot drawn by swans with the intensity of a fighter pilot. He shoots beams of beatitude from his palms onto the receiving heads of Nehru and his deputy, Sardar Patel. Other images that circulated in the wake of Gandhi's death showed a muscular Mahatma tearing open his chest to reveal the godhead within. On January 31, 1948, the god of nonviolence was given a military funeral. Only days earlier, Gandhi had called for the Congress to disband; now the party organized the Mahatma's cremation, and used it to consolidate its grasp on power, in a ceremony that drew heavily on British pomp. Overlaid with flowers, Gandhi's body was borne on a carriage accompanied by four thousand soldiers in uniform, regiments of paratroopers, Rajputana Rifles, and Gurkhas, to the sound of a blown conch shell. Seated beside the sacrosanct body of the Mahatma was Prime Minister Nehru, in a supreme display of state authority. People climbed up trees and lampposts for *darshan* as the Mahatma passed, while millions of mourners gathered at vigils across the country.

In death, Gandhi was bestowed with the heightened sanctity of those who die in violent ways. By the side of the Yamuna River at Raj Ghat, his pyre was lit to the chanting of verses from the Vedas. The surging crowds broke through the cordon of barbed wire and nearly ran into the flames. When the fire had subsided, people scrambled for twigs and chips of the wood, any relics they could find. "Many were seen with the greatest reverence picking up withered and trodden rose petals," reported the newspaper the *Pioneer*. Telegrams to Nehru poured in:

```
Gandhiji's ashes alone may be dissolved. Request
preservatio n of bones as sacred relics. Recalling
preservation of Buddha's relics. Pray issue
instructions.
```

Gandhi's death was a national sin for which all India would have to atone, as Nehru made clear in his speeches. The shock alone was said to have quelled the violence of Partition, returning people to their senses. Through the sacrificial death of India's unwilling god, it was said that secularism was at last making its ascent. New currents of religious tolerance suffused the nation, while at the same time hundreds of thousands of ultraright Hindu activists and opponents of the Congress were rounded up and arrested. Although Gandhi had been against the idea of the nation-state, framed as it was by European history, it was through the rituals of grieving him that India first consolidated its identity as a nation. Gandhi's ashes set off on a train journey through Uttar Pradesh, echoing the trip Mohandas had taken in 1922 and which first sparked his deification. Surrounded by flowers and Indian flags, lit by electric light bulbs, Gandhi's urn could be clearly seen through the window by the millions of spectators eager for *darshan* who lined the route of the sepulchral train.

With border disputes ongoing with Pakistan, China, and Nepal, as well as the local rulers of princely states, the Congress party had the idea to divide up the Mahatma's ashes. A small urn was given to provincial governors and ministers from each region of the fragile new republic. The offerings of incandescent dust traced the imagined outline of India. The ashes were to be scattered in India's rivers, networking the subcontinent through the flowing streams of Gandhi's bodily remains, from the Hooghly River in Calcutta to the southernmost shore of Cape Cormorin.

The relics became a kind of political currency, as the Congress used them to trade for favors and to win leaders over to their side as they jostled for an urn. The ashes were dispatched to war-torn regions, such as the Partition-ravaged Punjab, and to Muslim-majority areas, using Gandhi's cremains as a balm for peace. His limbs divided and apportioned like the Sacred Man, the Mahatma was in a hundred places at once.

◆ ◆ ◆

If Gandhi's assassination was the nation's original sin, secularism was its atonement. As prime minister, Jawaharlal Nehru strove to purge religion from the political sphere, building what would become the world's largest democracy. Despite the mystical origins of the Indian National Congress, inspired by Blavatsky's Mahatmas and the spiritual bureaucracy they controlled, Nehru led the party as India's secularizing force. In the midst of the fratricide wrought by the barbed edges of faiths, the prime minister preached tolerance of all spiritual proclivities, rather than the eradication of religion itself. India's constitution, adopted in 1949, enshrined the freedom to practice and preach religion as a fundamental right. For his own part, Nehru would maintain that he abhorred "organized religion," a phrase that dated back only to the mid-nineteenth century. "Almost always it seemed to stand for blind belief and reaction, dogma and bigotry, superstition and exploitation," Nehru recalled in his *Autobiography*. The prime minister soon found a fitting, secularist guru for himself—in an irreverent, renunciate god.

In the wake of the Holocaust, Theosophy had become discredited and vilified, for so easily did its occult exaltations of the Aryan root-race shade into Nazism, providing incendiary fuel for anti-Semitism. Blavatsky's "discovery" of the ancient Indian swastika was adopted by early groups of German esoterics such as the Ariosophists, before becoming the emblem of the Third Reich. Nonetheless, while membership in the Theosophical Society had plummeted, Jiddu Krishnamurti's star was rising, as he reinvented himself as a teacher of a modernist, spiritual humanism. Drawing upon his own experience, the ex-deity taught that religion was enslavement of the mind, and gods but a figment of man's fantasy. Only weeks after India's independence, Krishnamurti traveled from California to the subcontinent, where he found a large following of Indians eager to embrace his new message, Prime Minister Nehru among them. In their private meetings, the weary politician despaired of the violence that gripped India. His guru advised him that the nation's regeneration could only come from the transformation of its individuals: through silence, stilling the soul's chaos and awakening to the present. In his teachings, Krishnamurti replaced anthropomorphic deities with a spirituality both practical and abstract. Yet whenever they listened to him, his followers would often confess they still felt the rushing presence of something beyond human in the room.

The year 1957 marked both the tenth anniversary of independence and the centenary of the Indian Mutiny. One of the myriad ways India celebrated was by evicting the Delhi statue of John Nicholson from the land. Nikalsain had stood, with sword dangling unsheathed, for decades, keeping watch over the Kashmere Gate, as his color slowly turned from bronze to green. When Indian activists began to threaten his destruction, the brigadier's former high school in Northern Ireland arranged for its deified alumnus to be brought home, during what the *Times* of London decried as a "holocaust of British statues." In Benares, an idol of Queen Victoria was injured in a scuffle, while in Bombay, the statue of Richard Wellesley, once worshipped at Elphinstone Circle, was decapitated. Wellesley was later moved to the statue graveyard of an ethnographic museum, displayed like so many specimens of fetish worship. He joined another Victoria, missing a nose, as well as the old, vermilion-smeared statue of Charles Cornwallis, once so adored it had required an iron fence to defend it from excessive *puja*, but now headless too.

On May 10, 1957, over fifteen thousand people gathered at Ramlila Gardens in Delhi to hear Nehru give an expansive account of India's history and its invaders, from the ancient Aryans to the British. "When the British entrenched themselves strongly on Indian soil, a rift between the Hindus and Muslims developed. Is that not strange?" Nehru asked. It was a history written by Englishmen, the prime minister declared, because Indians had lived in fear. Nehru told of how the British had come to India in search of trade and gradually taken control of the

LORD MARQUIS OF WELLESLEY

country, "under the cloak of commerce," before anyone realized what was happening. In Nehru's view, Indians had been shackled by archaic superstitions that were "extremely stupid," and prevented them from keeping up with a swiftly modernizing world. "All the emphasis was on rituals and shibboleths. How could a people whose attention was constantly absorbed by such trivial matters hope to progress?" In his address, Nehru went through his rather prosaic five-year plan, which involved establishing steel plants and irrigation systems, fiscal loans and new taxation schemes. "Even today it is extremely dangerous to bring religion into politics," the arch-secularist declared.

✦ ✦ ✦

Asleep on the serpent, in Vishnu's dream, full of violence and nihilism and humor, it was only a matter of time before the prime minister would become ensnared in the godhead. In November 1958, reports began appearing in local newspapers that a cult devoted to Nehru had been uncovered in the district of Sabarkantha, near Ahmedabad. Proclaiming Nehru the latest incarnation of the pale-blue, four-armed Creator, the sect had built idols of Nehru, and were performing daily *pujas* to their new god. A booklet of hymns had been published and was being distributed secretly to initiates. It was reported that Nehru, outraged by the news, had gone to the chief minister of Bombay, Y. B. Chavan, to protest that his administration, which he had always considered quite enlightened, was tolerating such an absurdity in the district. But given that Nehru himself had enshrined the right to freedom of worship in India's constitution, there was little that Chavan could do. And the chief minister, too, seemed moved by the Nehruvian spirit. "In the glow of his presence," Chavan wrote of Nehru that same year, "something of the strength and tenderness, youth and maturity, defiance and humility of his being entered into me and lifted me high above the ordinary and humdrum plane of this earth."

In the pages of the *Times of India*, amused columnists and outraged subscribers began to take sides on the new deity. One reader, adept in conspiracy theory, claimed it was a propaganda campaign carried out by social workers with ties to the Congress, to exploit the villagers' gullibility and secure their positions in the next elections. He called for the vindication of Nehru, "perhaps the most secular-minded of all our leaders." The Hindu extremist N. B. Khare gleefully proclaimed it "a nice psychological revenge on a declared agnostic." In a column titled "BASIC RIGHT," the politician Rafiq Zakaria noted that, since the constitution guaranteed religious freedom, even if Chavan attempted to suppress the cult, he would be blocked by the high court. Zakaria then wondered aloud as to why Nehru should be so annoyed at being venerated as a god in the first place. "Almighty apart, there can be many divine manifestations on this earth. After all what is God but, as the Bible has proclaimed, 'love'? And what is Mr. Nehru if not love?" At a press conference in New Delhi, Nehru, questioned about his apotheosis, indignantly retorted that newspapers shouldn't give publicity to such "nonsense." The *Times of India* noted, "A correspondent then asked him to explain the 'melancholy touch' in his voice in Parliament of late. Mr. Nehru's answer was that he was recovering from a bad throat."

Twenty years earlier, in 1937, Nehru had gone so far as to write an essay, under a pseudonym, warning people not to deify him or even re-elect him. A mysterious op-ed appeared in a Calcutta journal by a certain "Chanakya," a fourth-century sage and kingmaker known as the Indian Machiavelli, who authored the *Arthashastra*, the Sanskrit manual on the art of rule. The ancient scribe warned that Nehru, in his immense popularity and vertiginous rise, was quickly becoming a dictator: "Watch him again. There is a great procession and tens of thousands of persons surround his car and cheer him in an ecstasy of abandonment. He stands on the seat of the car, balancing himself rather well, straight and seemingly tall, like a god. . . . What lies behind that mask of his, what desires, what will to power . . . ?" The article urged readers not to elect Nehru for a third term. "Men like Jawaharlal, with all their capacity for great and good work, are unsafe in democracy," Chanakya intimated from the afterlife. "He might still use the language and slogans of democracy and socialism, but we all know how fascism has fattened on this language."

Elected once more as president of the Congress, Nehru did indeed find his lionization an obstacle to his democratic message. He fought off embarrassing nicknames like *Bharat Bhushan* ("Jewel of India") and *Tyagamurti* ("O, Embodiment of Sacrifice.") He strove to diffuse wild legends of his bravery that distracted from his civic agenda. An entrepreneur even infused his aura into a line of cosmetic products with names like "Nehru Brilliantine." Disturbed and exhausted by the limelight, Nehru contemplated a retreat from politics. Chanakya had already dropped hints: "In spite of his brave talk, Jawaharlal is obviously tired and stale and he will progressively deteriorate if he continues as President. He cannot rest, for he who rides a tiger cannot dismount." When he rose to become the first prime minister of India, Nehru made few concessions to his new altitudes of power. He insisted on being greeted with a single flower rather than a garland, and refused to sit on a preposterously cushioned, gold-and-silver chair that resembled a throne.

"True, Mr. Nehru is no competitor to God, though he has made it clear that he is not afraid of Him," Rafiq Zakaria wrote. "He has, however, no time to make God in his image; though God in his infinite wisdom made Mr. Nehru in His image." Unable to imprison his worshippers under the same constitution he had helped to draft, Nehru may have been India's arch-secularist, but his power to move people was still sacred. It was Gandhi who had pronounced that Nehru was nearer to God than anyone else the Mahatma knew. "There could have been no greater praise," Zakaria argued, "and hence Mr. Nehru should develop a greater spirit of tolerance towards those who see in him God Himself!"

✦ ✦ ✦

The curtain rises on a scene.

In the darkness of a temple, footsteps are approaching. The crashing of iron and stone breaks the hallowed silence of the night. A group of monks, convened in a cloud of incense, are terrified to see the prime minister, a certain Mr. Zahmu, creeping through the corridors and smashing likenesses of his own face with an axe. Fearfully and adoringly, the monks confront their God.

> ABBOT: How merciful Thou art! How great is Thy glory! *[He lowers his head and covers his face with the palm of his hand.]* My eyes have not the strength to gaze upon the splendour of Thy light.
>
> ZAHMU: What is he talking about? A light? *My* light? It's all so dark that I can hardly see my hand.

The prime minister must be unable to see the light emanating from Himself, the monks reason. Fulfilling an age-old prophecy, the hour has come in which God would take His human vessel, whether Zahmu likes it or not. "Anything is possible," the incredulous politician protests, "except that I should be a god in spite of myself—without previous notice, even! Why, if I was a vacant room, the landlord's consent would have to be obtained before I was occupied!" His deification, Zahmu insists, must be a plot engineered by his rivals to disgrace him, to exile him from politics to the distant province of religion. For the apostles, however, everything that Zahmu says or does can be explained away as further proof of his divinity. "Do reconsider the decision," Zahmu begs. "Perhaps it is the Leader of the Opposition who is intended to be the god." But the monks cannot be shaken from their devotion. When Zahmu attempts to escape from the temple, he finds himself surrounded on all sides by throngs of his worshippers—including his own secretary and members of his cabinet. Caught in an unusual impasse, the perplexed prime minister despairs:

ZAHMU: What have I done that I should be robbed of my humanity? . . . Let me be human! I am not a god! [He paces back and forth, shouting] I am a man . . . I am a man . . . I am a man . . .

In Cairo, a playwright had been saving clippings of news stories about Nehru's plight, which appeared in the Egyptian papers. The story seemed to speak to the predicament of any nation trapped in a leadership cult. Ever since Gamal Abdel Nasser had succeeded in expelling the British in 1952 in a military coup, Egypt had been in the grip of a state-enforced passion for its own leader. Like being in love, one saw—or imagined one did—the face of the handsome lieutenant everywhere. His hawkish nose and reassuring mustache graced shop windows, living rooms, and dusty office walls. Nasser's disembodied voice emanated from the Voice of the Arabs, the state radio station, broadcast twenty-two hours a day, and his spirit entered the pantheon of the Sudanese *zar*. At the cinema, state-sponsored films depicted Nasser as a man so virtuous, so noble, that no one could hope to emulate him, only to worship him. Some of those closest to him claimed the man himself was actually rather lacking in charisma, but it didn't matter; a formidable propaganda machine was in place.

When he was younger, Nasser had learned to act in the theater, playing the role of Julius Caesar at school. Two decades later, when a member of the Muslim Brotherhood fired eight bullets at him while he was delivering a speech in Alexandria, Nasser, unscathed, kept on speaking, and proclaimed to his panicked audience, "If Gamal Abdel Nasser should die, I will not die—for *all of you are Gamal Abdel Nasser.*" It was rhetoric ripe for satire:

THIRD MONK: Your function tomorrow will be that of a god . . .
The poor shall take refuge in you; you shall live with the weak
and hear the complaint of the nameless, the downtrodden, the
banished . . .
ZAHMU: But this is precisely my party's programme. This is what I
have been doing ever since I entered politics.

If all were Nasser and Nasser was all, those who dared to disagree were excluded from this Oneness. In the aftermath of the assassination attempt, much as after Gandhi's death, religious movements and opposition parties were banned in the name of secularism and stability, and critics of the regime were imprisoned.

In 1962, the playwright who had been captivated by Nehru's apotheosis published a one-act play in Arabic, called *A God in Spite of His Nose.* Appearing with little fanfare in a book of short stories, and almost certainly never performed, the play seemed to be a trenchant satire of the uses and abuses of religion in politics. It appears to warn of what might happen were one to follow the rhetoric of any politician to its logical end. Even the most splendidly manipulative campaign to capture and control the hearts of the people cannot entirely avoid the risk of being taken at its own word.

Yet the author of *A God in Spite of His Nose* was none other than Nasser's chief propagandist and speechwriter, the ultranationalist politician Fathi Radwan, who had been a founding father of Young Egypt, a fascist-inspired paramilitary youth movement in the 1930s. As Nasser's first minister of "national guidance," and later as minister of culture, Radwan was responsible for devising the rhetoric and public image of the dictatorship. Almost militantly prolific, Radwan wrote over forty books, many of them hagiographies of great men. His first, in 1934, was a biography of Gandhi, whom he hailed as the spiritual leader of both India and Egypt's common struggle against the British. It was Radwan who wrote the words Nasser proclaimed right in the midst of the assassination attempt—"*All of you are Gamal Abdel Nasser*"—and some say he even staged the entire affair.

The paradox that the mastermind of Nasserist propaganda, a champion of autocracy and state-controlled media, had written a play about the dangers of deifying a politician, is striking. He was, perhaps, a satirist in spite of himself. In the script, Zahmu's endless objections to his own divinity nearly drive the monks into a crisis of belief. But by the end, having concluded that Zahmu's blasphemies must be the last gasps of human vanity escaping the sacred vessel, the monks remain, as ever, in adoration. Just so, Fathi Radwan remained a believer in Nasser, even after the humiliating defeat of the Six-Day War in 1967, when in a single night, Israel destroyed the entire Egyptian air force before it had even left the ground. Despite Nasser's failures, Radwan never recanted his faith in either the man or the machinery he had set in motion. The nation was his religion, one that Radwan loved too much.

FIRST MONK: Your coming was mentioned in the Holy Scriptures from the start, before you were born. Your characteristics are known to us, and the hour of your incarnation is precisely determined—it cannot be put forward by a moment or delayed for a second.

ZAHMU: And has the incarnation taken place?

SECOND MONK: It has started.

ZAHMU [*looking down at his chest, and at his hands which he turns over and over*]: Started?? Started without any signal or warning? I don't think that's fair.

✦   ✦   ✦

"HINDUS SEE VISHNU REBORN IN PRESIDENT" announced the headline in the *Los Angeles Times* on December 10, 1959. On the maiden

voyage of Air Force One, Dwight Eisenhower touched down in Delhi, as the first US president in office to visit India. Ike had come, bearing a bust of Abraham Lincoln as a gift, to help Nehru fight the incursions of Chinese communism. It was, however, to be more than a brief diplomatic visit: on the tarmac, that runway of accidental divinity, the American president joined the Indian prime minister in the godhead of Vishnu. As a crowd of thousands pressed around him, Eisenhower took off his hat to receive an enormous garland that snaked around his shining bald head. "'Do you think we were fools to travel from 10 to 100 miles to see anyone but Vishnu Ka Avatar?'" asked Kanthi, a seventy-year-old woman interviewed by reporters from the *New York Times*. "Her family, clustering around her in a bullock cart, nodded assent," the report continued, "and her daughter Shanthu, added, 'Does not this avatar also smile like Vishnu—a divine, radiant smile?'" It was said there were powerful healing properties in the sand of the dirt roads over which the Cadillac carrying Eisenhower and Nehru had passed. A man called Ramchandri, from Soni village, thirty miles away, was unable to bring his wife because she was ill, but he had collected a vial of sacred gravel. "I shall apply this on my wife's head and she is sure to be cured," the good husband said.

"IKE ACCLAIMED AS INDIAN GOD...COUNTRY FOLK INSIST HE IS MIGHTY DEITY," the *Chicago Tribune* proclaimed. The paper quoted Ram Swarup, aged twenty, from Gurgaon, who shed tears at the sound of Eisenhower's voice echoing from a white podium. "I do not understand English, but I can sense the depth of sincerity in his speech—he spoke from his heart," Swarup said. Even Christians were moved by the holy spirit: Reverend E. C. Anthony, from Meerut, avowed, "The sight I saw today is for angels to see and bless." In its own take on the events, the *Pittsburgh Press* told of how Eisenhower, on Air Force One, had traced the epic route of Alexander the Great. "Asia understands powerful men in terms of gods and kings, frequently combining the two," the paper noted. "Democratic self rule is wholly alien to ages-old Asiatic tradition. . . . Though Asiatic political leaders experiment with democratic forms, the new principle is hard to grasp." Nonetheless, "the Indian people have shown to us and to the world that their affection for America runs deep—a dividend of priceless value from the President's trip."

In the twilight of the British empire, the Hindu deification of Eisenhower was proof of the inexorable rise of the American empire across the world. If the British gods, the myriad colonial officers thirsting for gin and Havana cigars, could barely scrape the bottom of heaven's ring, the American gods were on the ascent. Eisenhower, who had once served as assistant to the great hunk of god Douglas MacArthur, was spreading the doctrine of liberalism over the earth like solar rays in the chill of the Cold War. If transforming Ike into a Supreme Being seemed a little at odds with the concept of democracy, the impulse to worship America was still, at least in American eyes, correct. Only a year earlier, the president had established NASA, in the wake of the Soviet Union's launch of Sputnik; clearly Eisenhower was a celestial being who had his sights properly set on outer space.

"Association of Mr. Eisenhower with Vishnu seems to indicate the 'image' of America has gotten through, at least dimly, among the vast, unlettered masses who get their news by word of mouth and tend to relate it to legend," the *Pittsburgh Press* opined. For their readers at home, the American papers offered a primer on the "Hindu trinity": Brahma, Vishnu, and Shiva. Vishnu was the "Protector of the world in epochs of danger," the *Pittsburgh Press* noted, who would descend to earth in different avatars "always for a wholesome purpose." In the body of blue-eyed Ike, Vishnu had come to protect and preserve a globe now facing its most acute threat of annihilation yet, nuclear weapons—a danger that peasants such as Kanthi understood, the *New York Times* reported. Kanthi, the seventy-year-old villager, recognized Eisenhower as avatar for two reasons: like Vishnu, the American president was "a great bene-factor," who had sent wheat to India and constructed dams. But more cosmically, Ike also held the power of Vishnu "to destroy the world by a mere wish." Like the pale-blue protector, Eisenhower "never used it and instead kept it as a final trump card against evil," Kanthi explained.

It was the moment in human history when politics itself first began to possess the ultimate capacity of a divinity: the ability to annihilate the entire earth in a flash, on a whim. A new age had been ignited ever since Robert Oppenheimer, after watching the first atom bomb detonate in the desert of New Mexico, quoted the *Bhagavad Gita*, "Now I am become Death, the destroyer of worlds." The power of divinity is that it is able to withstand its own contradictions: American imperium held the force of a new apocalyptic violence, but it was using it to spread peace. For the first time in American history, the president was to be accompanied everywhere by a black leather briefcase, like Poseidon with his trident, containing the nuclear codes, lest he suddenly need to use them.

"The violence which nuclear weapons can inflict makes any other kind of violence completely meaningless," Nehru had warned in 1957. Yet he was asking Indians to keep religion out of the public sphere just at the moment when politicians had reached a new apex of godliness. The doctrine of secularism proselytized rationality and commanded believers to eschew irrational faith, yet rational, calculated violence was unleashing more destruction than the irrational kind ever had. The atom bomb was the clearest indication of how states could become omnipotent. Like any so-called organized religion, the secular state was developing its own priestly castes, its legions of experts, scientists, and administrators. The state had new sacred tenets—nationalism, security, technological progress—and it demanded blind faith in them. Those who crowded around Eisenhower in Delhi for a glimpse of *darshan* were not wrong to see in him a god with a gleaming bald pate. Beneath the surface of secularism was the animating antagonism between friends and enemies, men and gods: the space of mythopolitics.

While Nehru strove to excise religion from India's public sphere, Eisenhower was injecting a new religiosity into American public life, deploying faith as a political weapon to defeat the godless enemy of communism. In 1954, he approved the motion to add "under God" into the Pledge of Allegiance, and two years later, made the official motto of the nation "In God We Trust," although America was still to be considered a secular state. Born a Mennonite, Ike was the first US president to be baptized in office, becoming a Presbyterian ten days after his inauguration. He instituted the ritual of the National Prayer Breakfast, and retained as his spiritual advisor the Reverend Billy Graham, the evangelist whose popularity was soaring among an American people, in his words, "hungry for God." As Eisenhower tried to weed out queer "subversives" in the government in the name of Christian morals, the pale-blue avatar presided over the "lavender scare." Meanwhile, the CIA was gaining ever greater powers of surveillance. The paradox of secularism, of removing the old gods from the public sphere, or co-opting them toward state ends, was that it left the people with no superpowers to protect themselves against the violence of the state. There were no checks or balances on the state's all-seeing divinity.

✦ ✦ ✦

For several years, the temple in Rajkot had been open, and embraced a shuffle of pilgrims beneath its thatched canopy. But the problem was no one had yet created a perfect likeness of the god enshrined within. Artists faltered on how to capture his keen eyes, rimmed by Bulgari specta-

cles, his full lips, framed by a downy but groomed white beard, his soft
features and round face like a lion cub's: friendly on the surface. How
also to project his fearsome, cold-blooded, authoritarian strength? At
the Gujarati temple, the faithful worshipped before a photograph until,
in February 2015, it was announced that sculptors from Odisha had at
last created, at great expense, an idol that was, almost miraculously, a
perfect copy. It looked "exactly like Modi," marveled one of the fundrais-
ers, Ramesh Undhad, of the marble bust of the hard-line prime minister,
a Hindu supremacist prone to describing himself as "secular."

In a navy vest and a saffron scarf embroidered with lotuses, the likeness of Narendra Modi received heaps of marigolds in his temple. It was
constructed on government-owned land by supporters of the Bharatiya
Janata Party, the ultraright, Hindu nationalist movement that swept to
power in 2014, in a consummate defeat of the Congress party. Now that
the statue had at last been unveiled, the newspapers reported an official
inauguration was planned, which ministers of agriculture and industry
would attend. Soon the flood of media coverage reached the flesh and
blood politician himself. Where once gods would have voiced their wrath
through storms, whirlwinds, or bird entrails, Modi took to a new channel
of divine communication to vent his displeasure to his followers:

> @narendramodi *Have seen the news about a Temple being built in
> my name. I was appalled. This is shocking and against India's great
> traditions.*

> @narendramodi *Building such Temples is not what our culture
> teaches us. Personally, it made me very sad. Would urge those doing
> it not to do it.*

"If our God is unhappy, we will remove his statue and worship him
in our heart," Undhad told reporters. A district inspector was brought
in and announced that the structure itself was illegal; the temple was
swiftly demolished. Yet it was not the first house of worship to be
raised to the politician of humble birth, the son of a chai-wallah from

Vadnagar, from a caste characterized by the government as "Other Backward Class." In Bhagwanpur village, a medieval temple devoted to Shiva had been reconsecrated to *NaMo*, a Sanskrit term of obeisance. A less realistic likeness of a cross-legged Narendra Modi had taken up residence with the Shiva lingam, in what was said to be the first temple devoted to a living god in the state of Uttar Pradesh. Surrounded by incense, offerings of rupees, and a conch shell, *NaMo* listened to the *Modi chalisa*, or devotional hymn, composed in His honor, as a Modi look-alike priest, a certain Pandit B. N. Misra, presided in a kurta and jacket modeled after the prime minister's own. A light was kept aflame at all times in front of His portrait. Newspapers reported that the *NaMo* shrine received a steady foot traffic of worshippers, until a dissenter broke the nose of the god.

Although it might have seemed, for Nehru and others, as though secularism should point the way to an inevitable death of religions, it has led only to the empowerment of a religiously extreme core. Some of his adepts call Modi, who trained as a military cadet in the RSS, the "god of politics," hailing him as Kalki, the final avatar of Vishnu, who comes to bring about a new age. Others chant *Har Har Modi*, a war cry to Shiva rewritten as a battle song against an enemy with two heads: Muslims and liberal Hindus of the Congress party. As chief minister of Gujarat, Modi had been infamous for inciting sectarian hatred; in 2002, while he was in power, an organized pogrom took place in which police and state officials participated, and over a thousand Muslims were slaughtered in cold blood. With Modi's approval, the Gujarat State Board published school textbooks glorifying the earlier avatar of Vishnu, Hitler; chapters extolled Nazi ideology and portrayed the Führer as a model of good leadership. Translations of *Mein Kampf* became required reading for business school students. In 2014, after Modi became prime minister, the Hindutva faithful began a campaign to apotheosize Gandhi's assassin, Nathuram Godse, by consecrating new holidays, constructing idols, and attempting to build a temple to the executed criminal.

In Varanasi, posters were spotted on which a Sanskrit chant to the goddess Durga had been rewritten as a paean to the far-right god: *Ya*

*Modi Sarvabhuteshu, Rashtrarupen Sansthita, namastasye, namastasye Namo Namah.* "We worship Modi, who resides in every human being in the form of the nation."

*I am born again and again, age after age,* Lord Vishnu says.

✦ ✦ ✦

On the opposite side of the earth, in a gilded resort in Palm Beach, Florida, the sleeping god took one last avatar. Just as the US president had joined the Indian prime minister in the godhead in 1959, history replayed itself in 2018, from tragedy to farce. "My family and village people call me mad," a thirty-one-year-old farmer named Bussa Krishna told the reporters who swarmed to his dusty village of Konne, sixty miles from Hyderabad. "Once they suggested I should visit a psychologist. I told them 'I don't require any, maybe you should go' because he is my god and I am not bothered about stuff others say." If a religion, as William James once defined it, was the experience of standing in relation to *whatever* one considered the divine, for Krishna it took the form of Donald J. Trump.

It was reported that Krishna carried Trump's portrait everywhere with him, on errands and into the fields; he was spotted holding it as he meditated under a tree, and prayed to it several times a day, with offerings of turmeric, marigolds, and candles with orange flames. Krishna posted photos and videos of himself online doing Trump *puja*, and claimed to have received a message from the god. He built a life-size idol of the deity, dressed in a navy suit and red tie, in his front yard, and inscribed the sacred syllable of TRUMP on the walls in red paint, repeated again and again in an incantation. Despairing of his strange brand of worship, Krishna's parents, who had lived with him, decided to move out. "Nobody took me seriously and some people even called me a mad fellow, wondering how prayers in a remote village would reach Trump. But I have a strong faith in what I am doing," Krishna said of the man-god he worshipped for his imperious, invincible strength.

Even though it was only a few years old, the Trump religion had already accrued several conflicting accounts of its origins. The *Hindustan Times* reported that Krishna had the idea of worshipping Trump after his inauguration, which had provoked a torrent of hate crimes against Indians in the United States. Krishna spoke of Srinivas Kuchibhotla, a software engineer from Hyderabad, who, a month after Trump took office, was killed at a bar in Kansas by a navy veteran shouting, "Get out of my country." "I was very much pained at the incident. I thought the only way the US president and his people could understand the greatness of Indians is to display our love and affection toward them. That is why I started worshipping Trump with a hope that the prayers would reach him one day," Krishna said. The murder of the engineer was only one of numerous violent attacks against Indians across the country, from South Carolina to Washington State. In Krishna's telling, his religion of Trump was apotropaic—its purpose was to avert and appease the divine wrath unleashed by the white supremacist god. But according to his neighbors, Krishna had been worshipping Trump even before he became president. "He's been doing this for the last three years," a villager, Sathayalkshimi, told reporters, leading them to speculate as to whether Krishna's prayers might have helped the reality TV mogul get elected. "I believe Indians can win over anyone with their spiritual powers," Krishna maintained.

"When you cannot take on a mighty person directly, you can win over him with love and worship, and that is what I am doing."

"Life is not worth living without a theory, however imperfect, of transcendence," the Indian political psychologist Ashis Nandy wrote in 1988. The distinction of religion versus politics was "not working well," he noted. This was something of an understatement: not only in India but in any allegedly secular society, it had led neither to the eradication of religion from politics nor to greater tolerance of different spiritual leanings. Where "religion" had succeeded, secularism had failed: "It is not an adequate consolation to the faithful, to whom religion is what it is precisely because it provides an overall theory of life," Nandy argued. "Facts are not enough," wrote the American white nationalist Greg Johnson in 2011. "We need a myth, meaning a concrete vision, a story of who we are and who we wish to become. Since myths are stories, they can be understood and appreciated by virtually anyone. And myths, unlike science and policy studies, resonate deeply in the soul and reach the wellsprings of action. Myths can inspire collective action to change the world." Johnson has been a chief architect of the resurrection of Savitri Devi in the twenty-first century, publishing new editions of her work. Her ashes are enshrined in Arlington, Virginia, watched over by American neo-Nazis, and her theories of white people as "children of the sun" are invoked at Trump rallies.

In early October 2020, when news was released that Trump had been infected with the novel coronavirus, Bussa Krishna began a hunger fast. On October 11, the day the US president announced his unusually swift recovery, Krishna collapsed of cardiac arrest and died en route to a hospital. Widely reported in the international media, the story of an Indian man doing *puja* to Trump, ultimately offering himself as blood sacrifice, gave a recognizably "religious" form to the parallel currents in America among those who believe in Trump. From tiki torch processionals, to theories of Trump as messiah, to the POTUS Prayer Shield, a network of millenarian Christian prayer warriors that protected the president, political power remains staked to the divine. Eisenhower once said: "Our form of government has no sense unless it is founded in a deeply felt religious faith, and I don't care what it is."

The first task of any god, whether Vishnu, Brahma, or Elohim, is to create what all other creatures will come to recognize as real. "We're an empire now," a senior advisor at the White House remarked in 2004, "and when we act, we create our own reality. And while you're studying that reality—judiciously, as you will—we'll act again, creating other new realities, which you can study too." This is mythopolitics. The avatars of the god are always changing: an endless stream of administrators, politicians, prime ministers, and presidents who serve their terms, or wilt with fever, or are assassinated. "I have a very great relationship with God," Donald Trump said in an interview during his presidential campaign. He was backtracking on an earlier claim that he never asked God for forgiveness, in comments that invoked a Eucharist of liquor and crumbs.

> *You know, when we go in church and when I drink my little wine, which is about the only wine I drink, and have my little cracker, I guess that is a form of asking for forgiveness.*
> *And I do that as often as possible, because I feel cleansed, OK?*

Long before Vishnu, in his avatar as Krishna, appeared in the killing fields of the *Bhagavad Gita* and urged Arjuna on, the god spent his childhood as the son of cow-herders, and was occasionally known to eat dirt. Once, the boy Krishna was playing with his friends when they tattled on him to his mother. She took Krishna by the hand, and scolding him, asked him why he had eaten dirt. "I didn't do it," Krishna protested. When she ordered the boy to open his mouth for proof, she saw the entire universe inside it. There were the heavens, the sun, stars, and clouds, the oceans and the islands, the altars and the palaces of kings, her entire village, and herself. It was all an illusion, the dream of a god asleep on a mattress of iridescent serpent scales. Because she had understood too much, the woman lost her memory of everything that she had just seen. She took her baby god onto her lap, and the Lord Vishnu spread his illusion in the form of love.

III

# WHITE GODS

Entered, according to Act of Congress in the year 1865, by J. A. Arthur, in the Clerk's Office of the District Court for the Eastern District of Pennsylvania.
WASHINGTON & LINCOLN. (APOTHEOSIS.)
J. Ferris, Pinxt. Photo. and Pub. by Phil. Pho. Co., 720 Chestnut St.

*We must lull hatred to sleep like a captive snake.*

—Fernando Pessoa, *The Book of Disquiet*, 1913

## THE BEATITUDES CONTINUED.

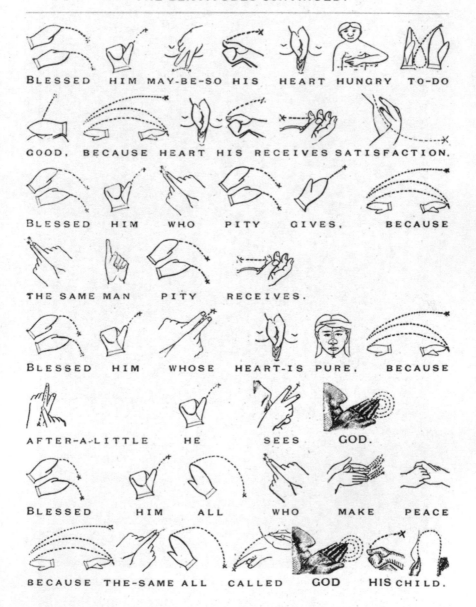

BLESSED HIM MAY-BE-SO HIS HEART HUNGRY TO-DO

GOOD, BECAUSE HEART HIS RECEIVES SATISFACTION.

BLESSED HIM WHO PITY GIVES, BECAUSE

THE SAME MAN PITY RECEIVES.

BLESSED HIM WHOSE HEART-IS PURE, BECAUSE

AFTER-A-LITTLE HE SEES GOD.

BLESSED HIM ALL WHO MAKE PEACE

BECAUSE THE-SAME ALL CALLED GOD HIS CHILD.

# 11

# Serpents

*So God created man in His own image,*
*in the image of God He created him,*
*male and female He created them . . .*

—Genesis 1:27

"We were superior to the god who had created us," recalled Adam, not long before his death at seven hundred years of age. "After God created me out of earth, along with your mother Eve, I went about with her in glory," he told his son Seth, as preserved in *The Revelation of Adam*, a Coptic text dating from the late first century CE and unearthed in Upper Egypt in 1945. According to a rabbinic commentary on Genesis, Adam was such a perfect likeness that the angels mistook him for God. They were about to cry out "Holy!" before the first man, and so, to differentiate Himself, God created sleep, sending Adam into a nightly, ungodlike stupor. The commentary records that Adam was once so large he reached from one end of heaven to the other, slipping into the hollow spaces of the earth. In Adam's account, he and Eve were a single, magnificent being. The fall was a plunge from unity into human difference. "God angrily divided us," Adam recounted in his *Revelation*. "And after that we grew dim in our minds . . ." Paradise was a lost sense of self, and it was a place that appeared on maps wistfully imagined by generations of Adam's descendants. In the fifteenth century, European charts located Eden where the sun rises, to the farthest east, an island ringed by a wall of fire. With the coordinates in their minds, Europe's explorers sensed they might someday return, and find their way back to wholeness, to transcendence, to the godhood that once belonged to man. Here begins the origin story of how whiteness became divine.

✦ ✦ ✦

The light appeared in the darkness of a maritime night. Like a candle it flickered and rose, guiding the navigator to make landfall. On October 14, 1492, Christopher Columbus recorded in his diary that crowds of astonished natives gathered on the shore, bearing sacrificial offerings for the strangers they mistook for divinities descended from the sky. As he explored the islands later known as Cuba, Haiti, and the Bahamas, Columbus recorded again and again that "Indians" confused him and his crew for celestial beings. Two sailors sent to survey the wild interior of an island were received with great solemnity, the captain reported. "The people touched them, kissed their hands and feet, marveling and believing that they came from heaven." The tribe gave them everything they had to eat, and the women eyed the sailors, "looking to see if they were of flesh and bones like themselves." The Indians conveyed through gestures that, if the strangers wished to take them aboard their ships, "more than 500 men and women would have come, because they thought the Spaniards were returning to heaven." Through this sign language, Columbus understood he had reached Cipangu, or Japan, the island so heavy with gold it might sink into the sea.

Every time he stepped off the ship's rowboat and onto the soft sand, Columbus walked on the clouds. Anchoring in a cove on December 3, he traded beads for darts with other islanders "with the same belief that we came from heaven." On the thirteenth, he reports that a chieftain told a crowd of two thousand kinsmen, who trembled in fear, that "the Christians were from heaven." The Indians put their hands on their heads, in "a sign of great reverence," and left offerings of yams, parrots, and fish. Three days later, off the coast of Haiti, Columbus noted that a chief and his men refused to believe the ships belonged to people named Ferdinand and Isabella: "They maintained that the Spaniards came from heaven, and that the Sovereigns of Castile must be in heaven, and not in this world." Every tribal leader Columbus met seemed to share the same conviction. Approached by an envoy of two hundred islanders on December 18, Columbus again recorded their belief in the celestial status of the visitors, although he noted the chief and his advisors "were very sorry that they could not understand me, nor I them. However," he continued, "I knew that they said that, if I wanted anything, the whole island was at my disposal." At each new territory he encountered, Columbus took possession for Spain, by reading out a proclamation none of its inhabitants could understand.

"Hast thou not dropp'd from heaven?" Caliban asks the shipwrecked Stephano, the butler who has washed up on shore in *The Tempest*. "Out o' th' moon, I do assure thee," Stephano replies. Shakespeare immortalized the trope of Europe's age of discovery, wherein the savage beseeches the civilized: "I prithee, be my god." In writing the play, Shakespeare drew upon published accounts of the voyage of Ferdinand Magellan, the first explorer to circumnavigate the globe. In 1520, sailing off the desolate coast of what is now Patagonia, the Portuguese captain sighted a male giant in the nude, dancing and singing as he poured sand over his painted face, according to the journal kept by his sailor Antonio Pigafetta. Magellan dispatched his tallest man to the beach, who reached only the waist of the person the explorers mythologized as a *patagon*, a fictional dog-headed monster who had starred in a recent chivalric tale. The sailor sang and leaped alongside the titan, to convey that he came in peace, and then led him to the captain. Pigafetta recalled, "When the giant stood before us he began to be astonished and afraid, and he raised one finger upwards, thinking that we came from heaven." Even the behemoths of the uncharted lands believed the Europeans were celestial beings, according to Pigafetta's report. More giants appeared: two were taken captive aboard the ship, baptized, and given the names Juan and Pablo.

Afloat in a strange new world, Magellan and his men were relieved to find that the Patagons seemed to possess some notion of God. They had their own wild deity to whom they prayed. Pigafetta recorded they became enraged, "foaming like bulls," when Magellan shackled them in leg irons, and they called out to "*Setebos*." From what the explorers understood, Setebos was a horned deity with long hair down to his feet who breathed fire through both his mouth and his rump. In *The Tempest*, Caliban cries out to the same god. That the natives had some prior idea of divinity, and connected the explorers in some way with it, was for both Magellan and Columbus the essential first step toward their conversion. "They are credulous and aware that there is a God in heaven," Columbus noted in his diary, "and convinced that we come from the heavens . . . they say very quickly any prayer that we tell them to say, and they make the sign of the cross." As he attempted to teach the gargantuan Juan the rudiments of the Christian faith, Pigafetta remarked, "The giant pronounced the name of Jesus, the Paternoster, the Ave Maria, and his own name as clearly as we did. But he had a terribly strong and loud voice."

Though he was never quite sure what land he had discovered, after his first voyage Columbus began signing his name *Christoferens*, the Christ-bearer. He informed his patrons that the profits from his voyages must go not only toward himself but to the conquest of Jerusalem, the ultimate mission, and offered his services for the liberation of the Holy Land. He became convinced that his discovery fulfilled the prophecies of Revelation and that only a century remained until the apocalypse. Spiraling into madness in the years before his death, Columbus saw himself propelled by a heavenly fire, and compiled a collection of eschatological writings he called his *Book of Prophecies* in a feverish rage. It was, to him, no coincidence that his last name meant "dove," the bird of the Holy Ghost. "Over the waters of the ocean, like the dove of Noah's ark, he bore the olive branch and oil of baptism," his son wrote. In 1498, on his third voyage, off the coast of what is now Venezuela, the dove had the realization that the earth is not perfectly round. It had "something like a woman's nipple," Columbus wrote in a letter—and he was there, approaching the very tip. All his calculations indicated that this was the location of the lost Eden. He felt his ship was rising upward as he sailed the breast, getting closer and closer to the sky. He was the Adam who had found his way back to paradise.

The stories of natives mistaking European explorers for deities would become foundational myths of the colonization of the Americas, a way to justify conquest and maintain European supremacy in the fragile settlements. The myths ushered in a new century in which nearly sixty million inhabitants of the New World would be killed, enough to cast a chill across the earth, as the forest crept back over once-inhabited lands, cooling the globe and blanketing Europe in snow. Whiteness was a divinity forged in flesh and blood and language gone astray. The altar was the sand.

✦ ✦ ✦

A comet sailed through the noonday sky and split into three. There was a sound like that of a thousand tiny bells, emanating either from the comet or from the people in their confusion. Two-headed men kept appearing, and then vanished. A temple burst into flames; another was struck by silent lightning in a clear sky. A tongue of fire hovered in the air each night for a year, emitting sparks. The great lake foamed and boiled over, flooding the houses. At midnight the voice of a woman was heard wailing, "*Now we are about to go.*" A fisherman caught a strange bird and brought it to the emperor. Its eyes and beak had been chopped off; in their place was a round mirror reflecting the constellations. When Moctezuma looked into it, he saw an army marching across the sky, dressed for battle and riding deer.

The descriptions of these omens appear in the sixteenth-century *Universal History of the Things of New Spain*, a text often held to be the authoritative account of the Spanish conquest of the New World, reproduced in textbooks and travel guides up to the present day. Compiled by the Franciscan friar Bernardino de Sahagún, it is a bilingual history in Nahuatl and Spanish, and often referred to as the *Florentine Codex* after the manuscript in which it was preserved. The text records that in the year Thirteen Rabbit, or 1518, a temple was spotted drifting off the coast of the gulf port of Xicalango. Five curious villagers paddled out to it in canoes filled with gifts. There they found the Spanish navigator Juan de Grijalva and his crew. "When they arrived next to the ships and saw the Spaniards, they all kissed the prows of the canoes as a sign of worship," the *Codex* narrates. The Spanish explorers gave the men strings of beads in return for the gifts, but had no intentions of coming ashore. The five villagers journeyed to the Aztec capital of Tenochtitlan to report to the emperor Moctezuma: "*We have seen some gods in the sea.*" According to the *Codex*, "They thought it was the god Quetzalcoatl who was returning, whom they had been and are expecting, as appears in the history of this god." The name Quetzalcoatl means "Feathered Serpent." It was said the serpent had created the earth in an act of discovery: he lifted up the sky and revealed the world beneath. He made the sun by throwing his own child onto a fire. Then Quetzalcoatl had sailed off toward the east on a raft of snakes, promising he would return.

A year later, temples were again sighted gliding over the waves. When Moctezuma's emissaries reached the Spanish ships, a ladder was sent down and they climbed aboard with offerings from the emperor. At the sight of the stout commander Hernán Cortés, they fell to their knees and kissed the ground. They said, "May the god, whom we come to worship in person, know from his servant Moctezuma, who rules and governs his city of Mexico for him, that he says the god has had a difficult journey." They dressed the weary deity in the gifts they had brought: a turquoise serpent mask with a crown of parrot feathers, gold medallions and jaguar skins, a shield and scepter of precious stones, a breastplate of seashells, obsidian sandals, and strings of gold bells to tie around his ankles. They laid out three more outfits before him. But when they had finished, Cortés asked, "Is this all you've brought?" The captain ordered the men to be chained with irons around their necks and feet. He fired the ship's cannon, making them faint with fear. Then he revived them with wine. "Aggression," wrote Emil Cioran, "is a trait common to men and new gods."

When the messengers raced back to Moctezuma, they told him of gods with bodies wrapped in iron, such that only their faces could be seen—faces so white they might have been carved from limestone. The terrified Moctezuma felt as if his heart had been washed in chili water, the *Florentine Codex* records. Prisoners were sacrificed and their blood sprinkled over the messengers, "as was only fitting for those who had ventured to dangerous places and seen and spoken to the gods." The emperor sent warriors to the port of Xicalango, bearing turkeys, eggs, sweet potatoes, and fruit, along with captives in case the gods demanded blood to drink. "Moctezuma did this because he took them for gods, considered them gods, worshipped them as gods. They were called and given the name of gods who have come from heaven," or *teules* in Nahuatl, the *Codex* relates. When the Aztecs offered the Spaniards torti-llas sprinkled with human blood, accidentally parodying the Eucharist, the new deities became sick to their stomachs.

The Spanish left the port and made their way across the valley of Anahuac. "Many came to gape at the strange men, now so famous, and at their attire, arms and horses, and they said, '*These men are gods!*'" Cortés's secretary, Francisco López de Gómara, recalled. The captain's second-in-command, Pedro de Alvarado, quickly proved himself to be the cruelest and most violent of them all. The blond conquistador was given the name of the sun god Tonatiuh, Nahuatl for "He who goes along getting hot." Later Alvarado traveled to Lake Atitlán, where he took on aspects of the old Maya god, the Mam. The Dominican friar Diego Durán, in his *History of the Indies of New Spain*, writes that the emperor Moctezuma asked an artist to render these strange divinities advancing toward his capital, based on the messengers' descriptions. The emperor was unconvinced they were Quetzalcoatl and Tonatiuh, and asked his subjects if any of them possessed pictures handed down from their ancestors that might explain who they were. Someone brought the emperor a portrait of one-eyed giants; someone else a drawing of men with fish tails. Others showed him an image of creatures who were half man, half snake. None solved the mystery of who the new arrivals were.

When the Spanish reached Tenochtitlan, they were unsure whether it was real or a dream. Gazing down into the valley at the island cities built upon the lake, the towers and monuments rising from the water, palaces and gardens with unimaginable flora, connected by bridges, with canoes gliding through the canals—it was as if out of a legend. The *Codex* describes Hernán Cortés coming face-to-face with Moctezuma, surrounded by his chiefs and noblemen on the causeway. "Our lord, I am not asleep or dreaming; with my eyes I see your face," Moctezuma proclaimed as if telepathic, prostrating himself in reverence. "For some time my heart has been looking in the direction from which you have come, having emerged from within the clouds and mists, a place hidden to all," he said as he laid a garland on Cortés. "You have come to sit on your throne, which I have kept a while for you," the emperor continued. "Here are your home and your palaces; take them and rest in them." The conquistador Bernal Díaz del Castillo reported that the Spanish were led to a storehouse for temple statues, for the Indians supposed the gods should be lodged with their own kind. The Spanish were delighted to discover that their accommodation had an interior chamber filled with gold. According to the history, recounted, as always, by the aggressors, within days Cortés had managed to bind Moctezuma in chains. Holding the emperor prisoner in his own home, the captain consolidated his rule over the fallen kingdom.

✦ ✦ ✦

A trope, in the medieval church, was a recurrent verse that served to embellish the songs of the liturgy. It conveyed a holiness that grew fat with repetition. Thirteen years after Cortés was hailed as Quetzalcoatl, the Spanish conquistador Francisco Pizarro was mistaken by the Incas for their own bristly and vanished god. The sixteenth-century chronicler Juan de Betanzos tells the story in his *Narrative of the Incas*. It was said that a white, bearded deity had risen from Lake Titicaca to create the earth, the sky, and mankind, though some of the first humans were made not of flesh but of stone. They were prototypes for future tribes who would emerge from rivers and caves, and the god gave predictions of their fates. Then the Creator set off walking upon the sea and disappeared.

The Spanish navigator Pedro Sarmiento de Gamboa, in his *History of the Incas*, recounts that because the god walked over the water, they called him *Viracocha*, a word meaning "sea-foam" or the "grease" that sits on top a lake. The god sent out minions of lesser viracochas in various directions to call upon the stones to come forth and turn to flesh at the appointed times, peopling the earth. "These barbarians have this ridiculous fable of their creation, and they state it and believe in it as if they had actually seen it happen," Sarmiento concludes. According to Betanzos, "We could have written much more that the Indians have told me about Viracocha, but I did not do so to avoid prolixity and great idolatries and beastliness."

When Francisco Pizarro and his sailors landed on the beach, the people watching them from afar thought they had risen up from the sea. Messengers carried the news to the Incan king Atahualpa that the creator Viracocha had returned, Betanzos relates. They described the Spaniards' appearance, how they were white and bearded, and mounted on improbably large sheep. They could kill from a distance. King Atahualpa, who at the time was deep in a war of succession against his half-brother Huáscar, was overcome with fear and considered fleeing into the jungle, but his advisors convinced him to send an envoy to determine whether the gods were benevolent or evil. The king recovered his courage, remarked "that he was happy that in his age and time gods would come to his land," and sent a messenger to meet and observe the sea-foam deities. The Incan emissary reported back that at first sight he had taken the stranger to be Viracocha, but the deity soon revealed himself to be entirely ignorant of the land. These beings carried their own water with them in gourds, the messenger observed, rather than creating springs and rivers as they went. They stole women, and gold and silver to feed their sheep, and they forced the Incan men into servitude. They were not gods but wild robbers, he reported, and suggested burning them in their sleep.

King Atahualpa still refused to believe that the conquistador was not Viracocha, and ordered the messenger to invite the god for a meeting face-to-face. When Pizarro reached the Inca's encampment deep in the mountains of Cajamarca, and soon after captured Atahualpa, the king's Incan adversaries rejoiced. According to Betanzos, for the rival faction it was as if a divine hand were at work, miraculously intervening in the war of succession just at the moment when all seemed lost. It was as if the creator gods had returned to restore the Andes to their original order and their rightful king, Huáscar. When three Spaniards went on a mission to Cusco to collect the king's ransom, they found themselves worshipped along the route, the conquistador Pedro de Cieza de León recounted. Upon arriving in the city, Huáscar's men received them with joyous festivities and gestures of veneration, and assigned them each a virgin from the Temple of the Sun. Wrote Cieza de León, "They believed that some deity was enclosed within them. The Christians were amazed to see such great reason in the Indians." Much as Cortés and his men had done before them, the conquistadors soon disgraced themselves, by raping the priestesses and peeling gold from the temple walls. Yet if their alleged holiness quickly dissipated, the story lingered and spread. The conquistadors' texts, particularly the one penned by Betanzos, circulated widely in Europe, were taken as authentic accounts, and underwent myriad reprintings. With every retelling, the myth bloated and swelled. Divinity feeds on the repetition of the trope.

✦  ✦  ✦

It will surprise no one that a woman is usually held to blame for the original mistake. The slave woman Malinche, whom Cortés took for his interpreter and his concubine, and who like a Mexican Eve would become mother to the first mestizo, is often said to have been the first to call the Spanish men gods. Ordinarily, a person in Anahuac was given a name based on where he came from, or what function in society he fulfilled. But these strangers who washed up on the beach came from nowhere in the known world, and their purpose was unknown. The slave woman, hailed ever after as both heroine and traitor, had to find a word for the inscrutable arrivals, and it was unclear what that should be. Malinche translated from Nahuatl to Maya, and then a Spaniard who had spent years marooned in the Yucatán translated from Maya to Spanish. According to the friar Diego Durán, one of Malinche's first acts of interpretation was to inform the Indians, "These *teules* say that they kiss your hands and that they will eat." *Teules*, or *teotl*, translated via Maya into Spanish as *dios*, became the name the Nahuas would use, at first, to denote the strangers.

*Teotl* became God, but the word originally did not mean anything like the Christian sense of it. It was more akin to a many-sided principle of divinity, responsible for the cosmos in its chaos and order. It could manifest itself in anything: from idols to images to human impersonators of gods, sometimes destined for sacrifice. A *teotl* could be a goddess, a sorcerer, a priest, or anyone commanding authority and respect. The word could be combined with others to qualify it as "fine, fancy, large, powerful." The Franciscan Toribio de Benavente, also called Motolinía, wrote that the natives referred to the Spanish as *teotl* for several years, "until we friars gave the Indians to understand that there is only one God." The disheveled Motolinía was one of the first twelve missionaries to journey, in 1524, from Spain to the nascent colony, where they erected makeshift classrooms. To convey Christian concepts in Nahuatl, the friars used the word *teotl* to mean *God*, and then attempted to entirely reshape its sacred associations. Where for the Nahua divinity existed along a spectrum, shared and overlapping with humankind, the friars sought to impose a binary of man and god. They made God singular, omniscient, all-powerful, masculine; His will was manifest everywhere yet somehow detached from the world. He was One and yet He was also three—this last concept proved especially complicated for the friars to explain in Nahuatl.

Another enslaved translator, named Felipillo, is alleged to have been the first to identify the Spanish in Quechua as *viracochas*, the sea-foam spirits—a name not unsuitable for mysterious beings who arrived by sea. The word became singularized in the narratives of the early Spanish chroniclers such as Betanzos and the Jesuit missionary José de Acosta, who explained that Viracocha was the Incan prime mover, a white, bearded god who formed humanity out of clay and modeled it after Himself. The name would become so associated with the new religion brought by the conquistadors that in the first Quechua dictionary, from 1560, *viracocha* was translated as *Christian*. It came to be used as a general term for "white men" or those of privileged status. Yet originally it was not the name of a single, all-powerful God or those who worship Him, but a plural category of primordial, ancestral beings, the founders of cities and villages across the Andes. *Viracocha*, like *teotl*, became vessels of the Europeans' own monotheism; two words for *god* made in their own image. Among the Taíno who first sighted Columbus, to describe a thing as "from heaven," or *turey*, was merely a word for the exotic, unusual, or valuable. For other peoples who discovered European explorers deposited on their shores, to say a thing "came from the sky" was just a way to speak of something you could neither understand nor explain.

Was it a metaphor, a mistranslation? What dangers lie in giving a thing the name that belongs to something else? The first friars in New Spain, messengers from a kingdom in the midst of the Inquisition and its witch hunts for heresy, would not have invented a claim that the Spanish were gods. But perceiving there had been a mistake, they seized upon it as proof that their arrival in the New World was providential. Shaking off the heavy defeat of the Crusades, the Christian missionaries had come "to build a New Jerusalem at the antipodes of the Old," as the historian Jacques Lafaye would write. The friar Motolinía, writing in the 1530s, argued that acts of mistaken apotheosis were evidence the Indians had anticipated Christ's emissaries would arrive. This was God's plan, visible in the omens He had sent: the comet, the tongue of fire, the strange bird. That the natives, living in a state of primitive darkness, mistook the Christians for gods was a sign that their conversion was preordained and legitimate. The Indians were misguided, but they were correct to sense that the Spanish had a privileged access to God, the friars surmised.

It was a reenactment of Saint Paul bitten by the viper, wrote José de Acosta in his widely circulated 1590 account: how the Gentiles hailed the unscathed apostle as a god. The Incans were right, as it were, to mistake Pizarro for their deity, Acosta mused. Huáscar's supporters had entreated Viracocha to deliver them from the tyranny of King Atahualpa; they saw the Spanish as the answer to their prayers, and hence called them *viracochas*. And they were correct, for "the lofty aim of Divine Providence" had indeed sent the Spanish to save them. God divided the natives in war and ensured "the great respect in which the Christians were held as folk who had come from Heaven," Acosta wrote. "In winning the lands of the Indians their souls were all the more splendidly won for Heaven," the Jesuit father concluded. In their chronicles, the friars strove to present their own evangelizing efforts as justified and inevitable. Their writings were sent back to Spain, where they were avidly consumed by an Old World hungry for news from the unmapped continent that had captivated its imagination. Like a chant, the trope echoed and spread.

People likely did use *teotl* and *viracocha*—words that became redefined to mean *God*—to describe the Spanish at first, but beyond this, little else in the narrative is certain. There are no firsthand Nahuatl accounts dating back to the conquest, for the indigenous records of the past, preserved in pictorial codices, were largely burned or destroyed by the Spanish during the violence that ensued. Into the silence, the mythmakers stepped in. The first friars in Anahuac established the Colegio de Santa Cruz in Tlatelolco, where they set out to educate a new generation of Aztec elites in Spanish and Latin, and taught them to write in Nahuatl in the Roman script. The friars, with the help of their students, began to author histories of the conquest and the pre-Hispanic past, as did a number of aging conquistadors. Among the first to publish a text was Cortés's secretary in Spain, Francisco López de Gómara, whose *General History of the Indies* appeared in 1552. Yet Gómara, while clearly in thrall to Cortés, had never set foot in the Americas. Bernal Díaz del Castillo, an elderly conqueror in Guatemala, wrote his own account to contest what he saw as grave errors in Gómara. But Díaz del Castillo may not have been there either, for his name is absent from the official lists of conquistadors held in archives in Spain.

The only sources dating to the time of the conquest, and written by someone who was unquestionably there, are Cortés's letters to King Charles V. In them, Cortés describes his impressions of Mexico, the march to Tenochtitlan, and his meeting with Moctezuma on the causeway. But his writings are full of contradictions and apparent fictions, as though they had been composed in self-defense. The slippery captain had set out on his voyage from Cuba without government authorization, and the Crown had never appointed him to act as ambassador. To justify his actions, he would have to present his rogue mission as a stunning success. In recalling Moctezuma's speech, Cortés needed to show that the emperor had transferred his territories voluntarily to Spain, for by law a European power could only annex land that was willingly submitted or won through a legitimate war. According to Cortés, Moctezuma had told him:

> *For a long time we have known from the writings of our ancestors that neither I, nor any of those who dwell in this land, are natives of it, but foreigners who came from distant parts; and likewise we know that a chieftain, of whom they were all vassals, brought our people to this region. And he returned to his native land . . . And we have always held that those who descended from him would come and conquer this land and take us as his vassals. So because of the place from which you claim to come, namely, from where the sun rises, and the things you tell us of the great lord or king who sent you here, we believe and are certain that he is our natural lord, especially as you say he has known of us for some time. So be assured that we shall obey you and hold you as our lord in place of that great sovereign of whom you speak.*

In language infused with medieval European rites of vassalage, references to the Castilian legal code, and the Aristotelian doctrine that some men are slaves by nature, the Aztec emperor had, apparently, relinquished his throne to Cortés. There are no testimonies to confirm or deny his account, for all the later works rely on this letter, published soon after it was received in Spain. Cortés makes no mention of his alleged divinity, or his mistaken identification with Quetzalcoatl. King Charles V would not have been pleased to hear that his renegade subject was being worshipped as a god. But Cortés was the first to record an Aztec prophecy of a returning king, and his account improbably makes room for Charles V within it. The Aztec emperor properly recognizes Charles, an unknown, unseen king across the sea, as the returning lord, rather than the arrogant commander standing in front of him. This is how Cortés explained Moctezuma's improbably swift and compliant surrender, an event often challenged by scholars. It is uncertain where Cortés got the story of the reappearing king from, though in Renaissance Europe, lost sovereigns—an Arthur, Barbarossa, or Charlemagne—were always on the verge of returning.

A story began to take shape with a forked tongue. In 1545, the friar Bernardino de Sahagún started to write a history of everything pertaining to the new people among whom he found himself, from their constellations to their farming practices, their gods to their insect bites. To collect the local lore before it was forgotten, Sahagún recruited his best pupils at the college in Tlatelolco to the task, young Mexican noblemen who had become fluent in Spanish and Latin and were able to write in Nahuatl. Over the course of two decades, they created the *Florentine Codex*, the twelve-volume illustrated history that became the seemingly authoritative resource for anyone studying the history of Mexico in the centuries to follow. Yet the *Codex* preserved a past that was being creatively imagined as it was written down.

It told of the omens prophesying the Spanish arrival in Mexico. But the signs—the monstrous prodigies, the celestial oddities, the inauspicious bird—almost exactly resembled those contained in certain Latin and Greek books available on the shelves of the small library at Tlatelolco. The comet that divides as it crosses the sky and the freak lightning flashes without thunder are both found in Lucan. In Plutarch, before the death of Caesar, things spontaneously burst into flames. The tongue of fire in the heavens is in Josephus, where it appears over Jerusalem, spelling the destruction of the city. Josephus tells of a vision of armed warriors on horseback galloping through the clouds, and of a voice that wailed in the streets, "*We are leaving here.*"

Into the prophecy slithered the plumed serpent, though it is unknown exactly when or how. Quetzalcoatl was an old god, but never particularly prominent in Tenochtitlan. Archeology dates his worship as early as 400 BCE. The serpent is recognizable in ruins by his spiraling, geometric body, his crown of feathers, fangs, and gaping smile. The *Florentine Codex* records that Cortés was mistaken for this god, but it also splits off in a second direction, and relates that Cortés was mistaken for a character known as Topiltzin, or "Prince" Quetzalcoatl, a mortal who was deified as a manifestation of the god. In an echo of the prophecy that Cortés attributed to Moctezuma, it was said Topiltzin Quetzalcoatl had ruled the great city of Tollan and then vanished, promising he would return. Bartolomé de Las Casas described him as Christlike, a tall white man with large eyes, a long forehead, flowing black hair, and a perfectly rounded beard. For the friar Diego Durán, this "Pope Topiltzin" was a saintly figure who eschewed violence, performed penance, planted altars, and taught the people how to pray. Other Franciscans wrote of how the hero had an immaculate conception, and how he survived a great flood. Whoever Quetzalcoatl had been before the arrival of the Spanish; he or it was forever changed. Durán recalled, "When I questioned another old Indian about Quetzalcoatl's exile, he began to tell me the content of chapter fourteen of Exodus . . . I did not bother to ask him other questions."

The notion that Topiltzin Quetzalcoatl must have been an early Christian apostle offered an answer to the question that troubled the friars as they contemplated the millions of unbaptized bodies, the work that lay before them. Why would God have left all these souls in darkness until now? There must have been some prior visitation of a Christian saint in the New World, and most likely, it was Saint Thomas, who was rumored to have traveled even "beyond the Ganges." *There is no speech nor language, where their voice is not heard*, Psalm 19 had proclaimed. *Their line is gone out through all the earth, and their words to the end of the world.* Searching for evidence, the friars began to see crosses everywhere, in the geometry of Aztec art, on Quetzalcoatl's cloak, crosses that more likely represented the cardinal directions, for one of his attributes was as wind god. Diego Durán cited Pope Topiltzin's reputation as preacher and legends of his miracles as proof that he was Saint Thomas who had carried the Gospel across the sea centuries before Cortés's arrival. *Quetzalcoatl* means "feathered serpent," but it can also mean "precious twin," and Thomas is the Aramaic word for twin—a convergence the friars seized upon, preaching that the two were twin brothers of Christ.

From Anahuac, the apostle made his way to the Andes, a Jesuit priest reported in a letter. The Indians living around Lake Titicaca informed him that, in ancient days, a bewhiskered Thomas, flanked by twelve disciples, had encountered their ancestors and left behind a large, apparently indestructible wood cross. In 1561, Augustinian friars reported that a statue had been found in Collao, resembling an apostle, sporting a tonsure and sandals, who people claimed was Viracocha. They told of how, when Viracocha tried to convert the villagers to Christianity, "they threw him out of the land." Pedro Sarmiento related that when they tried to kill Viracocha by pushing him off a cliff, the saintly figure knelt and, raising his hands to the sky, rained fire from the heavens so that the land burned like straw. The Augustinians explained that the Indians now understood the arrival of the marauding, pillaging Christians as revenge for this history. It was said that the godly Quetzalcoatl, like Viracocha, was driven into exile across the sea because the people chose to follow the devil instead. If this were true, the presence of an early Christian saint reversed the terms of the conquest: the Indians were the original aggressors, and the Christians were the real victims. That the Indians should mistake Cortés or Pizarro for this apostle was proof that he once had come, and that he had been kept alive somewhere deep in the collective memory.

It might have seemed merely the fantasy of friars far from home. Yet at stake in the question of Quetzalcoatl's—and indeed Viracocha's—identity was no less than what rights and protections the indigenous people would receive under the new regime. If the Indians had, in fact, been visited by an early apostle but had rejected him, they were fallen peoples, corrupted idolaters with a status akin to that of Jews and Muslims under Castilian law. If the Indians had once scorned the Word, it was uncertain whether they could ever be successfully converted. In the eyes of the Inquisition, even Jews and Muslims who had adopted Catholicism generations before, and claimed to uphold the faith, were seen as inveterate and stained. But if no early evangelization had in fact taken place, the Indians were innocents, in a state of pure, natural reason, like the pagans before Christ. In that case, the Indians deserved respect, for they had made religious progress in total isolation from the revealed faith, deducing the existence of a Viracocha through reason alone. Weighing the evidence, Sahagún pointed to the total absence of wheat in the New World as evidence that there had been no prior evangelization. It was impossible to imagine that the Word could have been planted without the grain that was the body of Christ.

The official stance taken by the Catholic Church and the Crown of Castile was that the Indians were in a state of natural grace. In 1493, Pope Alexander VI issued a papal bull decreeing that the right to annex territory in the New World rested upon the conversion of its natives to the Catholic faith. The Indians were innocent neophytes—it had to be so, for if they were as incorrigible as Muslims or Jews, then on what grounds could Spain justify its colonization of the New World? The Crown took on the role of protective father: legally, the Indians were deemed to be minors, and after the laws passed in 1542, they could not be enslaved. However, despite the official position, many Spaniards continued to believe that the Indians were fallen people, idolaters who practiced a degenerate version of Christianity. Citing practices such as human sacrifice and the ever-present accusations of cannibalism, the theologian Juan de Sepúlveda argued that Indians were less than human; they were to the Spanish "as apes to men." They must be treated like the followers of other irredeemable religions, he argued; it was legitimate to wage war against them and enslave them. The conquistador Gonzalo Fernández de Oviedo pronounced, "Who can deny that the use of gunpowder against pagans is the burning of incense to Our Lord?"

For evangelists such as Sahagún, an apostle may not have graced the continent, but there had undoubtedly been a visit from another early traveler—the devil himself. With the emergence of Christianity in the Old World, Satan had been exiled to the New, Sahagún surmised. The indigenous deities were not figments of a pagan imagination but actual demons, minions of Satan, the founder of this strange brand of worship. In their missionary work, the friars appear preoccupied with the question: How to kill a god? One method was baptism: the friars taught their pupils that when you are submerged under the holy water, the demons clinging to you drown. But water alone was not enough for an execution.

The missionaries had to redefine *teotl* and remake divinity in a moral sense, to sift out the good and strip evil of its sacred status. Their task was to break open the syllables of language itself, so that whatever was hallowed inside would perish.

In the 1530s, the friars selected an obscure word to mean *devil* or *demon*, which they used to categorize all the indigenous deities: *tlacatecolotl*, a Nahuatl word for "human owl." It referred to a malignant, shape-shifting shaman who took the form of the horned owl, the bird of the underworld, at night. This ominous midnight sorcerer was known to inflict illness and death, but he was not considered a *teotl*, the friars discovered. By identifying the native divinities "with something that, though having superhuman powers, was essentially human," as the scholar Louise Burkhart writes, the friars hoped the new name would desacralize them. Under the friars' guidance, Nahua writers began using the word frequently in their own texts, and in time it caught on. Old gods became owls.

There was a second species the Spanish priests would have to undeify: themselves. The Indians continued to call the Spaniards *teules*, Fray Motolinía relates, until the friars disabused them of the notion, teaching them that there was only one God. Baptism was one way to drown the concept; after undergoing the rite many of the Indians "then called the conquerors Spaniards," Motolinía writes. But "some foolish Spaniards took offense at this and complained. Filled with indignation against us, they said that we were depriving them of their name. The fools did this in all seriousness, not considering that they were usurping a name that belongs to God alone." Their indignation masked a deeper anxiety: if the Spanish were no longer gods but men, and if the Indians had now joined them as fellow Christians, then on what grounds could the distinction between the two populations be maintained? If all belonged to a universal brotherhood of man under Christ, as Saint Paul had preached, what right did the Spanish have to exploit indigenous labor and land? It was a question famously debated in Valladolid in 1550, when Bartolomé de Las Casas challenged Juan de Sepúlveda over Spain's moral rights and obligations toward the peoples of the New World. If native peoples were becoming Christians, and could not be enslaved, by what means would

European supremacy be maintained in the fragile new colony? Some other kind of divinity would have to step into the breach.

✦ ✦ ✦

Several shades of god arrived in the New World at the same moment. A fact often omitted from histories is that men from West Africa, kidnapped and enslaved, also participated in the Spanish conquest. "They were called and given the names of gods who have come from heaven," the well-known passage from the *Florentine Codex* relates. The awkward second half of the sentence is rarely quoted: "and the blacks were called soiled gods." In the century that followed the conquest, over two hundred thousand Africans survived the journey across the Middle Passage to toil largely as servants in Spanish homes. The population of enslaved Africans soon vastly outnumbered that of the conquistadors, and threatened to overturn the precarious balance of power in the colony. On both sides of the Atlantic, the myth of European divinity grew; tales of Cortés's godhood as Quetzalcoatl or Pizarro's as Viracocha gained currency and became increasingly elaborate as they were retold, preserved in history books, and taught in schools. That Moctezuma mistook the Spanish for gods became the primary explanation as to why an empire of millions had collapsed soon after the arrival of a small band of foreigners. Tales spread that the Aztecs thought the horses were deities, the ships were temples, the guns were gods breathing fire. But any mention of "soiled gods," or deified African slaves, was erased from the story.

From the arteries of the Inquisition, the idea of clean blood, or *limpieza de sangre*, flowed from Spain to the New World. By the end of the fifteenth century, Muslims and Jews had been expelled from the Iberian Peninsula or forced to convert to Catholicism. But many "Old Christians" were suspicious of the new converts, and accused them of still harboring old beliefs and practices, sullying and subverting the faith. How to determine whether a conversion was false or sincere? How can one ever know for certain what another person believes? To exclude New Christians from the institutions of power and prestige, Spanish officials implemented a system of access through ancestry. To gain entry into universities, guilds, and ecclesiastical positions, one would have to demonstrate *limpieza de sangre*—that one's blood was utterly free of any Jewish or Muslim taint. Relying on archival records and the testimony of neighbors, the officials of the Inquisition would undertake rigorous reviews of a candidate's genealogy. If it was determined that one had even a drop of Jewish or Muslim blood, it was said one had *raza*, or race, a word used primarily for breeds of horses and dogs. In order for the Eden of the New World to remain pristine and undefiled, if a Spaniard hoped to gain permission to travel there, he had to prove the unsullied contents of his veins.

In the Americas, the Indians were considered *gentiles no infectados*: innocents uncontaminated by Saracen heresy. They were "soft wax," a friar proclaimed, a people "willingly" and easily impressed by the Catholic faith and ready to be shaped. It was thought that these "children of the Crown," their numbers already ravaged by European diseases and war, must not be corrupted by too close contact with the Spanish, or especially their black slaves. The enslaved Africans were often alleged to be Muslims (and many were), or inveterate people who, though they had been taught the rudiments of the Catholic faith, had failed to take to it. At the same time, the Spanish surmised that they themselves shouldn't mix too much with the Indians—even the climate and the change in constellations were said to be having a degenerative effect on their fine European stock. Two separate republics were established, with segregated villages and churches, one for the Indians and one for the Spanish and the slaves who worked in their homes. In each society, different duties and privileges prevailed. A legal fiction emerged defining three types of bloods that must not mix—"pure Indian," "white Spanish," and "black"—and divided New Spain into an apartheid state.

It did not take long before the specter of miscegenation began to threaten the very structure of the nascent colony. It was fragile, for it was built only upon fictions, as all societies are. The first children born from transgressive unions were ostracized and banished, as they had no place in the Spanish scheme of rights and obligations accorded to each republic. Yet as the mestizo population grew, exile became untenable, and the boundaries of each sphere became more difficult to police. The Spanish, the minority population, were fearful that an alliance of Indians and black laborers could easily overpower them. Threatened by demographics, access to power and prestige became determined by proving purity of blood, as in Spain. To gain an education or a non-menial job, Indians would have to prove they were "pure Indian." Arriving in the Americas, *limpieza de sangre* shifted in meaning, from a conception of purity of blood based on theological lineage to a biological concept, based on skin tone. Race ceased to lurk in the obscurity of what one's great-grandparents had believed, and became visible, for all who were taught to see it.

If in Inquisition Spain sermons inveighed against contamination by the blood of Muslims and Jews, in the colony the vilification shifted to blackness. In his classroom, Fray Alonso de Molina spoke of sins before they are purged in confession as *motliltica, mocatzahuaca*, "your blackness, your dirtiness." Revelation 21:27, translated into Nahuatl, comes out in English as, "Nothing black, nothing dirty will enter heaven." The friars discovered that in Nahuatl, moral values were often expressed in terms of hygiene and filth; a broom, or matted, disheveled hair, were potent symbols of right and wrong. And so they seized upon indigenous concepts of cleanliness, preaching sin as squalor and setting apart the Christian sacred in its white, unsullied purity. Fray Juan de la Anunciación, the author of Christian hagiographies in Nahuatl, described how, when Saint Anthony was racked by temptations, God revealed to him the devil in his true form. He was *ce tliltic piltontli*, "a small black child." For the congregant about to receive communion, the friar suggested the prayer: "I am mud, I am earth, I am worth nothing. How will I dare to receive you? . . . For I am very dirty, I am very fetid, I am very black with sin." In the wake of sin, shame must follow. The friars adopted the Nahuatl term *pinahuiztli*, a word that meant "to chide, reprimand," or "timidity, bashfulness," for shame. It was visible in the natural world in the *pinahuizatl*, or "shame-water," Sahagún observed, a kind of river that ceased to flow when humans crossed it, as if shrinking in shyness from their gaze.

By the eighteenth century, a new style of oil painting came into fashion in New Spain that depicted every possible combination of human fauna, with names inspired by the zoo. The *casta* paintings, a word, like *raza*, that was primarily used for animal breeds, presented in hierarchical quadrants all the various family types, dressed up for their portraits in their Sunday best. There were the white-skinned Spanish, and then the myriad categories of everyone else, who were of *mano prieta*, or "dark hand": among them mestizos, mulattoes, moriscos, coyotes, wolves, and a mixture called "I don't understand you." When a white and a semi-white person produced a darker baby, it was called a "return backward"; a child born to two mestizos was *tente en el aire*, "suspended in the air," for they were neither moving toward nor away from whiteness. Blackness would never entirely disappear, the paintings proposed, even after generations of breeding. In 1735, an observer noted the strained relations between New Spain's "pure Indian" and mixed populations, and remarked, "But the notable discord and lack of affection that exists between the two groups is God's providence, because poorly inclined as they are, the day this disunion were to cease, they would annihilate the Spaniards who are least in number." In this common view, the schisms between races that maintained the Spanish in power were evidence of God's will.

Racial difference was divinely sanctioned, inevitable, as natural as the fact that, to European audiences, savage peoples should mistake white men for gods. Columbus was lowered from the heavens, Cortés grew scales and feathers, and Pizarro glided over the white foam of the sea. With each retelling, the stories crafted a narrative that justified European power. Apotheosis was the natives' mistake, and so Europeans could claim no responsibility for it. It was a mistake in need of correction, yet it also became a potent myth, preserving the colonists' supremacy as they faced the precarity ever beneath power. It is a basic ability of a god to conjure things into existence that did not exist before. With the arrival of the new deities, the modern concept of race had come into the New World. Forged in flesh and blood and exclusion, it would become indelible, this thing we call race—a fiction that has deified whiteness.

Morning of the Creation of Man.

Heaven.

Direct Line Of Kinship With God.

ADAM AND EVE
IN THE GARDEN OF EDEN.

*Lord, I fashion dark gods, too.*

—Countee Cullen, "Heritage," 1925

# 12

# Adam Blushed

It was Sir Francis Drake who told them they were naked. In the summer of 1579, on a mission to circumnavigate the world, the English explorer landed on the coast of northern California. Catching sight of the fleet of five ships, a tribe came rushing down from the hills, attired with bows, arrows, and spears and little else. Spying the Englishmen, they froze, "as men ravished in their minds, with the sight of such things as they never had seen, or heard of," according to Drake's nephew, in *The World Encompassed by Sir Francis Drake*, based largely on the journals of the mission's chaplain, Francis Fletcher. "Their errand," Fletcher recalled, was "rather with submission and fear to worship us as Gods, than to have any war with us as with mortal men." The Englishmen gave shirts and linen cloth to the prelapsarian natives and advised them, "we were no Gods but men, and had need of such things to cover our own shame." To further demonstrate their humanness, the explorers ate and drank heartily in the enraptured natives' presence, but it was to no avail. "Nothing could persuade them, nor remove that opinion, which they had conceived of us, that we should be Gods," Fletcher recounted, though neither the captain nor any of his men could understand a word of the Miwok language.

"They are a people of a tractable, free, and loving nature, without guile or treachery," Drake's nephew wrote. The Miwok lavished their visitors with gifts, feathers and fawn-skin quivers, headdresses and animal pelts. "They came forward with various offerings for the new-found gods, prostrating themselves in humble adoration and tearing their breasts and faces in a wild desire to show the spirit of self-sacrifice," narrated William Charles Henry Wood in his popular 1918 history *Elizabethan Sea-Dogs*. "Drake and his men, all Protestants, were horrified at being made what they considered idols," Wood continued. "So kneeling down, they prayed aloud, raising hands and eyes to Heaven, hoping thereby to show the heathen where the true God Lived." Drake read from the Bible, his crew sang psalms, and the Indians, at every pause, reportedly exclaimed, "Oh!"

In addition to the gifts, the Miwok presented the Englishmen with their ailments—"old aches, some shrunk sinews, some old sores and cankered ulcers," along with "wounds more lately received"—in the belief the new gods could cure them. "In the most lamentable manner," Fletcher records, they cried for help, "making signs, that if we did but blow upon their griefs, or but touched the diseased places, they would be whole." The Miwok crowded around Drake, waiting to be healed by the touch of the navigator's hand. Any doctor in the pantheon would do: they "expected to be cured by inhaling the divine breath of any one among the English gods," Wood writes. The Englishmen, according to Fletcher, did attempt to help, using lotions, plasters, and unguents, but stuck to "only ordinary means," lest they give the wrong impression of their powers.

During the second week of the Englishmen's stay, the Miwok chieftain paid them a visit. The native king instructed the captain to sit, and then delivered several speeches, "or rather indeed if we had understood them, supplications," Fletcher recorded, although the mariners still could not understand their language. The chieftain, "with great reverence, joyfully singing a song," placed a crown upon Drake's head, and honored him with the new name "Hyoh." He beseeched the English captain to "take the Province and kingdom into his hand, and become their king and patron: making signs that they would resign unto him their right and title in the whole land, and become his vassals in themselves and their posterities."

Like Moctezuma before him, the Miwok chief had, apparently, somehow learned the language of feudal vassalage, and become an advocate of Aristotle's doctrine that some men are naturally born to be slaves. After weighing this generous offer, Drake thought it "not meet to reject, because he knew not what honor and profit it might be to our Country." Appropriation followed apotheosis: Drake accepted the Miwok crown in the name of Queen Elizabeth. As the chieftain abdicated his throne, the Indians let loose "a song and dance of triumph," for "the great and chief God was now become their God, their king and patron."

Amid the uncomfortable festivities, "Drake's Protestant scruples were quieted by thinking 'to what good end God had brought this to pass,'" Wood writes. According to his nephew, Drake only permitted his worship out of a desire that "so tractable and loving a people" would eventually be made piously aware and obedient to the true Almighty. Momentary godhood was a travail the English navigator would have to bear, a temporary yet necessary misstep in the transfer of affection from the wrong to the right object. "We groaned in spirit to see the power of Satan so far prevail, in seducing these so harmless souls," Fletcher recalled, "but so mad were they upon their Idolatry." The Englishmen tried to train them: when the Miwok reached out to them in gestures of aggressive adoration or with hands fanning in reverence, the Englishmen would forcibly restrain them, "by violent withholding of their hands from that madness." They steered the natives' hands up toward heaven "to the living God whom they ought to serve." But their attempts to reroute Miwok passions failed, for as soon as their hands were freed they would violently reach out again to their terrestrial target. When the object of their devotion withdrew to his tent, the natives continued to "with fury and outrage seek to have again" their Drake.

When, after five weeks, it was time for the Englishmen to continue their journey, Drake erected a wooden post so that all those who came after him—specifically Spaniards—would see that the territory belonged to the queen of England. He nailed to it a coin with Her Majesty's portrait, along with a brass plate, engraved with a notice "of the free giving up of the province and kingdom, both by the king and people, into her majesty's hands." He proclaimed the land Nova Albion—the first English colony in the Americas. Upon learning that the Englishmen were about to depart, the Miwok were inconsolable, Fletcher wrote. Overcome with sadness, the Indians saw themselves as "castaways," "those whom the gods were about to forsake," and went about in tears. "The last the English saw of them was the whole devoted tribe assembled on the hill around a sacrificial fire, whence they implored their gods to bring their heaven back to earth," *Elizabethan Sea-Dogs* narrates. On a 1595 map of Nova Albion, a Latin inscription reads, "By tearing of the bodies of young goats, and through repeated sacrifices on the mountaintops, the inhabitants of Nova Albion mourned the loss of Drake, already twice crowned."

In 1596, Drake died off the coast of Panama and was buried at sea in a lead coffin. The same year, a twenty-year-old Oxford student, Charles Fitz-Geffry, eulogized him in a book-length poem. In over a hundred pages, the enthralled Fitz-Geffry erected a pagan apotheosis for Drake so numinous as to rival the Miwok devotion: *Be thou religious to renowned* DRAKE,/ *And place him in thy catalogue of saints./ Instead of Neptune god of sea him make.* A legend arose that should England ever require a savior to come to its rescue, one only need beat the drum that Drake carried with him on his voyages, and the navigator would resurrect from his grave, wherever on the ocean floor it may be.

> *Tomb? ah no tomb, but Neptune's frothing waves!*
> *Waves? ah no waves, but billow-rolling seas!*
> *Seas? ah no seas, but Honour's hallowed graves:*
> *Graves? ah no graves, but bones' eternal ease:*
> *Ease? ah no ease, but rest born to displease:*
> *Whate'er it be, where worthy* DRAKE *doth lie;*
> *That sacred shrine entombs a Deity.*
>
> *. . . Cease, fondlings, henceforth to idolatrize*
> *With Venus, your Carpathean sea-born queen;*
> *And to heroic* DRAKE *do sacrifice*
> *Of expiation for your former sin,*

*Erect his statue whereas her's hath been:*
*Make* DRAKE *your saint, and make the shrine his hearse,*
*Yourselves the priests, the sacrifice your verse.*

Drake was *England's Dragon, thy true turtle-dove,* Fitz-Geffry wrote, a feathered serpent whose greatest foe, the Spanish, fled from him in fear. In the English mariner's presence, even the great rivers of Spain overflowed in panic or hastily shrank back in shame:

*Iberus, river in Cantabria,*
*Oft wish'd he had still kept him underground,*
*His head-spring near to Juliobrica*
*Thrice hid himself, and could no where be found,*
*Thrice overwhelming, all the land was drowned,*
*For hearing that the conquering* DRAKE *came by,*
*Poor coward river knew not where to fly.*

✦ ✦ ✦

The men were sailing toward the nipple. In 1595, Europe's explorers returned to the place Columbus considered the vicinity of the lost Eden, the breast-shaped bulge of the earth near today's Venezuela. Navigating the labyrinth of rivers in the Orinoco basin, Sir Walter Ralegh spotted armadillos, iguanas, birds of every color, and painted men living in houses on stilts. In his attempt to reach a mythical city of gold, Ralegh soon discovered that the Spanish gods had been there first. None of the natives wanted to speak to them, Ralegh recalled in his 1596 account, *The Discoverie of the Large, Rich, and Bewtiful Empyre of Guiana,* for the Spanish who had come before them had "persuaded all the nations that we were man eaters and *Canibals,*" he wrote. The English explorers lavished the wary natives with nonhuman meat and gifts of things "rare and strange," Ralegh reported, and "they began to conceive the deceit and purpose of the *Spaniards.*" Having won their trust, the English were regaled by the Indians with tales of Castilian cruelty, especially at the hands of Antonio de Berrío, an explorer who was Ralegh's greatest rival in the search for gold. They told how Berrío had made slaves of the old Orinoco chiefs, how he kept them in chains and "dropped their naked bodies with burning bacon, & other such torments." They lamented bitterly that the Spanish were raping their wives and daughters. The upright English, Ralegh maintained, were determined to distinguish themselves by never touching the native women, even though many "very young, and excellently favoured . . . came among us without deceit, starke naked," and without shame.

Two rival godheads, Spanish and English, were battling for power in the New World. To sway the Indians to the English imperium, Ralegh told them of a different divinity, Astraea, Gloriana, the Virgin Queen. She could be seen in the moon and in the constellation Virgo, the very embodiment of virtue and peace, as foretold in Virgil's Fourth Eclogue: *Iam redit et virgo, redeunt Saturnia regna.* The golden age of Saturn would begin anew with a virgin who returns. Queen Elizabeth had fulfilled the prophecy, bringing with her all the qualities of justice and righteousness long banished from the earth. *Most sacred vertue she of all the rest,/ Resembling God in his imperiall might*, intoned Edmund Spenser in *The Faerie Queene*. She had two bodies, one natural, one political. Elizabeth was the crystallization of Dante's dream of a sacred empire, a single sovereign who ruled over church and state. She was *a comet to the eye of Spaine*, a poet sang; when the Spanish fleet came to invade England, she shipwrecked them all. In the 1590s, the immortal Phoenix was old in years but "still bright, *still one*, still divine," Thomas Dekker wrote. Elizabeth had once locked up Ralegh in the Tower of London for marrying one of her ladies-in-waiting, but the explorer didn't mention this.

In *The Discoverie*, Ralegh relates how, speaking to a group of tribesmen through an interpreter, he informed them that Elizabeth was the great chief, or cacique, of the North, "and a virgin," with more chiefs beneath her than there were trees in the land. She was the great enemy of Castilian tyranny, and having freed the entire northern world from their oppression, now she had sent Ralegh to free them too. When he showed them Her Majesty's portrait, they devoured the sight with "idolatrous" admiration. To every group of Indians he met, he would repeat the lecture, Ralegh reported back to the queen, with the result that Elizabeth was now known and revered all across the Orinoco basin. To crown her list of epithets, the Indians gave her a new name: Ezrabeta Cassipuna Aquerewana. Ralegh ended *The Discoverie*, a text intended to convince his monarch to fund the full-scale colonization of Guiana, with an invocation: "I trust . . . that He which is King of all Kings and Lord of Lords, will put it into her heart which is Ladie of Ladies to possess it." She had already won over "the love & obedience" of the people of Guiana, Ralegh remarked, and the Spanish were losing their grasp on the territory.

As if to prove that the English possession of Guiana was inevitable, and God's will, Ralegh ended his text with a prophecy. He had heard it, improbably, from none other than his Castilian nemesis Antonio de Berrío: "And I further remember that *Berreo* confessed to me and others (which I protest before the Majesty of God to be true) that there was found among prophecies in Peru (at such time as the Empyre was reduced to the Spanish obedience) in their chiefest temples . . . that from *Inglatierra* those *Ingas* should be again in time to come restored, and delivered from the servitude of the said Conquerors." The Peruvian vision divined that men from *Inglatierra* would invade Guiana, freeing it from Spanish despotism and heralding the final victory of the English in the Americas. Though Ralegh likely invented the prophecy as a literary device, it took on a life of its own in Guiana. A year later, a Dutch expedition in Orinoco reported that an Indian chieftain, about to be hanged by the Spanish, claimed that he had spoken with an oracle called Wattopa. This mysterious savant had promised him that the chieftain's people would be liberated by the English from Spanish oppression.

"My name hath still lived among them," wrote Ralegh in a letter to his wife upon his return to Guiana in 1617. "To tell you that I might be here King of the *Indians* were a vanitie," but "here they feed me with fresh meat, and all that Country yields, all offer to obey me." The following year, with the immortal Queen Elizabeth long dead and Ralegh fallen from royal grace, the explorer returned to England, where he was executed. But the names he had been given in Guiana—Walterali,

Gualtero—lived on, and it was said they continued to be bestowed as honorific titles in local dialects for over a century. In 1769, Edward Bancroft, a young doctor working in what had now been transformed into sugar plantations, wrote in *An Essay on the Natural History of Guiana in South America* that nearly two hundred years after Ralegh's first voyage, the natives "retain a tradition of an English chief, who many years since landed among them and encouraged them to persevere in enmity of the Spaniards, promising to return and settle among them, and afford them assistance." The prophecy of Walterali had endured. Even more remarkable, Bancroft wrote, "they still preserve an *English* Jack, which he left them, that they might distinguish his countrymen." It was lucky that they did, given Bancroft's next topic in his *Essay*: a lengthy discourse on how the Indians cannibalized their enemies.

The Peruvian prophecy persisted into the late nineteenth century, when it was deployed again by an unlikely cult of believers—the British government—at a time of border disputes between British Guiana and the newly independent Venezuela. The British government appended a translation of the 1597 account of the Dutch expedition to Orinoco to the British legal argument. To the hanged chieftain's last words, the translator added that the spirit Wattopa promised the natives "deliverance through the English *and the Dutch*." At the time, British Guiana was seeking to strengthen its claims to a continuity of administration with the earlier Dutch colony of Essequibo, which was alleged to have predated any Spanish settlement in the area. That the Dutch had been there first, and that the British colony was a continuation of the Dutch, was "a significant legal point in sustaining the British boundary claim against Venezuela," writes the scholar Neil Whitehead. National borders, then as now, were propped up by prophecies of return.

✦ ✦ ✦

In the glow of hindsight, it seemed a perfectly American mistake: the people saw guns and thought their owners were gods. In 1585, Ralegh sent Thomas Harriot, a young Oxford mathematician and astronomer who already knew some Algonquian, on an expedition to Roanoke Island, in what is now North Carolina. Harriot spent a year at the English colony, recording his observations of the region, its silkworms and sassafras trees, and its peoples, in his *Briefe and True Report of the New Found Land of Virginia*. He had brought along his gadgets—spring clocks and compasses, magnets and mirrors, rifles and books—and delighted in astonishing the Indians he met by demonstrating their functions. Gazing at the charmed objects, the Algonquians "thought they were rather the works of gods than of men, or at the least wise they had been given and taught us of the gods," Harriot recounted. "Which made many of them have such opinion of us, as that if they knew not the truth of god and religion already, it was rather to be had from us, whom God so specially loved than from a people that were so simple, as they found themselves to be in comparison of us." From their guns and clocks, the Algonquians gathered that the strangers must be closer to Him, or even divinities themselves.

The path to God must, Harriot supposed, be paved with idolatry. "Some religion they have already, which although it be far from the truth, yet being as it is, there is hope it may be the easier and sooner reformed," he wrote. Although he told them that the Bible as an object was of no value, only the doctrine inside, the Indians tried "to touch it, to embrace it, to kiss it, to hold it to their breasts and heads, and stroke over all their body with it; to show their hungry desire of that knowledge." With time, their wild affections would be tamed, the Englishman hoped: "Through discreet dealing and government" they would be brought "to the embracing of the truth, and consequently to honour, obey, fear and love us." Harriot swore a double oath—that the Indians would find salvation in God, and that the English would have supremacy over them. It was a vow with a familiar paradox at its center, which the Spanish had also run up against: How can one seek supremacy through a faith that teaches the universal brotherhood of man? But, of course, the mark of divinity is that it can weather its own contradictions.

When the Algonquians began dropping dead for no reason, the astronomer interpreted this "marvelous accident" as a sign of divine protection and authorization of the fragile English colony. In each village that the Englishmen passed through, a strange disease struck the Indians, while the English remained unscathed. Harriot supposed that the deaths only occurred where certain natives had in some way conspired against them. The Algonquians were bewildered; the medicine men had never seen anything like it before and had no idea how to cure the mysterious illness. Observing that none of the English died, "some people could not tell whether to think us gods or men," Harriot recounted. Noticing that all the strangers were male, other Algonquians concluded that "we were not born of women and therefore not mortal, but that we were men of an old generation many years past then risen again to immortality." The Englishmen must have been resurrected from the dead, an entire colony of Christs. Others blamed the sickness on a passing comet.

In the grip of the illness a second prophecy was made. The Algonquians foresaw "that there were more of our generation yet to come, to kill theirs and take their places." These multitudes, Harriot recorded, "they imagined to be in the air, yet invisible and without bodies, and that they by our entreaty and for the love of us did make the people to die . . . by shooting invisible bullets into them." Some supposed that the ammunition could reach its target no matter the distance from which it had been launched, whether from far-flung towns or across the sea. The bullets were attached to strings, the medicine men of Roanoke surmised; when they sucked blood from the bodies of the dying, they told their patients they were drawing out the threads to which the invisible bullets were tied, though the cure was to no avail. Waiting in the air, the future generations of strangers would continue to arrive: men who saw themselves as possessors of the right, given by a god, to kill on a whim.

✦ ✦ ✦

Along the same coast, several hundred miles to the north, the strangers climbed down from the moon. In 1609, Henry Hudson reached the river that now bears his name, on the Dutch ship the *Half Moon*, with a half English, half Dutch crew. The Lenape people were watching from the shore, as the Dutch colonist Adriaen van der Donck, a lawyer and advocate for New Netherland's claim on the land, narrated in 1650. "When some of them first saw our ship approaching at a distance, they did not know what to think about her, but stood in a deep and solemn amazement, wondering whether it were a ghost or apparition, coming down from heaven, or from hell," van der Donck related. "Others of them supposed her to be a strange fish or sea monster. When they discovered men on board, they supposed them to be more like devils than human beings." Van der Donck heard the story from the Indians themselves, who were known, he added, for their keen memory for oral history. It was proof, he wrote, that the *Dutch* had been there first, for the Indians had never before seen people so different in appearance from themselves.

Was it an enormous floating house, or an unusually shaped whale, the people wondered, according to John Heckewelder, who recorded his own version of the encounter in his 1819 *History, Manners, and Customs of the Indian Nations Who Once Inhabited Pennsylvania and the Neighboring States*. His narrative would become the most widely reproduced account of Hudson's arrival in Manhattan, recounted in generations of history books. Heckewelder lived among the Lenape people as an evangelist with the Moravians, the earliest Protestant mission in the Americas. When the *Half Moon* appeared off the coast of the island, the people "concluded that this wonderful object . . . must be an animal or something else that had life in it," Heckewelder related. Warriors gathered on the banks, ready for battle. As the unknown craft moved into the bay, the people determined that it was "a remarkably large house in which the Mannitto (the Great or Supreme Being) himself was present, and that he was probably coming to visit them." The Lenape were torn, Heckewelder wrote, "between hope and fear" at the approach of their god.

In his bestselling 1643 *Key into the Language of America*, Roger Williams translated *Mannitto* as *God*. However, like the Nahua *teotl* or the Quechua *Viracocha*, there is no evidence the word meant anything resembling the Christian concept of divinity. Rather, it connoted a spectrum of powers and prized qualities. It appeared to be used, Williams noted, in an all-purpose way; he observed "a generall Custome amongst them, at the apprehension of any Excellency in Men, Women, Birds, Beasts, Fish, &c. to cry out *Manittóo*, that is, it is a God, as thus if they see one man excell others in Wisdome, Valour, strength, Activity &c. they cry out *Manittóo* A God." Williams went on, "When they talke amongst themselves of the English ships, and great buildings, of the plowing of their Fields, and especially of Bookes and Letters, they will end thus: *Manitôwock,* they are Gods: *Cummanittôo,* you are a God, &c." Perhaps *Mannitto* was a compliment taken too seriously. The New World became imbued with its colonizers' animism: new gods were found in translation.

"Who is a *manito*?" asked an Algonquian chant. "He who walketh with a serpent." According to Heckewelder, people who were able to write, in particular, manifested *Mannitto.* When "thoughts etc. are put down on paper & conveyed to a distant friend," the evangelist reported, it is considered "as a piece of *Manittowoagan,* the writer being endowed with a supernatural power." But, Heckewelder supposed, even literary deities must be far inferior to the "Great" *Kitchi Mannitto,* "our Almighty Creator." The Moravian evangelist attempted to map the concept of *Mannitto* onto the Christian binary of good and evil, claiming that alongside the Supreme Being there must exist the bad, or *Matschi Mannitto*: the devil, in other words. The task of the missionaries was then to sift out the power of *Mannitto* from the quotidian world of men, beasts, and fish, to push the Christian heaven away from the baseness of the earth, and segregate the sacred from the profane.

Catching sight of *Mannitto* off the shore, Heckewelder wrote, the Lenape leaders assembled on what is now Manhattan to welcome the god. They brought offerings of meat, laid out idols, and decided that a ceremonial dance would not only "be an agreeable entertainment for the Great Being" but "might, with the addition of a sacrifice, contribute to appease him if he was angry with them." As they waited, scouts arrived announcing that the craft was full of beings, "of quite a different colour from that of the Indians." The messengers noted that one of the figures, in particular, was dressed in red, "who must be the Mannitto himself." This must have been Henry Hudson, historians assume, wearing a color that, to the Lenape, evoked vitality and warfare. "They took every white man they saw for an inferior Mannittoo attendant upon the supreme Deity who shone superior in the red and laced clothes," Heckewelder continued. And the Lenape marveled of

Hudson, "He, surely, must be the great Mannitto, but why should he have a white skin?" However, as the scholar Evan Haefeli has written, it seems unlikely that the strangers would have appeared "white" to Lenape eyes. The white skin that Heckewelder's nineteenth century would come to imagine was not the same hue as things customarily seen as white, the color of wampum shells and flint. The Dutch, for their part, did not identify themselves as "white" during their control of New Netherlands; they called themselves Christians.

Writing two centuries later, Heckewelder was projecting a contemporary racial sensibility onto his imagined version of the Lenape people's first impressions. Their own early accounts tend to fixate on the peculiar hairiness of the Europeans, rather than their skin color, for in a society of men who did not grow beards, the new arrivals were more akin to otters or bears. Or they remarked upon the color of their eyes, for where they lived, only wolves had blue or green irises. It was as if the strangers had surfaced from the waterlogged underworld, where a grandfatherly, half-man half-serpent presided amid a host of salamanders, otters, and snakes. The Lenape called the new arrivals *Shuwanakuw*, or *Swannekens*, in the Dutch spelling. The modern Delaware-English dictionary defines the word as "white person." Yet *Shuwanakuw* derives not from the word for *white*, *waapii*, as Haefeli notes, but from *shuwanpuy*, meaning "ocean, sea, or saltwater." White people were those who came from the sea.

There is a tendency among new gods to get their worshippers drunk. When Hudson visited the Lenape chieftains on shore, like Cortés before him he filled a cup with wine, took a sip, and passed it around. Everyone was too afraid to drink, except for one warrior who, fearing the wrath of *Mannitto*, downed the entire cup, staggered, collapsed to the ground, and promptly passed out, to everyone's horror. It was a sacrifice "for the good of the nation," Heckewelder writes. But soon the man awoke, declared that "he had never before felt himself so happy," and begged for more. The other chieftains, following his lead, drank themselves into a stupor under the auspices of Hudson, liquor flowing like the river that would be christened for him. And so it was, Heckewelder recounts, that

Manhattan got its name: *Mannahatanink*, meaning "the island or place of general intoxication." This moment of riotous communion, a drunken Eucharist before the conquest of what became New York, was consecrated in the island's new name.

✦ ✦ ✦

In South Carolina in 1725, a Cherokee medicine man explained to an English trader that there were four gods, corresponding to the four cardinal directions. In the north was "a black god colored like the negro," who was ill-tempered and had to be supplicated with offerings of meat, lest he blow his icy winds. The deity in the east was a "better" god, red in hue, "the color of us Indians." In the south was the most benevolent god, "white as you English are," the sage reportedly told the Englishman, and "so mild that we love him out of measure." There the Cherokee's tale tapered off. When the trader pressed him as to who was the fourth god, the storyteller replied that he was "... the color of the Spaniards." In the summertime, he explained, the three gods gang up against the "black petty god" and "make him so afraid that he cannot send forth his winds," and so the climate stays warm. This was a reinvented version of the old Cherokee myth of four guardian spirits, said to lord it over the four winds. Each was associated with a color—red, white, and black—and the fourth was blue. But blue men had no analogue in the embryonic racial divisions of America.

According to records from the early eighteenth century, natives and new arrivals in the British colonies rarely remarked on the hue of each other's skins or identified one another in such terms. By the mid-eighteenth century, however, comments about skin color had become widespread, as had the division of peoples into a trinity of white, black, and red. Barbados, England's first plantation colony, was the first to witness the transition from "Christian" to "white," as the British settlers, much like the Spanish, sought to separate themselves from their slaves, the islanders, and the small but growing caste of people with mixed ancestry. Like a wind from the south, whiteness traveled north and into the Carolinas, as colonialists from Barbados emigrated there. It took a decade to reach the colonies in the northeast. Around

the early 1720s, indigenous people in the South first began to appropriate the label *red*. Long before it became a slur, it was a term of empowerment, signifying ardor, joy, and prowess in war, a color that certain
tribes already associated with themselves. When in 1740 Carl Linnaeus
classified the peoples of the New World as "red" in his *Systema Naturae*,
red skin became enshrined as a scientific category, though it is no more
grounded in biology than in the wind.

With the creation of race came a pressing set of questions, keenly debated
on both sides of the Atlantic. According to Acts 17:26, God *hath made
of one blood all nations of men*. Yet the discovery of the myriad previously unknown peoples of the New World seemed to undermine the
biblical narrative. If all men were of one blood, what hue was Adam,
and how did mankind's physical variations come about? If Adam had
indeed been created in God's image, did it confer holiness on his particular race? What color is God? "We must consider white as the stock
whence all others have sprung," declared the physician and astrologer
Ebenezer Sibly, in his 1794 treatise, *The Universal System of Natural
History*. The German naturalist Johann Blumenbach had a collection
of skulls he called his "Golgotha." The most beautiful among them, a
skull of "extreme elegance," belonged to a woman from the Caucasian
land of Georgia. When he came to naming the white race—the race of
Adam—in his new system of classification, he called it *Caucasian*, after
this perfect specimen, believing that the Caucasus was the region from
which mankind had spread out after the Flood.

For others, a tawny shade between white and black seemed more
plausible as the original hue. The black abolitionist Martin Delany reasoned that, based on his name, Adam's skin must have been red: "It is,
we believe, generally admitted among linguists, that the Hebrew word
Adam (*ahdam*) signifies red—dark-red, as some scholars have it. And
it is, we believe, a well-settled admission, that the name of the Original
Man was taken from his complexion." The Pequot activist William Apess
declared in 1829, "We are the only people who retain the original complexion of our father Adam." An origin story began to spread among the
Cherokee that the god Yehowa had created the first man out of red clay.

If Adam's skin was white or red, then where did blackness come from? Among the many burgeoning racial theorists there was a widespread belief in the effects of climate and the heat of the sun. In a 1787 essay, Samuel Stanhope Smith, a Presbyterian minister and future president of the College of New Jersey (later Princeton University), surmised that blackness "may be considered a universal freckle." The British scientist William Whiston proposed the existence of "a network tunicle" under the skin "with small cavities full of a black juice." In the biweekly London paper *Athenian Mercury*, readers would often write in with questions about the nature of race, and the editors would respond, grasping by turns at the biblical and the biological in their replies. Perhaps, it was suggested, blackness was the fierce, psychosomatic power of the maternal imagination: Lot's white daughters may have conceived the first black children when they pictured the smoke and flames they had fled in Sodom. Blackness was, according to the pages of the *Mercury*, "an accidental imperfection." When mankind resurrects on the day of Judgment, the Negro would "not arise with that complexion, but leave it behind him, in the darkness of the grave, exchanging it for a brighter and better at his return again into the world."

Moving into the twentieth century, the Jamaican liberationist and reluctant Rastafari prophet Marcus Garvey argued that Adam and Eve were black. For Garvey, whiteness was a curse: the punishment of Cain for killing Abel. "When Cain slew Abel and God appeared to ask for his brother he was so shocked that he turned white," he narrated. The instant the blood drained from Cain's face, Adam's son "became the progenitor of a new race out of double sin." Guilty and ashamed, Cain's white race "hid in caves for centuries," Garvey explained. "Therefore, their white skin became fixed because most of the time they were hidden from the light." The Detroit bishop Albert Cleage Jr. reasoned that if God created man in His image, God Himself must be some combination of white, black, red, and yellow. But in America, he wrote, "one drop of black makes you black." By the standards of the racial integrity laws codified across America in the early twentieth century, God was black. *And why not* asked the African Methodist clergyman Henry McNeal

Turner. "We do not believe that there is any hope for a race of people who do not believe that they look like God."

+  +  +

The book of Genesis gives not one but two accounts of the creation of man: in Genesis 1:27, where God creates him on the sixth day after the plants and animals have been formed, and then again in Genesis 2:7, where God creates Adam out of dust *before* any flora or fauna. When the Dutch navigator Bernard Romans washed up in Pensacola, Florida, in 1771, he found the people he encountered there very strange. They built fires not by laying wood parallel but by standing it upright in a circle. They carried their babies not at their breasts but on their backs. The men urinated sitting down and the women standing up. Florida must have had its own Adam and Eve, Romans concluded in his *Concise Natural History of East and West Florida*. "Without doubt *Moses's* account of the Creation is true," he reasoned, "but why should this Historian's books, in this one thing, be taken so universally, when he evidently has confined himself to a kind of chronicle concerning one small part of the earth?" Across the ocean, God must have created another original pair, "of different species," Romans theorized. Adam was only the progenitor of the white race; his story, and those of his descendants, belonged exclusively to one lineage of man.

This was a theory with a notorious past: the French theologian Isaac La Peyrère was famously forced to repent his 1655 treatise *Prae-Adamitae*, or, *Men Before Adam*, as heresy. Reading the two accounts of creation in Genesis, La Peyrère argued that God must have created the Gentiles in the first act, and Adam, father of the Jews, in the second. If there were men who existed before Adam, it would explain other seeming inconsistencies in the Biblical narrative, such as the woman Cain married, and the origins of the people living in the Land of Nod, which is mentioned in Genesis. Polygenesis seemed to resolve the questions, posed by laymen and theologians alike, that had become more pressing with the discovery of the New World. If all men descended from Adam, how did racial difference come about? Why did the Holy Book give no mention of these unknown civilizations? And how had these peoples survived the Flood? The theory of two separate creations provided one answer, yet it stood in tension with the universalist claims of the Bible itself.

In the mid-eighteenth century, native Americans embraced this theory as they forged resistance movements against European encroachment onto their land. Old tribal affiliations were superseded by a new unity of first peoples, traced back to the red Adam and Eve. "Take up the Hatchet against the White People, without distinction," someone shouted at a joint council of Delawares, Shawnees, and Iroquois, "for all their Skin is of one Colour and the Indians of a Nother." During negotiations with the British over disputed land, an Iroquois chief warned that since the worlds on either side of the Great Water were created separately, "that which you call Justice may not be so amongst us." Different creations meant different laws and customs.

The theology of separation stood as a challenge to any indigenous people who had converted to the faith of Christ, or were thought to have grown too intimate with the Europeans. In 1763, a council of Delaware chiefs agreed to adopt a seven-year diet of emetic tea, to purge their bodies of the ways and manners of whiteness. When Presbyterians attempted to establish a mission among them, the Delaware chiefs repelled them with their own myth:

> In the beginning God created three men and three women: red, black, and white.
>
> But He gave the Bible only to the white man—black and red were never intended to read such a book.

When a Moravian evangelist asked a Seneca leader if he had heard how God came to earth as a human and died on the cross, the Seneca responded curtly: "The Indians are certainly not guilty of His death, as the whites are." To the Seneca, the clergyman's bizarre doctrine was further proof of the anathema of white people, who confessed to having tortured and killed their own God.

For the worshippers of an executed deity, the theory of separate origins threatened to unravel the entire fabric of their faith. If there were many Adams, if mankind did not arise from a single racial source, then the temptation in the Garden and the subsequent transmission of original sin could not be a stain on all mankind. The arc of the biblical narrative—the atonement of Christ, the redemption—would not apply to other peoples. *For as in Adam all die, so in Christ shall all be made alive*, reads Corinthians 15:22. Nothing less than universalism, the central tenet of Christianity, was at stake. Nor was it only Christian theology that was under threat—polygenesis risked imperiling the foundations of the Enlightenment. What does it mean "to be human" if humans are not all descended from the same root? "How could philosophers reason about the human condition or construe universal principles of morality," asks the scholar Colin Kidd, "if humankind turned out to be sprung from plural origins?" Without Adam and Eve, we cannot speak of "the human," Samuel Stanhope Smith warned in 1787: "The science of morals would be absurd; the law of nature and nations would be annihilated; no general principles of human conduct, of religion, or of policy could be framed, for human nature, originally, infinitely various, and, by the changes of the world, infinitely mixed, could not be comprehended in any system." If Adam was not, in fact, the "first man," the very foundations of "human knowledge" seem to cave in. We are fallen with Adam, we are fallen without him.

To fight off the threat of polygenesis, certain theologians turned to an unlikely ally to help demonstrate the racial unity of all mankind. In the mid-nineteenth century, a number of books and treatises began to appear which attempted to prove that the worship of the serpent could be found in every culture and place in time. The omnipresence of ophiolatreia was proof that the Fall was universal: all peoples preserved some ethnic memory of the drama in the Garden of Eden, and all races had subsequently diffused from this single point. Idolatry stood as the unwitting defense of Christian truth, as John Bathurst Deane, grandfather of P. G. Wodehouse, argued in his 1833 work *The Worship of the Serpent Traced Throughout the World*. Over five hundred pages, Reverend Deane slithered with the serpent-god "from Paradise to Peru," from the Celtic dracontiums to the great feasts of Hindustan, where villagers left rice outside their doors as offerings for the hooded snake. In Persian myth, two serpents, good and evil, contended for "the mundane egg" that represented the universe, each grasping an end in its mouth. In New Zealand, Māori fables recalled adders that spoke; in Louisiana, Indians sported tattoos of snakes coiled around the sun. To the ancient Greeks, the ouroboros—a snake biting its tail—was the symbol of eternity. The veneration of the serpent, Deane argued, was both irrational and natural. "*Irrational*, for there is nothing in common between deity and a reptile . . . and *natural* because, allowing the truth of the events in Paradise, every probability is in favour of such a superstition springing up."

In archaic Bacchic rites, devotees held asps to their breasts and "with horrid screams called upon *Eva! Eva!*" then "crowned themselves with these reptiles," narrated Matthew Bridges as he followed a serpentine path through history in his 1825 *Testimony of Profane Antiquity*. The unknown author of the 1889 treatise *Ophiolatreia* appealed to the authority of the philologists, claiming that the very name of *Europe* itself derives from *Aur-ab*—Hebrew for the "solar serpent." Moving west, the native American principle of divinity Manitou could also be translated as "snake." "How an object of abhorrence could have been exalted into an object of veneration must be referred to the subtlety of the arch-enemy himself," Reverend Deane wrote. Through the worship of the snake, the Devil not only received "the homage which he so ardently desired from the beginning" but was also "perpetually reminded of his victory over Adam." It was the Devil's device that through the adoration of the snake, mankind should continue to fall.

The worship of the serpent may be universal, Reverend Deane argued, but so too is the hope that he will be vanquished—the desire "to bruise the serpent's head," as cited in Genesis 3:15. Adam sought redemption after his transgression, but he could never rise to Paradise again. If it was by his sinful disobedience that man forfeited the earthly Eden, it was only by the *sinless* obedience of man that the heavenly Paradise would be attained. No atonement was enough, except the blood sacrifice of a perfect man. Everywhere on earth humankind is awaiting this "sinless man," who by definition could not be a natural man, or even an angel, for angels, too, are prone to "folly": it could only be God Himself manifest in the flesh. And so, Deane continued, we find in every culture the universal expectation that a god will arrive, incarnated as a man. Apollo came to slay Python; Krishna killed the scaly Naga king. Perhaps it is indeed because of the serpent that, in every place and time, we find men deified by mistake. The snake's prophecy, in its hissing sibilance, came true: *Ye shall be as gods*—with an emphasis on the simile.

The serpent, the ultimate intruder, adored and loathed, may also be God himself incarnate. In *Ophiolatreia*, the anonymous author tells of Quetzalcoatl, the "Feathered Serpent," a Great Teacher who came to the people of Mexico to instruct them in the art of civilization, and possessed both a divine and a human nature. Through the wise guidance of this demigod, who was "tall, of fair complexion, open forehead, large eyes and a thick beard," the cotton grew in a rainbow of colors, and gourds sprouted up the size of humans. "Under his benign administration the widest happiness prevailed amongst men." But soon the Feathered Serpent mysteriously disappeared; some said he was killed on the beach. In 1726, just as the Spanish Inquisition was at its height, an inquisition of snakes took place in the West African kingdom of Benin, then known as Whydah, and one of the epicenters of the transatlantic slave trade. The gods were of three classes, "*the serpent, tall trees,* and *the sea*," the Reverend Deane relates. When the territory was conquered by the neighboring kingdom of Dahomey, the invaders targeted Whydah's sacred serpents. Seizing every snake they could find, they "held them up by the middle and said to them, '*If you are gods, speak and save yourselves.*'" When the snakes didn't answer, or refused to, the conquerors cut off their heads, roasted them, and ate them.

While the serpent was enlisted to defend the singularity of man's origin, the fork-tongued creature was also enrolled in an opposing project: to prove the races were different species and that miscegenation was the true cause of the Fall. "The question is pressing home upon us too heavily to wait," declared the New Orleans physician Samuel Cartwright in

1860, on the eve of the Civil War. "Abandon the slow, uncertain, and torturous paths of proud Science," the doctor urged, writing a year after Darwin's *Origin of Species* first appeared. Cartwright argued that the Bible clearly revealed the two distinct creation stories. The true meaning of the first creation at Genesis 1:24—the birth of "the negro" alongside cattle and creeping things—had been lost in translation, he argued: the Hebrew phrase *naphesh chaiyah*, often translated as "living creatures," actually refers to this "inferior species" of human. The word *man* itself was originally meant to refer only to the descendants of Adam, Cartwright claimed: "The abolition delusion is founded upon the error of using the word *man* in a generic sense, instead of restricting it to its primary specific sense. But after a large part of the Adamic race had been corrupted by amalgamation with the inferior races, the term *man* was used to designate the *hybrids*, and the term *god* to designate the pure-blooded white man." The influential doctor—who served as a surgeon under then-general Andrew Jackson—traced the conflict dividing America to the mistake of calling creatures *men* to whom the name did not properly belong. According to Cartwright, it was almost as if the white man had been forced to become a god, to retreat to the heavens, in the face of the dark specter of racial integration.

In 1867, as the clouds of gunpowder parted over the defeated South, a pamphlet appeared as if out of *The Tempest*, authored by a mysterious "Ariel," that further articulated the American doctrine of white divinity. "The negro is not a *human* being—not being of Adam's race," it declared. "The step from the negro to Adam," Ariel wrote, "consists of change of color, hair, forehead, nose, lips, etc., and *immortality*." Only the white race was created in God's image; Adam's progeny alone were the sons of God, they alone were granted immortal souls and access to the heavenly afterlife. "Adam was to have *dominion* over all the earth," Ariel continued, yet the miscegenation of his descendants—a "horrible crime . . . immortal beings allying themselves with the beasts of the earth"—forced God to purge His creation of the monstrous hybrids. During the Flood—the original act of ethnic cleansing—the black race had indeed been aboard the ark, Ariel argued, but in the guise of beasts, not men. The repellent phantom behind the influential tract was

Buckner H. Payne, a Nashville clergyman, who pretended that the pamphlet had been published in a bipartisan spirit in the northern climes of Cincinnati.

A year later, a second pamphlet began to circulate, titled *Caliban: A Sequel to "Ariel,"* and written under the pseudonym "Prospero." Building upon Ariel's earlier tract, Prospero argued that the serpent in the garden must have been a pre-Adamite man—his legendary attribution as a reptile was only a slur. The original Hebrew text "presents a vivid picture of an African medicine-man, conjurer, with his 'grey dissimulation,' whispering his diabolical temptation into the ear of unsuspecting Eve," Prospero imagined. Who was in the garden with Eve? The question was posed by numerous anti-abolitionists, who projected their deepest fears all the way back to Eden as they contemplated the potential fall of white supremacy. Samuel Cartwright cited the British Methodist scholar Dr. Adam Clarke, who, from his close readings of the Bible, had been "forced to the conclusion" that the articulate creature that had beguiled Eve must have actually been an orangutan. But Clarke was mistaken, the Confederate physician Cartwright argued—it was Eve's "negro gardener" who was the serpent, and whom she had questioned, out of curiosity, about the fruit of the forbidden tree. In *Nachesh: What Is It?* a Georgian minister argued that the curse on *Nachesh*, the Hebrew word for "serpent" used in the Bible, was a divine justification for black enslavement, and for political subjugation in the wake of the Civil War.

"Does the adder speak, or does the boa-constrictor give utterance to language?" asked A. Hoyle Lester in his 1875 book *The Pre-Adamite, or Who Tempted Eve?* "Preposterous thought! The fall of man as revealed to us in Genesis is no metaphor." Eve, "the fairest queen that ever graced the courts of earth, made her *début* on the arena of life in the romantic shades of Eden." Yet "Eden's garden bird" soon wearied of monotonous daily life in paradise. "The presence of Adam had no doubt become irksome"; Eve was tired of his voice, and craved something new. The serpent arrived erect, in the shape of a man—Lester supposed he was Mongolian—and Eve "rose from the mossy couch a wiser but a fallen creature." She returned to Adam disrobed of her virtue, and pregnant

with Cain. The word *adam* means "red" in Hebrew, Lester wrote, and
he was given the name because he was the father of the white race—for
only whites can blush. "If the darker races blush, with whom we claim
no kindred blood, then, like the wild-flower in its native wilderness, it
blushes unseen and wastes its virtue on the desert air," Lester philoso-
phized. "The only immortal soul beneath the wide-expanded canopy of
heaven" was Adam, "whose cheeks gushed the crimson blood to manifest the intense shame of conscious guilt!" Lester is silent as to whether
Eve, the "first Caucasian damsel," blushed too.

The serpent was a woman, Charles Carroll argued in his mammoth
1902 tome *The Tempter of Eve*. Carroll was already infamous for his
malevolent *The Negro a Beast*, which had been widely read throughout
the Cotton Belt. Nachesh was Eve's black servant, Carroll claimed, who
"instilled into the woman's mind distrust of God; engendered in her heart
discontent with her position; and aroused in her nature the unholy ambition that she and her husband 'be as gods.'" In *The Tempter of Eve*, which
was still in print in Alabama as late as the 1970s, Eve's original sin was
treating the black servant as a confidante rather than as a beast of burden:
she "descended to social equality with her." Their transgressive friendship
"reveals the startling fact that it was man's social equality with the negro
that brought sin into the world," Carroll declared; her second offense was
tasting the forbidden fruit. Carroll may have based his black temptress
on Ida B. Wells, the civil rights activist who had taken up the fight against
lynching as punishment for interracial love. Wells argued that alliances
between white women and black men were usually consensual, and aimed
to restore to women an agency denied them in the myth of the black rap-
ist. Projecting her all the way back to the Garden of Eden, Carroll erased
everything that had since taken place: the conquest of the Americas, the
horrors of the Middle Passage, enslavement, and so-called freedom.

✦  ✦  ✦

Sailing the curve of the brain, tacking north from SUBLIMITY and HOPE
and diagonally from IMITATION, one reaches the point of VENERATION—

the place, near the crown of the skull, where the religious impulse originates. So surmised the nineteenth-century science of phrenology, which charted the regions of the mind with the enthusiasm and accuracy of a cartographer tracing sunken continents at the bottom of the sea. The size and shape of this zone of worship was said to vary among the different races. "The upper and middle part of the head, where is the organ of veneration, is generally high" in the black race, argued John Wilson, author of the pocket-sized *Phrenology Consistent with Reason and Revelation*, but it showed deficiency in the area where one grasps higher spiritual concepts. "Consequently, the mind is left more to the sensible creature rather than to the unseen Creator," Wilson wrote; such a brain might accidentally venerate any old thing. The geologist Peter Lesley, in a lecture in 1865, described how the black races "seem never to have had the ability to lift their spiritual life out of the bogs and swamps of Fetichism upon the firm land of Theism." It was the white race alone, Lesley contended, who possessed the "powers of imagination to devise symbols to represent abstract thought." Meanwhile, Charles Carroll was literally weighing brains: the average of "the black race" came in at 1,178 grams, which he compared to the brain of Lord Byron, tipping the scales at 1,807 grams.

While Christian theologians had once supposed that mankind's multiple spiritual predilections were the result of the corruption over time of a single ancient faith dating back to Adam, nineteenth-century thinkers began to explain religious phenomena as manifestations of a deeper reality, that of race. They believed there were not only variations in skin color but profound psychic distinctions between the races, as the scholar Colin Kidd writes, "which manifested themselves in the varieties of religion found throughout the world." Even the Christian heterodox revealed intrinsic racial differences: Protestants tended toward dolichocephaly, some scientists observed, while Catholics were brachycephalic. The Oxford philologist Max Müller located "the real Theogony of the Aryan races" in Vedic hymns, using language as his light to unearth racial origins from the sacred text. The influential Sanskritist Émile Burnouf, in *La science des religions*, argued that the Aryan brain, unlike those of the other races, never ceases to grow and transform itself, "up till the very last day of life by means of the never-changing flexibility of the skull bones." Burnouf maintained that this led to the white expertise for "transcendent speculations." Because of innate biological differences, whites could elevate themselves higher, and thus closer to God.

If religion, beginning with the arrival of the first Christian missionaries in the New World in the sixteenth century, had given rise to race, it was now subsumed into a myth, or an error, of its own making. Religion had become "an epiphenomenon of race," Kidd writes, which many took to be the underlying human reality. The scholars of empire had classified and reified sets of beliefs and rituals into distinct "world religions," with new names and boundaries, but these divisions, in turn, could be seen as reflecting the racial essence of people, as the deeper truth. "Hinduism" was the proper spiritual domain of the Indian, "Islam" was for the Arab race, "Confucianism" for the Chinese. For William James, belief was a mystical germ, lodged in the body and unable to be seen; now the yoking of religion to race meant that belief was no longer hidden or submerged—it could be read in the pigment of a person's skin, as if it was enough to scan someone's face to know what they believed. With religious tendencies bound to racial differences, the two were thus profoundly immutable. Under the influence of late-nineteenth-century racial science, true religious conversion came to be seen as, in a sense, biologically implausible. There was something suspicious and unconvincing about the convert, as if such transformations went against the order of the natural world.

✦ ✦ ✦

At an ill-starred moment in 1984, Ella Rose Tucker-Mast was knocked down by a shopping cart. Confined to a wheelchair with a broken hip, she consoled herself with a book that she had found in the library of Dr. Wesley Swift, the late husband of her friend Lorraine. Titled *In Quest of the White God*, and written by a mysterious Pierre Honoré, it had been translated from German to English in 1963. In the book, Honoré argued that an ancient race of Caucasians had once sailed from Crete, and brought to the native Americans the gifts of civilization, science, and law. "They arrived in huge foreign ships with swan wings, hulls gleaming so brightly that it looked as if gigantic serpents were gliding over the water," he wrote. The white men were immortalized in Indian lore. Centuries later, they boarded the ships of the celestial Columbus, the mighty Cortés, and the redoubtable Pizarro. Honoré described how, when the captains anchored in the New World, they were hailed as the white gods returning. The Americas were still teeming with such legends, according to Honoré: the author recalled tales of white deities the Indians had told him as they sat around a jungle campfire. He himself was greeted as *Viracocha*. Ella's husband placed a board across her wheelchair so she could use it as a desk to take notes on the book. "With such a subject to work on, I forgot my pain," she wrote.

"There is coming a day when your race puts back on immortality," Wesley Swift, a former Klu Klux Klan organizer and founder of the Church of Jesus Christ-Christian, announced in a radio sermon in 1963. As a swelling tide of hundreds of thousands, led by Martin Luther King Jr., marched on Washington to demand an end to black oppression, Swift described a future in which the white race would be bathed in light. In sermons broadcast across California and circulated widely on cassette tapes, he told of how America was in the midst of a race war, a combat as old as the Fall. The history of the world is the battle of two racial seedlines, Swift declared: the white race of Adam against the race of the Jews, the descendants of the union of Eve and Satan-as-serpent who, beginning with Cain, intermarried with the black pre-Adamites, the "beasts of the field." Only Adam's race possessed an "implanted spirit," a "stream of celestial life" rendering it eligible for salvation. "This race of YAHWEH transplanted from heaven to earth, is growing up into a mighty Empire in the midst of earth," Swift avowed to his listeners. "And I do not think that there has even been a period when it was more necessary for us to wake up than NOW." In his sermon the previous week, Swift told of Quetzalcoatl, and of the white gods who had sailed across the sea to the New World. It is possible the reverend had just received a copy of Honoré's recently published book. In 1963, along with *In Quest of the White God*, numerous other titles appeared that pursued the same thesis, from L. Taylor Hansen's account of a "Pale God" with a white halo in *He Walked the Americas*, to Constance Irwin's *Fair Gods and Stone Faces*.

Wesley Swift and the Church of Jesus Christ-Christian (for Christ, according to Swift, was not a Jew), became a major fountainhead of white extremism in the United States, influencing generations to follow. After Swift's death in 1970, the Church was taken over by his wife Lorraine, and Ella Rose Tucker-Mast became its chief archivist, tirelessly transcribing the tapes of his innumerable sermons and writing reports on her favorites from his library of eight thousand books. Swift's teachings and his library came to dictate the core curriculum of white supremacist theology, essential reading for its radicalized followers to this day. His most notorious protégé, Richard Girnt Butler, formed his own branch of the church, the Aryan Nations, which he ran out of a compound in Idaho; he was tried (but never convicted) of attempting to overthrow the US government. In his imagined constitution for an Aryan state, Butler noted that the translation of the Hebrew word *adam* in Genesis means "to show blood in the face." Taking up Butler's ideas, the neo-Nazi writer and activist Harold Covington advocated for the establishment of a new Aryan homeland in the Pacific Northwest. In radio broadcasts, YouTube videos, and a series of galvanizing adventure novels, Covington called for the mass migration of the people who blush.

Robert Marx, a shipwreck hunter once knighted by the Spanish government, traced a similar path to that of Honoré in his 1992 book *In Quest of the Great White Gods*. It was published by Crown, a respected publishing house. In 1995, the British writer Graham Hancock chased after the same white celestials in the bestselling *Fingerprints of the Gods*; two years later, Terry J. O'Brien wrote *Fair Gods and Feathered Serpents: A Search for Ancient America's Bearded White God*. Useful chapters cover subjects such as "How to Host a Returning God," a question perhaps answered by the section that follows it: "Daily Blood Baths." In 2007, Honoré's *Quest* was reprinted as a "classic," but with a more subtle title, *In Search of Quetzalcoatl*. Excerpts and summaries of the book, often in his acolyte Tucker-Mast's words, can be read on the internet, on sites ranging from that of a pro-apartheid political party in upstate New York, to the white nationalist forum Stormfront, which proclaims itself the "voice of the new, embattled white minority." A thread posted on Stormfront by user Aryan7314 tells of the white gods who came down from the sky: the explorers and conquerors, soldiers of Quetzalcoatl, who claimed America for the white race alone. "MAY THE LORD BLESS THE WHITE GODS THAT ROAM THE EARTH!!" a thread with images of white bodybuilders proclaims. *Bless* is appropriate, as it comes from *bledsian*, an Old English word used for animal sacrifices meaning, "to splatter with blood."

On Stormfront, mythopolitics churns as if in a washing machine, on a cycle of eternal return. Aryan7314 speaks of the "god self" of Adam's race, of the ophiolatreia tracked by Reverend Deane, how the serpent slithered into the Nag Hammadi gospels, buried in the sand. Elsewhere, Savitri Devi appears in a faded photograph wearing an orange sari, giving a Nazi salute with her eyes closed against the blinding sun. There are excerpts from her writings about the Hitler avatar, the *Bhagavad Gita*, Annie Besant and her "poisonous milk." On multiple threads users debate and condemn the black godhood of Haile Selassie I, pointing out that even he refuted it. Master Koot Hoomi appears. It all seethes and foments, becoming scriptural material for the religion of whiteness. "God is in our aryan DNA . . . So we must do everything to be eternal," Aryan7314 godsplains.

✦ ✦ ✦

*I can say today that I am completely racially aware,*

wrote Dylann Roof, a few hours before he killed nine black churchgoers in Charleston, in hope of igniting a race war. The first missionaries who arrived in the Americas were preoccupied by a question; now I find I am asking it too. How to undeify someone else's god? How do we kill the doctrine that has made gods out of white men? White supremacy will not leave us until we reject the divinity of whiteness. White is a moral choice, as James Baldwin wrote. Faced with the choice, I blush and refuse.

An Indian inhabiting the Country. N.th West of Louisiana. in 1741.

London. Published by J.G. & F. Rivington, St Pauls Church Yard, & Waterloo Place. 1833.    S. Baxer. sc

Man, then, lives by a kind of periodic deicide.

—Marshall Sahlins

It was the whiteness of the whale that above all things appalled me.

—Herman Melville, *Moby-Dick*

# 13

How to Kill a God

"Wherever he goes he plants English gardens," noted a Sri Lankan anthropologist, not without some disgust, of that most revered of British seamen, Captain James Cook. His ship was an ark, heavy with sheep, cattle, and potted plants, ready to domesticate any savage land he spied. Whenever he took possession of a new South Pacific island for the Crown, Cook would sow seeds and set loose pairs of animals "almost in a loving fashion." Among his crew, Cook was allegedly adored as a father, who cared deeply for his sailors' health, and rarely lost a man. In England, he was renowned as the navigator who determined the boundaries of the habitable world, and was praised for his humane conduct in dark, faraway waters. But on his third voyage, on the quest to find the Northwest Passage, Captain Cook began to drown in some unseen, interior deluge. He sank into a black mood, seemed to lose touch with reality, and began to inflict punishments on his crew at the slightest whim. He paced the deck and flew into rages that the sailors called *heivas*, after a Tahitian stomping dance. On the islands at which they stopped, he spread terror, torching entire villages and carving crosses into natives' flesh in revenge for petty crimes. Even before he became a god Captain

Cook had staked out the true space of divinity: violence, of the arbitrary kind. After weeks at sea, as supplies of food and water began to run low, his ship the *Resolution* sighted a paradisal shore. Rather than landing, Cook insisted, for no reason at all, that they keep sailing, interminably, around the coast. As the unhinged captain circled the island, the year turned from 1778 to 1779. Eyes watched from the beach.

When on January 17, a Sunday, the ark cast anchor at last in a black-sand bay, a crowd of ten thousand had gathered to await it. Five hundred canoes, laden with sugar cane, breadfruit, and pigs, glided up to it, as the islanders sang and rejoiced. Histories narrate that for the people of Hawaii, the arrival of Captain Cook was no less than an epiphany. "The men hurried to the ship to see the god with their own eyes," wrote the nineteenth-century Hawaiian historian Samuel Kamakau. "There they saw a fair man with bright eyes, a high-bridged nose, light hair, and handsome features. Good-looking gods they were!" Their speech sounded like the trilling of the *'o'o* bird, with the prolonged cooing of the *lali* bird, both native to the islands.

The strangers were white, the Hawaiians observed, according to the missionary Sheldon Dibble. "'Their skin is loose and folding,'" they noted "(as they themselves in their ignorance of civilized manners had no conception of a well-fitted garment)," Dibble explained. They mistook the Englishmen's hats for misshapen heads, and their pockets for doors in their sides. "'Into these openings they thrust their hands, and take thence many valuable things—their bodies are full of treasure,'" Dibble ventriloquized. Like volcanoes, fire and smoke appeared to pour from their mouths. An elderly, emaciated priest went on board the *Resolution* and led the cigar-smoking deity ashore. Thousands fell to their knees as Cook passed by. The priest led the captain to a thatched temple, where he wrapped Cook in a red cloth and sacrificed a small pig to him, as the people recited lines from a creation myth:

> Born was La'ila'i a woman
> Born was Ki'i a man
> Born was Kane a god

*Born was Kanaloa the hot-striking octopus*
   *It was day.*

The Hawaiian epic *Kumulipo* relates that, after the sea urchins, seaweed, lobsters, and birds were created, woman, man, god, and octopus were formed. God and man, Kane and Ki'i were born together as brothers, yet they became locked in a battle over who had the right to procreate with La'ila'i, the first woman. She chose to mate with Ki'i first, marking an original victory for mankind that has to be renewed each year through a set of rites known as the Makahiki. In the ritual, the god Lono, a fertility deity, is said to reappear from the distant land of his exile and to retake the earth from the king for a period of time.

According to the anthropologist Marshall Sahlins, among others, Cook's arrival marked an extraordinary coincidence: the Makahiki was taking place on Hawaii at the time and the *Resolution*, as it circled the island in a clockwise direction, was inadvertently tracing the path of the effigy of Lono as it was borne in a procession around the coast. The idol is made of a pole and crosspiece with white cloth hanging from it, resembling a sail. And Cook, as if following the script of a myth he could not have known, had landed in the very bay said to be the god's home, which lodges a shrine consecrated to him. In their journals and logbooks, the sailors reported that the captain was hailed variously as Orono, Rono, Eroner, Arrona, Lono—"a Character that is looked upon by them as partaking something of divinity," the ship's surgeon related, echoing a biblical phrase describing Christ. Another word used to greet Cook was *akua*, a Hawaiian term that was translated as "god." In a scholarly disagreement with Sahlins in the early 1990s, Gananath Obeyesekere contested this identification on the grounds of universal common sense. How could the Hawaiians possibly have mistaken an Englishman for a Polynesian deity? Don't all people think it is they themselves who resemble the gods?

The Hawaiians fashioned a special idol in Cook's honor, recorded Heinrich Zimmermann, a German sailor aboard the *Resolution*. "This god was made after the pattern of the others but was adorned with white feathers instead of red, presumably because Cook being a European had a fair complexion." With the arrival of the new deities, it is supposed that a nascent awareness of racial difference must have dawned in the Hawaiian world as well. The mariner John Ledyard wrote that the natives "observed that the colour of our skins partook of the red from the sun, and the white from the moon and stars," concluding that these ruddy strangers must have some connection with the heavenly bodies. According to Ledyard, the islanders marveled at how these celestial beings had rendered the power of fire subservient to them: they could use it to kill others without themselves being harmed.

The white men remained on the island for three weeks. They dismantled part of the temple at Hikiau for firewood, and turned the rest into an observatory housing their astronomical equipment, which they would take out, now and then, to stare up at the sky. Each day the priests ceremoniously presented the British with a barbecued hog. The people would gather all the fruits of their land—sweet potatoes, coconuts, bananas, and taro—for these gods from a heaven where food had run out.

✦  ✦  ✦

There is a prayer, recorded in the mid-nineteenth century, that goes,

> *Your bodies, O Lono who are in heaven,*
> *Are a long cloud, a short cloud,*
> *A cloud that guards, a cloud that peers,*
> *A cloud in cumulus form in the sky . . .*

A god may do well to pray to himself, for he can lay himself low. He can burn in the sun he created. On February 3, Captain Cook and his crew left Hawaii to continue their explorations in the north. A week later, Cook was struck by another manifestation of Himself as Lono: a particular type of severe storm believed to coincide with the exiled god's return. The mast of the *Resolution* was broken in the gale, forcing the captain to turn back. When the British anchored again in Kealakekua Bay, eight days after they had departed, they found none of the warmth of their earlier reception. No one flocked to greet them, which "in some measure hurt our Vanity," Lieutenant James King noted in his journal. A fog of suspicion and hostility settled over the island as the people attempted to discern the strangers' reason for returning. It was clear "that our former friendship was at an end," reported Ledyard, "and that we had nothing to do but hasten our departure to some different island where our vices were not yet known, and where our extrinsic virtues might gain us another short space of being wondered at." The tension soon erupted into violence. A Hawaiian chief, accused of theft, was thrown overboard the *Resolution*, then a second chief was shot and killed. When the ship's small boat was stolen, Cook decided to take the king, Kalani'ōpu'u, hostage. It was said that the king had intended to surrender, until his wife, Kānekapōlei, pleaded with him to resist. Meanwhile, three thousand warriors armed themselves in preparation to defend their king.

During the Makahiki festival, after the Lono effigy has sailed around the island, a ritual called *kali'i*, meaning "to strike the king," is performed. As the figure of Lono waits on the shore, the king paddles in a canoe to meet the god. When he approaches Lono, the king is symbolically pierced by a spear. His warriors rush ashore to fight the devotees of Lono in a theatrical sham battle. The king, as an outsider trying to seize the land, dies a symbolic death and is reborn as the rightful Hawaiian sovereign. In an act of reconciliation, the king visits the temple with the gift of a pig for Lono and welcomes him to the "land of Us-Two." Then the effigy of Lono is taken apart, marking the end of the festival season. According to Sahlins, Cook continued, unwittingly, to perform the Makahiki script. What happened next was "the climactic ritual battle, the *kali'i* but played in reverse," as the god Lono-Cook waded ashore with his sailors to confront the king. "For one brief and decisive moment," Sahlins wrote, "the confrontation returned to the original triad," of the god [Cook], the king [Kalani'ōpu'u], and the woman [Kānekapōlei], "with the issue again decided by the woman's choice," in a replay of the creation myth of *Kumulipo*. Captain Cook's fatal end, according to the anthropologist, was "the historical metaphor of a mythical reality." It was not premeditated by the Hawaiians, "but neither was it an accident, structurally speaking."

Can one become trapped, unaware, inside another person's myth? On February 14, 1779, whose script was played: that of the Hawaiians, the British, an anthropologist not yet born in Chicago? Captain Cook fired upon the crowd. Hundreds of Hawaiians fell upon him with clubs and the iron daggers the British had forged aboard the ship and traded with them. The islanders snatched the daggers from each other's hands, Lieutenant James Burney recalled, "out of eagerness to have their share in killing him." "The final homage to Cook is tendered in missiles that include stones and clubs among the pieces of breadfruit and coconut," Sahlins describes. More than a hundred Hawaiians "rushed upon the fallen god to have a part of his death." In the first published engraving of the scene, Cook is depicted face down on the beach, hatless and separated from his gun, surrounded by Hawaiians about to bludgeon him to death as his sailors flee. In the days that followed, the captain was accorded the traditional rituals for a vanquished chief. His corpse was dismembered, his flesh roasted, and his bones separated and portioned out, with his lower jaw going to King Kalaniʻōpuʻu, his skull to somebody else, and so on. The bones were placed in baskets and covered with red feathers.

Among Cook's sailors, who had fled back to the ship, "a general silence ensued," wrote the officer George Gilbert; it was "like a Dream that we could not reconcile ourselves to." A pair of Hawaiian priests rowed to the ark with a bundle containing a large chunk of the captain's thigh. Along with their charred offering, they brought with them "a most extraordinary question." They wished to know when Captain Cook would return to the vessel "and resume his former station." Would it be in—a very Christlike estimate—"three days' time?" The two men "shed abundance of tears at the loss of the Erono," King recorded, and they asked "what he would do to them when he return'd." On shore, others "asserted that he would return in two months & begged our mediation with him in their favor," according to midshipman James Trevenan. The German sailor Zimmermann recorded that islanders announced, "*The god Cook is not dead but sleeps in the woods and will come tomorrow*," as translated by an interpreter the British had taken on board in Tahiti. Over the following years, the idea seemed to persist that Cook would resurrect. Joshua Lee Dimsdell, who arrived in Hawaii as a settler in 1792, recalled a conversation with a man named Pihore who claimed to have slain Cook. He "added with tears that he hoped the Oroner (so they term Cap' C) would forgive him as he had built several Morais to his Memory & sacrificed a number of Hogs," Dimsdell related. "It is their firm Hope & Belief that he will come again & forgive them."

According to the sailor Edward Bell, who visited the bay in 1793, Captain Cook's death had become the definitive frame for the Hawaiian sense of time. "The Natives seem to consider that melancholy transaction as one of the most remarkable events in their History," Bell wrote, and reported that they used it as a date to assist their calendrical calculations. "They still in speaking of him style him the Orono and if they are to be believ'd, most sincerely regret his fate." The accounts by later British travelers to Hawaii, and those of historians who took up the narrative, emphasize the surprise and guilt felt by the islanders at Cook's death, as if they had imagined it to be a play, with no consequence. "The natives had no idea that Cook could possibly be killed, as they considered him a supernatural being, and were astonished when they saw him fall," reported the English explorer William Mariner in 1806; despite having killed him, "they esteem him as having been sent by the gods to civilize them."

These stories, told and retold over generations, ignore one obvious fact: Cook was killed because he acted rashly and violently, slaughtering chiefs, kidnapping the king, and giving the impression the British had returned to conquer the island. In 1825, Lord Byron's cousin commanded the HMS *Blonde* on its voyage to Hawaii, with the artist Robert Dampier on board to paint lush oil portraits of the natives. Encountering a chief who said he witnessed the killing, the Englishman reported that the man who struck the fatal blow was a commoner from a distant part of the island, "ignorant of Cook's attributed Divinity,'" Dampier explained. "They even now look upon this event as a sort of national stigma upon their character." What atonement was to be done?

The fur trader James Colnett, who arrived in Hawaii in 1791 aboard the *Argonaut*, reported that ever since the British first appeared, the islanders had been constantly at war and devastated by strange, unknown illnesses, all of which they attributed to Cook's revenge. Two volcanoes had awakened and burned, night and day, pouring out lava—the work, they contended, of the vengeful god. "They made strict enquiry of me, if ever he would come back again, and when I saw him last," Colnett wrote. He replied that Captain Cook, to avenge his death, was sending the Spaniards to colonize their land and turn them all into slaves. *For the LORD is a god of retribution*, warns the book of Jeremiah.

> *I will stretch out my hand against you,*
> *roll you off the cliffs.*

✦  ✦  ✦

When the first missionaries arrived in Hawaii from New England in 1820, they used the cautionary tale of Captain Cook as a potent parable for their teachings. "How vain, rebellious, and at the same time contemptible, for a worm"—meaning Cook—"to presume to receive religious homage and sacrifices from the stupid and polluted worshippers of demons," thundered Hiram Bingham, the Calvinist leader of the first evangelical mission, which set sail from Boston. After six months at sea, the Calvinists anchored at the archipelago, and found it beset by the "thickest heathenism," its sun-drenched landscapes masking terrible despair. Viruses introduced by the British were killing off entire families and villages, and survivors had taken to drinking themselves to death. The great Kamehameha, founder and first king of the newly unified Kingdom of Hawaii, had died the previous year, and his son had recently abolished the *tabu* system, the strict codes that had structured daily life for centuries, and which had unraveled in the wake of the British arrival. A crisis of faith seemed to grip the islands, as temples fell into ruin and the totems of the old gods were destroyed. "The nation, without a religion, was waiting for the law of Jehovah," according to one early missionary. The Calvinists blamed the rampant disease and malaise on the Hawaiians' immorality, sexual promiscuity, idol worship, and on their reverencing of Cook.

Into the disarray, the stern Bingham inserted himself and strove to exercise command over all aspects of Hawaiian life. Under the Calvinists, the Hawaiian language was alphabetized, the Bible was translated, and novel

Christian concepts were mapped onto old Hawaiian words. Schools and seminaries were opened, and draconian morality laws introduced across the islands. The queen of Hawaii was among the first to convert, and much of the population followed her; a broom dipped in water served to baptize five thousand Hawaiians at once. The myth of Cook-as-Lono lived on in the history books and school primers the evangelists produced, a tale that perpetuated the whiteness of divinity, while simultaneously affirming that Cook and all those who worshipped him were idolaters of the worst kind. Many Hawaiians accepted the story as a fact of their history.

In 1836, Reverend Sheldon Dibble gathered together his best students at the Lahainaluna Seminary in Maui for an ambitious project along similar lines to the *Florentine Codex*. He sent out his pupils with a questionnaire to interview the elders on the islands, in order to record Hawaiian traditions, mythology, and history before they were irreparably forgotten. Collated and edited by Dibble, the resulting text, *Ka Mooolelo Hawaii*, became an authoritative resource for scholars of Hawaiian history. It told of how, in the beginning, the people lived in darkness, "led by Satan to do his will," until the foreign ships bearing emissaries of Christ arrived and intervened. "They had sunk very low—were very degraded—animals were higher, they were lower." In the *Mooolelo*, Cook is represented as the archvillain, the Herod who allowed himself to be worshipped as a god, raped a Hawaiian princess, and spread venereal disease. But it is thanks to divine providence, not the armed resistance of Hawaiians, that the impostor was killed. "*God struck him dead.*"

Along with their indignations, the Calvinist missionaries brought with them a novel concept of private ownership, simply appropriating whatever land they desired. They were, after all, apostles of a God who *possesses* the earth. *To the LORD your God belong the heavens . . . the earth and everything in it*, Moses had declared, gripping tablets of stone. Their children went on to establish enormous sugar plantations, securing international markets for their lucrative crop. "The world is to be Christianized and civilized," the evangelist Josiah Strong would assert, capturing the mood of the century, "and what is the process of civilization but *the creating of more and higher wants?* Commerce follows the missionary." In 1840, with the looming threat of an invasion by France, Hawaii sought to clarify its ambiguous territorial status and seek nationhood. The king sent a delegation to the United States and Europe, and three years later Hawaii was officially pronounced an independent nation. However, the plantation owners, eager to sell their crop tax-free in the United States, deeply resented the prospect of Hawaiian sovereignty.

During the US Civil War, with sugar production halted in the South, the wealth of the white Hawaiian oligarchy soared, enabling it to consolidate its grip on the archipelago's economy, from banks, utilities, and steamships to local commerce and trade. Beset by illness and poverty, the native Hawaiian population had shrunk to a fifth of its former size. The industrialists deemed Hawaiian workers to be lazy and unemployable, casting them aside in favor of laborers from China and Japan whom they could pay even smaller wages. In 1893, the sugar cartel, along with a regiment of US Marines, overthrew the Hawaiian queen Liliʻuokalani, in an act that the US president at the time, Grover Cleveland, condemned as unconstitutional. Although he promised to reinstate the queen, the matter remained stalled in Congress for several years. When President William McKinley took office, he drafted a unilateral resolution to annex Hawaii, in spite of the warning by one congressman that "to do so will be not only to subvert the supreme law of the land but to strike down every precedent in our history." The American military occupation of the archipelago had begun.

"No darker cloud can hang over a people than the prospect of being blotted out from the list of nations," Hawaii's deposed queen Liliʻuokalani lamented. "No grief can equal that of a sovereign forcibly deprived of her throne." Kept under house arrest, the queen set about translating the creation myth of the *Kumulipo* as her own act of resistance. She arranged for the text to be published, in hope that it would demonstrate to the United States that Hawaiians had their own deep and intricate history—time had not begun with Captain Cook—as a way of countering the discourse that sanctioned the occupation of her kingdom. The *Kumulipo* catalogs an epic genealogy linking the reigning monarch to the birth of the universe, thus both consecrating the ruler and assuring the people they were governed by the rightful hands. In the myth, time is divided into epochs, the first seven the ages of *po*, or darkness, and the latter nine periods of *ao*, or light. Decades earlier, missionaries had appropriated the words and combined them with the word for *mind*, *na'au*, to create *na'auao* and *na'aupo*, the twin notions of "civilization" and "savagery." If she was unable to retake her land, the queen would at least wrest back these words through translation, restoring to them their original meanings.

In the American press, racist cartoonists deployed their anti-black arsenal of caricatures to sketch the Hawaiian sovereign as an African harlot, grinning as she heats a cannibal cooking pot. The papers claimed that Lili'uokalani was the bastard child of a "mulatto shoemaker," who illegitimately lorded over her "heathenish" people. With such coloring, it was argued, she was clearly unfit by nature to rule. Along with the queen, the US occupiers arrested newspaper editors who supported her and clamped down on the opposition press. This meant that the only news that came out of Hawaii was delivered by the coup's spokesmen, who announced that the queen had willingly surrendered both her kingdom and her claim to the land.

To this day, the myth that Hawaiians passively accepted the loss of their nation, without resistance, lives on. Historical accounts make little mention of the fact that some forty thousand Hawaiians petitioned against the occupation and protested in the streets. A century later, in 1993, thousands of Hawaiians marched on the queen's former palace in Honolulu, again calling for independence. The struggle is absent from textbooks and not taught in schools; Lili'uokalani appears as little more than a shadow in a footnote. The American public imagination rarely questions whether Hawaii wants to be part of the United States; there is the assumption that Hawaiians, in their distant paradise, must be content. Didn't they venerate a white man as a god? Didn't they prostrate themselves before him, dress him, and feed him with all the fruits of their land? They killed him in a ritual but, not knowing what they had done, didn't they, with guilty tears, impatiently await his return?

✦ ✦ ✦

In a type of neoclassical painting one might call *The Apotheosis of X*, the dead hero is bundled up to heaven by a host of angels, usually in a windswept tumult of robes, wings, and clouds. A crowd of grieving mortals watches from below. There is the sense of a celestial scramble: in Rubens's sumptuous *Apotheosis of James I*, heaven is chaos and James looks terrified at having arrived. In Barralet's *Apotheosis of George Washington*, the dead president has his arms outstretched in a crucified pose, while Father Time and the angel of immortality bear him up to heaven on a shaft of light. The white daughters of the nation weep at his feet, alongside an eagle and a native chief with a tomahawk. In a mid-1860s *Apotheosis*, a freshly assassinated Lincoln joins Washington in the sky, and clings to him in a tight hug. Washington has taken off his own laurel crown and is holding it over Lincoln's head like a halo. In the *Apothéose Napoléons*, the angels are few: it is as if the petite general has sprung up to heaven of his own accord, where he poses sprightly on parting clouds. The new god is less eager in Fragonard's *Apotheosis of Benjamin Franklin*: he seems to be reaching out toward something back on earth with one hand while a stern angel, grasping his other hand, drags him upward.

In 1785, in a Covent Garden theater, a spectacle premiered depicting Captain Cook's voyages in the South Pacific. During the final scene of *Omai, or A Trip Around the World*, at the words "Cook, ever honour'd, immortal shall live!" an enormous oil painting descended from the ceiling—Philippe Jacques de Loutherbourg's *Apotheosis of Captain Cook*, commissioned for the occasion. Cook is carried up to heaven by the angels Britannia and Fame, but his gaze is directed back at the vertiginous earth, where ships and canoes are facing off in the bay. His expression is queasy and his eyes seem to plead: "*Don't drop me!*"

When news of Cook's death finally reached London in January 1780, eleven months after the captain was killed, it was met not with a public outpouring of grief but a rather morbid fascination at the exotic details. The success of *Omai*, which starred alongside the oil painting eighty dancing "savages," some in blackface, inaugurated a new European ritual of slaying Cook onstage. In 1788, the wildly popular *Death of Captain Cook; A Grand Serious-Pantomimic-Ballet* premiered in Paris, before going on to tour the Continent, England, and the United States.

*... Lord, how you'll look,*
*And stare, and clap, Oh! such a Captain Cook!*
*You'll bleed when he is stabb'd, die at his fall ...*

By all accounts, the *Grand Serious-Pantomimic-Ballet* was violent, chaotic, "horrid," overwrought with emotion—and a great triumph. In his
memoirs, an oboist recalled that one of the dancers accidentally stabbed
an actor to death onstage during the scene where the savages are attacking Cook, while the audience cried, "Bravo!" Year after year, the ballet
was revived, and the captain's death reenacted, like a blood offering the
imperial powers continued to make to guarantee their own ascendance.
Cook was killed in Yarmouth, Bungay, Leeds, and nine times in Norwich;
he was bludgeoned to death in Dublin, clubbed in Quebec, speared on
Greenwich Street in Manhattan and again in Charleston, South Carolina. Navy men got death-of-Cook tattoos, and aristocratic women wore
dresses inspired by "the Indian who killed Capt'n Cook with His Club,"
as the society diarist Mrs. Hester Thrale noted. By the mid-nineteenth
century, P. T. Barnum would joke that the celebrated blunt instrument
had multiplied itself, securing a treasured place in every museum vitrine.
Cook was a scapegoat, yet, as the French theorist René Girard wrote, it
is the scapegoat—like Christ in his sacrificial guise as the tender Lamb
of God—who is deified. "I could not imagine that extraordinary man in
any other fashion than clothed in light," raved the poet-botanist Adelbert von Chamisso. The poet Anna Seward heaved him up to heaven in
her 1780 *Elegy on Captain Cook, to Which Is Added, an Ode to the Sun.*
"To put it bluntly," writes Obeyesekere, "I doubt that the natives created
their European god; the Europeans created him for them."

The swelling legend of Cook channeled the Greco-Roman apotheosis
of dead emperors and heroes, scenes of heavenly ascent preserved in
marble friezes across Rome and copied by the Enlightenment's neoclassical painters. Cook joined the pantheon of great men, long ago exalted
in imperial cults of state. Yet his story also partook of the Christological
myth: of the dying and resurrected Son of God, the hallowed atonement,
and also the original sin, the temptation of godhood dating back to the

Garden and the serpent's ruse. Cook, both sinner and savior, could not but appear biblical. In 1889, on his travels in the South Seas, Robert Louis Stevenson met the ruler of the tiny atoll of Abemama, who told him that he had heard about James Cook from the captain of a passing ship. The chief recounted how he had been intrigued by the story, and had looked for more information by turning to his copy of the Bible. "Here he sought long and earnestly," recalled Stevenson, but there was "no word of Cook," the disappointed chief reported. "The inference was obvious; the explorer was a myth."

Deification happens when a man is on his knees or flat on his face, in an epiphany or in prostration. It also happens through history-writing, through painting and pantomime, through edits, omissions, and translations. What word do you take for god? The Hawaiian syllables were *akua*, but again this is misleading, for in its original sense the word could refer to any number of sacred beings, objects, or living persons—anything possessing immense power. So too with the word *Lono*: the crew of the *Resolution* was never able to figure out its precise meaning. "Sometimes they applied it to an invisible being, who, they said, lived in the heavens. We also found that it was a title belonging to a personage of great rank and power in the island," Lieutenant King recalled. Not only Cook but the Hawaiian king, too, was greeted with shouts of "Lono!" Misinterpretations and deletions create gods.

The historian Samuel Kamakau wrote of the coming of Captain Cook in his 1866 *Mo'olelo* or "History," a text widely esteemed as the authoritative "native" account. It was eventually published in English in 1961, after decades of work by a team of translators that included the nineteenth-century Australian-born settler and former sugar plantation worker Thomas Thrum. In the English edition, the story was heavily doctored, ostensibly to conform to "Western" standards of history-writing, as the Hawaiian scholar Noenoe Silva has shown. Before his description of the arrival of Cook, Kamakau details, over seventeen pages, other foreigners who had already arrived by sea, some with pale skin, some with brown. The translators, however, omitted the entire section, transforming the narrative of the appearance of Cook and his ark into a magical, utterly unprecedented event. In the original, Kamakau emphasizes the violence, fighting, and hostage taking that culminated in the killing of the captain, and concludes with a list.

The fruits and seeds that Cook's actions planted sprouted and grew, and became trees that spread to devastate the people of these islands:
1. Gonorrhea together with syphilis.
2. Prostitution.
3. The false idea that he was a god and worshipped.
4. Fleas and mosquitoes.
5. The spread of epidemic diseases.
6. Change in the air we breathe.
7. Weakening of our bodies.
8. Changes in plant life.

"The best part of Cook's visit was that we killed him," the Hawaiian activist Lilikalā Kameʻeleihiwa writes. Violence has a peculiar property of simplifying things.

"Man has created gods in his own likeness," writes James Frazer in *The Golden Bough*, "and being himself mortal he has naturally supposed his creatures to be in the same sad predicament. Thus the Greenlanders believed that a wind could kill their most powerful god." If man imagines that a god resembles himself, then the god, eventually, must die. Captain Cook has been killed again and again, on the beach, in the theater, on the page, but the myth of his alleged divinity lives on. With every new death, it persists.

Deicide is on my mind. How do you kill a god, if not by bludgeoning, stabbing, piercing, splitting, dismembering, boiling, roasting, distributing? Is it through rewriting history, by exposing the machinations beneath myths, by breaking open syllables so that whatever is sacred inside spills out?[1] Is it by tearing down His image? In the twenty-first century, across New Zealand, Australia, and Hawaii, statues of Captain Cook have been defaced. They are not carved from white marble but cast

---

1 Can you kill Him by banishing Him to a footnote?

in dark bronze, as if the fact of their whiteness is so uncontestable that there is no need for it to be reproduced. The idols demand of the viewer a suspension of disbelief. Though they depict their subject in blackened metal, as if to belie the very notion of racial difference, we know we are meant to apprehend him as white, much as we are made to see racial difference that biologically does not exist. Strutting across a pedestal in his breeches, telescope in hand, a defaced Cook wears a spray-painted bikini; around the neck of another Cook hangs a large canvas sign that reads, simply, SORRY. The forecast calls for more. White gods will fall like raindrops. It feels as though the heavens are about to open up.

◆   ◆   ◆

It may have been the New World's earliest attempt at deicide. On Thursday, June 5, 1539, the people of Mexico staged a pageant of revenge against Hernán Cortés. The setting of their liberation was Jerusalem. On top of the foundations of the half-built town of Tlaxcala, the people erected a model of the holy city, with towers, ramparts, and crenellations. When they could build no higher with stone and mud they fashioned upper stories out of painted cloth and palm mats. They decorated the city with roses and divided themselves into armies.

The first to enter the stage were the uniformed regiments from Spain, an army of thousands commanded by an actor playing Charles V. They were joined by their allies, battalions from Germany and Rome, followed by militias from Peru and the Caribbean islands in tribal dress. Then came the forces of New Spain, the army that called itself "the Christians," attired in the regalia of Aztec warriors. They massed at the gates of the city; the armies of the Moors and the Jews were already concealed and waiting onstage. Leading the infidel army, as the "Great Sultan of Babylon and Tetrarch of Jerusalem," was none other than Cortés, played by a Tlaxcaltecan actor. Starring as "Captain General of the Moors" was an actor playing Pedro de Alvarado, the blond commander so hot-tempered he was taken for the deity of the sun. (The two actual conquistadors were absent from the scene: Alvarado was in Honduras, and Cortés was recovering from a wound.)

As the trumpet sounds, the army of Spain is the first to besiege the city. Sultan Cortés commands his troops on the defensive; the army of New Spain rushes in, fighting valiantly against the Moors. The Caribbeans are the first to be captured by the enemy. The Christian armies manage to liberate a herd of sheep from Jerusalem, only to be driven back by the Sultan's army. In the midst of the fighting, an actor playing Saint Santiago rides in on a white horse. The Christians attack again and the Moors retreat inside the walls of the city, in fear of the saint. The allies attempt to force their way inside but are again driven back by the Moors. The soldiers of New Spain resort to prayer, and soon an angel appears above their camp. "Although you are newcomers to the faith," the angel lectures them, "God has allowed you to be conquered in order that you might know that without His help, you can do little." A Tlaxcaltecan actor, playing Saint Hippolytus, gallops in on a brown horse.

The Christians, roused by the appearance of the saint, renew their assault, hurling thick stalks of corn and cannonballs made of reeds. They bombard the Moors with prickly pears, and fire bullets made of dried earth and filled with a wet, crimson mud, so that they appear to spill blood wherever they land. A straw pavilion on top of the towers is set on fire, igniting the upper stories of canvas and painted wood. As Jerusalem burns, the archangel Michael suddenly appears and announces that it is time for the Moors to allay God's anger with tears and penance. Sultan Cortés is terrified by the sight and cries out to his troops that he has been greatly blinded in sin. "We thought we were fighting with men. But now we see that we have been fighting with God and his saints and angels!" he exclaims. Pedro de Alvarado advises the Sultan to sue for peace. Cortés sends a letter of surrender to the armies of the Christians. *We are your natural vassals*, it reads. Sultan Cortés kneels before his conqueror, played by a Tlaxcaltecan lord, and kisses his hand. The liberation of Jerusalem is always about more than itself.

Sultan Cortés is informed that his life, and those of his men, will be spared if they agree to be baptized. The infidels—played by the thousands of villagers of Tlaxcala who in actuality have not yet received the sacrament—are led in procession to the priest, dissolving the distinction between the theatrical and the real. The priest will perform the holy rites for thousands this day, but first he plunges the head of Cortés beneath the water and pulls it out, allowing the rivers of revenge and redemption

to run
down
his
face.

It was said that in the Aztec afterlife there were different heavens for those who died in different ways. Heaven was divided into regions; one belonged to the sun god and another to the god of rain. Warriors who were killed in battle or in sacrifice went to the east side of the sun god Tonatiuh's heaven, which was warm and bright. The spirits of women who died in childbirth went to the west, where the sun goes down each evening, to a heaven where the light was dim. In the uppermost heights grew the blossoming *chichihuacuahuitl*, or nursing tree. The souls of babies sucked at its nectar until they were ready to be sent to a new womb. Those who had drowned, been struck by lightning, or died of illnesses like leprosy went to Tlālōcān, the wet heaven of the rain god. Mictlan, which meant simply "among the dead," was where everyone else went, the mundane underworld of those who had died in unexceptional ways.

As they attempted to translate the concepts of their Christian faith into Nahuatl, the early friars of New Spain had tried to strike fear of Mictlan into the hearts of their congregation, embellishing it with their own infernal imaginations. The Augustinian friar Antonio de Roa liked to demonstrate the torments of hell upon his own body, by asking his pupils to choke and whip him, to bathe him in boiling water, and drip searing pine resin onto his open wounds. The Franciscan friar Luis Caldera burned animals alive in an oven to try to convey the sounds and scents of hell.

Where do the men go who die as gods? Their heaven is white, I imagine, and it is crowded.

# Liberation
# (Last Rites)

"Think not, as you read these pages, that they were conceived in certainty and ease," wrote the Reverend Dr. William R. Jones. "Fear and trembling, confusion and doubt gave them birth." When in 1973 he published *Is God a White Racist?* bookshops wouldn't sell it and librarians kept it far away from their shelves. In the late sixties and early seventies, as Confederate monuments to whiteness were being erected in parts of the United States, a group of theologians in churches and seminaries began to forge a new movement. It was "a *religious* protest against the misuse of *religion* to establish and maintain oppression," as Jones defined black liberation theology, first charted by thinkers such as James Cone, Joseph Washington, and Bishop Albert Cleage. Jones contended, however, that none of its leading lights had wrestled with the "unsavory, and some will say, blasphemous question," which the reverend posed in his book's title. If the modern concept of race had proved challenging for Christian doctrine (did all men share an ancestor in Adam?), for Jones, more crippling for theology than the abstract idea of race were its real-life consequences—the immense, inordinate suffering of one race at the hands of another. In the face of black oppression, Jones argued, one might legitimately speculate as to whether God isn't at work for the supremacy of the white race.

Although Jones considered a different history than my own, he, too, recognized how ideas of divinity lie beneath white supremacy. "A theology of liberation," Jones wrote, "must provide persuasive grounds for removing the sanctity and hallowed status from those segments of the culture it seeks to reform." The starting point, he argued, was the problem of theodicy: if God is all-powerful and benevolent, then how to explain the evil of racial suffering in this world? Why did God allow slavery and injustice; why did He stand by as innocent men were lynched? How could the black believer know for certain that his God did not hate him for the color of his skin? Any coherent theology must address the question of why God permits evil; the black theologian, Jones insisted, must begin by refuting the charge of divine racism before further work can be done.

One option was to take the common escape route: to argue that God's motivation is beyond man's comprehension. But that, too, is a tool of oppression, Jones argued, a ruse to force blacks into quietism by recourse to a lofty, celestial unknown. Instead, the black believer must radically reappraise every aspect of his faith. "Each of our most cherished beliefs, every element of the creed and canon, must be ruthlessly probed and tested" according to the question, "What supports *black liberation*?" In *Is God a White Racist?* Jones systematically scrutinizes the work of the major liberation theologists, Cleage, Washington, and Cone, concluding that none of them could convincingly answer "no" to the question he poses in the book's title.

Bishop Cleage said to God in a prayer: "Certainly thou must understand that as black people, it would be impossible for us to kneel before thee, believing thee to be a white God." Cleage argued that if man was created in God's image, then God himself could not be white—according to America's one-drop law, He must be black. It was a theory that went some way toward dispelling accusations of divine racism, but it led "to very dubious consequences," Jones averred. The problem was with the "combination" theory of *Imago Dei*: if God is a mixture of all humanity's hues, then presumably the same theory had to be applied to "the category of weight, size, sex, intelligence, etc," leading logically to anthropomorphism—and a divinely average God. Further, given that Cleage had declared that as a black man he could not kneel to a white god, "would not a plurality of gods, each with a different color, be necessary to accommodate the human family of worshippers?" The right coloring would never be enough. "God might be an 'Oreo' God, black on the outside but white on the inside," Jones wrote mischievously. We would end up with raucous polytheism, or a strange theophagy, and without having resolved the question of black oppression.

For Bishop Cleage, black suffering must somehow have been deserved, as punishment for some inarticulated sin. Yet it was difficult, Jones countered, to identify or even imagine so grave a sin that would justify the oppression blacks have faced since arriving in America. Worse, Cleage's view would consign black people to suffer without end. For the theologian Joseph R. Washington, black misery was the mark that they were God's chosen people. Slavery was a necessary part of the divine plan, "the means for inextricably binding the Negro and the Caucasian," Washington wrote in his 1967 book *The Politics of God*. "Without this binding the immeasurably more bruising work of releasing whites from their blasphemous bondage to whiteness and racial superiority cannot be done." In Washington's view, black suffering is the Christlike sacrifice that makes it possible for white people to be released from their own shackles and stop worshipping their own supremacy. The suffering slave possesses a kind of power that the oppressor lacks, Washington claimed, and will be redeemed and liberated on Judgment Day. But as Jones points out, we cannot know whether this state of affairs is truly the case until the moment of liberation actually occurs, for only then will we witness the proof. This leaves the question of whether or not God is a white racist unresolved until the eschaton, the end of days, and Jones didn't want to wait so long.

Is divinity the ability to commit violence in its purest, most arbitrary form? Or is it the ultimate liberation from violence, which properly belongs to the profane earth? James Cone believed it was the latter, writing in 1970 that liberation "is not an afterthought, but the very essence of divine activity." He agreed with Washington that black people, due to the very fact of their oppression, are in a favored position in the eyes of God. For Cone, divine racism was impossible, as a contradiction in terms. He drew his portrait of God's character from His historic acts of liberation in the past, such as the abolition of slavery—proof, Cone argued, that God is on the side of black justice. In his view, paradise awaits those who die in the struggle. But, Jones countered, we can only be certain that it is God who is the liberator if we can clearly discern His hand at work in acts of black liberation. Jones again raises the specter of evil: "Consider: the promise of a future reality after death motivates blacks to make the ultimate sacrifice for their liberation, and this is the means by which a racist God beckons blacks to suicidal efforts and thus accomplishes black genocide." Perhaps it is unduly dark, but we cannot know. Besides, Cone himself had offered a startling response to the possibility that he might be wrong: "If God is not for us, if God is not against white racists, then God is a murderer, and we had better kill God."

With the problem of God's racism still unresolved, the Reverend Jones reached the conclusion that two of his deepest beliefs must be abandoned. He would have to relinquish the notion that God is sovereign over history, or even active in it. There is no politics of God. Instead Jones turned to secular humanism, which does, after all, solve the problem of divine racism by simply removing God from the equation. Man is the ultimate agent in history, and racism is his alone. Jones's conclusion silenced the centuries of justifications of white supremacy and imperialism—from the papal bull of 1493 that made conquest conditional on Catholic conversion, to debates over the nature of Adam— and cut off any theological excuses the white nationalist might reach for. "What is being done, some will say, is to remove all hope from black religion," Jones wrote. "But it must also be considered that to speak of God as the ground for black hope—without the prior refutation of divine racism—is sheer theological illusion." If God exists, He is at a remove from the world. He is up there on a higher branch, with the owls who once were gods too.

✦ ✦ ✦

On February 26, 2012, George Zimmerman shot and killed the black teenager Trayvon Martin. When Zimmerman was acquitted of the boy's murder, it reminded a professor of a book she had read when she was a student. Reverend Jones's treatise shocked her at the time, but now, looking back, "I have to say: I get it," Anthea Butler wrote. "I know that this American god ain't my god. As a matter of fact, I think he's a white racist god with a problem . . . He is carrying a gun and stalking young black men." In 2014, in two separate incidents, white police officers killed two unarmed black men, Michael Brown and Eric Garner, and faced no consequences. In response, two scholar-activists in the Black Lives Matter movement, Stephen Finley and Biko Mandela Gray, decided to pick up where Reverend Jones had left off. In their 2015 essay "God *Is* a White Racist," they argued that, in the face of state-sanctioned violence against black people, and given the state's absolute power to arbitrate innocence and guilt, it was the state itself that must be understood as the white racist god. "The vindication of police officers is a form of theodicy," they wrote, "one that protects the divine state from charges of injustice and, more bluntly, evil." Like any god, the state is not bound by the laws it sets, and ever eludes any self-indictment.

Race, the scholar-activists remind us, is not only a word but a sentencing, of who can live and who will die. The divine state's transcendence masks "an insidious, covert form of white supremacy coded as 'law and order,'" Finley and Gray write. The only possible response, they argue, is atheism: not the traditional refutation of the existence of God, but a humanism that refuses the deification of the state "as divine and above reproach." Echoing Reverend Jones's systematic questioning of his own religious beliefs, they assert the obligation to radically reappraise every tenet and mechanism of the state. It will require an act of deicide toward what is considered sacred in the United States, including the right to wield guns and the militarization of the police. "We must destroy," the activists write, "the state-gods that continue to make our lives matter negatively." After all, as Job taught, the conscience of man is finer than that of a god. *Now that my eyes have seen you, I shudder with sorrow for mortal clay*, Job said, in words that reduced God to silence.

✦  ✦  ✦

They would meet at eight o'clock sharp, for the dead berated anyone who showed up late. Around a table in New Orleans, a circle of Afro-Creole teachers and government clerks, blacksmiths, cigar makers, scholars, and poets convened each night to contact the afterlife. They called themselves the Cercle Harmonique. Their unofficial leader was Henry Louis Rey, a politician and civil rights activist who had been skeptical until he tried to levitate a table, and discovered that he could. Between 1858, not long before the Louisiana state legislature passed "An Act to Permit Free Persons of African Descent to Select Their Masters and Become Slaves for Life," and 1877, after the Civil War and the failed Reconstruction had come to an end, the group recorded over seven thousand pages of messages from the dead. At the séance, the spirits of Moctezuma, Swedenborg, Confucius, deceased Confederate lieutenants, Parisian revolutionaries, and members of the circle's own dead relatives described, in French, the nature of the next life. Those who had left earth in the flurry of an apotheosis—George Washington, Napoleon, and the newcomer Abraham Lincoln, among them—conversed with the spirits of war martyrs and slaves. Saint Augustine argued with the infamous Judge Roger Taney of the *Dred Scott* case. John Wilkes Booth and Robert E. Lee arrived with apologies for their past mistakes. Jesus announced he was delighted to be there. Some of the spirits, especially the women, said they had trouble making it to the table, for so many spirits were crowding around it, trying to speak.

There is no such thing as heaven, the spirits reported, and no hell, though they sometimes used these words to make their surroundings intelligible to the living. The inferno all along was an invention of exploitative priests, relayed the spirit of the philosopher Lamennais. There are no angels, no torments, no rewards of paradise, only a celestial Ladder of Progress to climb. The spirits of dictators roamed like shadows as they worked on their self-improvement from the bottom rung. "You, the first on earth, will be the last here," a spry Napoleon lamented. "You will regret the royal mantle you draped over your shoulders." In the Spiritual Republic, everyone lived together in harmony, bound by laws

that controlled its citizens without violence. The spirits received whatever education they required. "We have houses for every taste," the souls
related, "every desire, all arranged in an admirable, intelligent, and har-
monious fashion. Each receives that which is due him, and exists with
the sublimity of new organs, prodigious new sensations, infinite, admirable, appreciable." It was all "perfect and delicious."

The dead of every generation reported that there is no such thing as
race. When the soul leaves the body, it sheds its "envelope," leaving its
racial identity, its skin color, its hair, and its nationality behind. "I am
not an American," the spirit of George Washington declared. The French
historian and slave owner Moreau de Saint-Méry, who invented racial
taxonomies and wrote panegyrics to white supremacy while he was alive,
appeared at the séance to renounce the concept of race. A spirit calling
himself "A Black Man, Once" recited a poem imploring white America
to put aside the notion of race once and for all. Having been a black
man in America, in the afterlife he was now incandescent, composed of
pure, bright light. The soul emits a glow depending on its inner nature,
its moral beauty or ugliness, he explained. Martyrs glow the brightest.

"I paid, strangled with a rope," announced the radical abolitionist
John Brown, who was sent to the gallows in 1859. "And I am free from
your atrocities; Brown is luminous!" The spirit of a former slave named
Jean Pierre reported that when he abandoned his "black envelope," all
the hatred and vengeance he had felt toward his cruel master remained
behind, attached to it. In the afterlife he went by the new name of "The
Sublime One." He was "another myself," with a phosphorescent, almost
metallic appearance. One must not confuse the quality of light with
whiteness.

There is no race, no heaven, no hell, the spirits explained, only the
Idea that all people are equal and free and share the same rights and
opportunities, an Idea that structures the afterlife and must be replicated
on earth. The evening after the Battle of Liberty Place, in September
1874, when White League militants led a violent uprising against the
state not far from where the circle gathered, a slain Confederate insur-
rectionist came to the table to atone for his mistakes. Having seen what
the Spiritual Republic looked like, he now realized that everything he

had fought for was wrong. John Brown breezed in to announce that his hanged, limp body was the flag of Equality, hoisted on top of the mast of Liberty, waving in the wind. ("Weird John Brown," Herman Melville had called him.) Appearing in the darkness, Abraham Lincoln chimed in, "Like me, thou hast killed him; but the Idea has progressed. . . . A man may disappear! But the Idea never stops advancing."

Night after night, the spirits showed up to a séance in New Orleans to urge the living to imitate the republic up above. Look at us, they said. The dead had organized themselves into a perfect democracy. Their system of voting was sublime. They always elected "the most dignified" to lead them, the spirits noted, and no one in power ever abused their authority. There was no injustice, abjection, or poverty. No souls were struggling and slipping down. They had crushed the serpent who was all along, as the spirit of Lamennais reported, merely human greed and fear. The dead gave true meaning to emancipation. "Liberty is not an empty word," announced George Washington, cradling the recently assassinated Lincoln in a tender, iridescent embrace. Every evening the spirits crowded around the table, unfurling the pent-up centuries of divine advice. But everyone they lobbied is now long dead, and still we have so far to go. Until race becomes a relic, white divinity a curiosity of a pagan past. Until the day someone, catching sight of a woman, will turn and say,

*The infinite suits you.*

# NOTES

## FIRST RITES

2     *so to you we pray*: For Demetrius Poliorcetes and a translation of Douris of Samos's hymn, see "Incarnate Human Gods," in Sir James George Frazer's *The Golden Bough*, vol. 1 (London: Macmillan, 1922), 91–106. See also Kenneth Scott, "The Deification of Demetrius Poliorcetes: Part I," in *American Journal of Philology* 49, no. 2 (1928): 137–66, as well as "The Deification of Demetrius Poliorcetes: Part II," in *American Journal of Philology* 49, no. 3 (1928): 217–39; for the quotation from Demochares, 236. See also Plutarch's life of Demetrius in *Lives*, trans. Bernadotte Perrin, Loeb Classical Library (Cambridge, MA: Harvard University Press, 1920), 21–35.

3     **Euhemerus:** See S. Spyridakis, "Zeus Is Dead: Euhemerus and Crete," in *Classical Journal* 63, no. 8 (May 1968): 337–40.

3     **Lysander and Epicurus:** The Spartan general Lysander was, according to S. R. F. Price, "the first known case of divine cult of a living human," arising in Samos, "out of the confused situation at the end of the Peloponnesian War." See *Rituals and Power: The Roman Imperial Cult in Asia Minor* (Cambridge: Cambridge University Press, 1984), 26. It was strange that Epicurus should be deified postmortem by his followers, as Cicero pointed out in his *Tusculan Disputations*, for the Epicureans believed death was utter extinction, with no chance of any hereafter.

3     **the god-making of Julius Caesar:** There is intricate debate over when and how, but according to most sources, Caesar's deification happened in stages, with the lines between his manhood and godhood increasingly blurred. Julius received

divine rights while still alive, according to the histories of Cassius Dio and Suetonius, after the battles of Thapsus and Munda (46–45 BCE), further deifying
decrees a few months before his death, and a posthumous apotheosis at his
funeral. Many of these were modeled after the celestial honors heaped upon the
man-god Demetrius. See Stefan Weinstock, *Divus Julius*, vol. 1 (Oxford: Clarendon Press, 1971), 133–62. For the inscription erased, see Cassius Dio, *Roman
History*, trans. Earnest Cary, vol. 4, bk. 43, Loeb Classical Library (Cambridge,
MA: Harvard University Press, 1916), 43.14.6 and 43.21.2. See also Spencer
Cole, *Cicero and the Rise of Deification at Rome* (Cambridge: Cambridge University Press, 2013), 111–16, 122, 185. For the phases of Caesar's living deifica-
tion and how it led to his assassination, see Ittai Gradel, *Emperor Worship and
Roman Religion* (Oxford: Clarendon Press, 2002), 54, 68, 108; and Gwynaeth
McIntyre, *Imperial Cult* (Leiden: Brill, 2019), 14–24.

3       **what the virtues of a god *should be*:** See Anna J. Clark, *Divine Qualities: Cult
and Community in Republican Rome* (Oxford: Oxford University Press, 2007);
Cole, *Cicero*, 115–16, 122.

4       **emperors would demur:** On Rome's autocrats slinking from divinity while
alive, see Gradel, *Emperor Worship*, 142–44, 232. For Vespasian, see Suetonius,
*Lives of the Caesars*, trans. J. C. Rolfe, Loeb Classical Library (Cambridge, MA:
Harvard University Press, 1914), 293.

4       **an eagle was released:** Mary Beard and John Henderson, "The Emperor's New
Body: Ascension from Rome," in *Parchments of Gender: Deciphering the Bodies
of Antiquity*, ed. Maria Wyke (Oxford: Clarendon Press, 1998), 208: "There has
to be a wing as well as a prayer; but what sort of wing—and whose?"

4       **love and devastation:** See Gwynaeth McIntyre, *A Family of Gods: The Worship
of the Imperial Family in the Latin West* (Ann Arbor: University of Michigan
Press, 2016). For Drusilla, see Susan Wood, "Diva Drusilla Panthea and the
Sisters of Caligula," in *American Journal of Archaeology* 99, no. 3 (July 1995):
457–82. For a "roll-call" of deified Roman relatives, see Beard and Henderson, "Emperor's New Body," 191–219. "What did deification do to marriage?"
they ask.

4       **Cicero's apotheosis of Tullia:** See Cole, *Cicero*; for Cicero's letter to Atticus, 3. In
the fifteenth century, a Roman tomb was unearthed that people said belonged to
Tullia, with a body inside that had not deteriorated at all. A lamp next to her had
reportedly remained lit across the centuries.

5       **The century that reset time:** The literature on the historical Jesus and whether
he considered himself divine is vast and contentious. See John P. Meier's *A
Marginal Jew: Rethinking the Historical Jesus*, 2 vols. (New York: Doubleday,
1991–1994). For an account of Jesus deflecting claims of his divinity, and rival
understandings of his nature, see Reza Aslan, *Zealot: The Life and Times of Jesus
of Nazareth* (New York: Random House, 2013), 132–36. On how the nature of
Jesus's divinity magnifies from the earliest to the final Gospels, culminating in

John, see Bart D. Ehrman, *How Jesus Became God: The Exaltation of a Jewish Preacher from Galilee* (San Francisco: HarperOne, 2013).

6     **"God," "Son of God," "the Lord":** On how Jesus's apotheosis responded to the cult of Roman emperors, see John Dominic Crossan, *God and Empire: Jesus against Rome, Then and Now* (San Francisco: HarperOne, 2007). On how the same titles were used for the pagan emperors as for Christ, see John Dominic Crossan and Jonathan L. Reed, *In Search of Paul: How Jesus's Apostle Opposed Rome's Empire with God's Kingdom* (San Francisco: HarperOne, 2005), 234–41. The notion of resetting time, measuring it from Christ's birthdate, was predated by a similar initiative from the birth of Augustus Caesar, who was seen as "Lord of History" and the calendar.

6     **he emptied himself:** On "kenotic" divinity, see Crossan, *In Search of Paul*, 242, 288–90. For a survey of Greco-Roman and early Christian understandings of deification, see M. David Litwa's *Becoming Divine: An Introduction to Deification in Western Culture* (Eugene, OR: Wipf and Stock, 2013). See also Litwa, *Iesus Deus: The Early Christian Depiction of Jesus as a Mediterranean God* (Minneapolis: Fortress Press, 2014).

6     **the Ophites:** James H. Charlesworth, *The Good and Evil Serpent: How a Universal Symbol Became Christianized* (New Haven, CT: Yale University Press, 2010), 2, 469.

6     **"a god going about in flesh":** For Clement of Alexandria, see Elaine Pagels, *Adam, Eve, and the Serpent: Sex and Politics in Early Christianity* (New York: Random House, 1988), 39–46. Scandalized by the cult of Antinous, the theologian lambasted how people worship "often the worst of humankind!"

6     ***theosis* versus *apotheosis*:** On how Christian writers avoided apotheosis, see Michael J. Christensen and Jeffery A. Wittung, eds., *Partakers of the Divine Nature: The History and Development of Deification in the Christian Traditions* (Grand Rapids, MI: Baker, 2008), 61, 95. See also Stephen Finlan and Vladimir Kharlamov, eds., *Theosis: Deification in Christian Theology* (Eugene, OR: Wipf and Stock, 2006).

6     **a deified counterpart or divine twin:** See Charles M. Stang's study of angelic other halves, lost twins, and syzygia in *Our Divine Double* (Cambridge, MA: Harvard University Press, 2016). In the Gospel of Thomas, Jesus asks, cryptically, "But when you become two, what will you do?"

7     **"I asked the sea . . .":** Saint Augustine, *Confessions*, trans. R. S. Pine-Coffin (London: Penguin Classics, 1961), 212.

7     **"like a small wax candle . . .":** *The Diario of Christopher Columbus's First Voyage to America, 1492–1493*, trans. Oliver Dunn and James E. Kelley Jr. (Norman: University of Oklahoma Press, 1989); entry for October 11, 1492, 59; for October 14, 75. See also *The Journal of Christopher Columbus (during His First Voyage, 1492–93)*, trans. and ed. Clements R. Markham (London: Hakluyt Society, 1893); for October 14, 41; for October 21–22, 54–56.

8     **"We are all direct descendants . . .":** Tzvetan Todorov, *The Conquest of America: The Question of the Other*, trans. Richard Howard (Norman: University of Oklahoma Press, 1999), 5.

8     **Columbus killed a serpent:** See Valerie I. J. Flint, *The Imaginative Landscape of Christopher Columbus* (Princeton, NJ: Princeton University Press, 1992), 138.

8     **"No opposition was offered to me":** For Columbus's letter to Luis de Santángel, see Stephen Greenblatt, *Marvelous Possessions: The Wonder of the New World* (Chicago: University of Chicago Press, 1992), 52; for the rituals of (dis)possession, 56–61.

9     **"Who will wipe this blood from us?":** Friedrich Nietzsche, *The Gay Science*, ed. Bernard Williams, trans. Josefine Nauckhoff (Cambridge: Cambridge University Press, 2001), 120.

10    **a spectrum:** For a few "Essential Characteristics of a Divinity," see James Leuba, *A Psychological Study of Religion: Its Origin, Function, and Future* (New York: Macmillan, 1912), 111–25.

10    **meta-persons:** I first came across this term listening to Marshall Sahlins's 2016 Inaugural A. M. Hocart Lecture, "The Original Political Society" (SOAS, London, April 29, 2016). See also David Graeber and Marshall Sahlins, *On Kings* (Chicago: Hau Books, 2017).

11    **"It should be known that it is impossible . . .":** *Origen*, trans. Rowan A. Greer (New York: Paulist Press, 1979), 228.


## PART ONE: LATE THEOGONY

## 1. IN THE LIGHT OF RAS TAFARI

17    **cake, a refrigerator, rose bushes:** "Abyssinia: Coronation," *Time* (November 3, 1930). The *New York Times* ran its own coronation coverage the same day with the subhead: "5,000 Cattle Slaughtered for Feast of 25,000 on Raw Meat and Wine—Americans at Ceremony."

18    **"The studded doors . . .":** Addison E. Southard, "Modern Ethiopia," *National Geographic,* June 1931, 679–746; W. Robert Moore, "Coronation Days in Addis Ababa," *National Geographic,* June 1931, 738–46.

19    **"Arise and shine . . .":** For Leonard Howell and early police reports of his sermons, see Robert A. Hill, *Dread History: Leonard P. Howell and Millenarian Visions in the Early Rastafarian Religion* (Chicago and Kingston: Research Associates School Times Publications/Frontline Distribution and Miguel Lorne, 2001). See also Clinton A. Hutton, "Leonard Howell Announcing God: The Conditions That Gave Birth to Rastafari in Jamaica," in *Leonard Percival Howell and the Genesis of Rastafari*, ed. C. A. Hutton et al. (Kingston, Jamaica: University Press of the West Indies, 2015), 10–15; James Robertson, "'That Vagabond George Stewart of England': Leonard Howell's Seditious Sermons, 1933–1941," in Hutton et al., *Leonard Percival Howell*, 69–106; for the May 30, 1933, police

report by Corporal Robert E. Coombs, Appendix B, 86; for the flier, Appendix C, 91. See also Hélène Lee, *The First Rasta: Leonard Howell and the Rise of Rastafarianism*, trans. Lily Davis (Chicago: Lawrence Hill Books, 2003); for "a stupid ranter," 65–66.

21    **Ethiopianism:** See Anthony Bogues, *Black Heretics, Black Prophets: Radical Political Intellectuals* (New York: Routledge, 2003), 153–86; Charles Reavis Price, "'Cleave to the Black': Expressions of Ethiopianism in Jamaica," *New West Indian Guide* 77, no. 1/2 (2003): 31–64. For Robert Alexander Young's *Ethiopian Manifesto*, see Wilson Jeremiah Moses, ed., *Classical Black Nationalism: From the American Revolution to Marcus Garvey* (New York: New York University Press, 1996), 60–67.

22    **the Shepherd Athlyi:** Robert Athlyi Rogers, *The Holy Piby: 1924–1928* (Global Grey ebooks: 2019), 4, 17, 29–30, PDF. For more on Athlyi and the context of the anti-immigration Johnson-Reed Act, see Allison Paige Sellers, "The 'Black Man's Bible': The *Holy Piby*, Garveyism, and Black Supremacy in the Interwar Years," *Journal of Africana Religions* 3, no. 3 (2015): 325–42. See also Michael A. Barnett, "Interrogating Leonard Howell as the 'First Rasta,'" in Hutton et al., *Leonard Percival Howell*, 67n18.

23    **the occult Hibbert:** See Barnett, "Interrogating Leonard Howell," 56; as well as Barry Chevannes, *Rastafari: Roots and Ideology* (Syracuse, NY: Syracuse University Press, 1994), 124–26. See also M. G. Smith, Roy Augier, and Rex Nettleford, *The Ras Tafari Movement in Kingston, Jamaica* (Kingston: Institute of Social and Economic Research, University College of the West Indies, 1960), 9–14.

24    **"snow fell same time . . .":** From an interview with Henry Archibald Dunkley, conducted by Robert A. Hill in 1976. See D. A. Dunkley [no relation], "Rastafari: Race and Spirituality," in *Black Resistance in the Americas*, ed. D. A. Dunkley and Stephanie Shonekan (New York: Routledge, 2019), 20–29; see also Barnett, "Interrogating Leonard Howell," 57.

25    **the Bedwardites:** For many of his followers, Alexander Bedward was the manifestation of the Biblical prophet Aaron. See W. F. Elkins, *Street Preachers, Faith Healers, and Herb Doctors in Jamaica, 1890–1925* (New York: Revisionist Press, 1977). See also Edward White, "Rise Up: Why Alexander Bedward Promised to Fly to Heaven," *Paris Review*, October 6, 2015.

26    **Haile Selassie as *Nzambi a Mpungu*:** See Hutton, "Leonard Howell Announcing God," 37–40, 50n91. For more on "zombie," see "The Colors of Christ in the Diaspora of Africana Religions," a roundtable between Edward J. Blum, Keri Day, Rabia Gregory, Paul Harvey, Elizabeth McAlister, and Charles Price, *Journal of Africana Religions* 2, no. 3 (2014): 379–433. In the early sixteenth century, when Portuguese traders landed in the Kongo, they determined *Nzambi a Mpungu* was the closest word in Kikongo to the Christian Almighty; in their catechisms, Jesuit missionaries used this name for "Deus," or God.

27    **His portrait as passport:** *Daily Gleaner*, December 16, 1933. For the steamships, see Robertson, "'That Vagabond George Stewart of England,'" 75. For parting waters, see *Daily Gleaner*, July 9 and August 20, 1934. See also Hill, *Dread History*, 26.

On the back of the cards, it read, "Presented by Leonard Howell—Traved. [*sic*] the World Through." Known as the "Prince of Peace" photograph, some scholars argue it was given to Howell by Annie and David Harvey, a Jamaican couple who lived as missionaries in Ethiopia for six years and may have witnessed the coronation firsthand. According to Archibald Dunkley, the Harveys were among the first to declare the divinity of Haile Selassie, although less information about them is known. The Harveys considered themselves black Israelites and set up a revivalist healing practice on Paradise Street in Kingston. Like the other early preachers, they were subjected to surveillance by the colonial police and arrested numerous times. See Charles Price, "The Cultural Production of a Black Messiah: Ethiopianism and the Rastafari," in Blum et al., "The Colors of Christ," 422, 429–30. For the Harveys, see also Barnett, "Interrogating Leonard Howell," 63.

27    **his umbilical cord:** Born on July 23, 1892, the future Conquering Lion of Judah was a Leo, albeit on the cusp. The most detailed biography of Haile Selassie to date is by the emperor's great-nephew, the political analyst Asfa-Wossen Asserate. See *King of Kings: The Triumph and Tragedy of Emperor Haile Selassie I of Ethiopia*, trans. Peter Lewis (London: Haus, 2015); for Makonnen's letter from his deathbed to Emperor Menelik II, 11. See also Harold Marcus's study, *Haile Selassie I: The Formative Years, 1892–1936* (Asmara: Red Sea Press, 1996).

28    **The orphaned Tafari:** As some Rastafari tell the story of the emperor's early life, the child Tafari was sent to boarding school in England, where he was a classmate of the future King George V. One day, the Ethiopian prince threw an apple into the air and sliced it into thirty-two pieces before it fell to the ground. When George returned home to Buckingham Palace, he told his parents, "I met God today." See interview with Mykal Rose in William David Spencer's *Dread Jesus* (Eugene, OR: Wipf and Stock, 1999), 41.

28    **"like Sleeping Beauty . . .":** Quoted in Angelo Del Boca, *The Negus: The Life and Death of the Last King of Kings*, trans. Antony Shugaar (Addis Ababa: Arada Books, 2012), 78.

29    **forty Armenian orphans:** See Ani Aslanian, "In the Company of Emperors: The Story of Ethiopian Armenians," *Armenite*, October 6, 2014. For Haile Selassie's state tours, see Theodore M. Vestal, *The Lion of Judah in the New World: Emperor Haile Selassie of Ethiopia and the Shaping of Americans' Attitudes toward Africa* (Santa Barbara, CA: Praeger, 2011).

29    **"There is nothing that is human . . .":** For the proclamation, see Asserate, *King of Kings*, 74; for the account of R. E. Cheesman, 77. In 1928, following a series of coup attempts, Tafari had pressured the Empress Zauditu to elevate his title to *Negus*, or King. He began using the royal pronoun "We," although he would be inconsistent at times, slipping back into "I."

30    **in a bad mood:** Ellen N. La Motte, "A Coronation in Abyssinia," in *Harper's Monthly Magazine*, April 1, 1931, 574–84; Evelyn Waugh, *The Coronation of Haile Selassie* (London: Penguin, 2005), 41.

31    **the National Geographic Society:** See Robert M. Poole's history, *Explorers*

*House:* National Geographic *and the World It Made* (New York: Penguin Press, 2004), 61–63.

31    **"God is the grief of irony":** E. M. Cioran, *The New Gods*, trans. Richard Howard (Chicago: University of Chicago Press, 2013), 6. For Waugh on fines for calling the emperor "Tafari," *Coronation*, 11.

32    **an anthropologist:** George Eaton Simpson, "Personal Reflections on Rastafari in West Kingston in the Early 1950s," in *Chanting Down Babylon: The Rastafari Reader*, ed. Nathaniel Samuel Murrell, William David Spencer, and Adrian Anthony McFarlane (Philadelphia: Temple University Press, 1998), 217–30. See also Simpson, "Political Cultism in West Kingston, Jamaica," *Social and Economic Studies* 4, no. 2 (June 1955): 133–49; Simpson, "The Ras Tafari Movement in Jamaica: A Study of Race and Class Conflict," *Social Forces* 34, no. 2 (December 1955): 167–71. Attending Rastafari meetings, Simpson recorded a call-and-response: "How did we get here?" *Chorus:* "Slavery." "Who brought us from Ethiopia?" *Chorus:* "The white man."

32    **"the book is a underwater book . . .":** Brother Yendis interviewed by Charles Price in his study *Becoming Rasta: Origins of Rastafari Identity in Jamaica* (New York: New York University Press, 2009), 50.

34    *Look to Africa:* For the apocryphal prophecy attributed to Garvey, see Hill, *Dread History*, 6–14. Hill notes the words can only be traced to Paul Earlington, a Rastafari leader interviewed in 1960. See also Chevannes, *Rastafari*, 94–95. For Garvey's editorial in the *Blackman*, see Hutton et al., *Leonard Percival Howell*, 19; for Garvey as "but a John the Baptist," see Bob Blaisdell, ed., *Selected Writings and Speeches of Marcus Garvey* (New York: Dover, 2004), 132.

34    **Marcus Garvey as John the Baptist:** For a biography of Garvey, see Colin Grant, *Negro with a Hat: The Rise and Fall of Marcus Garvey and His Dream of Mother Africa* (Oxford: Oxford University Press, 2008.) For Athlyi's prophecy, see *The Holy Piby*, 26. See also Rupert Lewis, "Marcus Garvey and the Early Rastafarians," in Murrell, Spencer, and McFarlane, *Chanting Down Babylon*, 145–58; Horace Campbell, *Rasta and Resistance: From Marcus Garvey to Walter Rodney* (London: Hansib, 2007). For "There will be no democracy in the world . . ." see Moses, *Classical Black Nationalism*, 244. For "the spectacles," Amy Jacques Garvey, ed., *The Philosophy and Opinions of Marcus Garvey: Africa for the Africans* (London: Routledge, 1989), 44. For "the Almighty in sable hue," see "A New Religion," in *Daily Gleaner*, June 6, 1927.

35    **"white supremacy":** T. S. Winn, *Emancipation: or Practical Advice to British Slave-Holders* (London: W. Phillips, 1824), 57. For Lothrop Stoddard, see *The Rising Tide of Color against White World-Supremacy* (New York: Charles Scribner's Sons, 1921), 91, 148.

36    **"Now we are Perfectly DISGUSTED OF THEM":** "White Peoples Mind is the Snake's Mind," the reverend relates. Fitz Balintine Pettersburg, *The Royal Parchment Scroll of Black Supremacy* (Kingston, Jamaica: self-pub., 1926). For a "weird doctrine," see Hutton et al., *Leonard Percival Howell*, 21.

38    **"I had visions in my sleep . . .":** Jephet Wilson interviewed by Hill, *Dread History*, 31.

38    **cross-examination:** For the 1934 trials of Howell and Hinds, see coverage in "Leonard Howell Being Tried for Sedition in Saint Thomas," *Daily Gleaner*, March 14, 1934, 21; "Leonard Howell, On Trial, Says Ras Tafari Is the Messiah Returned to Earth," March 15, 1934, 20; "'Ras Tafari' Disciple Found Guilty of Sedition," March 16, 1934, 16; "Prisoner Declares That King of Abyssinia Will Deliver Him," "Howell Given 2-Year Term for Sedition," March 17, 1934, 1. For Howell's trial, see also Lee, *The First Rasta*, 71–79; for the rooster, 79. See also Bogues, *Black Heretics*, 159–62.

40    **"oh come let us adore him":** Howell, an admirer of Gandhi, self-published *The Promised Key* under the mystical Hindu pen name Gangunguru Maragh and noted the place of publication as Accra, Ghana. See also William David Spencer, "The First Chant: Leonard Howell's *The Promised Key*," in Murrell, Spencer, and McFarlane, *Chanting Down Babylon*, 361–89.

42    **"He did not seem to know . . .":** From the account of George Steer, cited in Asserate, *King of Kings*, 124. For the Italian invasion, 112–118; see also Anthony Mockler, *Haile Selassie's War* (Oxford: Oxford University Press, 1984). For Garvey's criticisms of Haile Selassie during the war, see Hutton et al., *Leonard Percival Howell*, 27.

42    **"the said same Romans":** L. F. C. Mantle, "In Defense of Abyssinia and Its History," *Plain Talk*, November 2, 1935; see also Hill, *Dread History*, 20.

43    **"Snakes, caterpillars, scorpions . . .":** From a report written by Ranny Williams, quoted in Hill, *Dread History*, 44. See also Hutton et al., *Leonard Percival Howell*, 29.

43    **Haile Selassie as Dr. Belsidus:** See George Samuel Schuyler, *Black Empire*, ed. Robert A. Hill and R. Kent Rasmussen (Boston: Northeastern University Press, 1991), 1–142. For Robert Hinds's scriptural exegesis, see Chevannes, *Rastafari*, 133–34. For more on Schuyler, see Mark Christian Thompson, "George S. Schuyler and the God of Love: Black Fascism and Mythic Violence," in *Black Fascisms: African American Literature and Culture between the Wars* (Charlottesville: University of Virginia Press, 2007), 72–86. See also Lara Putnam, *Radical Moves: Caribbean Migrants and the Politics of Race in the Jazz Age* (Durham: University of North Carolina Press, 2003), 218.

43    *Nyabinghi:* Frederico Philos [pseud.], "Nya-Binghi," *Jamaica Times*, December 7, 1935, 22–23. See also "Appendix III: Niyabingi Men," in Smith, Augier, and Nettleford, *The Ras Tafari Movement*, 43–47; Ken Post, *Arise Ye Starvelings: The Jamaican Labour Rebellion of 1938 and Its Aftermath* (The Hague: Martinus Nijhoff, 1978), 172–74; as well as Lee, *The First Rasta*, 91–94.

44    **Sin was not personal . . . but structural:** For the Rastafari concept of Babylon, see Anna Kasafi Perkins, "The Wages of (Sin) Is Babylon: Rastafari versus Christian Religious Perspectives of Sin," in *Rastafari in the New Millennium: A Rastafari Reader*, ed. Michael Barnett (Syracuse, NY: Syracuse University Press, 2012), 240. For Haile Selassie's 1936 remarks at the League of Nations, see Asserate, *King of Kings*, 134.

45    **"(the bores, the bowing) . . .":** It was said among Rastafari that Hinds, in a letter
      from prison, had warned Edward not to ascend the throne or else he would be
      assassinated, and Edward sent him the *Coronation Commentary* in thanks. See
      Chevannes, *Rastafari*, 136–43; for Hinds "washed in bare blood," 139.

45    **If God was alive . . . what was the nature of death?:** For Garvey's demise while
      reading his own obituaries, see Grant, *Negro with a Hat*, 450. For Hinds's empty
      funeral, see Chevannes, *Rastafari*, 142; as well as Michael Barnett, "Rastafari
      and the Coming of Age," in Barnett, *Rastafari in the New Millennium*, 19. For
      myths of Garvey still alive, see Barry Chevannes, "Garvey Myths among the
      Jamaican People," in *Garvey: His Work and Impact*, ed. Rupert Lewis and Patrick
      Bryan (Trenton, NJ: Africa World Press, 1991), 123–34.

46    **"Would I not go to hell . . .":** Marcus Garvey, "First Message to the Negroes of
      the World from Atlanta Prison," February 10, 1925, in Garvey, *The Philosophy
      and Opinions of Marcus Garvey*, 237–39.

46    **Pinnacle:** See Clinton Hutton's interview with Leonard Howell's sons Bill and
      Monty in Hutton et al., *Leonard Percival Howell*, 220–26; Lucy McKeon, "The True
      Story of Rastafari," *New York Review of Books*, January 6, 2017. For Howell's dream
      before the 1941 raid, see Lee, *The First Rasta*, 145–47. Bill (nicknamed "Blade")
      recalled that, during the Pinnacle years, his father was sometimes taken for divine.
      "One day when I was about eight or nine years old, an older friend said to me, 'Sir
      Blade, don't you know that your father is a god?' I told him that I'd never heard
      anything like that. He was amazed. 'You really don't know how powerful he is?'
      He laughed so hard that he almost fell over." "Dadda never claimed to be God.
      He was a believer . . ." Lee, *The First Rasta*, 169.

47    **myriad factions, mansions, and sects:** On Rastafari doctrinal differences, see
      Michael Barnett, "The Many Faces of Rasta: Doctrinal Diversity within the Ras-
      tafari Movement," in *Caribbean Quarterly* 51, no. 2 (June 2005): 67–78. A new
      breakaway faction of Rastafari arose in February 1957, when forty Rastas in Mon-
      tego Bay apostatized from Haile Selassie to a new god. The brethren joined a new
      sect led by Leonard Morle on Railway Lane, who determined that King Saud Ibn
      Abd al-Aziz of Saudi Arabia was the true messiah. Further information is scarce,
      however, on the unwitting Jamaican divinity of King Saud. See Frank Jan van
      Dijk, "Sociological Means: Colonial Reactions to the Radicalization of Rastafari in
      Jamaica, 1956–1959," in *New West Indian Guide* 69, no. 1/2 (1995): 67–101.

47    **"very 'dreadful'":** For Brother Wato, see Chevannes, *Rastafari*, 156. For Sylvia
      Wynter, see "A Dream Deferred: Will the Condemned Rasta Fari Ever Return to
      Africa?" in *Tropic*, October 1960, 50–51.

48    **speaking in tongues:** His follower Jephet Wilson recalled that when Howell "start to
      tear the language, we couldn't catch it, as he talk it so deep." Hill, *Dread History*, 41.

48    **Iyaric:** Velma Pollard, "Dread Talk: The Speech of the Rastafarian in Jamaica,"
      *Caribbean Quarterly* 26, no. 4 (December 1980): 32–41; Pollard, "The Social
      History of Dread Talk," *Caribbean Quarterly* 28, no. 4 (December 1982): 17–40.
      Iyawata Farika Birhan, "Iyaric Glossary," in *Itations of Jamaica and I Rastafari*, ed.

Millard Faristzaddi (Miami: Judah Anbesa, 1987). See also G. E. Simpson, "Religion and Justice: Some Reflections on the Rastafari Movement," *Phylon* 46, no. 4 (1985): 286–91; Adrian Anthony McFarlane, "The Epistemological Significance of 'I-an-I' as a Response to Quashie and Anancyism in Jamaican Culture," in Murrell, Spencer, and McFarlane, *Chanting Down Babylon*, 107–24.

49    **a telegram:** For Prince Emmanuel's message to the Queen, see van Dijk, "Colonial Reactions," 82–83.

49    **"Lepers' Government":** For the "Claudius Henry affair," see Bogues, *Black Heretics*, 166–72. See also Barry Chevannes, "Rastafari and the Exorcism of the Ideology of Racism and Classism," in Murrell, Spencer, and McFarlane, *Chanting Down Babylon*, 62–63; Chevannes, "Rastafari and the Coming of Age," 26; van Dijk, "Colonial Reactions," 90–94.

50    **restored to the throne:** When Italy aligned with Nazi Germany, the British military belatedly mobilized to support Ethiopia's freedom fighters, liberating Addis Ababa on May 5, 1941, the same day of Jamaica's proverbial "discovery" by Columbus. Outside the emperor's palace at Guenete Leul, the Italians had built a large concrete spiral staircase as if ascending to heaven, each step representing a year of Fascist rule in Italy and abroad. Instead of destroying the hateful symbol, Haile Selassie reappropriated it, much like his devotees would do. He placed a modestly sized Lion of Judah on top, as if to put an end to the whole affair.

50    **Shashamane:** Even before Haile Selassie's reign, the emperor Menelik, inspired by the project of Liberia, had earmarked land for anyone in the black diaspora who wished to repatriate, although his initiative never got underway. For a study of Shashamane, see Erin C. MacLeod, *Visions of Zion: Ethiopians and Rastafari in the Search for the Promised Land* (New York: New York University Press, 2014).

51    **the "Apostles of the Negus":** See "Majority Report" and "Minority Report of Mission to Africa," letters addressed to N. W. Manley, Premier of Jamaica, Kingston, 1961 (unpublished). The mission was also warmly received by Kwame Nkrumah in Accra, who commended them for fulfilling the prophecies of Marcus Garvey. In Liberia, the delegation visited President William Tubman's private zoo, and dined with him at the Coo Coo's Nest. The president asked the Rastafari brethren to bless the table and to explain their spiritual conceptions to him. Years earlier, on Tubman's 1954 state visit to Jamaica, he was hailed as an avatar of the divine Garvey, returning to earth. See Chevannes, "Garvey Myths," 125.

51    ***Travel with the Lord of Love:*** For Mortimo Planno's lyrics, see *The Earth Most Strangest Man: The Rastafarian* (Kingston, Jamaica: self-pub., 1969). Accessible at https://www.cifas.us/new/caribbean/PDFs/TheEarthMostStrangestMan _Original.pdf. Planno included his own illustration of Columbus and enslaved Arawaks, to tell a history of Jamaica "both modern and mad."

52    **"We would have been very proud of you . . .":** On the 1960 coup, see Asserate, *King of Kings*, 222–42. On Haile Selassie's inability to prevent the deaths of his loved ones, see Spencer, *Dread Jesus*, 42–43, 224, 226, 241.

53    **a pressing matter:** For the visit with the Abuna Basilios, see "Minority Report,

Appendix 'A,'" 13; Leonard E. Barrett Sr., *The Rastafarians* (Boston: Beacon Press, 1988), 108.

53    **the matted Magi:** "Minority Report," 13–17. In their memo, the apostles argued against the idea, maintained by Garvey and *National Geographic*, that the emperor didn't consider himself black.

54    **a doubting Thomas:** For Clyde Hoyte, see Frank Jan van Dijk, *Jahmaica: Rastafari and Jamaican Society* (Utrecht: ISOR, 1993), 158–59. "Those who were serious in their declaration that they believed Haile Selassie to be God will now have a vacancy in their lives which must be filled," Hoyte crowed. "Who will take it from here?"

55    **"I didn't want to go":** For Abba Laike Mandefro (later styled as the Abuna Yesehaq), see interview with Barbara Blake Hannah in the *Daily Gleaner*, November 25, 1984, 2–3, 11; Abuna Yesehaq, *The Ethiopian Tewahedo Church: An Integrally African Church* (Nashville: J. C. Winston, 1997). See also van Dijk, *Jahmaica*, 190–94; Spencer, *Dread Jesus*, 47–50.

55    **to read aloud the letters:** According to the late Ajai Mansingh, professor at the University of the West Indies and a friend of Haile Selassie's secretary. See Lee, *The First Rasta*, 272.

55    **Shashamane as stolen land:** On its Oromo inhabitants, see MacLeod, *Visions of Zion*, 50, 98, 120. For "a people without history," see Asafa Jalata, "The Struggle for Knowledge: The Case of Emergent Oromo Studies," *African Studies Review* 39, no. 2 (September 1996): 95–123.

57    **"WILD WELCOME FOR NEGUS":** Haile Selassie's landing would become known as Grounation Day. See coverage in the *Daily Gleaner*, April 22, 1966, 1–2, 14, 22; April 23, 1966, 24; the *Sunday Gleaner*, April 24, 1966, 1; April 25, 1966, 1. See also Rebecca Tortello, "All Hail: The State Visit of Emperor Haile Selassie I," *Kingston Gleaner*, March 25, 2002. For the story of Planno's lost voice, see Jeanne Christensen's interview with Ras Ivi in *Rastafari Reasoning and the RastaWoman: Gender Constructions in the Shaping of Rastafari Livity* (Lanham, MD: Lexington Books, 2014), 106. See also Joseph Owens, *Dread: The Rastafarians of Jamaica* (London: Heinemann, 1979), 250–53. For the Jamaican government's intentions and schedule of events, see van Dijk, *Jahmaica*, 171–79.

58    **the black stigmata:** Rita Marley with Hettie Jones, *No Woman No Cry: My Life with Bob Marley* (New York: Hyperion, 2004), 42–46.

58    **"I am not God":** For the first person singular disavowal, see Barbara Makeda Blake-Hannah, *Rastafari: The New Creation* (Kingston: Jamaica Media Productions, 1981), 34–35, 59. For the first person plural, see Asserate, *King of Kings*, 258–60. See also van Dijk, *Jahmaica*, 191.

58    **"I am who you think I am":** See Colin Grant, *I & I: The Natural Mystics; Marley, Tosh, and Wailer* (London: Vintage, 2012), 135.

58    **"He lifted us from the dust . . .":** "An Interview with Professor Leonard Barrett," 415–28, in Murrell, Spencer, and McFarlane, *Chanting Down Babylon*; see also Barrett, *The Rastafarians*, 160.

58    **"politricks":** For Howell's boycott, see Hutton et al., *Leonard Percival Howell*, 123.

59    **"We are the vanguard . . .":** Ras Sam Brown, "Treatise on the Rastafarian Move-
      ment," *Caribbean Studies* 6, no. 1 (April 1966): 39–40.

60    **Manley's "Rod of Correction":** Manley was often likened to the biblical prophet
      Joshua. See Chevannes, "Rastafari and the Exorcism," 66; for Henry's pamphlet,
      see van Dijk, *Jahmaica*, 203.

60    **eightieth birthday party:** For the twilight Jubilee amid the famine, see Asserate,
      *King of Kings*, 276–82.

61    **"swollen with forgetfulness":** Oriana Fallaci, "Journey into the Private Universe of
      Haile Selassie," *Chicago Tribune*, June 24, 1973. For "full-a-cheese," see Ras Iadonis,
      "Selassie I Tempted by Devil & Ms. Oriana Fallaci?!" accessed June 16, 2017, at
      https://www.youtube.com/watch?v=VvhHighsVRQ; user account since deleted.

61    **prostrating to the telephone:** See Asserate, *King of Kings*, 292–97. Asserate notes
      that when he meets Rastafarians, he is occasionally addressed as "God's Nephew."
      "I tell them that Haile Selassie was a man, and moreover a devout Christian," he
      writes. "It makes little impression upon them, I must confess" (260).

62    **Lulu's tombstone:** To add insult to injury, the chihuahua Lulu had perished in
      1969 on the emperor's birthday.

62    **a sky-blue Beetle:** "It's a shame that I'm so old, otherwise I could have led the rev-
      olution myself," the emperor remarked. On his dethronement, see Del Boca, *The
      Negus*, 321–33. See also the account of former Derg officer Michael Ghebrenegus
      Haile, *Downfall of an Emperor: Haile Selassie of Ethiopia and the Derg's Creeping
      Coup* (Trenton, NJ: Africa World Press, 2018), 140–49; for the "108 emperors,"
      268. See also John Ryle, "Burying the Emperor," *Granta* 73 (Spring 2001).

62    **no fortune was to be found:** "See that 30 million they say the Emperor Selassie
      I stole? The 30 million?" the reggae musician Duckie Simpson laughs. "Oh, we
      got it, spend it. Rasta been spending it. We used to live in caves one time? Now
      we living in mansions." Simpson interviewed by Spencer, *Dread Jesus*, 57.

62    **Eshetu's testimony:** After the fall of Mengistu's reign in 1991, Eshetu Tekle-Mariam
      gave two nearly identical interviews, with Asfa-Wossen Asserate and Paulos
      Milkias. For Milkias, see *Haile Selassie, Western Education, and Political Revolution
      in Ethiopia* (Amherst, NY: Cambria Press, 2006), 248–49. For Asserate, see *King of
      Kings*, 307–08. For Haile Selassie as a bird, see Haile, *Downfall of an Emperor*, 149.

63    **"Ya cyaan kill God":** Bob Marley quoted in Spencer, *Dread Jesus*, 54; for Ras
      Michael Henry's vision, 60.

63    **beneath a latrine:** For the discovery of Haile Selassie's remains, see Del Boca,
      *The Negus*, 26.

64    **fresh-squeezed orange juice:** For Howell's death in the Sheraton, see Lee, *The
      First Rasta*, 293.

64    **"I'll show you mystery":** For Dermot Fagan, see Perkins, "The Wages of (Sin),"
      242–48.

64    **Ras Iadonis:** "RasTafari School, Divinity Class: Is Haile Selassie I Divine?–
      Webster's Word Study by Ras Iadonis," accessed June 16, 2017, at https://www
      .youtube.com/watch?v=9OC7Ga2Ys0U; user account since deleted.

64   the exegesis of *National Geographic*: Abba Yahudah Berhan Sellassie, *A Jour-
     ney to the Roots of Rastafari: The Essene Nazarite Link* (Bloomington, IN: Traf-
     ford, 2014), 171. In 1983, not long before Joseph Nathaniel Hibbert's death, the
     journalist and photographer Derek Bishton sought out the octogenarian patri-
     arch in his home in Bull Bay, and Hibbert went and changed into his green
     satin robe and Masonic turban for the occasion. Father Hibbert made Bishton
     promise to mail him a copy of the June 1931 issue of *National Geographic*, for
     he had lost his old one. See Derek Bishton, "An Audience with Joseph Nathaniel
     Hibbert, Rastafari Patriarch (July 23, 1983)," at DerekBishton.com.

65   **"Bless, barakat, you understand?":** From the film *Negus*, directed by Inver-
     nomuto, 2017, DCP, color, sound, 70 min.

65   **"I am a man . . .":** Haile Selassie interviewed by Bill McNeil for CBC/Radio-
     Canada, broadcast in June 1967. For audio, see "Haile Selassie Denies Being
     Christ—1967," at https://www.youtube.com/watch?v=TZ4cvQlXMzg/. For Ras
     Iadonis's analysis, see "HAILE SELASSIE I Never Denied Being CHRIST!" at
     https://www.youtube.com/watch?v=rVCxZ5NzVcE.

66   **Māori Rastas:** Edward Te Kohu Douglas and Ian Boxill, "The Lantern and the
     Light: Rastafari in Aotearoa (New Zealand)," in Barnett, *Rastafari in the New
     Millennium*, 35–65; for interviews with Ras Gideon and Ras Arama, 47–48.
     See also Dave Robinson, "Continuity, Communion and the Dread: The Maori
     Rastafari of Ruatoria, Aotearoa-New Zealand" (PhD diss., London School
     of Economics, 2013), accessible at http://etheses.lse.ac.uk/3217/1/Robinson
     _continuity_communion.pdf. Through the efforts of the dreads and other activ-
     ists, the Ngāti were able to repossess Hikurangi, transforming the mountain
     from an undignified state park to Māori-restored land.

66   **the ends of the earth, or the beginning:** The Māori Rasta sense of origins dif-
     fers from the evolutionary anthropologists, who would say that New Zealand
     was the last inhabitable place to be settled by human life, late into the thirteenth
     century CE. But then again, *The first will be last and the last first.*

67   **the cherubs:** Hone Heeney interviewed by Robbie Shilliam in *The Black Pacific:
     Anti-Colonial Struggles and Oceanic Connections* (London: Bloomsbury, 2015),
     128; for the pronoun *tatou tatou*, 29; on the Ngāti sense of blackness, 146.

67   **his name shall be on their foreheads:** Ras Arama reports his parents were not
     pleased. For the Māori Rasta facial tattoos, see Douglas and Boxill, "The Lantern
     and the Light," 55–58; for Ras Arama's prophecy, 59–60; for Io, see Shilliam, *The
     Black Pacific*, 133.

## 2. THE GOSPEL OF PHILIP

68   **a parchment scripture:** For the Nag Hammadi scrolls, see Elaine Pagels, *Adam,
     Eve, and the Serpent: Sex and Politics in Early Christianity* (New York: Random
     House, 1988), 65; Marvin Meyer, ed., *The Nag Hammadi Scriptures* (San Fran-
     cisco: HarperOne, 2008), 157–79.

69    **emitting sparks:** James Cook, *The Voyages of Captain James Cook Round the World*, vol. 4 (London: Sherwood, Neely, and Jones, 1813), 35–77; *The Resolution Journal of Johann Reinhold Forster, 1772–1775*, ed. Michael E. Hoare, vol. 4 (London: Haklyut Society, 2016), 615–31.

70    **from nowhere on earth:** The anthropologist Jean Guiart, who lived on Tanna and later became director of the Musée de l'Homme in Paris, preserved stories and interviews with islanders in his study, *Un siècle et demi de contacts culturels à Tanna, Nouvelles-Hébrides* [*A Century and a Half of Cultural Contact in Tanna, New Hebrides*] (Paris: Musée de l'Homme, 1956). See also Matthew Baylis, *Man Belong Mrs. Queen: Adventures with the Philip Worshippers* (London: Old Street, 2013), 189.

71    **"I saw him standing on the deck . . .":** See Paul Chapman, "Why a Tribe in Vanuatu Believes Their God Prince Philip Is Set to Visit," *Telegraph*, April 25, 2015.

71    **a hotbed of mythopolitics:** For Frum and the messianic history of the New Hebrides, see Peter Worsley, *The Trumpet Shall Sound: A Study of "Cargo" Cults in Melanesia* (New York: Schocken, 1968), 146–69; Edward Rice, *John Frum He Come: A Polemical Work about a Black Tragedy* (New York: Doubleday, 1974). Some accounts hold that Frum and Rusefel were divine cousins.

73    **USS *Echo*:** Guiart, *Un siècle et demi*, 184. See also Lamont Lindstrom, "Working Encounters: Oral Histories of World War II Labor Corps from Tanna, Vanuatu," in *The Pacific Theater: Island Representations of World War II*, ed. Lamont Lindstrom and Geoffrey M. White (Honolulu: University of Hawai'i Press, 1989), 406; Paul Raffaele, "In John They Trust," *Smithsonian Magazine*, February 2006.

73    **George Bristow as Noah:** Guiart, *Un siècle et demi*, 213–14; Baylis, *Man Belong Mrs. Queen*, 207. For Bristow in retirement, see Margaret Critchlow Rodman, *Houses Far from Home: British Colonial Space in the New Hebrides* (Honolulu: University of Hawai'i Press, 2001), 159–64.

74    **Political tides:** See Marc Tabani, "Dreams of Unity, Traditions of Division: John Frum, *Kastom* and Inter-Manipulation Strategies as Cultural Heritage on Tanna (Vanuatu)," *Paideuma* 55 (2009): 27–47. For Fornelli, see Brian J. Bresnihan and Keith Woodward, eds., *Tufala Gavman: Reminiscences from the Anglo-French Condominium of the New Hebrides* (Fiji: University of the South Pacific, 2002), 116–19; Baylis, *Man Belong Mrs. Queen*, 248.

74    **a dining room table in Corfu:** Philip Eade, *Young Prince Philip: His Turbulent Early Life* (New York: HarperCollins, 2012); for the "bloody amoeba," 255–72. For Crawfie's account, see Marion Crawford, *The Little Princesses* (London: Cassell, 1950), 131–36.

75    **power decreases, pageantry increases:** See David Cannadine, "The Context, Performance and Meaning of Ritual: The British Monarchy and the 'Invention of Tradition,' c. 1820–1977," in *The Invention of Tradition*, ed. Eric Hobsbawm and Terence Ranger (Cambridge: Cambridge University Press, 2012), 101–64.

76    **"a Body natural, and a Body politic":** On the divine right of kings, see Ernst

H. Kantorowicz's magisterial work, *The King's Two Bodies: A Study in Medieval Political Theology* (Princeton, NJ: Princeton University Press, 1997); for Edmund Plowden, 7.

78    **pig-killing stick:** For the exchange of gifts, see Baylis, *Man Belong Mrs. Queen*, 56.

78    **"The French do not seem to get implicated . . .":** Joël Bonnemaison, *The Tree and the Canoe: History and Ethnogeography of Tanna*, trans. Josée Pénot-Demetry (Honolulu: University of Hawai'i Press, 1994), 246. For further French intimations of Britain's cultic involvement, see Andrew Stuart, *Of Cargoes, Colonies and Kings: Diplomatic and Administrative Service from Africa to the Pacific* (London: Radcliffe Press, 2001), 188–92.

78    **"He is a god . . .":** For a clip of Siko Nathuan's interview with Ian Woods for Sky News, see https://news.sky.com/story/when-i-stood-in-for-prince-philip-the-south-pacific-god-10863077.

79    **an alchemy of black and white:** Tuk Noao interviewed by Baylis, *Man Belong Mrs. Queen*, 17; for the severed islands, 79, 259; for the Tannese divine double, 32. For the interview with Kasonipo, see "Vanuatu: The Return of Prince Philip," program for French 24, available at https://www.youtube.com/watch?v=jOOoKXpwxRI.

79    **federal taxes:** For the incident, Baylis, *Man Belong Mrs. Queen*, 261.

79    **Captain Lloyd's head:** See Stuart Barton Babbage, *Hauhauism: An Episode in the Maori Wars, 1863–1866* (Wellington, NZ: Reed, 1937), 27–37; Julia Blackburn, *The White Men: The First Response of Aboriginal Peoples to the White Man* (New York: HarperCollins, 1979), 143–45. For the Pai Mārire movement (called by the British "Hau-Hau"), see Michael Adas, *Prophets of Rebellion: Millenarian Protest Movements against the European Colonial Order* (Chapel Hill: University of North Carolina Press, 1979).

80    **Jake Raites . . . another name for Jesus Christ:** See Baylis, *Man Belong Mrs. Queen*, 106.

80    **"Bilip . . .":** Jack Naiva interviewed by Baylis, *Man Belong Mrs. Queen*, 12. For Nako Nikien's remarks, see interview with the AP, "Islanders Worship Britain's Prince Philip," May 31, 2015, accessible at https://www.youtube.com/watch?v=2mi34ARHvws.

80    **"cargo cult":** For its origins, see Lamont Lindstrom, *Cargo Cult: Strange Stories of Desire from Melanesia and Beyond* (Honolulu: University of Hawai'i Press, 1993); as British attack on the Australian Labour Party, 21. See also Peter Lawrence's *Road Belong Cargo* (Manchester: Manchester University Press, 1964), a book that itself was allegedly deified. It was translated into Tok Pisin and said to have been considered a scripture of the Yali movement in Papua New Guinea. See also G. W. Trompf, ed., *Cargo Cults and Millenarian Movements* (Berlin: De Gruyter, 1990); Holger Jebens, ed., *Cargo, Cult, and Culture Critique* (Honolulu: University of Hawai'i Press, 2004).

81    **the German Wislin:** See E. W. P. Chinnery and A. C. Haddon, "Five New Religious Cults in British New Guinea," *Hibbert Journal* 15 (London: Sherman,

French, 1917), 460–63; Worsley, *The Trumpet Shall Sound*, 94–97. See also Nonie Sharp, *Stars of Tagai: The Torres Strait Islanders* (Canberra: Aboriginal Studies Press, 1993), 117–19; Jeremy Beckett, "Whatever Happened to German Wislin?," in *Metaphors of Interpretation: Essays in Honour of W. E. H. Stanner*, ed. Diane E. Barwick, Jeremy Beckett, and Marie Reay (Canberra: Australian National University Press, 1985), 52–73.

82    **the worship of LBJ:** The 1960s movement had a second wave in the mid-1980s, although LBJ himself had died of a heart attack in 1973. See Dorothy K. Billings, *Cargo Cult as Theater: Political Performance in the Pacific* (Lanham, MD: Lexington Books, 2002); as well as Lamont Lindstrom's review in *Contemporary Pacific* 16, no. 1 (Spring 2004): 201–3. See also the tabloid story by Benjamin Gunn, "Ex-President Worshipped as a God—By Jungle Tribe!," *Weekly World News*, November 2, 1993, 44.

83    **myth-dreams:** Thomas Merton, "Cargo Cults of the South Pacific," in *Love and Living* (New York: Farrar, Straus and Giroux, 1979), 80–96. The monk was inspired by his conversations with his close friend Edward Rice, who would author *John Frum He Come*.

83    **money's sacred origins:** On Juno *Moneta*, see Karl-Heinz Kohl, "Mutual Hopes: German Money and the Tree of Wealth in East Flores," in Jebens, *Cargo, Cult, and Culture Critique*, 84. For readings on the divinity of capitalism, see Harvey Cox, *The Market as God* (Cambridge, MA: Harvard University Press, 2019); Devin Singh, *Divine Currency: The Theological Power of Money in the West* (Stanford: Stanford University Press, 2018); as well as Eugene McCarraher, *The Enchantments of Mammon: How Capitalism Became the Religion of Modernity* (Cambridge, MA: Harvard University Press, 2019).

84    **the construction site of heaven:** Peter Brown, *The Ransom of the Soul: Afterlife and Wealth in Early Western Christianity* (Cambridge, MA: Harvard University Press, 2015), 27, 79.

86    **xeroxed scriptures:** For Baylis's reading of the origin myth, see *Man Belong Mrs. Queen*, 53–56; for the myth about Philip begging his father to go to war, 135; for "Lisbet's" hospital, 166; Crawfie's myth, 159; "our thing isn't like that," 234. The sacred archive remained on Tanna after Baylis departed the island.

89    **"Is the pawpaw ripe . . .":** For the meeting at Windsor Castle, see *Meet the Natives*, Episode 3, Channel 4, 2007, 48 min., available at https://www.youtube.com/watch?v=Yz5gjUN9bN8.

89    **a cyclone:** Patrick Sawer, "Island Cult Who Worship Prince Philip Believe Cyclone Is Omen Sent by Weather Gods," *Telegraph*, May 4, 2017.

90    ***Jojbus*:** For Chief Isak Wan's theory, see Tabani, "Dreams of Unity," 14; see also Paul Theroux, *The Happy Isles of Oceania: Paddling the Pacific* (London: Penguin, 1992), 266.

90    **"the spirit in Prince Philip won't die":** Nako Nikien interviewed in 2015 by the AP, "Islanders Worship Britain's Prince Philip."

90    **Philip the Apostle:** For his life, see "The Acts of Philip," in Philip Schaff, *Ante-*

*Nicene Fathers* (1885), vol. 8 (Grand Rapids, MI: Christian Classics Ethereal Library), 1535–60. See also Rev. Alban Butler, *The Lives of the Fathers, Martyrs, and Other Principal Saints*, vol. 5 (Dublin: James Duffy, 1845), 2–4.

91    **the world was drowned**: For the myth of Tanna rolled like a leaf, as narrated by Yoma, see Robert J. Gregory and Janet E. Gregory, "Myth and Social Control: Extending a Tannese Case," *Anthropologist* 6, no. 2 (2004): 91–95; Baylis, *Man Belong Mrs. Queen*, 149.


## 3. MACARTHUR, 4 WAYS

94    **balsa wood**: For the MacArthurs made in San Blas, see Paolo Fortis, "General MacArthur among the Guna: The Aesthetics of Power and Alterity in an Amerindian Society," *Current Anthropology* 57, no. 4 (August 2016). See Leon S. De Smidt, *Among the San Blas Indians of Panama: Giving a Description of Their Manners, Customs, and Beliefs* (Troy, New York: 1948), 37. See also Michael Taussig, *Mimesis and Alterity: A Particular History of the Senses* (New York: Routledge, 1992), 10, 40.

95    **MacArthur led the offensive**: For the *Apsoged* ritual, see Norman Macpherson Chapin, "Curing among the San Blas Kuna of Panama" (PhD diss., University of Arizona, 1983), 355–65; for the weeping octopus, 92. See also Carlo Severi, "Cosmology, Crisis, and Paradox: On the White Spirit in the Kuna Shamanistic Tradition," in *Disturbing Remains: Memory, History, and Crisis in the Twentieth Century*, eds. Michael S. Roth and Charles G. Salas (Los Angeles: Getty Research Institute, 2001), 178–206.

97    **"In the old days we worshiped . . ."**: For Soma Toyojiro's letter to MacArthur and translations of many more messages, see Sodei Rinjiro, *Dear General MacArthur: Letters from the Japanese during the American Occupation*, trans. Shizue Matsuda (Lanham, MD: Rowman and Littlefield, 2001), 224. For Hirohito's rescript, see John W. Dower, *Embracing Defeat: Japan in the Wake of World War II* (New York: W. W. Norton, 1999), 308–10.

97    **a "Humanity" tour**: Dower, *Embracing Defeat*, 330–36.

98    **"a face as infinite in aspect . . ."**: For the sculptor's letter, see Rinjiro, *Dear General MacArthur*, 117; for the mystical *Makkāsā*, 17; for the Japanese turkey, 127. For the letters and offerings, Dower, *Embracing Defeat*, 228–330.

99    **MacArthur's alleged Japanese ancestry**: See William Manchester, *American Caesar: Douglas MacArthur 1880–1964* (Boston: Little, Brown, 1978), 93.

99    **a deity that could compete**: On the Meiji Restoration and the invention of Shinto, see Jason Ānanda Josephson, *The Invention of Religion in Japan* (Chicago: University of Chicago Press, 2012).

100   **"The truth of Shinto is no small thing . . ."**: For Ōkuni Takamasa, see Josephson, *The Invention of Religion*, 125; for the Japanese god behind the light bulb, 160. For Itō Hirobumi, see Dower, *Embracing Defeat*, 601n. See also Emiko Ohnuki-Tierney, "The Emperor of Japan as Deity (Kami)," *Ethnology* 30, no. 3 (July 1991): 199–215.

100   **Oomoto:** See Nancy K. Stalker's study, *Prophet Motive: Deguchi Onisaburo, Oomoto, and the Rise of New Religions in Imperial Japan* (Honolulu: University of Hawai'i Press, 2007).

101   **"the *kami* will use a tough guy . . .":** A spreadsheet of "Onisaburo's General Prophecies" is available at http://onisaburo.net/gi/ph.html.

101   **"to cross from war to peace":** Dower, *Embracing Defeat*, 30.

101   *Jiji Shimpo:* For the censorship scandal, see Dower, *Embracing Defeat*, 405. See also William J. Coughlin, *Conquered Press: The MacArthur Era in Japanese Journalism* (Palo Alto, CA: Pacific Books, 1952), 51–52.

102   **the humiliating dismissal:** On Truman's firing of MacArthur, see Dower, *Embracing Defeat*, 548. For the reaction in Tokyo, see Rinjiro, *Dear General MacArthur*, 293.

102   **"Gee, do you suppose . . . ?":** E. J. Kahn Jr., "Letter from Korea," *New Yorker*, April 21, 1951, 122.

102   **"a great hunk of God":** Quoted in Stanley Weintraub, *MacArthur's War: Korea and the Undoing of an American Hero* (New York: Free Press, 2000), 6.

102   **"The reincarnation of St. Paul":** For Hoover's remarks, see Michael Schaller, *Douglas MacArthur: The Far Eastern General* (Oxford: Oxford University Press, 1989), 244. For the 1932 incident, see John K. Fairbank, "Digging Out Doug," *New York Review of Books*, October 12, 1978.

102   **"a boy of twelve":** Rinjiro, *Dear General MacArthur*, 299; Dower, *Embracing Defeat*, 550–51.

103   **a woman from Chejudo:** For the interview with Chaktu Posalnim, her biography, and encounters with the spirit-MacArthur, I am indebted to Joon Hyun Michael Choi's study "Orijinŏl Mansin: An Ethnography of Shaman Life in South Korea" (PhD diss., Harvard University, 2010); for Chaktu's first-person testimony, 69–88; for the origins of her name, 13.

106   **an amphibious god:** For the interview with Madame Chung Hak-Bong, the *kut*, and context of Hwanghae-do shamanism, see Heonik Kwon and Jun Hwan Park, "American Power in Korean Shamanism," *Journal of Korean Religions* 9, no. 1 (2018): 43–69; for Kim Kye-Sun, 45; for Lee Jong-Ja, 64.

106   **GI uniforms in their trance:** See Keith Howard, *Preserving Korean Music: Intangible Cultural Properties as Icons of Identity* (London: Ashgate, 2006), 139. See also Peter Knecht, "Aspects of Shamanism: An Introduction," in *Shamans in Asia*, ed. Clark Chilson and Peter Knecht (London: Routledge Curzon, 2003), 2.

106   **contraband Marlboros:** See Michael Breen, *The Koreans: Who They Are, What They Want, Where Their Future Lies* (London: Orion Books, 1998), 47.

107   **"is quite un-American":** Kwon and Park, "American Power," 67.

107   **Manarmakeri:** For the myth of the itchy old man and his baptism by fire, see Freerk Ch. Kamma, *Koreri: Messianic Movements in the Biak-Numfor Culture Area*, trans. M. J. van de Vathorst-Smit (The Hague: Martinus Nijhoff, 1972), 17–36. See also Danilyn Rutherford, *Raiding the Land of the Foreigners: The Limits of the Nation on an Indonesian Frontier* (Princeton, NJ: Princeton University Press, 2003), 157–60.

108   **"The dead will rise":** On *Koreri* and the 1889 prophecy, see Rutherford, *Raiding the Land*, 128, 143–47.

109   **"I descended and bathed at my spring":** For the song as recalled by the Papuan elder Nikanor A., see Rutherford, *Raiding the Land*, 151.

109   **"two luncheon tables":** See Manchester, *American Caesar*, 307.

109   **All the signs indicated:** On MacArthur as Manseren Mangundi, see Kamma, *Koreri*, 194.

109   **Angganeta Menufandu:** For the prophetess, her general, and the rise of the Koreri army, see Kamma, *Koreri*, 157–83; for MacArthur as Morning Star, 175. See also Rutherford, *Raiding the Land*, 188–96. Kamma relates that Angganeta herself was worshipped by some as a goddess.

110   ***Kapten Koki:*** Kamma, *Koreri*, 190–92; Rutherford, *Raiding the Land*, 198.

110   **"After the carnage came the cargo":** Rutherford, *Raiding the Land*, 200.

111   **Uncle Bert:** For Rutherford's visit with the prophet on Wundi, see *Raiding the Land*, 129–35. For the failed development projects on Biak and sightings of Manarmakeri, 138.

112   **"Your time has not come yet":** For the myth of finding Koreri in the cave, see Kamma, *Koreri*, 23–25; Rutherford, *Raiding the Land*, 151.

## 4. GODS IN UNIFORM

115   **"like trying to fit that police station":** J. Brent Crosson, "Catching Power: Problems with Possession, Sovereignty, and African Religions in Trinidad," *Ethnos* 84, no. 4 (2019): 588–614.

115   **"a kind of crazy wind":** My discussion of the *Hauka* is indebted to the research of Paul Stoller, *Embodying Colonial Memories: Spirit Possession, Power, and the Hauka in West Africa* (New York: Routledge, 1995), and *Fusion of the Worlds: An Ethnography of Possession among the Songhay of Niger* (Chicago: University of Chicago Press, 1989). Stoller was initiated into a spirit circle in the Niger region of Tillabéri in 1977 and encountered the *Hauka* spirits firsthand.

116   **"I am Corsasi":** For the incident in the jail, see John W. Adams, "Jean Rouch Talks about His Films to John Marshall and John W. Adams," *American Anthropologist* 80, no. 4 (December 1978): 1005–20.

117   **"the bloody skin":** See Jean Rouch's account from *La religion et la magie Songhay*, translated in Stoller, *Embodying Colonial Memories*, 22; see also Rouch, "On the Vicissitudes of the Self: The Possessed Dancer, the Magician, the Sorcerer, the Filmmaker, and the Ethnographer," *Studies in Visual Communication* 5, no. 1 (Fall 1978): 2–8. On the *bia*, see Stoller, *Fusion of the Worlds*, 31.

118   **"occult instability":** Frantz Fanon, *The Wretched of the Earth*, trans. Constance Farrington (London: Penguin Classics, 2001), 183.

119   **born at the crossroads:** On the early modern history of spirit possession, see Paul Christopher Johnson, "An Atlantic Genealogy of 'Spirit Possession,'" *Comparative*

*Studies in Society and History* 53, no. 2 (April 2011): 393–425; see also Johnson, "Introduction: Spirits and Things in the Making of the Afro-Atlantic World," in *Spirited Things: The Work of "Possession" in Afro-Atlantic Religions*, ed. Paul Christopher Johnson (Chicago: University of Chicago Press, 2014), 1–22.

119    ***potis + sedere*:** This etymology is from J. Brent Crosson's introduction, "What Possessed You? Spirits, Property, and Political Sovereignty at the Limits of 'Possession,'" *Ethnos* 84, no. 4 (2019): 546–56. Paul Christopher Johnson notes that the term "property" was used to refer to enslaved people before it was first applied to land ownership.

119    **politics of terror:** On the conquest of Niger and the transformations of the French regime, see Finn Fuglestad, *A History of Niger, 1850–1960* (Cambridge: Cambridge University Press, 1983), 107–46; Stoller, *Embodying Colonial Memories*, 57–74; on the Voulet-Chanoine mission, 97–113.

120    **"creative work in human material":** Jules Brévié quoted in Stoller, *Fusion of the Worlds*, 149.

121    ***Hauka* politics:** Stoller, *Embodying Colonial Memories*, 118–19, 125–27; on the Accra riots, see Adams, "Jean Rouch Talks."

121    **Prazidan di la Republik:** On Vincent Auriol, see David Drake, *Intellectuals and Politics in Post-War France* (London: Palgrave Macmillan, 2002), 36.

122    **"The Mad Masters":** The literature on *Les maîtres fous* is vast. See the study by Paul Henley, *The Adventure of the Real: Jean Rouch and the Craft of Ethnographic Cinema* (Chicago: University of Chicago Press, 2010); Paul Stoller, *The Cinematic Griot: The Ethnography of Jean Rouch* (Chicago: University of Chicago Press, 1992), 145–60; Matthias Krings, *African Appropriations: Cultural Difference, Mimesis, and Media* (Bloomington: Indiana University Press, 2015), 28–55; Kien Ket Lim, "Of Mimicry and White Man: A Psychoanalysis of Jean Rouch's *Les maîtres fous*," *Cultural Critique*, no. 51 (Spring 2002): 40–73; for Rouch's remarks on watching a dialogue between humans and an otherworld, 45. James G. Ferguson, "Of Mimicry and Membership: Africans and the 'New World Society,'" *Cultural Anthropology* 17, no. 4 (November 2002): 551–69; Gillian Goslinga, "Spirited Encounters: Notes on the Politics and Poetics of Representing the Uncanny in Anthropology," *Anthropological Theory* 12, no. 4 (April 2013): 386–406. See also Adams, "Jean Rouch Talks." After the possession ritual, Rouch gave the locomotive a ride back home: "Just like after a party, and there was an incredible smell of dogs and perfume in the car because they drink perfume during the ceremony," the filmmaker remembered.

123    **words ground into paste:** Stoller, *Fusion of the Worlds*, 100–101.

123    ***kizungu*:** See Linda L. Giles, "Spirit Possession and the Symbolic Construction of Swahili Society," in *Spirit Possession: Modernity and Power in Africa*, ed. Heike Behrend and Ute Luig (Madison: University of Wisconsin Press, 1999), 157.

124    ***varungu*:** Michael Gelfand, *Shona Ritual, with Special Reference to the Chaminuka Cult* (Cape Town: Juta, 1959), 121, 139–41; Fritz Kramer, *The Red Fez: Art and Spirit Possession in Africa*, trans. Malcolm R. Green (London: Verso, 1993), 77–78.

124 **ntambwe bwanga:** W. F. P. Burton, *Luba Religion and Magic in Custom and Belief* (Tervuren, Belgium: Musée Royal de l'Afrique Centrale, 1961), 173–77; Kramer, *The Red Fez*, 133–34.

125 **iskokin turawa:** Matthias Krings, "On History and Language of the 'European' *Bori* Spirits, Kano, Nigeria," in Behrend and Luig, *Spirit Possession*, 53–67; for Jamus, the deification of Germany, 61–63. In 1993, Krings tape-recorded interviews in Kano with incarnating spirits, including Jamus.

126 **zar:** On the early Ethiopian history, see Richard Natvig, "Oromos, Slaves, and the Zar Spirits: A Contribution to the History of the Zar Cult," *International Journal of African Historical Studies* 20, no. 4 (1987): 669–89; Enrico Cerulli's theory on the Cushitic god "reduced to minor rank," from his *zar* entry in the *Encyclopaedia of Islam*, cited in Natvig, 677.

128 **Gordel, Karoma:** P. M. Constantinides, "Sickness and the Spirits: A Study of the Zaar Spirit-Possession Cult in the Northern Sudan" (PhD thesis, University of London, 1972), 92, 322, 338, 343. Constantinides witnessed the spirits speaking through khaki-clad mediums in Khartoum and Omdurman and recorded the song to Lord Cromer. On Lord Cromer, see Hussein A. H. Omar, "The Rule of Strangers: Empire, Islam, and the Invention of 'Politics' in Egypt, 1867–1914" (PhD thesis, University of Oxford, 2016), 138–204.

128 **lurk in latrines:** My discussion here is indebted to Janice Patricia Boddy's ethnography *Wombs and Alien Spirits: Women, Men, and the* Zar *Cult in Northern Sudan* (Madison: University of Wisconsin Press, 1989); for her interview with Sadiya, 215; Bakheita, 250; Sittalbenat, 212; Haile Selassie as *zar*, 280; the *mayz*, 288. See also Susan M. Kenyon, "Zar as Modernization in Contemporary Sudan," *Anthropological Quarterly* 68, no. 2 (April 1995): 107–20; I. M. Lewis, *Religion in Context: Cults and Charisma* (Cambridge: Cambridge University Press, 1986). Lewis notes that Gamal Abdel Nasser, Egypt's charismatic socialist dictator, also manifested in the pantheon of the *zar*.

131 **fetishism:** Rosalind C. Morris and Daniel H. Leonard, *The Returns of Fetishism: Charles de Brosses and the Afterlives of an Idea* (Chicago: University of Chicago Press, 2017); for "In their fit of superstition," 48. On the history of the fetish, see William Pietz's classic series of articles "The Problem of the Fetish, I," *RES: Anthropology and Aesthetics*, no. 9 (Spring 1985): 5–17; "The Problem of the Fetish, II: The Origin of the Fetish," *RES: Anthropology and Aesthetics*, no. 13 (Spring 1987): 23–45; "The Problem of the Fetish, IIIa: Bosman's Guinea and the Enlightenment Theory of Fetishism," *RES: Anthropology and Aesthetics*, no. 16 (Autumn 1988): 105–24; Tomoko Masuzawa, "Troubles with Materiality: The Ghost of Fetishism in the Nineteenth Century," *Comparative Studies in Society and History* 42, no. 2 (April 2000): 242–67. On the *Hauka* as "fetishist agitation," see Stoller, *Embodying Colonial Memories*, 129.

132 **"The peculiarly African character":** G. W. F. Hegel, *The Philosophy of History*, trans. J. Sibree (New York: Dover, 1956), 110; for "no historical part of the World," 117.

132    **a disagreement . . . about the proper worth:** I draw here on J. Lorand Matory, *The Fetish Revisited: Marx, Freud, and the Gods Black People Make* (Durham: Duke University Press, 2018), 14.

132    ***waka snan:*** On the Baule *colon* figures, see Susan Mullin Vogel, "People of Wood: Baule Figure Sculpture," *Art Journal* 33, no. 1 (1973): 23–26; Stoller, *Embodying Colonial Memories*, 84–85.

134    **the colonizer-worm:** Herbert M. Cole, "Mbari Is Life," *African Arts* 2, no. 3 (Spring 1969): 8–17, 87; Stoller, *Embodying Colonial Memories*, 87–90. For an illustrated collection of renderings of white colonialists, see Julia Blackburn, *The White Men: The First Response of Aboriginal Peoples to the White Man* (London: Orbis, 1979); and Cottie Arthur Burland, *The Exotic White Man* (London: Weidenfeld and Nicolson, 1968).

134    **"He frightens me":** See Taussig, *Mimesis and Alterity*, 237; for "Why are they Other," 7–8; "The image is more powerful," 62. See also James Clifford's analysis in *The Predicament of Culture: Twentieth-Century Ethnography, Literature, and Art* (Cambridge: Harvard University Press, 1988), 189–214.

135    ***Kijesu:*** Gerhard Lindblom, *The Akamba in British East Africa* (Uppsala: Appelberg, 1920), 238–40; Katherine Luongo, "Prophecy, Possession, and Politics: Negotiating the Supernatural in 20th Century Machakos, Kenya," *International Journal of African Historical Studies* 45, no. 2 (2012): 191–216; Kramer, *The Red Fez*, 100. Kramer records a similar phenomenon in Angola in response to the invasions of the Portuguese (185): "At a time when very few whites came to Cokweland, just the sight of one made some people possessed," he wrote. "The spirit hosts infected themselves from the graves of dead Europeans; they danced with knives and forks." They carved likenesses of the Portuguese in wood, with long noses, pith helmets, and prudish postures. In possession rituals, the Chokwe spirit mediums offered the Portuguese fetish-selves a Eucharist of bread and wine.

135    **Europe's mirror:** On the fetish and commodity fetishism, see Masuzawa, "Troubles with Materiality"; David Chidester, *Empire of Religion: Imperialism and Comparative Religion* (Chicago: University of Chicago Press, 2014), 109–10.

135    **"it stands on its head":** Karl Marx, *Capital: A Critique of Political Economy*, trans. Ben Fowkes, vol. 1 (London: Penguin Classics, 1990), 163–64. On fetishism in the work of Marx and Freud, see Matory, *The Fetish Revisited*; for "transcendent, omniscient, panoramic," 35; for "no more universal, eternal 'truths,'" 22.

136    **Seyni Kountché:** On the coup and Kountché's *Hauka* past, see Stoller, *Embodying Colonial Memories*, 133, 165–90. For Kountché's wife filmed in a trance, see Henley, *Adventure of the Real*, 383, 443.

137    **"a strategy of mystical attack":** I. M. Lewis, *Ecstatic Religion: An Anthropological Study of Spirit Possession and Shamanism* (London: Penguin Books, 1971), 100–26.

138    **"Possession is in our blood":** Stoller, *Fusion of the Worlds*, 202.

## 5. THE APOTHEOSIS OF NATHANIEL TARN

139  **Nathaniel Tarn:** For an introduction to his work as poet, see Nathaniel Tarn, *Selected Poems: 1950–2000* (Middletown, CT: Wesleyan University Press, 2002). For autobiographic essays and an interview, *The Embattled Lyric: Essays and Conversations in Poetics and Anthropology* (Stanford: Stanford University Press, 2007). For an in-depth survey of Tarn's work up to the mid-1980s, see Lee Bartlett, *Nathaniel Tarn: A Descriptive Bibliography* (London: McFarland, 1987). See also Jed Rasula and Mike Erwin, "An Interview with Nathaniel Tarn," *Boundary 2* 4, no. 1 (Autumn 1975): 1–33; "A Portfolio of Work in Honour of Nathaniel Tarn," Dispatches from the Poetry Wars, updated November 5, 2020, https://www.dispatchespoetrywars.com/nathaniel-tarn/.

139  *Scandals:* On the Mam, the mask, and Tarn's fieldwork in Santiago Atitlán, see Nathaniel Tarn with Martín Prechtel, *Scandals in the House of Birds: Shamans and Priests on Lake Atitlan* (New York: Marsilio, 1997). See also Shamoon Zamir's review in *Jacket* 6 (January 1999), as well as Peter O'Leary's in *Chicago Review* 45, 1 (January 1999): 102–8.

142  **a four-foot-tall bundle:** See E. Michael Mendelson, "A Guatemalan Sacred Bundle," *Man* 58 (August 1958): 121–26; as well as "Maximon: An Iconographical Introduction," *Man* 59 (April 1959): 57–60. See also Mendelson, "Religion and World-View in Santiago Atitlán" (PhD diss., University of Chicago, 1956).

143  **holy crime:** For "robes aflutter," see "Devilish Deity" in *Time,* Latin American Edition April 2, 1951. On the battle waged between orthodox Catholics and Maya traditionalists, see E. Michael Mendelson, "The King, the Traitor, and the Cross: An Interpretation of a Highland Maya Religious Conflict," *Diogenes* 6, no. 21 (March 1958): 1–10.

144  **fumigated and restored:** For Tarn's acquisition of the mask, see *Scandals*, 27–28.

146  **husband as divine:** See Janet Rodney's poem "Under the Weight of Seasons (Guatemala)," from *Orphydice* (1986), collected in *Moon on an Oarblade Rowing* (Lawrence, KS: First Intensity Press, 2005), 73.

146  **"sliding, slithering, sidling up":** For Tarn's account of the mask's return, see *Scandals*, 144, 179–82.

146  **Francisco Sojuel:** See Tarn, *Scandals*, 206–7, 218–19. For stories of the prophet and myths that came after Tarn, see Allen J. Christenson, "Ancestral Presence at the Navel of the World: Francisco Sojuel and Santiago Atitlán," in *Landscapes of Origin in the Americas: Creation Narratives Linking Ancient Places and Present Communities*, ed. Jessica Joyce Christie (Tuscaloosa: University of Alabama Press, 2009), 99–104; as well as "Places of Emergence: Sacred Mountains and Cofradía Ceremonies," in *Pre-Columbian Landscapes of Creation and Origin*, ed. J. E. Staller (New York: Springer, 2008), 102–10. See also Christopher Jones, "Tekun Uman and Tata Mon Fistfight in Heaven: Indigenous Imaginaries and

Decolonization in Highland Guatemala" (PhD diss., Tulane University, 2013), 440–43.

146 **rain angel:** See Tarn, *Scandals*, 31–32.

147 **his earthly exit:** For Chiviliu's death and Prechtel's April 1980 letter, see Tarn, *Scandals*, 148–54.

149 **"A! E! O! Oh! Ay!":** For the story of the wood, see Tarn, *Scandals*, 33, 50–51.

150 **angels of Creation and Record:** See Tarn, *Embattled Lyric*, 80, 245.

150 **pantheon of anthropologists:** For Maclay, see N. M. Mikloucho-Maclay, *New Guinea Diaries 1871–1883,* trans. C. L. Sentinella (Madang, Papua New Guinea: Kristen Press, 1975), 171, 217, 256, 287. See also Marshall Sahlins, *How "Natives" Think: About Captain Cook, for Example* (Chicago: University of Chicago Press, 1995), 181. For Moszkowski, see Peter Worsley, *The Trumpet Shall Sound: A Study of "Cargo" Cults in Melanesia* (New York: Schocken, 1968). For Lepowsky, see Sahlins, *How "Natives" Think*, 188–89. For Boddy, see *Wombs and Alien Spirits*, 136. For Pehrson, see Ian Whitaker, "The Personal Equation in Fieldwork: An Assessment of the Work of Robert N. Pehrson (1926–1955)," *Arctic Anthropology* 15, no. 1 (1978): 36–57. For Taussig, see *Mimesis and Alterity*, 7–8.

151 **"turned into a god myself":** Matthew Baylis, personal correspondence, May 5, 2014. See also Baylis, *Man Belong Mrs Queen*, 216–18.

152 **"The Apotheosis of Augustus":** Claude Lévi-Strauss, *Tristes Tropiques*, trans. John Weightman and Doreen Weightman (London: Penguin Classics, 2001), 375–82. See also Patrick Wilcken, *Claude Lévi-Strauss: The Poet in the Laboratory* (London: Bloomsbury, 2010), 94–96.

153 **an auto-anthropology:** Nathaniel Tarn's *Atlantis: An Autoanthropology* is forthcoming from Duke University Press, 2022.

154 **"I am not God":** Nathaniel Tarn, "Fragments from the Prayers Made on Behalf of Nathaniel Tarn by the Zutuhil-Maya Priest N.C. of Tziquinaha, the House of Birds, Guatemala, 1953 & 1969," *Alcheringa*, no. 1 (Fall 1970).

154 **Don Pedro:** For the Mam as conquistador, see Tarn, *Scandals*, 204. For the Spanish invasion of Guatemala and the deification of Alvarado as Tonatiuh, see Matthew Restall and Florine Asselbergs, *Invading Guatemala: Spanish, Nahua, and Maya Accounts of the Conquest Wars* (University Park: Pennsylvania State University Press, 2007), 103–10. See also Garrett W. Cook, *Renewing the Maya World: Expressive Culture in a Highland Town* (Austin: University of Texas Press, 2000), 119, 139. See also Allen J. Christenson, *The Burden of the Ancients: Maya Ceremonies of World Renewal from the Pre-Columbian Period to the Present* (Austin: University of Texas Press, 2016), 115–16, 128–37.

156 **the civil war:** Tarn, *Scandals*, 327–28, 339, 346–48; for the Mam shot in the nose, 360.

156 **the images would go off to fight:** See Christenson, "Ancestral Presence," 103; for the war efforts of Sojuel and the rain angels, 118. For the three volcanoes, see "Places of Emergence," 97.

158 **"relatively late-appearing animal":** Tarn, *Embattled Lyric*, 251.

## PART TWO: THE RAGGED EDGES OF RELIGION

## 6. THE MYSTICAL GERM

163    **Pole, Powell, or Poole:** Rev. Robert Caldwell, *The Tinnevelly Shanars: A Sketch of Their Religion, and Their Moral Condition and Characteristics as a Caste* (Madras: Christian Knowledge Society Press, 1849), 27; Caldwell, "On Demon-' olatry in Southern India," *Journal of the Anthropological Society of Bombay* 1 (1886): 91–105; Caldwell, "Demonolatry, Devil-Dancing, and Demoniacal Possession," *Contemporary Review* 27 (December 1875–May 1876): 372–73; H. R. Pate, *Madras District Gazetteers: Tinnevelly* (Madras: Superintendent Government Press, 1917), 119; T. T. Perowne, *A Memoir of the Rev. Thomas Gajetan Ragland, B.D.* (London: Seeley, Jackson, and Halliday, 1861), 111–12. L. S. S. O'Malley collected numerous incidents of the deification of British officers in *Popular Hinduism: The Religion of the Masses* (Cambridge: Cambridge University Press, 1935), 170–87. See also Shubhangi Swarup, "India's Most Haunted," *Open*, January 1, 2011. Throughout, I use the old colonial spellings of places as the British used them at the time.

165    **Colonel William Wallace:** John Howison, *Foreign Scenes and Travelling Recreations*, vol. 2 (Edinburgh: Oliver and Boyd, 1825), 68–69; 152–79. "Officers' Tombs in India," a letter from H. G. Rawlinson to the *Times* (London) (September 15, 1934); "Gazetteer Department," Maharashtra State Gazetteers, updated 2014, https://gazetteers.maharashtra.gov.in. For the plague on three hundred cats, see K. R. N. Swamy and Meera Ravi, *British Ghosts and Occult India* (Calcutta: Writers Workshop Greybird, 2004), 94–96.

166    **"no such laws have been definitely ascertained":** Sir Alfred C. Lyall, *Asiatic Studies* (London: John Murray, 1899), 27.

167    **the idols of Wellesley and Cornwallis:** Preeti Chopra, *A Joint Enterprise: Indian Elites and the Making of British Bombay* (Minneapolis: University of Minnesota Press, 2011), 205–19. Murali Ranganathan, ed., *Govind Narayan's Mumbai: An Urban Biography from 1863* (London: Anthem Press, 2009), 128–30. James Douglas, Sheriff of Bombay, *Glimpses of Old Bombay and Western India, With Other Papers* (London: Sampson Low, Marston, 1900), 16.

167    **shoo any adorers away:** In Khandesh, it was reported the sepoys who served Sir James Outram had come across a figurine they thought resembled the commander, famous for having killed 235 tigers. "They set it up forthwith and worshipped it as 'Outram Sahib,'" reported Sir James's biographer, who found the aesthetics of the idol distasteful. See Sir F. J. Goldsmid, *James Outram, A Biography* (London: Smith, Elder, 1880), 97–98. The East India Company magistrate Henry Revell was venerated at his tomb in Revelganj, the town in Bihar he founded. See Anand A. Yang, *The Limited Raj: Agrarian Relations in Colonial India, Saran District, 1793–1920* (Berkeley: University of California Press, 1989), 92.

There was also Captain James Stewart, who was fatally shot in 1779 when he climbed up a tree to survey the position of opposing Maratha troops as the

British marched on Poona. Stewart was worshipped as *Ishtur Phakda*, or Stewart the Valiant, at three tomb shrines: an obelisk near Karla, where he died; a stone slab where his body was buried; and a site where his severed head was said to have been interred in an open field. When a police station was built on the land in the late nineteenth century, it incorporated the altar to the head inside it, draped with saffron garlands and a metal cross. Police officers would dutifully bring Ishtur weekly animal sacrifices, for the deity was said to notice when they slackened their gifts. See Charles Augustus Kincaid, *Ishtur Phakde a Gallant Englishman and Other Studies* (Bombay: Times Press, 1917); ed. Rosie Llewellyn-Jones, *Chowkidar* 4, no. 4 (1986): 64–66; Uday S. Kulkarni, "Ishtur Phakda: The Story of Captain James Stuart," eSamskriti, March 5, 2019; William Dalrymple, *The Anarchy: The Relentless Rise of the East India Company* (London: Bloomsbury, 2019), 244.

The young administrator Augustus Clevland had tried to leave Bihar, sailing for the Cape of Good Hope in 1784, but died at sea. Preserved in spirits, he was shipped back to India, where his white, domed monument at Bhagalpur became a shrine. On the sea voyage, Clevland had possibly been recovering from injuries sustained in an attack by resistance fighters in Bihar. He was buried beneath a highly questionable plaque commemorating how Clevland "*attached*" the locals "to the British Government by a conquest over their minds, the most permanent as well as the most rational mode of domination." See the Right Reverend Reginald Heber, *Narrative of a Journey through the Upper Provinces of India from Calcutta to Bombay, 1824–1825*, vol. 1 (Philadelphia: Carey, Lea and Carey, 1828), 184–97; "Monody on the Death of Augustus Clevland, Esq.," in Charles John Shore Baron Teignmouth, *Memoir of the Life and Correspondence of John, Lord Teignmouth*, vol. 1 (London: Hatchard, 1843), 88–96, 489. "Grief whispers to the soul—and shews his urn—" Lord Teignmouth lamented. "No more shall Clevland's social hour return."

167   **Sir Thomas Sydney Beckwith:** "An Englishman's Grave in India," letter from Mrs. Kathleen Steel to the *Times* (London) (September 1, 1934). See also R. B. D. B. Parasnis, *Mahabaleshwar* (Bombay: Lakshmi Art Printing Works, 1916), 113.

168   **Tilman Henckell:** Barbara S. Groseclose, *British Sculpture and the Company Raj: Church Monuments and Public Statuary in Madras, Calcutta, and Bombay to 1858* (Newark: University of Delaware Press, 1995), 23–24. See also L. S. S. O'Malley, *Bengal, Bihar and Orissa, Sikkim* (Cambridge: Cambridge University Press, 1917), 214. *Calcutta Gazette* of April 2, 1788.

168   **Patrick Maxwell:** O. S. Crofton, *List of Inscriptions on Tombs or Monuments in the Central Provinces and Berar* (Nagpur: Government Printing, 1932), ii.

168   **"Events, not intention":** "Farewell and Hail: End of the Indian Empire," *Manchester Guardian*, August 15, 1947.

168   **apotheosis of the dead:** See Stuart H. Blackburn, "Death and Deification: Folk Cults in Hinduism," *History of Religions* 24, no. 3 (February 1985): 225–74. On the veneration of accidents, see William Crooke, *The Popular Religion and*

*Folk-Lore of Northern India*, vol. 1 (Westminster: Archibald Constable, 1896), 235. "Many of these shrines to persons who have died by an untimely death are known by special names, which indicate the character of the accident. We shall meet again with the Baghaut, or shrine, to a man killed by a tiger. We have also Bijaliya Bîr, the man who was killed by lightning, Târ Bîr, a man who fell from a Târ or toddy tree, and Nâgiya Bîr, a person killed by a snake. General Cunningham mentions shrines of this kind; one to an elephant driver who was killed by a fall from a tree, another to a Brâhman who was killed by a cow, a third to a Kashmîri lady who had only one leg and died in her flight from Delhi to Oudh of exhaustion on the journey."

169 **"Hinduism lies in urgent need of a Pope":** Crooke, *Popular Religion*, 183–84, 228. For the alcoholic godling and the Frenchman, see "The Kindly Dead," in the later edition of Crooke published as *Religion and Folklore of Northern India* (Oxford: Oxford University Press, 1926), 172. For class mobility, see Lyall, *Asiatic Studies*, 25, 31.

170 **Colonel Dixon:** Lieutenant-Colonel C. J. Dixon, *Sketch of Mairwara: A Brief Account of the Origin and Habits of the Mairs; Their Subjugation by a British Force; Their Civilization, and Conversion into an Industrious Peasantry* (London: Smith, Elder, 1850). Sir Walter Roper Lawrence, *The India We Served* (London: Cassell, 1928), 38, 239, 273. The shrine at Dixon's tomb also included an ornate silk dress from Paris that belonged to his Indian wife Bibi, preserved in a glass vitrine.

171 **Max Müller:** "The Perception of the Infinite," from *Lectures on the Origin and Growth of Religion* (1878), in *The Essential Max Müller: On Language, Mythology, and Religion*, ed. Jon R. Stone (New York: Palgrave Macmillan, 2002), 166–91. See also "Lecture on the Vedas" (1865), 43–67; "Forgotten Bibles" (1884), 249–67. In a later lecture from 1890, Müller modified his definition of religion as "the perception of the infinite" to "from the moment, therefore, that the perception of something supernatural begins to exercise an influence *on the moral actions of man, be it for good or for evil,* from that moment, I maintain, and from that moment only, have we a right to call it religious."

173 **Jezeus Christna:** Godfrey Higgins, *Anacalypsis: An Attempt to Draw Aside the Veil of the Saitic Isis*, vol. 2 (London: Longman, 1836). Louis Jacolliot, *The Bible in India: Hindoo Origin of Hebrew and Christian Revelation*, trans. G. R. (London: John Camden Hotten, 1870). For a comparison of Hindu avatars and Christian incarnation, see Daniel E. Bassuk's study *Incarnation in Hinduism and Christianity: The Myth of the God-Man* (London: Palgrave Macmillan, 1987). See also Colin Kidd, *The Forging of Races: Race and Scripture in the Protestant Atlantic World, 1600–2000* (Cambridge: Cambridge University Press, 2006), 46. Max Müller, *Chips from a German Workshop*, vol. 2 (New York: Charles Scribner, 1869), 76.

173 **teeming ecology of apotheosis:** See Max Müller's lectures "Physical Religion" (1890) in *The Essential Max Müller*, 266; "The Divine and the Human" (1891), 321–322. Müller even found himself hailed as a solar deity by a scholarly satirist

who claimed, in a journal article, the word *Müller* derived from a Sanskrit root meaning "to grind." Armed with his "battle-axe of light," the professorial sun god was "crushing frost and clouds alike into impalpability." See "The Oxford Solar Myth," in Müller, *Comparative Mythology* (London: Routledge, 1909), xxxi–xlvii. For Lyall's ladder, *Asiatic Studies*, 37.

174   **"that marvelous harvest"**: Müller, "Religion, Myth and Custom," in *The Essential Max Müller*, 288; for the list of religions, "The Parliament of Religions in Chicago, 1893," 346; for "Every religion . . . suffers," see "Preface to *Chips from a German Workshop*," 75; for "rose to the surface," "The Perception of the Infinite," 171.

175   **enshrined by . . . Plato**: Plato himself turned divine in an unlikely way on the Konya Plain, in what is now south-central Turkey. In a Muslim tradition dating as early as the thirteenth century, the philosopher, said to possess magical abilities, was venerated at a tomb shrine and at Eflatun Pinar, the "spring of Plato," a site of pilgrimage and astrological divination. It was said Konya was once entirely underwater, covered by a vast sea that Plato made disappear; the suprahuman sage holds back a river from flooding it again. See F. W. Hasluck, "Plato in the Folklore of the Konia Plain," in *Christianity and Islam under the Sultans*, vol. 2 (Oxford: Clarendon Press, 1929), 363–69.

175   *religio*: My discussion here is indebted to Brent Nongbri's study *Before Religion: A History of a Modern Concept* (New Haven, CT: Yale University Press, 2013), 1–34, 85–131; for Alexander Ross, 120–22. See also Jonathan Z. Smith, "Religion, Religions, Religious," in *Critical Terms for Religious Studies*, ed. Mark C. Taylor (Chicago: University of Chicago Press, 1998), 269–84. For Müller's remark "Classify and conquer," see David Chidester, *Empire of Religion: Imperialism and Comparative Religion* (Chicago: University of Chicago Press, 2014), 59–90. See also Tomoko Masuzawa, *The Invention of World Religions: Or, How European Universalism Was Preserved in the Language of Pluralism* (Chicago: University of Chicago Press, 2005).

177   **"my mystical germ"**: William James, *The Varieties of Religious Experience: A Study in Human Nature*, ed. Martin E. Marty (New York: Penguin Classics, 1985), xxi–xxv; for "whatever they may consider the divine," 31. Italics are my own.

177   **"the world fills up with believers"**: Bruno Latour, *On the Modern Cult of the Factish Gods* (Durham: Duke University Press, 2002), 2.

177   *sraddha, dharma*: Müller, "Lecture on the Vedas," in *The Essential Max Müller*, 61; for "The real history of man," 52. See also Carlos A. Lopez, "Philological Limits of Translating Religion: Sraddha and Dharma in Hindu Texts," in *Translating Religion: What Is Lost and Gained?*, ed. Michael P. DeJonge and Christiane Tietz (London: Routledge, 2015), 45–69.

179   **worship of Lala Hardaul**: William Sleeman, *Rambles and Recollections of an Indian Official*, vol. 1 (London: J. Hatchers and Son, 1844), 211; Crooke, *Popular Religion*, 138–41.

179   **Anti-Idolatry Connexion League**: See Robert Eric Frykenberg, "Christian Missions and the Raj," in *Missions and Empire*, ed. Norman Etherington (Oxford: Oxford University Press, 2005), 107–31; Peter van der Veer, *Imperial*

*Encounters: Religion and Modernity in India and Britain* (Princeton, NJ: Princeton University Press, 2001), 20.

180    **cargo of Christ:** On British missionary activities in India, see Robert Eric Frykenberg, *Christianity in India: From Beginnings to Present* (Oxford: Oxford University Press, 2008), 243–300.

180    **worship of James Clow:** Douglas, *Glimpses of Old Bombay,* 14–15; Anne Hamilton, *Personal Life of James Clow: A Memoir* (Melbourne: Ramsay, 1937).

180    **worship of John E. Clough:** John E. Clough and Emma R. Clough, *Social Christianity in the Orient: The Story of a Man, a Mission, and a Movement* (New York: Macmillan, 1914), v–vi, 286–89, 394–97.

181    ***Hindooism . . . renounce:*** Letter to John Thomas cited in Henry Morris, *The Life of Charles Grant: Sometime Member of Parliament and Director of the East India Company* (London: Murray, 1904), 105; Geoffrey A. Oddie, *Imagined Hinduism: British Protestant Missionary Constructions of Hinduism, 1793–1900* (New Delhi: Sage, 2006), 67–71; Nongbri, 110, 208n10. Caldwell, *The Tinnevelly Shanars,* 6. On the expansive and contentious debate around the "invention" of Hinduism, see the essays collected in J. E. Llewellyn, ed., *Defining Hinduism: A Reader* (New York: Routledge, 2014). On the British as "transcendent arbiter" between religions, see van der Veer, *Imperial Encounters,* 23.

183    **soon to be flattened:** Sir Monier Monier-Williams, *Modern India and the Indians: Being a Series of Impressions, Notes, and Essays* (London: Trübner, 1879), 156, 196, 246, 302.

184    **Colonel-Shah Pir:** Lt. Col. William Carden, worshipped at his sepulcher in Kheda, was remembered as a compassionate officer who, during a famine, gave away government money to the poor and was punished by the British authorities. See Peter Nazareth, "A Dargah for a British Army Officer from the Raj," *Times of India,* March 24, 2013.

184    **animism, brandy, and cigars:** Edward Burnett Tylor, *Anthropology: An Introduction to the Study of Man and Civilization* (London: Macmillan, 1881), 353; Tylor, *Primitive Culture: Researches into the Development of Mythology, Philosophy, Religion, Language, Art, and Custom,* vol. 1 (London: J. Murray, 1871), 129. See also Jason Ā. Josephson Storm, *The Myth of Disenchantment: Magic, Modernity, and the Birth of the Human Sciences* (Chicago: University of Chicago Press, 2017), 98–99; Chidester, *Empire of Religion,* 11, 64.

185    **extracting the ore of religion:** Edward Burnett Tylor, "On the Limits of Savage Religion," *Journal of the Anthropological Institute of Great Britain and Ireland* 21 (1892), 283–301; Chidester, *Empire of Religion,* 120.

186    **ephemeral gods in encyclopedias:** "Apotheosis," entry in *The Encyclopaedia Britannica,* 9th ed., vol. 2 (Edinburgh: Adam and Charles Black, 1889), 199. "Pole, Captain," entry in Edward Balfour, *The Cyclopædia of India and of Eastern and Southern Asia,* vol. 3 (London: B. Quaritch, 1885), 241, see also "Spirit Worship," 723.

186    **"stones . . . to be propitiated":** Lawrence, *India We Served,* 166.

186    **worship of John Jacob's horse:** "A Horse's Grave in India," letter from Mrs. G. A. Thomas to *Times* (London), September 8, 1934, 8.

186    **a pantheon of distillers:** Sir Charles Grant, ed., *The Gazetteer of the Central Provinces of India* (Nagpur: Education Society's Press, Bombay, 1870), cxxi; Crooke, *Popular Religion*, 183.

186    **liquor licenses:** Edgar Thurston, *Omens and Superstitions of Southern India* (London: T. Fisher Unwin, 1912), 187.

186    **deification of silence:** F. R. Hemingway, *Madras District Gazetteers: Tanjore* (Madras: Government Press, 1915), 219; for "fêted wherever he went," see O'Malley, *Popular Hinduism*, 181.

186    **"to Christianity its right place":** Max Müller, "Preface to *Chips*," in *The Essential Max Müller*, 74; for "infinitely superior," see *Theosophy, Or Psychological Religion: The Gifford Lectures* (London: Longmans, Green, 1893), 26.

188    **"What constitutes a religion?":** W. L. Distant, "On the Term 'Religion' as Used in Anthropology," *Journal of the Anthropological Institute of Great Britain and Ireland* 6 (1877): 60–70. See also Chidester, *Empire of Religion*, 12; Jonathan Z. Smith, *Imagining Religion: From Babylon to Jonestown* (Chicago: University of Chicago Press, 1982), xi; Smith, "Religion, Religions, Religious," 281. See list of definitions of *religion* in James H. Leuba, *A Psychological Study of Religion: Its Origin, Function, and Future* (New York: Macmillan, 1912).

188    **a shadow where God had been:** Josephson Storm, *Myth of Disenchantment*, 120–21. Josephson Storm's translation from the French of the entry for *religion* in Denis Diderot's *Encyclopédie*.

189    **"Ragged edges of religion":** E. M. Forster, *A Passage to India* (New York: Knopf, 1991), 287.

190    **"the illusion":** Lawrence, *India We Served*, 42–43.

## 7. A TUMESCENT TRINITY

191    **two frogs:** Robert Baden-Powell, *Scouting for Boys: A Handbook for Instruction in Good Citizenship*, ed. Elleke Boehmer (Oxford, Oxford University Press, 2004), 241–43; for "slackers," 278. See also Michael Rosenthal, *The Character Factory: Baden-Powell and the Origins of the Boy Scout Movement* (New York: Pantheon, 1986).

192    **tumescence of the male:** On new spirits of Christian manliness, see Donald E. Hall, ed., *Muscular Christianity: Embodying the Victorian Age* (Cambridge: Cambridge University Press, 1994); Norman Vance, *The Sinews of the Spirit: The Ideal of Christian Manliness in Victorian Literature and Religious Thought* (Cambridge: Cambridge University Press, 1985). See also Daniel Boyarin's discussion in *Unheroic Conduct: The Rise of Heterosexuality and the Invention of the Jewish Man* (Berkeley: University of California Press, 1997). For Inman's trinity, see Thomas Inman, *Ancient Faiths Embodied in Ancient Names*, vol. 1 (London: Trubner, 1868), 88–89. See also Joscelyn Godwin, *The Theosophical Enlightenment* (Albany: State University of New York Press, 1994), 23–24.

193    **"heartfelt prostrate admiration":** Thomas Carlyle, *On Heroes, Hero-Worship, and the Heroic in History* (London: Oxford University Press, 1959), 15.

193    **"cast in a giant mould":** William Wotherspoon Ireland, *History of the Siege of Delhi: By an Officer Who Served There* (Edinburgh: Adam and Charles Black, 1861), 224.

193    **"a messianic element":** George L. Mosse, *The Image of Man: The Creation of Modern Masculinity* (New York: Oxford University Press, 1996), 44.

193    **"a commanding presence":** From the memoir of Reginald G. Wilberforce, *An Unrecorded Chapter of the Indian Mutiny* (London: John Murray, 1894), 25–30.

193    **"sceptered race":** From the poem by Walter Savage Landor, "Rose Aylmer," lamenting an Englishwoman who died of cholera in India in 1800. *Ah what avails the sceptred race, / Ah what the form divine!*

193    **An icon of manhood mistaken for divine:** The hagiographical literature on Nicholson is vast. See R. E. Cholmeley, *John Nicholson: The Lion of the Punjab* (London: Andrew Melrose, 1908); J. Claverdon Wood, *When Nicholson Kept the Border* (London: Boy's Own Paper, 1922); Hesketh Pearson, *The Hero of Delhi: A Life of John Nicholson, Saviour of India, and a History of His Wars* (London: Collins, 1939); Achmed Abdullah and T. Compton Pakenham, *Dreamers of Empire* (London: Harrap, 1930), 152. Nicholson also appears in L. S. S. O'Malley, *Popular Hinduism: The Religion of the Masses* (Cambridge: Cambridge University Press, 1935), 171. See also Ernest A. Gray, *Nikkal Seyn: A Tale of John Nicholson, Hero of Delhi, Saviour of India* (London and Glasgow: Collins, 1947). Gray presents an especially sensationalist and sinister scene in his book, published the year India gained independence. A British officer is in hysterics as he watches Nikalsainis in worship: "Roars of laughter, leaning helplessly against the doorpost, and wiping away the tears streaming down his cheeks . . . One of the fakirs shouts, 'I have our Lord's boot! . . . Come, my brothers, let us depart and build an altar around it, where all the world can come to wonder and to pray!'"

194    **"*Dark rouge, not black*":** The incident with Mehtab Singh was recorded by Lord Roberts of Kandahar, in his bestselling autobiography, *Forty-One Years in India* (London: R. Bentley, 1897), 137–38. For the Nicholson tableau, see Baden-Powell, *Scouting for Boys*, 279–81. See also Peter van der Veer, *Imperial Encounters: Religion and Modernity in India and Britain* (Princeton, NJ: Princeton University Press, 2001), 90. The offensive scene was removed from subsequent editions of *Scouting for Boys* by the publishers.

195    **blistered brigadier:** See Sir John William Kaye's biography of Nicholson, written in the decade after his death, in *Lives of Indian Officers*, vol. 2 (London: A. Strahan, 1867), 417–92. For Lionel James Trotter's canonical account, see *The Life of John Nicholson, Soldier and Administrator, Based on Private and Hitherto Unpublished Documents* (London: John Murray, 1898); for "grinding Sikh tyranny," 125. The most recent addition to the genre is Stuart Flinders, *Cult of a Dark Hero: Nicholson of Delhi* (London: I. B. Tauris, 2018).

195    **"the unique distinction of deification by his enemies":** Pearson, *Hero of Delhi*, 112.

195   **"god veiled in human flesh"**: Wilberforce, *Unrecorded Chapter*, 28–30. In *Dreamers of Empire*, Abdullah adds the implausible anecdote that Nikalsain, rejecting his godhood, was able to quote back to the Sikhs their own theology, "reminding them that their own Sikh doctrines lay great stress on the unity and omnipotence of God . . . that in the *Japji*, the Bible of the Sikhs, it is written:
    By thinking I cannot obtain a conception of Him,
    Even though I think hundreds of thousands of times.
    He hath no colour nor outline."

196   *creature-feeling*: Rudolf Otto, *The Idea of the Holy*, trans. John W. Harvey (London: Oxford University Press, 1952), 10.

196   **"this new god *Nikalsain*"**: Trotter, *Life of John*, 126–27. For "revolted and enormously irritated," and Abbott's account of the "Nicholsynie Priest," see Charles Allen, *Soldier Sahibs: The Men Who Made the North-West Frontier* (London: Time Warner Books, 2001), 217–20. For Nikalsain's violent persecution of his worshippers, Wilberforce, *Unrecorded Chapter*, 30; Pearson, *Hero of Delhi*, 117–18. For the attempted transfer of adoration to John Becher, see the account by Herbert Edwardes in Charles Raikes, *Notes on the Revolt in the North-Western Provinces of India* (London: Longman, 1858), 32.

196   **"'Dread' becomes worship"**: Otto, *Idea of the Holy*, 110.

197   **"the very incarnation of violence"**: See William Dalrymple, *The Last Mughal: The Fall of a Dynasty; Delhi, 1857* (London: Bloomsbury, 2009), 200. For "a bill for Flaying," see Michael Silvestri, *Ireland and India: Nationalism, Empire and Memory* (London: Palgrave Macmillan, 2009), 79. For "When an Empire is at stake," see Wilberforce, *Unrecorded Chapter*, 33.

198   **Under siege**: Dalrymple, *Last Mughal*, 341–85. For the words of Ghalib, see Frances W. Pritchett, *Nets of Awareness: Urdu Poetry and Its Critics* (Berkeley: University of California Press, 1994).

198   **Nicholson's funeral**: Wilberforce, *Unrecorded Chapter*, 214–16. For Sir Donald Macnabb's letter to Sir James Hogg, October 1860, see Trotter, *Life of John*, 314.

199   **Mrs. Clara Nicholson**: Trotter, *Life of John*, 315; Silvestri, *Ireland and India*, 77–78, 118–21.

199   **"very God to me"**: For the "Punjabi ballad," Trotter, *Life of John*, 318–19; Silvestri, *Ireland and India*, 91–92.

200   **"Energy and Courage"**: Samuel Smiles, *Self-Help* (London: John Murray, 1876), 118, 236–37. The Rastafari founding father Leonard Howell was inspired by Smiles, and cited *Self-Help* in the constitution of his Ethiopian Salvation Society. Considered a "holy book" of the Meiji era in Japan, *Self-Help* also influenced the prophet Deguchi Onisaburo, cofounder of the Oomoto religion, which recognized divinity in General MacArthur and L. L. Zamenhof.

201   **an orgiastic *puja***: Rudyard Kipling, "The Tomb of His Ancestors," first published in *Pearson's Magazine*, December 1897. See notes on the text edited by John Radcliffe at http://www.kiplingsociety.co.uk/rg_tomb1.htm; also Philip Mason, *Kipling: The Glass, the Shadow and the Fire* (London: Jonathan Cape, 1975), 135–36.

For Kipling in postcolonial scholarship see the essays collected in Caroline Rooney and Kaori Nagai, eds., *Kipling and Beyond: Patriotism, Globalisation and Postcolonialism* (London: Palgrave Macmillan, 2010). In Kipling's novel *Kim*, an Indian veteran of the 1857 mutiny praises Nicholson's bravery and sings lines from the same Punjabi ballad Mrs. Nicholson received in the mail.

202   **Whereas the Sikhs:** Pearson, *Hero of Delhi*, 117–18.

203   **Nikkasayn as Shia saint:** Personal correspondence with professor Omer Tarin and Dr. Ilyas Khan, June 5, 2017.

204   **"a longing for the father":** Sigmund Freud, *The Origins of Religion: Totem and Taboo, Moses and Monotheism and Other Works*, trans. James Strachey (London: Penguin Books, 1986), 104, 117, 204–19.

204   **a gold mine:** Sir James George Frazer, *The Golden Bough*, vol. 1 (London: Macmillan, 1922); for Nikkal Sen, 100; for "Eating the God," 479–94. For Frazer's influence on Freud, see Ronald E. Martin, *The Languages of Difference: American Writers and Anthropologists Reconfigure the Primitive, 1878–1940* (Newark: University of Delaware Press, 2005), 91–132.

205   **"*Mixing hate and love*":** From Louis O. Coxe's *Nikal Seyn and Decoration Day: A Poem and a Play* (Nashville: Vanderbilt University Press, 1966), 4. The poem's speaker calls Nicholson "the realest god I know."

207   **sexual repression:** Michael Edwardes, *Bound to Exile: The Victorians in India* (London: Sidgwick and Jackson, 1969), 100; Christopher Hibbert, *The Great Mutiny: India 1857* (New York: Viking, 1978), 293; see also Silvestri, *Ireland and India*, 107–8. Frank M. Richardson, *Mars without Venus: A Study of Some Homosexual Generals* (Edinburgh: W. Blackwood, 1981), 127–34, 151–52; for "common sense," 1, 4, and also 161 in praise of "the common sense of some wives who have discovered their husbands' transvestist practices, and quietly come to terms with them."

208   **"drunk with wine, and soma-juice":** Aleister Crowley, *The God-Eater: A Tragedy of Satire* (London: Watts, 1903). For the spell to end the Christian age, see John Symonds, *The Great Beast: The Life of Aleister Crowley* (London: Rider, 1951), 133–35. See also *The Confessions of Aleister Crowley*, ed. John Symonds and Kenneth Grant (New York: Hill and Wang, 1970), 807–9. See also Jason Ā. Josephson Storm, *The Myth of Disenchantment: Magic, Modernity, and the Birth of the Human Sciences* (Chicago: University of Chicago Press, 2017), 157–60. E. D. Starbuck quoted in William James, *The Varieties of Human Experience: A Study in Human Nature*, ed. Martin E. Marty (New York: Penguin Classics, 1985), 199.

## 8. PASSAGE

210   **young bulls, rams:** Kari Elizabeth Børresen, ed., *The Image of God: Gender Models in Judaeo-Christian Tradition* (Minneapolis: Fortress Press, 1995), 42. See also Kristen E. Kvam, Linda S. Schearing, and Valerie H. Ziegler, eds., *Eve and Adam: Jewish, Christian, and Muslim Readings on Genesis and Gender* (Bloomington: Indiana University Press, 1999).

211    **Joanna, the New Eve:** See Yvonne Petry, *Gender, Kabbalah and the Reformation:
       The Mystical Theology of Guillaume Postel (1510–1581)* (Leiden: Brill, 2004),
       39–46, 95–116. After her death, Postel said he fell into a coma wherein his body
       was possessed by Joanna's divine spirit for several weeks.

211    *la femme messie:* See Marwa Elshakry, "Free Love, Funny Costumes and a Canal
       at Suez," *Bidoun 10: Technology* (Spring 2007): 64–65. See also Naomi J. Andrews,
       *Socialism's Muse: Gender in the Intellectual Landscape of French Romantic Social-
       ism* (Lanham, MD: Lexington Books, 2006), 33–35. In contemporary feminist
       theology, some scholars use the term "Christa" to designate the female messiah.

211    **"the thin 'membrane'":** James H. Billington, *Fire in the Minds of Men: Origins of
       the Revolutionary Faith* (New Brunswick, NJ: Transaction, 2009), 219–21.

212    *Suez:* Translated by Pamela Pilbeam in her study *Saint-Simonians in Nineteenth-
       Century France: From Free Love to Algeria* (London: Palgrave Macmillan, 2013),
       112; for the quest to Egypt, 104–29.

212    *Bathe me O God in thee:* Walt Whitman, "Passage to India," *The Portable Walt
       Whitman,* ed. Michael Warner (New York: Penguin, 2004), 274–84.

213    **"the fresh blood":** Sir Alfred C. Lyall, *Asiatic Studies* (London: John Murray,
       1899), 53.

213    **Mrs. Clare Watson:** L. S. S. O'Malley, *Popular Hinduism: The Religion of the
       Masses* (Cambridge: Cambridge University Press, 1935), 178.

213    **shrine to the nameless "wife":** Recorded by H. P. Blavatsky, *From the Caves and
       Jungles of Hindostan* (London: Theosophical, 1908), 186–88.

213    **backward-facing feet:** See Alan Butterworth, *The Southlands of Siva: Some
       Reminiscences of Life in Southern India* (London: John Lane, 1923), 26.

213    **Mary Rebecca Weston:** See ed. Rosie Llewellyn-Jones, *Chowkidar* 13, no. 1
       (Spring 2012): 4–5. See also Shubhangi Swarup, "India's Most Haunted," *Open,*
       January 1, 2011; Man Aman Singh Chhina, "Dagshai's 'Mem ki qabr' Gets a
       Fresh Lease of Life," *Indian Express,* June 24, 2017; Rajeev Khanna, "A Fabled
       Grave in a Hill Town Cemetery," *Citizen,* August 16, 2019. It was said that the
       pieces of tombstone only had efficacy for fertility if they were chewed. The grave,
       known as *Mem ki Qabr,* or the "Englishwoman's Grave," was restored in 2017
       and is now fenced by an iron cage and surveilled by CCTV.

214    **"Esmiss Esmoor":** E. M. Forster, *A Passage to India* (New York: Knopf, 1991), 203.

215    **Queen Victoria as God:** Sir Walter Roper Lawrence, *The India We Served* (Lon-
       don: Cassell, 1928), 42, 239. See also "Queen Victoria as Goddess," *Spectator,*
       March 17, 1883, 10. For Victoria's anti-suffragism, see letter to Sir Theodore
       Martin, cited in Frank Hardie, *The Political Influence of Queen Victoria, 1861–
       1901* (London: Frank Cass, 1963), 140.

217    **Genda Bir, tired of life:** William Crooke, *The Popular Religion and Folk-Lore of
       Northern India,* vol. 1 (Westminster: Archibald Constable, 1896), 240.

217    **Vallavan's nagging god:** Rev. Samuel Mateer, *"The Land of Charity": A Descrip-
       tive Account of Travancore and Its People, with Especial Reference to Missionary
       Labour* (London: John Snow, 1871), 206.

217 **"Worship of Beings in Strange Shapes"**: Rev. William Ward, *A View of the History, Literature, and Religion of the Hindoos*, vol. 1 (London: Black, Parbury, and Allen, 1817), 247–48.

217 **Kumari:** See Isabella Tree's study *The Living Goddess: A Journey into the Heart of Kathmandu* (London: Eland, 2015); also Michael Allen, "Kumari or 'Virgin' Worship in Kathmandu Valley," in *Ritual, Power, and Gender: Explorations in the Ethnography of Vanuatu, Nepal, and Ireland* (New Delhi: Manohar Publishers, 2000).

217 **worship of dead daughters:** Mateer, *"The Land of Charity,"* 204–5.

218 **"* * * * * *":** For the "diabolical business," see Ward, *View of the History*, 246–48.

219 ***sahamarana*, or "dying with":** See Catherine Weinberger-Thomas, *Ashes of Immortality: Widow-Burning in India* (Chicago: University of Chicago Press, 1999), 21.

219 **goddess in the flames:** For a collection of colonialist accounts, see "Suttee/Sati" in *Archives of Empire*, vol. 1, ed. Barbara Harlow and Mia Carter (Durham, NC: Duke University Press, 2003), 337–90. See also Crooke, *Popular Religion*, 186–88; Sleeman's visit to "Suttee Tombs" in *Rambles and Recollections of an Indian Official*, vol. 1 (London: J. Hatchers and Son, 1844), 139–44.

219 **"*As long as fourteen Indras reign*":** Ward, *View of the History*, 237.

219 **"fire-eater":** My discussion of *sati* is indebted to the scholarship of Tanika Sarkar. See "Something Like Rights? Faith, Law and Widow Immolation Debates in Colonial Bengal," *Indian Economic and Social History Review* 49, no. 3 (2012): 295–320; for the possibility of the *sati* turning evil, 301. See also Sarkar, "Holy 'Fire Eaters': Why Widow Immolation Became an Issue in Colonial Bengal," in *Rebels, Wives, Saints: Designing Selves and Nations in Colonial Times* (Ranikhet, India: Permanent Black, 2009); for "the rules of deference," 62.

220 **Toolseboy:** An eyewitness testimony appears in "Papers Relating to East India Affairs Viz. Hindoo Widows and Voluntary Immolations," House of Commons Parliamentary Papers, July 10, 1821, 3–4. For Ward's snake, see *View of the History*, 245.

220 **Jesus as suicidal:** See Jack Miles's discussion in *Christ: A Crisis in the Life of God* (London: Arrow, 2003), 176, 183, 193.

221 **"a ceremony authorized":** For Charles Cornwallis, see Sarkar, *Rebels, Wives*, 47. For the changing British policy toward *sati*, see Lata Mani, *Contentious Traditions: The Debate on Sati in Colonial India* (Berkeley: University of California Press, 1998), 21–41.

221 ***Om!*:** Henry Thomas Colebrooke, "On the Duties of a Faithful Hindu Widow," in *Essays on the Religion and Philosophy of the Hindus* (London: Williams and Norgate, 1858), 70–72. According to Colebrooke, the *sankalp* derived from the words of the Vedic sage Angiras: "As the snake-catcher forcibly drags the serpent from his earth; so, bearing her husband [from hell], with him she shall enjoy heavenly bliss."

221 **excessive display of love:** See Sarkar, *Rebels, Wives*, 50–51; for the prevalence in Bengal in the early nineteenth century, 43, for *Rassoo* et al., 46n. "The woman was about to ascend to heaven, and yet she lacked a proper name," Sarkar writes.

222 **Digambari's protest march:** Sarkar, *Rebels, Wives*, 17–22. For "Controversially but recognisably," see Sarkar, "Something Like Rights," 296–300.

223    **Rammohan Roy:** On his life and ideas, see Amiya P. Sen, *Rammohun Roy: A Critical Biography* (London: Viking, 2012). For *sati* interpreted through the *Bhagavad Gita*, see Sarkar, "Something Like Rights," 314–15; *Rebels, Wives*, 54.

224    **"Rise, woman":** Max Müller, *Chips from a German Workshop*, vol. 2 (New York: Charles Scribner, 1869), 35–36. Müller draws upon Professor Wilson's "On the Supposed Vaidik Authority for the Burning of Hindu Widows, and on the Funeral Ceremonies of the Hindus," *Journal of the Royal Asiatic Society of Great Britain and Ireland* 16 (1856): 203–4.

224    **Purusha, the Sacred Man:** Translated by Laurie L. Patton in "Cosmic Men and Fluid Exchanges: Myths of Ārya, Varna, and Jāti in the Hindu Tradition," in *Religion and the Creation of Race and Ethnicity,* ed. Craig R. Prentiss (New York: New York University Press, 2003), 188. The translation has been slightly edited here.

225    **scattered pieces of Sati:** See John Stratton Hawley, *Sati, the Blessing and the Curse: The Burning of Wives in India* (Oxford: Oxford University Press, 1994), 31.

225    **martyred mothers to the nation:** Sarkar, "Something Like Rights," 312–13; Sarkar, *Rebels, Wives*, 51.

226    **Dayananda Saraswati:** "It was a small mouse, that in the middle of night came out of its hole and began to take liberties with the mighty God of the temple," writes M. A. Chamupati in *Glimpses of Dayananda* (Delhi: Sharada Mandir, 1937). On Dayananda, see also J. T. F. Jordens, *Dayananda Sarasvati: His Life and Ideas* (Oxford: Oxford University Press, 1997); Rachel Fell McDermott et al., eds., *Sources of Indian Traditions: Modern India, Pakistan, and Bangladesh*, vol. 2 (New York: Columbia University Press, 2014), 131–35; Peter van der Veer, *Imperial Encounters: Religion and Modernity in India and Britain* (Princeton, NJ: Princeton University Press, 2001), 50, 158.

226    **"Ladies, excuse me":** From the speech "The Future of India," given at Madras on February 14, 1897, in Swami Vivekananda, *Lectures from Colombo to Almora* (Almora: Advaita Ashrama, 1947), 207–29.

226    **Sarada Devi:** See "The Deification of Ramakrishna's Wife," in McDermott et al., *Sources of Indian*, 139–40. See also Narasingha P. Sil, *Divine Dowager: Life and Teachings of Saradamani the Holy Mother* (Selinsgrove, PA: Susquehanna University Press, 2003), 56–58. Despite her deification, Sarada remained in domestic servitude: "Her entire young adult life was spent cooking for and catering to her husband and his admirers." Ramakrishna's appetite was legendarily insatiable; Sarada would rise at three a.m. each day to begin cooking.

227    **"biceps":** From Vivekananda's speech "Vedanta in Its Application to Indian Life," Madras, February 13, 1897, in *Lectures from Colombo to Almora*; see also Sikata Banerjee, *Make Me a Man! Masculinity, Hinduism, and Nationalism in India* (Albany: State University of New York Press, 2005), 58–66; for "Make your nerves strong," 59.

228    **"The first Gods we have to worship":** Vivekananda, "Future of India"; see also Nandini Saraf, *The Life and Times of Swami Vivekananda* (New Delhi: Ocean Books, 2012), 108.

## 9. THE TYRANNY OF LOVE

231  **"the Wife of a Beneficed Clergyman":** For Besant's troubled married life and spiritual searching, see Arthur H. Nethercot's classic study *The First Five Lives of Annie Besant* (Chicago: University of Chicago Press, 1960), 34–59. See also Anne Taylor, *Annie Besant: A Biography* (Oxford: Oxford University Press, 1992); as well as Annie Besant's *An Autobiography* (London: T. Fisher Unwin, 1908), 65–130.

231  **birth control:** For Besant's advocacy and the trial, see Nethercot, *First Five Lives*, 107–44; Sripati Chandrasekhar, *"A Dirty Filthy Book": The Writings of Charles Knowlton and Annie Besant on Reproductive Physiology* (Berkeley: University of California Press, 1981); Besant, *Autobiography*, 205–40. See also Nancy Fix Anderson, "'Not a Fit or Proper Person': Annie Besant's Struggle for Child Custody, 1878–9," in *Maternal Instincts: Visions of Motherhood and Sexuality in Britain, 1875–1925*, ed. Claudia Nelson and Ann Sumner Holmes (London: Macmillan, 1997), 13–36.

232  **"special exhibit of specimens":** Nethercot, *First Five Lives*, 200.

233  **"Yours ever truly, K.H.":** Letter XXXIII, preserved in A. T. Barker, *The Mahatma Letters to A. P. Sinnett* (London: Rider, 1933), 245.

234  **sacrificial Pole rituals:** H. P. Blavatsky, *From the Caves and Jungles of Hindostan* (London: Theosophical, 1908), 186–88.

234  **"Oh, my dear Mrs. Besant":** For Besant's conversion to Theosophy, see *Autobiography*, 338–44; Nethercot, *First Five Lives*, 283–309, 363–75.

235  **a celestial bureaucracy:** For Blavatsky's Mahatmas and the historical personages beneath, see the study by K. Paul Johnson, *The Masters Revealed: Madame Blavatsky and the Myth of the Great White Lodge* (Albany: State University of New York Press, 1994). See also Roland Vernon, *Star in the East: Krishnamurti, The Invention of a Messiah* (Boulder, CO: Sentient Publications, 2000), 11–13; Gauri Viswanathan, "Conversion, Theosophy, and Race Theory," in *Outside the Fold* (Princeton, NJ: Princeton University Press, 1998), 177–208.

235  **rather bossy letters:** Barker, *Mahatma Letters*; see also Joy Dixon, *Divine Feminine: Theosophy and Feminism in England* (Baltimore: Johns Hopkins University Press, 2003), 26–29; for Morya's prophecy, 27–28. Besides rice paper, the letters were written on all kinds of stationery and scrap paper, or scrawled in the margins of other missives in red and blue crayons, whatever the shadowy beings had at hand. Forensic experts determined that the letters, in English, were written by someone for whom French was their first language. See the study by Geoffrey A. Barborka, *The Mahatmas and Their Letters* (Madras: Theosophical Publishing House, 1973).

237  **"highly pernicious":** Letter from K.H. reprinted in *Mahatma Letters*, 405. For the Masters' views against birth control, see Nethercot, *First Five Lives*, 210, 375; for the astral form at the foot of Besant's bed (it was Morya), 305.

237  **vampiric teeth:** For the life of the infamous priest, see Gregory Tillett, *The Elder Brother: A Biography of Charles Webster Leadbeater* (London: Routledge, 1982). See also Mary Lutyens's memoir *To Be Young: Some Chapters of Autobiography* (London: Rupert Hart-Davis, 1959), 153.

238    **the murdered (and invented) Gerald:** Charles Webster Leadbeater allegedly searched for the spirit of Gerald in numerous boys until he found the correct one. See Tillett, *Elder Brother*, 12–17; Vernon, *Star in the East*, 16.

238    **occult chemistry:** Besant and Leadbeater authored the textbook *Occult Chemistry: Investigations by Clairvoyant Magnification into the Structure of the Atoms of the Periodic Table and Some Compounds* (Adyar: Theosophical Publishing House, 1908). See also the second volume of Arthur H. Nethercot's biography, *The Last Four Lives of Annie Besant* (London: Rupert Hart-Davis, 1963), 49–53.

238    **root-races:** For the elaboration of this theory, see Blavatsky on "Anthropogenesis," in *The Secret Doctrine*, vol. 2 (London: Theosophical, 1888); Besant, *The Pedigree of Man* (Benares: Theosophical, 1904); see also Viswanathan, *Outside the Fold*, 197–99.

239    **the Director of Religion:** The prominent Theosophist Dr. Mary Rocke collected prophecies in *The Coming of the World Teacher* (London: George Allen and Unwin, 1917). In 1927, much like Forster's Mrs. Moore, Dr. Rocke died in the passage to India, aboard a steamship crossing the Suez Canal. Traveling with Besant and Krishnamurti, Rocke fell in a corridor and hit her head. She was buried in the Red Sea.

239    **"Mahatmosphere":** See Nethercot, *Last Four Lives*, 36; for "Laugh at us," 43. For anti-Theosophist polemic, see also John Murdoch, *The Theosophic Craze: Its History; The Great Mahatma Hoax; How Mrs. Besant Was Befooled and Deposed* (Madras: Christian Literature Society, 1894), which ends with a purifying coda, "Need of Prayer."

239    **wet dreams:** For Leadbeater's theory, see Rocke, *Coming of the World*, 42–45. A variant of this idea, that after Christ emptied himself of divinity to become human he was adopted by God as His Son, was espoused by the medieval Iberian sect the Adoptivi.

239    **"You may meet Him in the train . . .":** George Arundale in Rocke, *Coming of the World*, 28.

240    **Hubert Van Hook:** For the prep school messiah, see Nethercot, *Last Four Lives*, 144; Vernon, *Star in the East*, 39, 46.

240    **"teaching young boys to * * * * ":** Olcott to Leadbeater, January 1907, cited in Veritas [pseud.], *Mrs. Besant and the Alcyone Case* (Madras: Goodwin, 1913), 14.

240    **the most unusual aura:** For Krishnamurti's early life, see the account by his Theosophist tutor Russell Balfour-Clarke, *The Boyhood of J. Krishnamurti* (Bombay: Chetana, 1977); as well as the court testimony preserved in Veritas, *Mrs. Besant*, 18–21. See also Mary Lutyens, *Krishnamurti: The Years of Awakening* (New York: Avon, 1975); Vernon, *Star in the East*; Pupul Jayakar, *J. Krishnamurti: A Biography* (New Delhi: Penguin India, 2003); C. V. Williams, *Jiddu Krishnamurti: World Philosopher (1895–1986): His Life and Thoughts* (Delhi: Motilal Banarsidass, 2004); Radha Rajagopal Sloss, *Lives in the Shadow with J. Krishnamurti* (London: Bloomsbury, 1991). While on holiday in Normandy, a teenage Krishna began his own memoir, titled *Fifty Years of My Life* and left unfinished.

241    **Alcyone:** A Greek nymph who incurred Zeus's wrath and was transformed into a kingfisher, or halcyon bird. When she lays her eggs, it is said the god Aeolus

calms the winds and waves out of compassion, in lulls of tranquility known as halcyon days.

241 **"This is our Krishna":** Nethercot, *Last Four Lives*, 134.

241 **the initiation:** See Krishnamurti's description in a letter to Besant, preserved in Balfour-Clarke, *Boyhood*, 16–24; Nethercot, *Last Four Lives*, 147–49.

242 **"as a silk-worm":** Sir Alfred C. Lyall, *Asiatic Studies* (London: John Murray, 1899), 47. In a March 31, 1910, letter to Krishnamurti, Besant wrote, "My loved Krishna, blessed little son, I wonder if you see or feel me in the morning meditation where I come to you, *you* do in your astral, but do you in your brain down here? And very often in the day I sent a thought-form to wrap its wings round you."

242 **the grooming of a god:** The daily routine and controversial milk-drinking were recounted in the court proceedings preserved in Veritas, *Mrs. Besant*, 98, 196, 236. See also Balfour-Clarke, *Boyhood*, 7–8; Tillett, *Elder Brother*, 124–25; Vernon, *Star in the East*, 56–57; Jayakar, *J. Krishnamurti*, 27–28.

243 **"imperfect magnetism":** Vernon, *Star in the East*, 59; for Hubert's later life, 46.

243 **"to be a Christ—as a profession":** Sir Edwin Lutyens, quoted in Lady Emily Lutyens, *Candles in the Sun* (London: Rupert Hart-Davis, 1957), 50.

244 **"*Who were you in the Lives?*":** The genealogy of reincarnations was published by Annie Besant and Charles Leadbeater in two volumes as *The Lives of Alcyone* (Adyar, Madras: Theosophical, 1924). For the jealousies and rivalries, see Williams, *Jiddu Krishnamurti*, 22–24; Nethercot, *Last Four Lives*, 140–41.

244 **"You should make a nice little book":** The Rt. Rev. Charles Webster Leadbeater, *The Masters and the Path* (Madras: Theosophical, 1925), 65–66. See also Balfour-Clarke, *Boyhood*, 25–26; Nethercot, *Last Four Lives*, 153.

245 **a phosphorescent blue halo:** See Balfour-Clarke, *Boyhood*, 28–31; Veritas, *Mrs. Besant*, 108; Nethercot, *Last Four Lives*, 170–72.

245 **"*we put out delicate tendrils to each other*":** For Besant's letter to Krishnamurti, Vernon, *Star in the East*, 57–58.

245 **the Rishi Agastya:** Annie Besant, *The Theosophist*, January 1929. See Joy Dixon, "Of Many Mahatmas: Besant, Gandhi, and Indian Nationalism," in *Indian Critiques of Gandhi*, ed. Harold Coward (Albany: State University of New York Press, 2003), 67–86. For Besant's Indian activism, see also Nethercot, *Last Four Lives*, 208, 237–50.

246 **"the pangs of a parent":** For Narayaniah's plea to Besant, see Veritas, *Mrs. Besant*, 47; for the letter to "hand over my two sons," 58.

248 **the empire as family:** On maternal imperialists, see Kumari Jayawardena, *The White Woman's Other Burden: Western Women and South Asia during British Rule* (New York: Routledge, 2014). See also Viswanathan, *Outside the Fold*, 177–207; for Besant's "The genius of the Empire," 193; "a cry for freedom," 203. For Besant on the British Empire's "bonds of close affection," see Rocke, *Coming of the World*, 159. See also Nancy Fix Anderson, "'Mother Besant' and Indian National Politics," *Journal of Imperial and Commonwealth History* 30, no. 3 (2002): 27–54.

248   **"Deified and Defiled":** "Deified and Defiled. Two Boys and a Beast," *John Bull*,
      November 16, 1912. For Crowley, "no prude," see Dixon, *Divine Feminine*, 109.

248   **"The plaintiff":** For the trial proceedings, see "Mr. Narayaniah's Plaint," in Ver-
      itas, *Mrs. Besant*, 70–76.

249   **"they were half-starved, beaten":** Annie Besant to G. Narayaniah, February 7,
      1912, in Veritas, *Mrs. Besant*, 55–56.

249   **the verdict:** See "Judgement," in Veritas, *Mrs. Besant*, 248–64; Nethercot, *Last Four
      Lives*, 184–201. For "Bristling with indignation," see Vernon, *Star in the East*, 72.

250   **"*I want you to civilise them*":** Jayakar, *J. Krishnamurti*, 26. On the Mahatmas'
      approval of the regimen, see "The High Court Case," in Veritas, *Mrs. Besant*, 98–
      100; for the Master on the night train, 106.

251   **a profound paradox:** For the anti-colonial activism of Ranbir Singh and Tha-
      kar Singh Sandhanwalia, see Johnson, *Masters Revealed*, 120–75. Ranbir Singh's
      great-grandson would become Indian ambassador to the United States in 1989.

251   **occult practices for political insight:** For A. O. Hume, see Sir William Wedder-
      burn, *Allan Octavian Hume: Father of the Indian National Congress, 1829–1912:
      A Biography*, ed. Edward C. Moulton (New Delhi: Oxford University Press,
      2002). See also Mark Bevir, "Theosophy and the Origins of the Indian National
      Congress," *International Journal of Hindu Studies* 7, no. 1/3 (February 2003):
      99–115; Dixon, *Divine Feminine*, 26–29; Johnson, *Masters Revealed*, 234–41.
      For Hume's own writings on the Masters, see H—X—[A. O. Hume], *Hints on
      Esoteric Theosophy, Nos. 1 and 2* (Calcutta: Calcutta Central Press, 1882/1883).
      Wrote Hume to K. H., "even when I was fully persuaded you were a myth . . .
      even then my heart yearned to you as it often does to an avowedly fictitious
      character."

252   **an "army of the deluded":** Blavatsky's confessional letter to Franz Hartmann,
      April 1886, in Johnson, *Masters Revealed*, 9.

252   **souls lining up:** See Besant and Leadbeater on the WWI dead in Rocke, *Coming
      of the World*, 124–56. For Theosophy during the war, see Dixon, *Divine Femi-
      nine*, 87–90.

253   **scrubbed and coiffed:** For Krishnamurti's wartime years in England, see Ver-
      non, *Star in the East*, 74–78.

253   **"a brown Messiah":** For Balliol College's rejection, see Nethercot, *Last Four
      Lives*, 229; for Armine Wodehouse's remarks, 178.

253   **"Why did they pick me?":** Vernon, *Star in the East*, 74; for "a lusus naturae,"
      see Lutyens, *Awakening*, 117. Krishna recalled to a friend that once, when Koot
      Hoomi stood in front of him, he ignored what the Master was saying and aggres-
      sively walked right through the slender astral body (Jayakar, *J. Krishnamurti*, 39).

254   ***What kind of god art thou?:*** Shakespeare, *Henry V*, in *Four Histories*, ed.
      A. R. Humphreys et al. (London: Penguin Books, 2005), 4.1.220–21. For K.H.'s
      suggestion to read Shakespeare, see Nethercot, *First Five Lives*, 164, 345. Besant
      took the boys to a London production of *Julius Caesar*, for she felt the dictator's
      ego was soon to reincarnate on earth.

254 **"I did not feel at all sea-sick":** Mohandas K. Gandhi, *An Autobiography: The Story of My Experiments with Truth*, trans. Mahadev Desai (Boston: Beacon Press, 1993), 42; for his encounters with Theosophists, 67–69, 263–67.

255 **the Arctic Circle:** Bal Gangadhar Tilak, *The Arctic Home in the Vedas* (Poona: Tilak Bros., 1925). See also David Chidester, *Empire of Religion: Imperialism and Comparative Religion* (Chicago: University of Chicago Press, 2014), 46.

255 **fratricide among a hundred brothers:** On the *Gita*, a "humanization of God in the face of the inhumanity of war," see Shruti Kapila and Faisal Devji, eds., *Political Thought in Action: The Bhagavad Gita and Modern India* (Cambridge: Cambridge University Press, 2013).

255 **a violation of *swadeshi*:** See Dixon, "Of Many Mahatmas," 81. For Besant's "that *greater* work," see Vernon, *Star in the East*, 87.

256 **"the Mahatma of the majority":** For Tilak's remarks, see Jayawardena, *White Woman's Other*, 132. For Gandhi, "I long to belong," see Dixon, "Of Many Mahatmas," 70.

257 **"a wedding ring rather than by handcuffs":** Besant cited in Dixon, "Of Many Mahatmas," 80.

257 **"Har-har-har":** For the interview with Naujadi Pasin and other Chauri Chaura villagers, see Shahid Amin's history, *Event, Metaphor, Memory: Chauri Chaura 1922–1992* (Berkeley: University of California Press, 1995), 164. My discussion here is indebted to Amin's extensive collection of miracles attributed to Gandhi in Gorakhpur. See Shahid Amin, "Gandhi as Mahatma: Gorakhpur District, Eastern UP, 1921–2," in *Selected Subaltern Studies*, ed. Ranajit Guha and Gayatri Chakravorty Spivak (Oxford: Oxford University Press, 1988), 288–348.

259 **"the tyranny of love":** D. G. Tendulkar, *Mahatma: Life of Mohandas Karamchand Gandhi*, vol. 2 (Bombay: Times of India, 1951), 78. See also Amin, "Gandhi as Mahatma," 291; for "darshan was now demanded," 307.

259 **the loyal assistant:** Mahadev Desai, *Day-to Day with Gandhi*, vol. 3 (Varanasi: Sarva Seva Sangh Prakashan, 1968), 263–66; see also Amin, "Gandhi as Mahatma," 307–8.

259 **"What was I to do?":** Gandhi quoted in Amin, *Event, Memory, Metaphor*, 167. For "our own devilishness," see Amin, "Gandhi as Mahatma," 308.

260 **to overturn every sacrosanct hierarchy:** Amin, "Gandhi as Mahatma," 312; for "prompt disclaimers," 337.

260 **"*Blow the conch-shell of Swaraj*":** "The Great Fortune of Gorakhpur," *Swadesh*, February 6, 1921, translated in Amin, "Gandhi as Mahatma," 305.

260 **Gandhi Note:** For the alternative currency and the "drum of Swaraj," *Gyan Shakti*, April 1921, 34–5, translated in Amin, "Gandhi as Mahatma," 338–39.

261 **"*I am not God*":** A lifetime of Gandhi's writings are gathered in the hundred-volume series *Collected Works of Mahatma Gandhi* (New Delhi: Publications Division, Government of India, 1956–1994) (hereafter *CWMG*). For his denials of divinity, see "One Year's Time-Limit," *Navjivan*, December 11, 1921, *CWMG*, 21:559; "Bihar and Untouchability," *Harijan*, February 2, 1934, *CWMG*, 63:82; speech at Mill Hand's meeting, Ahmedabad, June 29, 1934, *CWMG*, 64:105; "Speech after Prayer

Meeting," *Amrita Bazar Partika*, December 3, 1945, *CWMG*, 88:413; "Letter to G. D. Birla," February 15, 1947, *CWMG*, 86:466.

261    **"Bullets have turned into water"**: Amin, *Event, Metaphor, Memory*, 15–17.

262    **"national sin"**: Gandhi, "The Crime of Chauri Chaura," editorial for *Young India*, February 6, 1922, in *Speeches and Writings of M. K. Gandhi* (Madras: G. A. Natesan, 1922), 679–88.

263    **"tempting violence"**: Faisal Devji, *The Impossible Indian: Gandhi and the Temptation of Violence* (London: Hurst, 2012), 4–8; for "the death of non-violence," 98.

263    **"'Mahatma' stinks in my nostrils"**: Gandhi, "Speech at Excelsior Theatre, Bombay," August 31, 1924, *CWMG*, 25:56.

263    **"I shall be bald"**: Nethercot, *Last Four Lives*, 402.

263    **"This striving striving"**: Krishnamurti to Lady Emily Lutyens, in a March 1922 letter written on an interminable sea voyage to meet Leadbeater in Sydney, in Lutyens, *Awakening*, 146; for "how I abhor the whole thing," 147.

263    **profane love:** For Krishnamurti's crush on Helen Knothe, see Vernon, *Star in the East*, 103–5.

264    **soft drinks for the gods:** Vernon, *Star in the East*, 113–14.

264    **The symptoms:** See the testimonies of Nityananda and Krishnamurti written for Leadbeater and Besant, reproduced in Lutyens, *Awakening*, 162–85; see also Vernon, *Star in the East*, 116–32. For a detailed narration of the Process and its relation to *kundalini* energy, see also Jayakar, *J. Krishnamurti*, 48–59. In the middle of his excruciating ordeal, Krishna took a trip to Hollywood to see a film of the life of Christ—the tickets had been bought long ago and he hadn't wanted to ruin the plans.

265    **"screams, snippets"**: Vernon, *Star in the East*, 124.

265    **"I am God"**: Jiddu Krishnamurti, *The Path* (Melbourne: Star of the East, 1924). For "We are sorry," see Lutyens, *Awakening*, 203.

265    **"Sorrow is wonderful"**: Cited in Vernon, *Star in the East*, 153.

266    **his voice swerved:** Recounted by Balfour-Clarke, *Boyhood*, 38–39; see also Nethercot, *Last Four Lives*, 373.

266    **"The coming has begun"**: Lutyens, *Awakening*, 242–43. For the creation of the World Religion and its myriad houses of worship, see Nethercot, *Last Four Lives*, 366. For "The Divine Spirit has descended," see Besant's statement to the AP, January 14, 1927, in Lutyens, *Awakening*, 259. Amid the fervor around the Coming, Krishnamurti and Besant took a much-publicized trip to New York City, passing through Ellis Island, where Immigration and Customs announced they would need to examine him and his luggage like any other mortal. "Krishnamurti Due with Besant Today," *New York Times*, August 25, 1926.

266    **"Krishnamurti . . . no longer exists"**: Quoted in Vernon, *Star in the East*, 166; for "I urge you to escape," 177.

267    **"a blending of the consciousness"**: Cited in Nethercot, *Last Four Lives*, 390; for the Dark Brotherhood, 383. See also Besant's pamphlet *The Work of the Ruler and the Teacher* (Adyar: Theosophical, 1930), 16.

267    **the World Mother:** For Besant's failed initiative, see Vernon, *Star in the East*, 174–75; Lutyens, *Awakening*, 276–77; Nethercot, *Last Four Lives*, 402–6; for Rukmini's "absence of . . . personality," 403.

267    **"The Coming has gone wrong":** Tillett, *Elder Brother*, 240.

268    **"Truth is a pathless land":** Reprinted in Jiddu Krishnamurti, *Total Freedom: The Essential Krishnamurti* (San Francisco: HarperSanFrancisco, 1996), 1–7.

269    **Annie Besant's pyre:** Nethercot, *Last Four Lives*, 452–55; Vernon, *Star in the East*, 194–96.

269    **he could remember nothing at all:** See appendix.


## 10. MYTHOPOLITICS

272    **"German Baba":** For the Oraon messianic movement, see Lt. Col. K. R. Kirtikar's 1916 report "The German Kaiser William in the Incantations of the Oraons of Chota Nagpur," *Anthropological Papers* (Bombay: British India Press, 1918), 234–47. For the hymn, composed by the Oraon leader Letho, see Ranajit Das Gupta, "Oraon Labour Agitation: Duars in Jalpaiguri District, 1915–1916," *Economic and Political Weekly* 24, no. 39 (September 30, 1989): 2197–2202. See also Heike Liebau, "*Kaiser kī jay* (Long Live the Kaiser): Perceptions of World War I and the Socio-Religious Movement among the Oraons in Chota Nagpur 1914–1916," in *The World in World Wars: Experiences, Perceptions and Perspectives from Africa and Asia*, ed. Heike Liebau et al. (Leiden: Brill, 2010), 251–76.

272    **"unhindered access . . . for the 'Spirit'":** Stephen Fuchs, *Godmen on the Warpath: A Study of Messianic Movements in India* (New Delhi: Munshiram Manoharlal, 1992), 48.

273    **"exploits in Belgium":** Quoted in Kirtikar, "German Kaiser William," 245.

273    **Hitler as avatar:** See Nicholas Goodrick-Clarke's study *Hitler's Priestess: Savitri Devi, the Hindu-Aryan Myth, and Neo-Nazism* (New York: New York University Press, 1998); for Hitler's racist views on Indians, 65–66; for Devi's astral travels to Göring, 128; her Hitler pilgrimage, 150. For Savitri Devi's own writings on the divine Adolf, see *The Lightning and the Sun* (Calcutta: Temple Press, 1958).

274    **Subhas Chandra Bose:** Stories began to circulate that Bose was not dead, that he would return as Kalki, the final avatar, commanding an army of men to free India from oppression and hardship. See Leonard A. Gordon, *Brothers against the Raj: A Biography of Indian Nationalists Sarat and Subhas Chandra Bose* (New York: Columbia University Press, 1990), 604–10; Goodrick-Clarke, *Hitler's Priestess*, 90.

274    **a transfiguration of the sacred:** Carl Schmitt, *Political Theology*, trans. George Schwab (Chicago: University of Chicago Press, 2006), 36; for "every myth is polytheistic," see Schmitt, *Political Theology* II, trans. Michael Hoelzl and Graham Ward (Cambridge: Polity, 2008), 23.

275    **a sleight of hand:** Milinda Banerjee, *The Mortal God: Imagining the Sovereign in Colonial India* (Cambridge: Cambridge University Press, 2018), 174.

276    **cosmic democracy:** B. G. Tilak, *Bal Gangadhar Tilak: His Writings and Speeches*

(Madras: Ganesh, 1918), 74–76, 80; Banerjee, *The Mortal God*, 86–87, 181. For the anatomy of the Sacred Man, see Bhudev Mukhopadhyay, "India's History Revealed in a Dream (1875)," trans. Sujit Mukherjee, *Indian Economic and Social History Review* 32, no. 2 (1995): 226; see also Banerjee, *The Mortal God*, 18–19.

277   **"Nationalism is a religion":** For Sri Aurobindo Ghose's 1908 remarks, see Rachel Fell McDermott et al., eds., *Sources of Indian Traditions: Modern India, Pakistan, and Bangladesh*, vol. 2 (New York: Columbia University Press, 2014), 281.

278   **"Mohammedan Hindus":** See Ashis Nandy, "The Politics of Secularism and the Recovery of Religious Tolerance," *Alternatives: Global, Local, Political* 13, no. 2 (1988): 177–94.

278   **acrid with powdered bleach:** See the account of Gandhi's grandniece and companion, Manubehn Gandhi, *The Miracle of Calcutta*, trans. Gopalrao Kulkarni (Ahmedabad: Navajivan, 1959). On Gandhi and Partition, see also Faisal Devji, *The Impossible Indian: Gandhi and the Temptation of Violence* (London: Hurst, 2012), 151–91.

279   **conundrum of sovereignty:** David Gilmartin, "Towards a Global History of Voting: Sovereignty, the Diffusion of Ideas, and the Enchanted Individual," *Religions* 3, no. 2 (2012): 407–23.

279   **A deep pit:** See Nathuram Godse's court testimony, "Why I Killed Gandhi," May 5, 1949, in *The Great Speeches of Modern India*, ed. Rudrangshu Mukherjee (New Delhi: Random House India, 2011).

280   ***Gandhiji's Journey to Heaven:*** For the works of Narottam Narayan Sharma and others, see Christopher Pinney, *'Photos of the Gods': The Printed Image and Political Struggle in India* (London: Reaktion Books, 2004). Pinney divides images produced in the aftermath of Gandhi's assassination into "apotheosis" versus "avatar cycle" styles: "The former depict Gandhi ascending to heaven in the manner of eighteenth-century European Imperial heroes, and the latter present a central atemporal form around which a biography in the form of 'descents' appears," often featuring Vishnu's earlier animal incarnations.

280   **a military funeral:** See Yasmin Khan, "Performing Peace: Gandhi's Assassination as a Critical Moment in the Consolidation of the Nehruvian State," *Modern Asian Studies* 45, no. 1 (2011): 57–80; "trodden rose petals," in *Pioneer*, February 2, 1948, cited in Khan, "Performing Peace," 69; telegram to Nehru, *Pioneer*, February 9, 1948, in Khan, "Performing Peace," 70.

281   **Gandhi's urn:** For the railway journey and the division of ashes, see Khan, "Performing Peace," 72–77.

282   **"blind belief":** Jawaharlal Nehru, *An Autobiography* (New Delhi: Jawaharlal Memorial Fund, 1982), 374–75. See also Sunil Khilnani, "Nehru's Faith," *Economic and Political Weekly* 37, no. 48 (2002): 4793–99.

282   **a modernist humanism:** For Krishnamurti's meetings with Nehru, see Pupul Jayakar, *J. Krishnamurti: A Biography* (New Delhi: Penguin India, 2003), 126–28; Roland Vernon, *Star in the East: Krishnamurti, The Invention of a Messiah* (Boulder, CO: Sentient Publications, 2000), 219.

283    **"holocaust of British statues":** On the falling idols of Nikalsain and others, see
       Michael Silvestri, *Ireland and India: Nationalism, Empire and Memory* (London: Pal-
       grave Macmillan, 2009), 134–36; Manimugdha S. Sharma, "What Statue-Topplers
       around the World Can Learn from India," *Times of India*, September 3, 2017.

283    **"Is that not strange?":** For Nehru's 1957 speech, see *Selected Works of Jawaharlal
       Nehru*, vol. 38 (New Delhi: Jawaharlal Nehru Memorial Fund, 2006), 3–15.

285    **ensnared in the godhead:** For the deification of Nehru, see "The Nehru Cult:
       Letter to the Editor from K. G. Dhru, Ahmedabad," *Times of India*, November
       28, 1958; "Worship of Mr. Nehru: 'Protest' to Bombay," *Times of India*, August 8,
       1959; Rafiq Zakaria, "Basic Right," *Times of India*, August 16, 1959.

285    **"the glow of his presence":** Y. B. Chavan, "The Unaging Youth," in *A Study of
       Nehru*, ed. Rafiq Zakaria (Bombay: Times of India Press, 1959), 203; for N. B.
       Khare's remarks, see "The Angry Aristocrat," in Zakaria, *Study of Nehru*, 221.

286    **"Chanakya":** The secret soon came out who the true author of the op-ed was. See
       "Rashtrapati" (from Sanskrit meaning "head of state"), first published in Calcutta's
       *Modern Review*, reprinted in *The Essential Writings of Jawaharlal Nehru*, ed. S. Gopal
       and Uma Iyengar, vol. 2 (New Delhi: Oxford University Press, 2003), 643–46.

286    **"Nehru Brilliantine":** For Nehru's off-brand beauty products and epithets,
       see Alex von Tunzelmann, *Indian Summer: The Secret History of the End of an
       Empire* (London: Simon and Schuster, 2008), 104.

288    **"Let me be human!":** Fathi Radwan, *Ilah raghm anfih*, translated by Pierre Cachia
       as "A God in Spite of Himself," *Journal of Arabic Literature* 5 (1974): 108–26.

289    **"all of you are Gamal Abdel Nasser":** On Nasser's theatrics, see Margaret Litvin,
       *Hamlet's Arab Journey: Shakespeare's Prince and Nasser's Ghost* (Princeton, NJ:
       Princeton University Press, 2011), 40.

289    **chief propagandist:** On Fathi Radwan's politics, see James P. Jankowski, *Egypt's
       Young Rebels: "Young Egypt," 1933–1952* (Stanford, CA: Hoover Institution
       Press, 1975). For an interview with Radwan about the play, see Fu'ad Dawwarah,
       *'Asharat Udaba' Yatahaddathun* [*Interviews with Ten Leading Writers*] (Cairo:
       Dar al-Hilal, 1965), 257. See also Radwan's memoir *72 Shahran Ma'a 'Abd al-
       Nasir* [*Seventy-Two Months with Nasser*] (Cairo: Dar al-Huriya, 1985).

290    **"VISHNU REBORN IN PRESIDENT":** For the deification of Eisenhower, see
       press coverage on December 10, 1959, in the *Los Angeles Times*; "Ike Hailed as
       Hindu-God Reincarnation," in the *Washington Post*; "President Called Hindu God
       Reborn: Villagers Go Miles to View 'Reincarnation' Who Has Given Them Wheat,"
       in the *New York Times*; "Ike Acclaimed as Indian God Vishnu Reborn," in the *Chi-
       cago Daily Tribune*; "Visit Moves Emotions: Ike Held Reincarnation of Hindu's God,
       Vishnu," in the *Spokesman-Review*; and "President Eisenhower as a Protector," in
       the *Pittsburgh Press*, December 13, 1959. For archival footage of Eisenhower on the
       Delhi tarmac, see https://www.youtube.com/watch?v=rmDg6BE8AYE.

294    **"hungry for God":** On Eisenhower and religion in American public life, see
       William I. Hitchcock, *The Age of Eisenhower: America and the World in the
       1950s* (New York: Simon and Schuster, 2018).

295    **the apotheosis of Narendra Modi:** Joanna Sugden, "'Modi Temple' Appalls
       Prime Minister Modi," *Wall Street Journal*, February 12, 2015; Shelly Walia,
       "Narendra Modi Has Been Elevated to the Status of a God—But He Is Not
       Pleased," *Quartz India*, February 12, 2015; "PM Modi Shocked over Temple
       Built in His Name in Gujarat," *Times of India*, February 12, 2015; Helen Nian-
       ias, "Indian Prime Minister Modi 'Appalled' by 'Shocking' Statue Built to Wor-
       ship Him," *Independent*, February 12, 2015; Kapil Dixit, "PM Modi's Statue
       Adorns Temple in UP's Kaushambi," *Times of India*, February 13, 2015. By some
       accounts, Modi's godhood was penance for the ostentatious pinstriped suit he
       wore featuring his own name, embroidered in tiny letters over and over again,
       for the occasion of Barack Obama's state visit.

296    **temple to *NaMo*:** Amita Verma, "Now, a Temple for Narendra Modi," *Deccan
       Chronicle*, January 29, 2014.

296    **a paean to the far-right god:** "After Har Har Modi Chant, It's Ya Modi
       Sarvabhuteshu in Varanasi," *Indian Express*, March 29, 2014; Swati Parashar, "Of
       Gods and Politicians," *Asian Currents* (June 2014).

297    **avatar in Palm Beach:** For Bussa Krishna and the deification of Trump, see
       Srinivasa Rao Apparasu, "Telangana Man Worships Photo of Donald Trump
       Every Day," *Hindustan Times*, June 21, 2018; Brendan Cole, "Trump Is Wor-
       shipped as a God by This Man—And He Is Not Even a Republican," *Newsweek*,
       June 27, 2018; video segment on 9 News Australia, "Indian Man Worships US
       President Donald Trump as a God," June 27, 2018. Another version of the reli-
       gion's origins holds that it began after Trump appeared to Krishna in a dream,
       and correctly prophesied that India would win the national cricket match
       against Pakistan the following day.

299    **"Life is not worth living":** Nandy, "Politics of Secularism," 183–85.

299    **"We need a myth":** Cited in David Lawrence, "Hindu Mysticism and the Alt-
       Right," Hope Not Hate, March 27, 2018, https://www.hopenothate.org.uk/2018
       /03/27/hindu-mysticism-alt-right/. For Savitri Devi in American white suprem-
       acist thought, see Mattias Gardell, *Gods of the Blood: The Pagan Revival and
       White Separatism* (Durham, NC: Duke University Press, 2003), 183–86.

299    **hunger fast:** For Krishna's death, see Shalini Venugopal Bhagat and Mike Ives,
       "He Built a Trump Statue and Worshiped It. Then He Collapsed," *New York
       Times*, October 14, 2020.

300    **"We're an empire now":** Quoted in Ron Suskind, "Faith, Certainty and the
       Presidency of George W. Bush," *New York Times Magazine*, October 17, 2004.

300    **"I feel cleansed, OK?":** "Trump Makes Fun of Communion," uploaded on July
       20, 2015, YouTube video, https://www.youtube.com/watch?v=7sWzJZMTNd4;
       Steve Benen, "Trump's Religious Talk Causes Unease among Social
       Conservatives," MSNBC, July 21, 2015; Dan Friedman, "Trump Touts 'Great
       Relationship with God,'" *Washington Examiner*, January 17, 2016.

300    **known to eat dirt:** *Bhagavata Purana* 10.8.21–45, trans. by Wendy Doniger in
       *Hindu Myths* (London: Penguin Classics, 1975), 220–21.

## PART THREE: WHITE GODS

## 11. SERPENTS

305   **"We were superior":** For Adam's own testimony of the Fall, see Marvin Meyer, ed., *The Nag Hammadi Scriptures* (San Francisco: HarperOne, 2008), 343–56. For the rabbinic commentary Genesis Rabbah, see Kristen E. Kvam, Linda S. Schearing, and Valarie H. Ziegler, eds., *Eve and Adam: Jewish, Christian, and Muslim Readings on Genesis and Gender* (Bloomington: Indiana University Press, 1999), 79.

306   **Columbus's clouds:** For the 1492 entries from November 5, December 3, 13, 18, *The Journal of Christopher Columbus (during His First Voyage, 1492-93)*, trans. and ed. Clements R. Markham (London: Hakluyt Society, 1893), 69–70, 96, 108, 114, 118.

307   **Magellan's giants:** The mythologized "Patagons" were Tehuelche hunters, who tended to be tall and wore large fur shoes. Antonio Pigafetta, *The First Voyage Round the World by Magellan*, trans. Lord Stanley of Alderley (London: Hakluyt Society, 1874); Charles Nicholl, "Conversing with Giants: Antonio Pigafetta in the New World," in *Traces Remain: Essays and Explorations* (London: Allen Lane, 2011). For Columbus's remarks, see the November 12 entry in *The Diario of Christopher Columbus's First Voyage to America, 1492-1493*, trans. Oliver Dunn and James E. Kelley Jr. (Norman: University of Oklahoma Press, 1989), 143.

308   ***Christoferens:*** Pauline Moffitt Watts, "Prophecy and Discovery: On the Spiritual Origins of Christopher Columbus's 'Enterprise of the Indies,'" *American Historical Review* 90, no. 1 (February 1985): 73–102. See also Valerie I. J. Flint, *The Imaginative Landscape of Christopher Columbus* (Princeton, NJ: Princeton University Press, 1992); Stephen Greenblatt, *Marvelous Possessions: The Wonder of the New World* (Chicago: University of Chicago Press, 1992), 51–83.

309   **the omens:** For the arrival of the conquistadors, appearing in Book XII of the *Florentine Codex*, see the parallel translations from the Spanish and Nahuatl in James Lockhart, ed. and trans., *We People Here: Nahuatl Accounts of the Conquest of Mexico* (Eugene, OR: Wipf and Stock, 2004); for the strange portents, 51–57; for Juan de Grijalva, 58–61; for the apotheosis of Cortés, 69–83.

311   **"*These men are gods!*'":** Francisco López de Gómara, *Cortés: The Life of the Conqueror by His Secretary*, ed. and trans. Lesley Byrd Simpson (Berkeley: University of California Press, 1966), 137.

311   **one-eyed giants, men with fish tails:** Diego Durán, *History of the Indies of New Spain*, trans. Doris Heyden (Norman: University of Oklahoma Press, 1994), 503–7.

312   **"I am not asleep or dreaming":** For Moctezuma's alleged welcome to Cortés, see Lockhart, *We People Here*, 116–17.

312   **a storehouse for temple statues:** "They took us to lodge in that house, because they called us Teules, and took us for such, so that we should be with the Idols or Teules which were kept there." Bernal Díaz del Castillo, *The History of the*

*Conquest of New Spain*, trans. Davíd Carrasco (Albuquerque: University of New Mexico Press, 2008), 150.

312  **bristly and vanished god:** For the apotheosis of Pizarro, see Juan de Betanzos, *Narrative of the Incas*, ed. and trans. Roland Hamilton and Dana Buchanan (Austin: University of Texas Press, 1996); for "prolixity . . . and beastliness," 11. My discussion here is indebted to Peter Gose's study *Invaders as Ancestors: On the Intercultural Making and Unmaking of Spanish Colonialism in the Andes* (Toronto: University of Toronto Press, 2008), 36–70; for a chart of all appearances of *viracocha* in sixteenth-century chronicles, 50. The "sheep" Betanzos describes the Spanish as riding would have been llamas or alpacas.

313  **sea foam:** Pedro Sarmiento de Gamboa, *The History of the Incas*, ed. and trans. Brian S. Bauer and Vania Smith (Austin: University of Texas Press, 2007), 54; for "ridiculous fable," 55.

314  **three Spaniards worshipped on the road:** Pedro de Cieza de León, *The Discovery and Conquest of Peru*, ed. and trans. Alexandra Parma Cook and Noble David Cook (Durham, NC: Duke University Press, 1998), 228.

314  **Malinche's word:** My discussion here is indebted to Camilla Townsend's study "Burying the White Gods: New Perspectives on the Conquest of Mexico," *American Historical Review* 108, no. 3 (June 2003): 659–87. See also Townsend, *Malintzin's Choices: An Indian Woman in the Conquest of Mexico* (Albuquerque: University of New Mexico Press, 2006), 49–50. For Durán, *History of the Indies*, 499–500.

315  **teotl:** On the Nahuatl word and missionary translations of the sacred, see Louise M. Burkhart's study *The Slippery Earth: Nahua-Christian Moral Dialogue in Sixteenth-Century Mexico* (Tucson: University of Arizona Press, 1989). For "fine, fancy, large," see Matthew Restall, *Seven Myths of the Spanish Conquest* (Oxford: Oxford University Press, 2003), 112.

315  **disheveled Motolinía:** Fray Toribio de Motolinía, *Motolinia's History of the Indians of New Spain*, trans. Francis Borgia Steck (Washington, DC: Academy of American Franciscan History, 1951), 223. To some villagers, Motolinía noted, the Spanish horsemen were centaurs: "Some imagined the man and the horse to be all one person," he wrote.

315  **Felipillo:** See Olivia Harris, "'The Coming of the White People': Reflections on the Mythologisation of History in Latin America," *Bulletin of Latin American Research* 14, no. 1 (1995): 9–24; Gose, *Invaders as Ancestors*, 56–62.

316  **"came from the sky":** On how incomprehensible things were often referred to as having "sky origins" in indigenous American languages, see Rolena Adorno, "The Negotiation of Fear in Cabeza de Vaca's *Naufragios*," *Representations*, no. 33 (Winter 1991): 163–99. The explorer Cabeza de Vaca wrote in 1542, "Among all these peoples, it was held for very certain that we came from the sky, because about all the things that they do not understand or have information regarding their origins, they say that such phenomena come from the sky" (183). For the Taíno, Fray Ramón Pané, who traveled on Columbus's second voyage, deter-

mined that "from the sky" "had no supernatural connotation but a geographical one: the Taínos located the sites of the before-life and the after-life on their own landmass," Adorno writes, 197n. See also William F. Keegan, *Taíno Indian Myth and Practice: The Arrival of the Stranger King* (Gainesville: University Press of Florida, 2007), 44–46.

316 **"to build a New Jerusalem":** Jacques Lafaye, *Quetzalcóatl and Guadalupe: The Formation of Mexican National Consciousness, 1531–1813*, trans. Benjamin Keen (Chicago: University of Chicago Press, 1976), 304.

316 **a reenactment of Saint Paul:** José de Acosta, *Natural and Moral History of the Indies*, ed. Jane E. Mangan (Durham, NC: Duke University Press, 2002), 366; see also Gose, *Invaders as Ancestors*, 71.

317 **Bernal Díaz del Castillo:** On how he might not have participated in the conquest, see Susan D. Gillespie, *The Aztec Kings: The Construction of Rulership in Mexican History* (Tucson: University of Arizona Press, 1989), 182.

317 **Cortés's letters:** As translated by Anthony Pagden in *Hernan Cortes: Letters from Mexico* (New Haven, CT: Yale University Press, 1986), 85–86, 467–69. See also J. H. Elliott, "The Mental World of Hernán Cortés," *Transactions of the Royal Historical Society* 17 (1967): 41–58; Townsend, "Burying the White Gods," 674.

319 **constellations to insect bites:** See *The Work of Bernardino de Sahagun: Pioneer Ethnographer of Sixteenth-Century Aztec Mexico*, ed. José Jorge Klor de Alva, Henry B. Nicholson, and Eloise Quiñones Keber (Albany: State University of New York Press, 1988).

319 **celestial oddities, inauspicious bird:** On the uncanny similarity of the Aztec omens to those of classical Greece and Rome, see Felipe Fernández-Armesto, "'Aztec' Auguries and Memories of the Conquest of Mexico," *Renaissance Studies* 6, no. 3/4 (1992): 287–305.

320 **Topiltzin Quetzalcoatl:** For variants of the myth, see Gillespie, *Aztec Kings*, 185–95; for Quetzalcoatl and Thomas as "precious twins," 184. See also Davíd Carrasco, *Quetzalcoatl and the Irony of Empire: Myths and Prophecies in the Aztec Tradition* (Chicago: University of Chicago Press, 1982); for Quetzalcoatl as Christ, see John L. Phelan, *The Millennial Kingdom of the Franciscans in the New World* (Berkeley: University of California Press, 1956); for Diego Durán and "Pope Topiltzin," see Lafaye, *Quetzalcóatl and Guadalupe*, 157–60.

321 **an indestructible cross:** For the Jesuit letter from 1599, see Gose, *Invaders as Ancestors*, 79; for the 1561 Augustinian account, 74; Sarmiento de Gamboa, *History of the Incas*, 52.

321 **at stake:** On the debates over whether New World peoples were idolaters or innocents in a state of natural grace, see Gose, *Invaders as Ancestors*, 26–27, 72–73. For Sahagún on the absence of wheat, see Rebecca Earle, *The Body of the Conquistador: Food, Race and the Colonial Experience in Spanish America, 1492–1700* (Cambridge: Cambridge University Press, 2012), 149–53, 175–76.

322 **"apes to men":** For Sepúlveda's comment, see Restall, *Seven Myths*, 131; for Oviedo's remarks, 105.

323    **"human owl"**: See Burkhart, *Slippery Earth*, 40–42; Townsend, "Burying the White Gods," 671.

323    **to undeify themselves:** Motolinía, *History of the Indians*, 223.

324    **"soiled gods":** Lockhart, *We People Here*, 82; see also Herman L. Bennett, *Africans in Colonial Mexico: Absolutism, Christianity, and Afro-Creole Consciousness, 1570–1640* (Bloomington: Indiana University Press, 2003), 15–32.

324    *limpieza de sangre*: My discussion here draws on María Elena Martínez's *Genealogical Fictions: Limpieza de Sangre, Religion, and Gender in Colonial Mexico* (Stanford, CA: Stanford University Press, 2008). See also Earle, *Body of the Conquistador*, 187–216. See also Ilona Katzew and Susan Deans-Smith, eds., *Race and Classification: The Case of Mexican America* (Stanford, CA: Stanford University Press, 2009).

326    **cleanliness and filth:** On mapping Christian concepts of sin into Nahuatl, see Burkhart, *Slippery Earth*, 28–38, 87–129; for Alonso de Molina, 104; for the Nahuatl translation of Revelation 21:27, 124; for Anunciación's Nahuatl hagiographies, 71; for "I am mud," 107–8; for "shame-water," 32.

327    **human fauna:** On the racial zoology of New Spain, see Martínez, *Genealogical Fictions*, 166; see also Claudio Lomnitz-Adler, *Exits from the Labyrinth: Culture and Ideology in the Mexican National Space* (Berkeley: University of California Press, 1993), 271–74.

327    **"the notable discord":** See Ilona Katzew, *Casta Painting: Images of Race in Eighteenth-Century Mexico* (New Haven, CT: Yale University Press, 2004), 42.


## 12. ADAM BLUSHED

329    **"ravished in their minds":** Francis Drake, ed., *The World Encompassed by Sir Francis Drake* (London: Hakluyt Society, 1854), 120–31. The text, originally published in 1628, was compiled by the younger Francis Drake (the explorer's nephew) from the journals of the ship's chaplain Francis Fletcher. I have attributed first-person quotations to Fletcher here, although Drake as editor may have modified them.

330    **"tearing their breasts":** William C. H. Wood, *Elizabethan Sea-Dogs: A Chronicle of Drake and His Companions* (New Haven, CT: Yale University Press, 1918), 138–40. On the deification of Drake, see also William M. Hamlin, "Imagined Apotheoses: Drake, Harriot, and Ralegh in the Americas," *Journal of the History of Ideas* 57, no. 3 (July 1996): 405–28.

331    **"not meet to reject":** Richard Hakluyt, *Voyages of Drake and Gilbert: Select Narratives from the "Principal Navigations" of Hakluyt* (Oxford: Clarendon Press, 1909), 218.

332    **Oxford student:** Charles Fitz-Geffry, *Sir Francis Drake: His Honorable Lifes Commendation, and His Tragicall Deathes Lamentation* (Oxford: Ioseph Barnes, 1596).

333    *Bewtiful Empyre*: Sir Walter Ralegh, *The Discoverie of the Large, Rich and Bewtiful Empyre of Guiana*, ed. Neil L. Whitehead (Norman: University of Oklahoma Press, 1998); for Berrio and the prophecy, 66–67; for the spirit Wattopa, 23.

334    **Astraea, Gloriana:** Frances A. Yates, "Queen Elizabeth as Astraea," *Journal of the Warburg and Courtauld Institutes* 10 (1947): 27–82. See also Hamlin, "Imagined Apotheoses," 417–19.

334    **"*a comet to the eye of Spaine*":** From John Lane's poem "An Elegie upon the Death of the High and Renowned Princesse, Our Late Soveraigne Elizabeth" (1603).

335    **"My name hath still lived . . .":** Ralegh to his wife Bess from the Cayenne River, November 14, 1617, in *Discoverie*, 59.

335    **Walterali, Gualtero:** Line Cottegnies, "'Waterali' Goes Native: Describing First Encounters in Sir Walter Ralegh's *The Discovery of Guiana* (1596)," in *British Narratives of Exploration: Case Studies on the Self and Other*, ed. Frédéric Regard (London: Pickering and Chatto, 2014), 51–62.

336    **"an *English* Jack":** Edward Bancroft, *An Essay on the Natural History of Guiana in South America* (London: T. Becket and P. A. De Hondt, 1769), 259.

336    **borders propped up by prophecies:** *British Guiana Boundary Arbitration, Appendix to the British Case* (I:21) (London: HMSO, 1896); see Whitehead's annotations to Ralegh, *Discoverie*, 112. The prophecy was deployed again in the eighteenth century by Incan revolutionary movements. See Nicholas A. Robins, *Genocide and Millennialism in Upper Peru: The Great Rebellion of 1780–1782* (Westport, CT: Praeger, 2002), 36–40.

336    **gun owners as gods:** Thomas Harriot, *Briefe and True Report of the New Found Land of Virginia* (London, 1588); Hamlin, "Imagined Apotheoses," 411–16. See also Stephen Greenblatt, "Invisible Bullets," in *Shakespearean Negotiations: The Circulation of Social Energy in Renaissance England* (Berkeley: University of California Press, 1988), 21–65. Harriot's spelling has been modernized here.

338    **the *Half Moon*:** My discussion of Hudson is indebted to Evan Haefeli's study "On First Contact and Apotheosis: Manitou and Men in North America," *Ethnohistory* 54, no. 3 (July 2007): 407–43.

339    **an apparition, a strange fish:** Adriaen van der Donck, *Description of the New Netherlands*, trans. Jeremiah Johnson (Boston: Directors of the Old South Work, 1896), 3.

339    **"the Mannitto . . . himself was present":** John Heckewelder, *History, Manners, and Customs of the Indian Nations Who Once Inhabited Pennsylvania and the Neighbouring States* (Philadelphia: Historical Society of Pennsylvania, 1881), 72–75.

339    **"they cry out *Manittóo*":** Roger Williams, *A Key into the Language of America* (London: Gregory Dexter, 1643), 126.

340    **"*Manittowoagan*":** John Heckewelder in an 1816 letter, cited in Haefeli, "On First Contact," 420.

340    **red, white:** On Lenape color perceptions, see Haefeli, "On First Contact," 425–26; for *Shuwanakuw*, 442n71.

342    **Mannahataninik:** Haefeli, "On First Contact," 430; John Heckewelder, "The Arrival of the Dutch," in *The World Turned Upside Down: Indian Voices from Early America*, ed. Colin Calloway (Boston: Bedford Books, 1994), 37.

342    **four colors of gods:** As told to the trader Alexander Longe by a Cherokee

narrator whose name was not recorded, cited in Nancy Shoemaker, *A Strange Likeness: Becoming Red and White in Eighteenth-Century North America* (Oxford: Oxford University Press, 2004), 133–34. For Longe's original "A Small Postscript on the Ways and Maners of the Nashon of Indians Called Charikees," see *Southern Indian Studies* 21 (October 1969). Longe's spelling has been modernized here.

342 **a trinity of white, black, and red:** For the spread of white identity from South to North, see Shoemaker, *Strange Likeness*, 129–32. The Iroquois word for the invaders had the literal meaning of "hatchet-makers"; it was first translated as "Christians," and later as "white people."

343 **what hue was Adam?:** My discussion here is indebted to Colin Kidd's study *The Forging of Races: Race and Scripture in the Protestant Atlantic World, 1600–2000* (Cambridge: Cambridge University Press, 2006); for Ebenezer Sibly, 30.

343 **Blumenbach's Golgotha:** See H. F. Augstein, "From the Land of the Bible to the Caucasus and Beyond: The Shifting Ideas of the Geographical Origin of Humankind," in *Race, Science and Medicine, 1700–1960,* ed. Waltraud Ernst and Bernard Harris (London: Routledge, 1999), 6–64.

343 **Adam (*ahdam*):** Martin Delany and William Apess cited in Kidd, *Forging of Races,* 31.

343 **red clay:** Emmet Starr, *History of the Cherokee Indians and Their Legends and Folk Lore* (Oklahoma City: Warden, 1921), 23.

344 **"universal freckle":** Samuel Stanhope Smith, *An Essay on the Causes of the Variety of Complexion and Figure in the Human Species* (New Brunswick, NJ: J. Simpson, 1810), 49.

344 **"black juice":** For a discussion of William Whiston, see Kidd, *Forging of Races,* 70–72.

344 *Athenian Mercury:* Cited in Kidd, *Forging of Races,* 68–69.

344 **Cain's curse:** Marcus Garvey, *Message to the People: The Course of African Philosophy,* ed. Tony Martin (Dover, MA: Majority Press, 1986), 104.

344 **"one drop":** Albert Cleage Jr., *The Black Messiah* (Trenton, NJ: Africa World Press, 1989), 43. See also Craig R. Prentiss, "Coloring Jesus: Racial Calculus and the Search for Identity in Twentieth-Century America," *Nova Religio: The Journal of Alternative and Emergent Religions* 11, no. 3 (February 2008): 64–82.

344 **Henry McNeal Turner:** Black was, Turner noted, more primordial than white: "Chaos floated in infinite darkness or blackness . . . before God said, *Let there be light.*" From *Voice of Missions* (1898), reprinted in Paul Harvey, *Through the Storm, through the Night: A History of African American Christianity* (Lanham, MD: Rowman and Littlefield, 2011), 165–66.

345 **Pensacola, Florida:** Bernard Romans, *A Concise Natural History of East and West Florida,* ed. Kathryn E. Holland Braund (Tuscaloosa: University of Alabama Press, 1999).

345 **polygenesis:** On Isaac La Peyrère, see David N. Livingstone's study *Adam's Ancestors: Race, Religion, and the Politics of Human Origins* (Baltimore: Johns Hopkins University Press, 2008); see also Kidd, *Forging of Races,* 62–64.

346  **"Take up the Hatchet":** Cited in Shoemaker, *Strange Likeness*, 135; for the Iroquois chief's comment on justice, 136.

346  **separate creations:** For the Native American embrace of the idea, see Gregory Evans Dowd, *A Spirited Resistance: The North American Indian Struggle for Unity, 1745–1815* (Baltimore: Johns Hopkins University Press, 1992), 30; for the emetic tea, 33.

346  **a people who killed their god:** For the Seneca's remarks, see Dowd, *Spirited Resistance*, 42.

347  **"How could philosophers . . . ?":** Kidd, *Forging of Races*, 106–7.

347  **an unlikely ally:** John Bathurst Deane, *The Worship of the Serpent Traced throughout the World* (London: J. G. and F. Rivington, 1833); for "irrational" and "natural," 35; see also Kidd, *Forging of Races*, 130.

348  **"*Eva! Eva!*":** Matthew Bridges, *The Testimony of Profane Antiquity to the Account Given by Moses of Paradise and the Fall of Man* (London: L. B. Seeley, 1825), 86.

348  **Europe, a solar serpent:** *Ophiolatreia: An Account of the Rites and Mysteries Connected with the Origin, Rise, and Development of Serpent Worship in Various Parts of the World . . .* (self-pub., 1889), 84. The text shields its authorship likely because of its ultimate aim: "The whole forming an exposition of one of the phases of phallic, or sex worship."

348  **a perfect man:** Deane, "Concluding Remarks on the Fall of Man," in *Worship of the Serpent*, 461–75.

349  **"Feathered Serpent":** *Ophiolatreia*, 45.

349  **inquisition of snakes:** Deane, *Worship of the Serpent*, 162–70.

349  **fork-tongued creature:** Samuel A. Cartwright, "Unity of the Human Race Disproved by the Hebrew Bible," *DeBow's Review* 29, no. 2 (August 1860): 129–36; see also Kidd, *Forging of Races*, 147–50. Cartwright contended that "the tribes of negroes which make the best slaves were, before they became the slaves of the white man, the slaves of a serpent," for they worshipped a snake god, particularly in Haiti. "The serpent, in every neighborhood, governs them more absolutely and tyrannically than any white man ever governed them," Cartwright theorized.

350  **as if out of *The Tempest*:** Ariel [Buckner H. Payne], *The Negro: What Is His Ethnological Status?* (Cincinnati, 1867). See also Kidd, *Forging of Races*, 149–50; Livingstone, *Adam's Ancestors*, 192–93. See also the study by Mason Stokes, "Someone's in the Garden with Eve: Race, Religion, and the American Fall," *American Quarterly* 50, no. 4 (December 1998): 718–44.

351  **a pre-Adamite man:** Prospero [pseud.], *Caliban: A Sequel to Ariel* (New York, 1868); reprinted in Kristen E. Kvam, Linda S. Schearing, and Valarie H. Ziegler, eds., *Eve and Adam: Jewish, Christian, and Muslim Readings on Genesis and Gender* (Bloomington: Indiana University Press, 1999), 491–95.

351  **orangutan:** For Adam Clarke, see Cartwright, "Unity," 130.

351  **curse on *Nachesh*:** A Minister [D. G. Phillips], *Nachesh: What Is It? or An Answer to the Question, 'Who and What Is the Negro?' Drawn from Revelation* (1868),

excerpted in Kvam, Schearing, and Ziegler, *Eve and Adam*, 486–91; see also Kidd, *Forging of Races*, 150.

351   **"Does the adder speak . . . ?":** A. Hoyle Lester, *The Pre-Adamite, or Who Tempted Eve?* (Philadelphia: J. B. Lippincott, 1875), 21–26; Stokes, "Someone's in the Garden," 724–26.

352   **the serpent a woman:** Charles Carroll, *The Negro a Beast, or, In the Image of God* (St. Louis, MO: American Book and Bible House, 1900); Carroll, *The Tempter of Eve—or—The Criminality of Man's Social, Political, and Religious Equality with the Negro, and the Amalgamation to Which These Crimes Inevitably Lead* (Marietta, GA: The Thunderbolt, n.d.), 404–6. See also Stokes, "Someone's in the Garden," 728; for the suggestion that the black temptress villainized Ida B. Wells, 731–32.

353   **"the organ of veneration":** John Wilson, *Lectures on Our Israelitish Origin* (London: James Nisbet, 1876), 125; Wilson, *Phrenology Consistent with Reason and Revelation* (Dublin: R. D. Webb, 1836); Kidd, *Forging of Races*, 206–8.

353   **"bogs and swamps of Fetichism":** J. P. Lesley, *Man's Origin and Destiny Sketched from the Platform of the Sciences* (London: J. B. Lippincott, 1868), 295.

353   **Carroll weighed brains:** Carroll, *Negro a Beast*, 47–49.

353   **a deeper reality, that of race:** Kidd, *Forging of Races*, 171–72.

353   **"the real Theogony":** Max Müller, *Chips from a German Workshop*, vol. 2 (New York: Charles Scribner, 1869), 76. The philologist later distanced himself from a racialist reading of *Aryan*, seeing it as a purely linguistic category, yet his scholarship continued to be used by others to further reify Aryan as a race.

354   **"flexibility of the skull":** Émile Burnouf, *The Science of Religions*, cited in Kidd, *Forging of Races*, 179; see also Masuzawa's discussion of Burnouf in *The Invention of World Religions: Or, How European Universalism Was Preserved in the Language of Pluralism* (Chicago: University of Chicago Press, 2005), 250–54.

355   **"hulls gleaming":** Pierre Honoré, *In Quest of the White God*, trans. Oliver Coburn and Ursula Lehrburger (London: Hutchinson, 1963), 15.

355   **"I forgot my pain":** Ella Rose Tucker-Mast's report on *In Quest of the White God*, archived at https://swift.christogenea.org/articles/erm-quest-white -god; see also "Autobiography of Ella Rose Tucker-Mast," Tape 78, at https:// covenantpeoplesministry.org/forum/entry.php?1328-ERM-Alexander-Of -Macedon&goto=prev.

355   **"There is coming a day":** From Wesley Swift's radio sermon "Amazing Grace to a Race," May 12, 1963, archived at https://swift.christogenea.org/articles /amazing-grace-race-5-12-63; for "This race of YAHWEH," see "The Racial River of God," February 24, 1963, at https://swift.christogenea.org/articles/racial -river-god-2-24-63. On Wesley Swift and Richard Girnt Butler, see also Douglas E. Cowan, "Theologizing Race: The Construction of 'Christian Identity,'" in *Religion and the Creation of Race and Ethnicity*, ed. Craig R. Prentiss (New York: New York University Press, 2003), 112–23.

356   **same white celestials:** See L. Taylor Hansen, *He Walked the Americas* (Amherst,

WI: Amherst Press, 1963); Constance Irwin, *Fair Gods and Stone Faces* (London: St. Martin's Press, 1963); Robert Marx, *In Quest of the Great White Gods* (New York: Crown, 1992); Graham Hancock, *Fingerprints of the Gods* (London: William Heinemann, 1995); Terry J. O'Brien, *Fair Gods and Feathered Serpents: A Search for Ancient America's Bearded White God* (Horizon Pub & Dist Inc., 1997).

357    **Stormfront:** For Aryan7314, https://www.stormfront.org/forum/t1258837/; "BLESS THE WHITE GODS" at https://www.stormfront.org/forum/t1262410–2; for the godhood of Haile Selassie, https://www.stormfront.org/forum/t15126/.

357    **"*I am completely racially aware*":** Dylann Roof's manifesto of June 17, 2015, posted at www.lastrhodesian.com (site discontinued).

## 13. HOW TO KILL A GOD

359    **"Wherever he goes . . .":** Gananath Obeyesekere, *The Apotheosis of Captain Cook: European Mythmaking in the Pacific* (Princeton, NJ: Princeton University Press, 1992), 12; for "almost in a loving fashion," 26.

360    **"Good-looking gods they were!":** S. M. Kamakau, *The Ruling Chiefs of Hawaii* (Honolulu: Kamehameha Schools Press, 1961), 99; for the 'o'o bird, 96. For Cook's ecstatic welcome in Kealakekua Bay, see Marshall Sahlins, *How "Natives" Think: About Captain Cook, for Example* (Chicago: University of Chicago Press, 1995), 47–50.

360    **"skin is loose and folding":** Sheldon Dibble, *A History of the Sandwich Islands* (Honolulu: Thos. G. Thrum, 1909), 22–23; see also Obeyesekere, *Apotheosis*, 172.

360    **a creation myth:** As translated by Martha Warren Beckwith in *The Kumulipo: A Hawaiian Creation Chant* (Honolulu: University of Hawai'i Press, 1972), 97–98.

361    **the Makahiki:** On the extraordinary coincidence of myth and action, see Sahlins, *How "Natives" Think*, 21–24; as well as Sahlins, *Historical Metaphors and Mythical Realities: Structure in the Early History of the Sandwich Islands Kingdom* (Ann Arbor: University of Michigan Press, 1981); Sahlins, *Islands of History* (Chicago: University of Chicago Press, 1985); Lilikalā Kame'eleihiwa, review of Obeyesekere's *Apotheosis* in *Pacific Studies Journal* 17, no. 2 (June 1994): 111–17. For Obeyesekere's counterargument on the Makahiki, see *Apotheosis*, 53–54, 95–97.

361    **"partaking something of divinity":** David Samwell, *A Narrative of the Death of Captain James Cook* (London: G. G. J. and J. Robinson, 1786), cited in Sahlins, *How "Natives" Think*, 58.

361    **"white feathers":** Heinrich Zimmermann's *Reise um die Welt, mit Captain Cook* (1781), cited in Sahlins, *How "Natives" Think*, 18.

362    **"white from the moon":** *John Ledyard's Journal of Captain Cook's Last Voyage*, ed. James Kenneth Munford (Corvallis: Oregon State University Press, 1963), 113; see also Obeyesekere, *Apotheosis*, 273; Sahlins, *How "Natives" Think*, 173.

362    **"*Your bodies, O Lono*":** Valerio Valeri, *Kingship and Sacrifice: Ritual and Society in Ancient Hawaii* (Chicago: University of Chicago Press, 1985), 208.

362 **another manifestation of Himself:** For the shipwrecking storm, see Sahlins, *How "Natives" Think*, 78.

363 **"hurt our Vanity":** From the journals of Lt. James King, cited in Glyn Williams, *The Death of Captain Cook: A Hero Made and Unmade* (Cambridge, MA: Harvard University Press, 2009), 31. For John Ledyard's observations, see *Ledyard's Journal*, 141; Sahlins, *How "Natives" Think*, 80.

363 **"the climactic ritual battle":** Sahlins, *How "Natives" Think*, 30–33, 82. For "historical metaphor of a mythical reality," see Sahlins, *Islands of History*, 105–6; "neither was it an accident," Sahlins, *Historical Metaphors and Mythical Realities*, 24. On the *kali'i*, see also Obeyesekere, *Apotheosis*, 53.

364 **"The final homage":** Sahlins, *How "Natives" Think*, 84; for Lt. James Burney's observation, 83. For "rushed upon the fallen god," see Sahlins, *Historical Metaphors*, 24. For an intricate debate on Cook's dismemberment, see Obeyesekere, *Apotheosis*, 89–91; Sahlins, *How "Natives" Think*, 144–45. According to scholar Greg Dening, history repeated itself thirteen years later, when a young astronomer, William Gooch, was taken to be a god in Oahu and then bludgeoned to death. See Greg Dening, *The Death of William Gooch: A History's Anthropology* (Honolulu: University of Hawai'i Press, 1995).

364 **"a general silence ensued":** Account of Midshipman George Gilbert, quoted in Williams, *Death of Cook*, 41.

364 **"a most extraordinary question":** For the alleged Hawaiian expressions of remorse, see Sahlins, *How "Natives" Think*, 85–86; for "The god Cook is not dead," 18; for Dimsdell's meeting with Pihore, 95; for Edward Bell's remarks, 87–88; see also Obeyesekere, *Apotheosis*, 151, 202.

365 **"sent by the gods to civilize":** William Mariner as edited by John Martin in *An Account of the Natives of the Tonga Islands*, vol. 2 (London: John Murray, 1818), 66–67; Sahlins, *How "Natives" Think*, 97.

365 **"national stigma":** Robert Dampier, *To the Sandwich Islands on H.M.S. Blonde* (Honolulu: University of Hawai'i Press, 1971), 67; Williams, *Death of Cook*, 106–7. For James Colnett, see Sahlins, *How "Natives" Think*, 92; Obeyesekere, *Apotheosis*, 140–41.

366 **"How vain":** Hiram Bingham, *A Residence of Twenty-One Years in the Sandwich Islands* (New York: Sherman Converse, 1848), 35, 56.

366 **"waiting for . . . Jehovah":** Rufus Anderson, *A Heathen Nation Evangelized: History of the Mission . . . to the Sandwich Islands* (Boston: Congregational Publishing Board, 1884), 19.

367 **a broom dipped in water:** On early missionary activities in Hawaii and the sugar cartel, see Bruce Cumings, *Dominion from Sea to Sea: Pacific Ascendancy and American Power* (New Haven, CT: Yale University Press, 2009).

367 **"They had sunk very low":** Sheldon Dibble, *Ka Mooolelo Hawaii: The History of Hawaii* (Honolulu: University of Hawai'i Press, 2005); Obeyesekere, *Apotheosis*, 159–60; Williams, *Death of Cook*, 143–44.

367 **"The world is to be Christianized":** Josiah Strong, *Our Country: Its Possible*

*Future and Its Present Crisis* (New York: American Home Missionary Society, 1885), 14.

368 **unconstitutional:** On the 1893 American coup and Hawaiian resistance, see Noenoe K. Silva, *Aloha Betrayed: Native Hawaiian Resistance to American Colonialism* (Durham, NC: Duke University Press, 2004).

368 **"to subvert the supreme law":** Remarks of Congressman Thomas H. Ball of Texas in the House of Representatives, June 15, 1898.

368 **"No darker cloud":** Queen Lili'uokalani, cited in Silva, *Aloha Betrayed*, 164; on her translation of the *Kumulipo* ("Source of Deep Darkness"), see 89–104; on *ao* and *po*, 99.

369 **cannibal cooking pot:** On racist depictions of the Hawaiian queen, see Silva, *Aloha Betrayed*, 173–78; on censorship of news, 181.

369 **1993 march:** See Lilikalā Kame'eleihiwa, "The Hawaiian Sovereignty Movement: An Update from Honolulu (January–August 1993)," *Journal of Pacific History* 28, no. 3 (1993): 63–72.

370 **"immortal shall live!":** On the play *Omai*, see Obeyesekere, *Apotheosis*, 129–30; Williams, *Death of Cook*, 79–80.

370 **slaying Cook onstage:** On the theatrical afterlives of Cook, see Ruth Scobie, "The Many Deaths of Captain Cook: A Study in Metropolitan Mass Culture, 1780–1810" (PhD diss., University of York, 2013); for the *Grand-Serious-Pantomimic Ballet*, 224–26; "Lord, how you'll look," *Whitehall Evening Post*, June 20, 1789.

371 **"Bravo!":** William Thomas Parke's account of how a real sword was negligently substituted for a prop in *Musical Memoirs*, vol. 1 (London: H. Colburn and R. Bentley, 1830), 115. Others say it happened at a different chaotic pantomime; see Scobie, "Many Deaths," 227. On Cook tattoos and fashions, 13; on Barnum's club, 274.

371 **"clothed in light":** Adelbert von Chamisso in *A Voyage around the World*, in Williams, *Death of Cook*, 97. For Robert Louis Stevenson's encounter, *In the South Seas* (London: Chatto and Windus, 1900), 311; Williams, *Death of Cook*, 129. For Obeyesekere's remarks, *Apotheosis*, 3. Anna Seward, in her elegy to Cook, exclaimed, "His bones now whiten an accursed shore!"

372 **the word *Lono*:** Captain James King, *A Voyage to the Pacific Ocean*, vol. 3 (London: W. and A. Strahan, 1784), 5n; Obeyesekere, *Apotheosis*, 94.

372 **heavily doctored:** On the editorial transformations of Samuel Kamakau's *Mo'olelo*, see Silva, *Aloha Betrayed*, 16–23. On Kamakau, see also Obeyesekere, *Apotheosis*, 166.

373 **"The best part of Cook's visit . . .":** Kame'eleihiwa, review of Obeyesekere's *Apotheosis*, 111–18.

373 **"same sad predicament":** Sir James George Frazer, "The Killing of the Divine King," in *The Golden Bough*, vol. 2 (London: Macmillan, 1922), 264–82.

374 **earliest attempt at deicide:** My description of the pageant draws on Max Harris, *Aztecs, Moors, and Christians: Festivals of Reconquest in Mexico and Spain* (Austin: University of Texas Press, 2000), 132–47.

376    **different heavens:** On the Aztec afterlife, and the friars' attempts to strike fear
       of hell, see Louise M. Burkhart, *The Slippery Earth: Nahua-Christian Moral Dia-
       logue in Sixteenth-Century Mexico* (Tucson: University of Arizona Press, 1989),
       50–54.


## LIBERATION (LAST RITES)

378    **"blasphemous question":** William R. Jones, *Is God a White Racist? A Preamble
       to Black Theology* (Boston: Beacon Press, 1997); and his earlier article, "The-
       odicy and Methodology in Black Theology: A Critique of Washington, Cone
       and Cleage," *Harvard Theological Review* 64, no. 4 (October 1971): 541–57.
       On Jones, see also Colin Kidd, *The Forging of Races: Race and Scripture in the
       Protestant Atlantic World, 1600–2000* (Cambridge: Cambridge University Press,
       2006), 262.

379    **"impossible for us to kneel":** Albert B. Cleage, *The Black Messiah* (New York:
       Sheed and Ward, 1968), 47.

380    **"bruising work":** Joseph R. Washington, *The Politics of God* (Boston: Beacon
       Press, 1969), 157.

380    **liberation "is not an afterthought":** James H. Cone, *A Black Theology of Lib-
       eration* (New York: Orbis Books, 2016), 64; for "then God is a murderer," 27.
       On Cone, see also Lilian Calles Barger, *The World Come of Age: An Intellectual
       History of Liberation Theology* (Oxford: Oxford University Press, 2018).

382    **"this American god":** Anthea Butler, "The Zimmerman Acquittal: America's
       Racist God," *Religion Dispatches*, July 16, 2013.

382    **"the divine state":** Stephen C. Finley and Biko Mandela Gray, "God *Is* a White
       Racist: Immanent Atheism as a Religious Response to Black Lives Matter and
       State-Sanctioned Anti-Black Violence," *Journal of Africana Religions* 3, no. 4
       (2015): 443–53.

382    **reduced God to silence:** See Jack Miles on Job in *God: A Biography* (New York:
       Knopf, 1996), 308–28.

383    **the Cercle Harmonique:** My discussion here is indebted to Emily Suzanne
       Clarke's scholarship and translations of the spirit messages in *A Luminous
       Brotherhood: Afro-Creole Spiritualism in Nineteenth-Century New Orleans*
       (Chapel Hill: University of North Carolina Press, 2016). See also the study by
       Robert S. Cox, *Body and Soul: A Sympathetic History of American Spiritualism*
       (Charlottesville: University of Virginia Press, 2003); for "We have houses for
       every taste," 177; as well as Melissa Daggett, *Spiritualism in Nineteenth-Century
       New Orleans: The Life and Times of Henry Louis Rey* (Jackson: University Press
       of Mississippi, 2017).

# APPENDIX

*Nobody can understand what went through this body. Nobody. Don't anybody pretend.*

*I repeat this: nobody amongst us or the public knows what went on,* the ninety-year-old Krishnamurti spoke into a tape recorder, ten days before his death. It was to be the final recording of his voice.

*For seventy years that super energy—no—that immense intelligence, has been using this body,* he said, in a swerve from his contention that he hadn't been the vessel of any divine power, nor even remembered the whole affair. *I don't think people realize what tremendous energy and intelligence went through this body. . . . And now after seventy years it has come to an end. . . . You won't find another body like this, or that supreme intelligence operating in a body for many hundred years. You won't see it again.*

*When he goes, it goes.*

On February 17, 1986, Krishnamurti died in Ojai, California, of pancreatic cancer. But for the next generation of Theosophist thinkers, signs persisted of a supernatural mind still at work in the world. Cryptic messages kept appearing on vegetables and fruit, a Lebanese girl wept crystal shards of glass, and stars would hover conspicuously in the daylight sky. On a September day in 1995, tens of thousands of people observed that statues of Hindu gods were suddenly able to drink milk fed to them on spoons and in cups, in a portent that began at dawn at a Delhi temple and was witnessed at numerous Hindu shrines abroad. For the Scottish painter and mystic Benjamin Creme, it was clearly the hand of the Maitreya, the Supreme Being who had entered Christ, Buddha, Krishna, the Imam Mahdi, and possibly Krishnamurti, and who would return to teach humankind the way of salvation from its self-made disasters. In the decades after Krishnamurti's death, there were sightings of this Director of Religion from Perth to Paraguay, in the outskirts of Nairobi and in Rabat. In pulling off the global milk omen, skeptically acknowledged in the *Guardian* and the *New York Times*, the Maitreya was aided by the shadowy, wrinkled Masters, Koot Hoomi and Morya among them, still known to melt in and out of shrubbery in their white robes.

A student of the writings of Madame Blavatsky and Annie Besant, and the founder of the British sect Share International, the esoteric Creme offered his hundreds of followers a few details about the Maitreya's current form. The World Teacher appeared to be of Indian descent. In 1977, he had left his celestial abode in the Himalayas, his residence for thousands of years, and caught a flight from Karachi to Heathrow on a 747 jet, returning to human society *on the clouds of heaven*, as Matthew 24:29 foretold. In 2010, Creme, now in his late eighties, made the sensational announcement that the Maitreya had recently appeared on an American television show, giving millions of viewers a prime-time glimpse of the figure who is born again and again, age after age.

"I had a dream early this January," an email began, crossing the ether on Saturday, January 23, at 2:57 p.m., "and in this dream people we're whispering 'it's Maitreya it's Maitreya' and I looked over and saw a man looking just like you."

The British Indian political economist Raj Patel had been promoting his new book, *The Value of Nothing*, with appearances on *Democracy Now!*, *The Colbert Report*, and other shows. With an unblinking stare and a slight stutter, the handsome, Oxford-educated author argued for the cameras that only a profound rethinking of pricing could end inequality and global hunger. Soon after the broadcasts, the San Francisco–based economist was in a taxi when messages began to pour into his phone. There were texts from friends asking if he had ever heard of Benjamin Creme, and peculiar emails with subjects such as: "Are you the One?" It was at first "a trickle, and then a flood," Patel recalled. Across the earth, seekers were parsing Patel's Wikipedia page for theological clues. Although Creme would neither confirm nor deny the identification, web pages and videos clips began to circulate that pointed out Patel's resemblances to the Maitreya—from the size of his nose, to his devotion to social justice, and even his stutter—proof that Patel was merely trying to seem human. In their emails, the seekers spoke of how they had awaited him, dreamed of him. Patel's instinct was to ignore the missives, but then strangely excited people began showing up in person at his lectures.

Bewildered, Patel took to his blog to dispel his divinity. "It frustrates me only a little less than it might disappoint those looking for Maitreya that, in fact, I'm just an ordinary bloke," he confessed. Attempting to skewer any sacredness, Patel embedded a clip of the "He's Not the Messiah" scene from *Monty Python's Life of Brian*. But among those who had identified Patel as divine, any renunciations and denials were merely reasoned away: as proof of His holiness, marks of His humility, or signs that He was testing the faithful. In his post, Patel revealed he had indeed flown from India to

London in the year 1977, on a return trip from a family holiday, fulfilling the prophetic criteria. Hundreds of comments, as if sacrificial offerings, inundated the reluctant deity's blog. "When I look into Raj Patel's eyes I see that which Maitreya is the embodiment of: Love," one reader wrote. The adoration of the media soon followed. "Mr. Patel's journey from ordinary person to unwilling lord is a case of having the wrong résumé at the wrong moment in history," a *New York Times* article announced. *The Colbert Report*, relishing its role in the making of a god, recorded a new episode, "I Can't Believe It's Not Buddha." The *New Yorker* writer Lauren Collins visited Patel at home in Potrero Hills, where she noted the messiah's Ikea furniture and his outfit of a hoodie and jeans. Patel's apotheosis was embraced by the American Institute for Stuttering as proof that, not only is stuttering not a barrier to success, but can even bestow divine status.

"When He who is Beauty and Love and Bliss shows a little portion of Himself on earth, encased in human form, the weary eyes of men light up," Annie Besant once wrote, well acquainted with the throes of such emotions. As if by a magnetic pull, people were drawn to Patel's book promotion events, with some pilgrims even traveling across the country. When a father-son pair spent $900 to fly from Detroit for the day to be in Patel's presence, the economist was distraught. "It broke my heart," Patel told the *New York Times*. "It's just absurd in many, many ways," he went on. "The guy who says, 'Don't wait for The One' is declared The One." His deification contradicted the principles of his activism, which urged people not to rely on saviors but to find democratic strategies to build a better world, taking matters into their own hands through grassroots organizing. "One doesn't need a messiah to show how capitalism has damaged our relationships, society, ecology, body politic and future," he wrote in an op-ed for the *Guardian*, "(and anyway it isn't me)." After weeks in the limelight of an otherworld, Patel was exhausted. With a book to promote, several deadlines, and a newborn baby at home, it was clear that only a god could survive being divine.

✦   ✦   ✦

Amid the media storm, the elusive Creme found himself under pressure to comment on Raj Patel. From his home in London's Tufnell Park, the occultist traveled to Berkeley, where, in August 2010, the unwilling deity and the man called by his followers John the Baptist met face to face in a closed-door meeting. While Creme's impression of Patel was that he was "very charming, very intelligent," for his own part Patel found the curly-white-haired mystic to be "like the Red Queen in *Alice in Wonderland* who said she could believe in six impossible things before breakfast." The meeting was by all accounts cordial, included a plate of cookies, and ended with both parties mutually agreeing the apotheosis had all been a mistake.

The 2010 episode was a premature misfiring, for it is said the Maitreya will reveal himself when catastrophe has clearly overtaken the earth. He will appear amid global financial ruin and economic collapse, in an age when even the very elements of nature itself are disturbed, to overturn the tyranny of the capitalist market and the governments that have followed it with fatal devotion. Jesus will also arrive, in a separate six-hundred-year-old Syrian body, to seize control of the Roman Catholic Church and lead it to accept the Maitreya as the return of Christ. Six months before his death in 2016, Creme received a message from the Director of Religion, delivered by telepathic means:

> Remember that we are at the beginning and the end of a civilization, an epic period in the history of the world, and understand thereby that men feel the pain of change. For some it is a release into freedom. For others it is a loss of surety and calm.

*Soon humanity as a whole will awaken to My presence*, the messiah told the mystic. His identity—always, his—remains unclear.

## ACKNOWLEDGMENTS

Precisely a decade before it became a book, *Accidental Gods* took its first birth as an essay for the "Soft Power" issue of *Bidoun*. To my colleagues at *Bidoun*, especially Negar Azimi and Michael Vazquez, I owe my earliest thanks. The second incarnation, an early avatar of Prince Philip, appeared in the *London Review of Books*, with thanks to Mary-Kay Wilmers, Paul Myerscough, and Christian Lorentzen. The artists of Invernomuto, Simone Bertuzzi and Simone Trabucchi, led me deeper into the divinity of Haile Selassie with an essay commissioned for *Negus*, published by Humboldt Books in collaboration with ar/ge kunst and Museion in 2014. My thanks to Jacques Testard and Ben Eastham for publishing it as well as an essay on Nehru, Nasser, and Gandhi in *The White Review*. Material from the book also appeared in "Five Words for 'God'" for the *Serving Library Annual 2018/2019*. At the Poetry Project at St. Mark's

Church in 2018, I performed a version of "White Gods," with thanks to Mirene Arsanios, Rachel Valinsky, and Kyle Dacuyan. Many thanks to Giles Edwards for producing my radio program, "Living with Gods," for BBC Radio 4 in January 2020.

Alexander Jacobs was the first apostle to believe my strange idea could turn into a book. He guided it from the astral plane into a more plausible, publishable form with thoughtfulness and care, and Alice Whitwham deftly shepherded the book's passage into print. To Elyse Cheney, Allison Devereux, and the team at the Cheney Agency, and to Natasha Fairweather at Rogers, Coleridge & White, I owe profound gratitude.

Editors are divinities, and none are more wise or all-seeing than the almighty Riva Hocherman at Metropolitan Books and Anne Meadows at Granta. My sincere thanks as well to Sara Bershtel, Brian Lax, Natasha Lehrer, Molly Bloom, Marinda Valenti, and Carolyn O'Keefe at Metropolitan/Henry Holt. At Granta, my thanks to Bella Lacey, Rowan Cope, Jason Arthur, and to Lamorna Elmer for her enthusiasm since day one. Thanks to Leah Paulos and Liv Walton, and to Benjamin Tear for his help with the book's images. Matthew Young designed the glorious, idolatrous cover.

The pantheon of this book would be incomplete without Nathaniel Tarn, my living god, and Janet Rodney. Thank you for welcoming me in Santa Fe, and letting me tear through the archives of the underground bunker.

I am grateful to all who pointed me toward inadvertent gods at early stages of the project, in conversations long ago but not forgotten, especially Faisal Devji, Pankaj Mishra, Richard Sieburth, and Marina Warner, who has a direct line to the divine. Tynan Kogane was the muse of MacArthur; Orlando Reade was the oracle of Walterali, and Thomas Wide the spark of Nikalsain. My thanks to friends who read drafts or offered their publishing wisdom: Michael Barron, Mieke Chew, Maud Doyle, Barbara Epler, Emmie Francis, Adrian Gregory, Will Heyward, Valerie Miles, Mary Mount, Yasmine El Rashidi, Thomas Roueché, Katherine Rundell, Emily Stokes, Drenka Willen. Special thanks to Ruth

Harris for her insightful comments on the chapters about India; to Omer Tarin for our correspondence on the Nikalsainis; and to Matthew Baylis and J. S. Tennant for stories of their visits with the Philip sect on Tanna.

More primordial still are my debts to my teachers, first at the University of Chicago and then at Harvard Divinity School. Daniel Raeburn was the first to encourage me to write. Wendy Doniger, David Shulman, Kimberley Patton, and the late Paul Friedrich gave me new ways of seeing the sacred. Charles Stang inspired me with his divine doubles. My thanks as well to the staff of Oxford's Bodleian Library, who let me rove for six years in the collections. In a book about mistakes of cosmic proportions, many undoubtedly remain in its pages, and they are all my own.

My deepest thanks are to my family in New York, and to the Cairo branch, Ahmed Omar, Yehia Omar, and Mona Fahmy, for their support over the years. Sana Barakat was always my sharpest reader and is greatly missed.

My father, Eliot Weinberger, showed me how the mythic, the poetic, and the political are ever intertwined. Stefan Weinberger and Faye Tsakas always bring the light. In 2020, Nina Subin, god of author photographs, quite literally resurrected, after a harrowing medical ordeal. My mother's strength and high spirits are proof that the miraculous is around us at each moment.

In the final months, Ismael kept me company from the womb as I finished the manuscript. The love and omniscience of Hussein Omar have illuminated every page.

—*Dublin, 2021*

# LIST OF ILLUSTRATIONS

# INDEX OF INADVERTENT DEITIES

# ABOUT THE AUTHOR

ANNA DELLA SUBIN is a writer and critic and independent scholar born in New York. Her essays have appeared in the *New York Review of Books*, *Harper's Magazine*, the *New York Times*, and the *London Review of Books*. A senior editor at *Bidoun*, she studied the history of religion at Harvard Divinity School. *Accidental Gods* is her first book.